James R .

People, Pattern and Process

People, Pattern and Process

An Introduction to Human Geography

Keith Chapman

Lecturer in Human Geography, University of Aberdeen

Edward Arnold

© Keith Chapman 1979

First published in Great Britain 1979 by
Edward Arnold (Publishers) Ltd, 41 Bedford Square, London WC1B 3DQ

Edward Arnold (Australia) Pty Ltd, 80 Waverley Road, Caulfield East,
 Victoria 3134, Australia

Edward Arnold, 3 East Read Stret, Baltimore, Maryland 21202, U.S.A.

Reprinted 1983 with corrections
Reprinted 1986

British Library Cataloguing in Publication Data

Chapman, Keith
 People, pattern and process.
 1. Anthropo-geography
 I. Title
 909   GF41

ISBN 0 7131 6242 4

Text set in 10 on 11 Times
Printed and bound in Great Britain by
Butler & Tanner Ltd, Frome and London

Contents

Spatial Process

Spatial Pattern

Acknowledgements

The author and publishers would like to thank the following for permission to reproduce or modify copyright material. Figure numbers refer to this book, full citations can be found by consulting captions and bibliography.

Allen and Unwin Ltd for fig. 6.12; the American Geographical Society for figs. 9.6, 9.9, 9.12 and 10.11; the Association of American Geographers for figs. 1.3, 1.4, 3.9, 4.7, 4.12 and 11.15; Cambridge University Press for figs. 4.4 and 8.12; Chicago University Press for fig. 4.5; *Economic Geography* for figs. 3.2, 5.4, 6.13, 7.9, 10.12 and 10.15; *Environment and Planning* for fig. 1.1; The Free Press, N.Y. for figs. 7.15 and 7.16; *Geographical Magazine* for fig. 9.13; *Geography* for fig. 4.10; Gleerup Bokforlag for figs. 6.1, 6.2, 9.8 and 11.6; Houghton-Mifflin Inc. for figs. 8.5, 10.1 and 10.14; the Institute of Australian Geographers for fig. 8.7; the Institute of British Geographers for figs. 5.2, 6.8, 6.9, 6.10, 6.14, 6.16, 11.5 and 11.14; *Irish Geographical Studies* for fig. 10.9; the Geographical Society of Ireland for fig. 6.17; Johns Hopkins University Press for fig. 4.11; the *Journal of Developing Areas* for figs. 5.9, 5.10 and 5.11; the *Journal of Regional Science* for fig. 8.1; the *Journal of Tropical Geography* for figs. 10.16 and 11.4; McGraw-Hill Inc. for figs. 3.3, 3.4, 6.5, 6.7 and 11.10; Macmillan Co. Ltd for fig. 11.3; the MIT Press for figs. 5.1 and 5.7; Northwestern University Press for figs. 7.5, 7.6 and 7.7; Ohio State University Press for fig. 7.3; Penguin Books Ltd for figs. 3.5 and 3.6; Prentice-Hall Inc. for figs. 1.2, 3.7, 4.8, 6.4, 7.8, 8.11 and 9.7; the Regional Science Association for figs. 3.10, 4.6 and 8.4; *Regional Studies* for fig. 5.6; the Royal Scottish Geographical Society for figs. 11.8 and 11.9; Shell International for fig. 8.2; the *South African Geographical Journal* for fig. 5.12; Syracuse University Press for fig. 7.17; *Tijdschrift voor economische en sociale geografie* for figs. 3.8, 7.18, 8.6, 10.2, 10.6, 11.11 and 11.13; University of Chicago, Department of Geography for figs. 8.9 and 9.3; the University of Oregon Bureau of Business Research for fig. 6.7.

Preface

This book, like many others before it, had its origins in a series of lecture notes. Students at the University of Aberdeen have been subjected for several years to this interpretation of human geography. Their adverse reactions to recommended textbooks provided a partial justification for this contribution to the literature which may now itself become just another regretted purchase! No textbook should be taken too seriously since it rarely contains anything new. The most it can hope to achieve is to provide a framework within which ideas and material from other sources may be structured. The need for such a framework seems to be particularly acute in the study of a field as broad as that of human geography. This book seeks to meet this need by outlining just one approach towards the ultimate objective of understanding the factors which affect the spatial distribution of human activities at the surface of the earth.

Numerous individuals have contributed to the formulation of the ideas contained in this book. I have never met most of these people and can only hope that the rather impersonal acknowledgement implicit in their inclusion in a list of references will suffice. The principle of the anonymity of academic referees is such that I cannot even guarantee to manage this for two or three individuals who commented upon an early outline of the book – it is a case of expressing thanks to persons unknown! Colleagues at the University of Aberdeen have also influenced, both directly and indirectly, the development of my own ideas. Some of the examples used to illustrate approaches to the analysis of networks were 'borrowed' from material prepared by Peter Stanley. David Sugden read and provided helpful comments on much of the manuscript whilst Patrick Hamilton was a particularly demanding and valued critic who stuck it out to the bitter end! Finally thanks to Edith Smith and Christina Morrison for translating my own handwriting into a form more acceptable to others.

Keith Chapman

Department of Geography,
University of Aberdeen.
9 May, 1978.

1 A World without Distance

Good science fiction should maintain a credible link between reality and imagination. A productive theme for writers of science fiction has been man's ability to jump beyond the barriers imposed by the dimensions which define his existence – space and time. Thus H. G. Wells's time traveller could project himself both forward and backward in time. The 'transporter' of the starship *Enterprise* enables Captain Kirk and his crew to travel through space instantaneously, although it has been known to permit simultaneous movement in both dimensions! Geography may appear to have little in common with such worlds of the imagination, but its position as an academic discipline is related to its explicit concern with spatial relationships of objects and events at the surface of the earth. The universal availability of the kind of technology at the disposal of the Startrekkers would transform these relationships by effectively nullifying the role of distance as an obstacle to movement between one place and another (Webber, 1963).

All contemporary transport systems would be redundant in a world of limitless and effortless mobility. There would be no need to live in towns and cities. The urban agglomerations characteristic of the contemporary world would virtually disappear as individuals searched for their own place in the sun. Property speculators would be extolling the virtues of desirable residences located on mountaintops or coral islands according to taste. The daily journey to work would give way to the commuter's 'materializing' at his console in one of the various industrial parks scattered around the globe. These parks would be designated for the purpose of keeping the planet tidy. Their location would be of no economic significance because such traditional location factors as the availability of raw materials and markets would be irrelevant since inputs could be assembled at no cost and outputs distributed just as easily.

Despite the rapidity of technical change, there is little prospect that anybody other than Captain Kirk and his colleagues will be able to enjoy the advantages of such a world-without-distance in the foreseeable future. Nevertheless, there is already some evidence of the emergence of new location factors with increasing human mobility. The pull of amenity is especially apparent in the US where the growth of areas such as Southern California and peninsular Florida may be related to the search for personal utopias (Zelinsky, 1974). Implicit in this trend is the breakdown of the influence of distance upon location. The same point may be made by adopting an historical rather than a futuristic perspective. Thus a valid interpretation of the history of civilization could be based upon those achievements in the field of transport and communications which have given meaning to the notion of a 'shrinking world'.

1.1 'A Shrinking World'

As far as the individual is concerned, the world 'shrinks' at a rate which is related to his level of personal mobility. An example is the way our attitudes towards and awareness of our surroundings change as we grow older, for the world becomes less formidable and seems somehow smaller as we pass from childhood to maturity. The progression is often reversed with the onset of old age as our ability or willingness to face long journeys declines. Contrasting views of the world are not only a function of the life-cycle and similar differences may also be observed between cultures.

Individuals within pedestrian societies have first-hand experience of a much more limited portion of the earth's surface than mobile members of twentieth-century post-industrial society. The bottom circle in Figure 1.1 translates the assumption of a 50-mile walking day into a 'known world' centred on Trafalgar Square in the heart of London (Adams, 1972). In practice, many societies operate within a much more restricted area than the 8,000 square miles incorporated within a circle of 50-mile radius. Ascending from the bottom circle are progressively larger 'known worlds' whose radii have been increased in the same proportion as the increase in the speed of transport available. The final circle indicates that the whole world is theoretically within the range of a day's journey travelling at supersonic speed, whilst the dot describes what might be called the 'electronic known world' of all those who are linked into the global telecommunications network. Many assumptions are incorporated in Figure 1.1. The supersonic traveller does not even see much of the world he crosses so that he can hardly 'know' it in the same sense that the inhabitant of a pedestrian society 'knows' the area around his village. Nevertheless, their differing abilities to move through space ensures that there is a tremendous contrast between their respective images of the world.

Although the notion of a 'shrinking world' may be appreciated at an individual or personal level, its significance in terms of the development of human society is perhaps greatest in the context of man's economic activities. Thus we may conceive of a merchant's view of the world related to changes in the technology of moving commodities between points of supply and demand. An extensive network of trading relationships has provided the basis of many important civilizations and these relationships have often been maintained through the operation of shipping fleets (see Couper, 1972). The overseas empires of the European colonial powers, for example, were all essentially based upon the trading capabilities of the sailing ship. Such ships had a dramatic effect on patterns of world trade between 1500 and 1850. Prior to the development of vessels capable of crossing the world's oceans with a reasonable probability of making the return journey, it had been easier to travel by land. Consequently, the major trade routes crossed the continental interiors. However, the sailing ship had the effect of turning the world inside-out by making the oceans more accessible than the land masses (Fig. 1.2), leading to the decline of inland trading centres such as Timbuktu and Samarkand and the rise of the ports of the great sea powers.

Changes in transport technology affecting movement between continents have

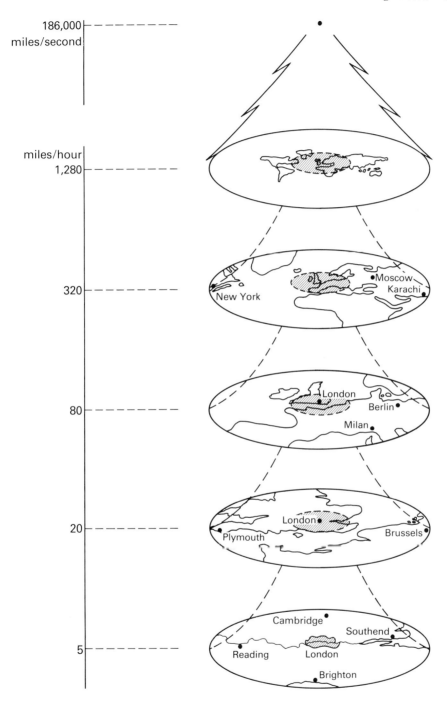

Fig. 1.1 A shrinking world (Adams, 1972, 386).

been paralleled by similar developments affecting movement within them. Many aspects of both the history and geography of 'new lands' such as North America (see Brook, 1976) and Australia (see Blainey, 1968) may be explained in terms of advances in methods of transport. As late as 1825, there was little long-distance movement in North America and most of the population remained concentrated along the northeastern seaboard facing the immigrant source of Western Europe. The opening of the Erie Canal began a period of 'canal mania' which promoted inland penetration towards the Great Lakes, but it was the railways which fostered large-scale transcontinental movement after 1870 and integrated the embryo urban regions of Atlantic and Pacific coasts. The origins of these urban regions may be directly related to different stages in the evolution of transport technology (Fig. 1.3).

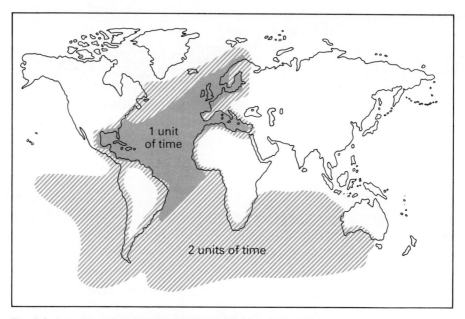

Fig. 1.2 A maritime world (Abler, Adams and Gould, 1971, 285).

Although the North American continent has 'shrunk' dramatically in response to developments in transport technology, the Australian land mass has been more resistant to this process. The legacy of isolated 'limpet ports' established to protect British trading interests is still reflected in the peripheral distribution of the population. Whereas the railway effectively integrated the North American economy, in Australia it initially strengthened independent regional economies as separate networks emerged to extend the interior hinterlands of already established ports. The first transcontinental line between the main railways of Western Australia and those of the southeastern states did not come until 1917 – almost 50 years later than the Atlantic–Pacific link was achieved in the US. The multiplicity of gauges was a further handicap and it was only in 1962 that the three largest Australian cities, Brisbane, Sydney and Melbourne, were joined by a common system. The

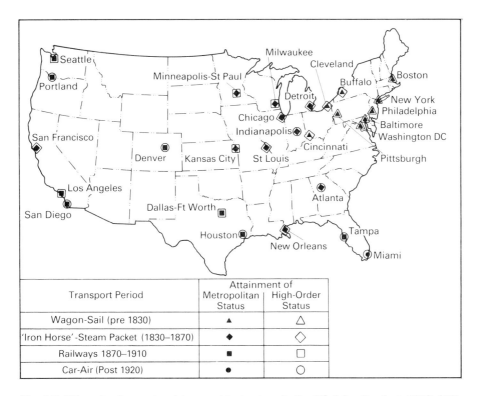

Transport Period	Attainment of	
	Metropolitan Status	High-Order Status
Wagon-Sail (pre 1830)	▲	△
'Iron Horse'-Steam Packet (1830–1870)	◆	◇
Railways 1870–1910	■	□
Car-Air (Post 1920)	●	○

Fig. 1.3 Urban development and transport technology in the US (after Borchert, 1972, 355).

growth of air travel has certainly facilitated movement between the major cities, but the vast transcontinental distances remain an obstacle to national integration and the Australian economy may still be regarded as a loosely connected amalgam of separate metropolitan-oriented regional systems.

1.2 Physical and Electronic Mobility

It is clear that human attitudes towards space and distance have changed considerably through time and, in certain respects, a world without distance has become a reality. With the advent of communications satellites, it is possible to be in two places at once as far as sight and sound are concerned. Events taking place on one side of the world can be seen and heard 'live' on the other. Such *telemobility* essentially involves moving the experience to the body, the reverse of 'normal' participation in events. Despite the potentially profound implications of this technology for the way in which people live and work (see Berry, 1970), telemobility does not in itself create a world without distance. Such a world would be characterized not only by the instantaneous transmission of information, but also by a similar facility in the movement of material objects. This capability remains confined to the realms of science fiction and a clear distinction must therefore be drawn between *transportation* and *communication*.

This distinction may be emphasized through a consideration of the phenomenon of *time/space convergence* (Janelle, 1968). 'Space may be the central concept on which geography as a discipline relies for its coherence' (Harvey, 1969, 209), but this dimension '... is interchangeable with, and often measured in terms of, time' (Ullman, 1974, 125). Time/space convergence extends this latter notion to consider change through time in the duration of a journey from one location to another. Figure 1.4a plots the trend in the time taken to travel between London and Edinburgh over a period of 300 years. Breaks of slope in the graph reflect such events as the introduction of the railway and inter-city air travel. However, rapid rates of time/space convergence can only be achieved if money is available to invest in modern transport facilities. In certain situations, spectacular changes may occur

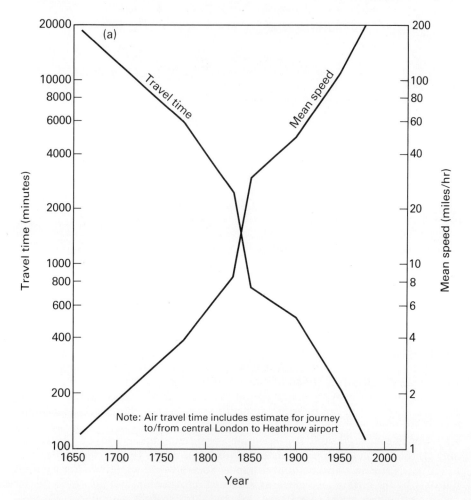

Fig. 1.4 Travel time: (a) between London and Edinburgh, 1650–1978 (air travel time includes estimate for journey to/from central London to Heathrow airport); (b) within Venezuela, 1936–1961 (Marchand, 1973, 509).

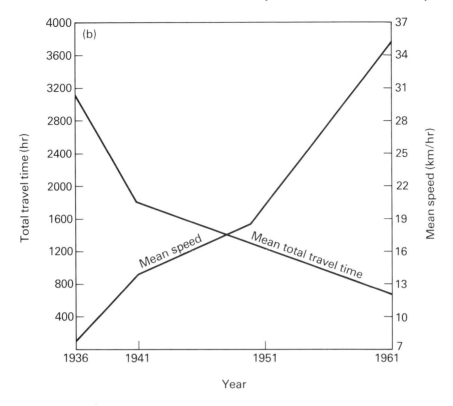

Year

very quickly. For example, Venezuela has spent large sums of money derived from its oil industry upon the improvement of the country's road network. On the basis of certain assumptions about the maximum feasible speeds on roads of differing quality, Marchand (1973) has shown how Venezuela has 'shrunk' dramatically in only 25 years. Figure 1.4b shows how the total time required to make a round trip from any one node to a specified number of other places on the Venezuelan road network fell from over 3,000 hours in 1936 to less than 700 hours in 1961.

Although developments in transportation have drawn places closer together through time, advances in communication have, in some respects, brought about total convergence. Thus a telephone call between London and Edinburgh is usually just as quick as a local call. However, this illustration assumes universal access to a telephone, which is far from reality in most countries. Furthermore, research into the business applications of communications technology has suggested that telephones and more sophisticated videophones are still widely regarded as a poor substitute for the traditional face-to-face exchanges around a table (Goddard and Pye, 1977). Yet another limitation on the flexibility implied by 'instant' communication is the fact that most systems such as telephones and computer link-ups rely upon the continued existence of cable-like distribution networks connecting transmitter with receiver. Access to information will depend upon location with respect to the network, leading to the emergence of critical terminals. Thus implicit in communications technology itself, quite apart from the inertial influence of existing patterns of human activity, are forces encouraging concentration rather than the dispersed distributions characteristic of a world in which distance is truly irrelevant.

The constraints upon complete time/space convergence are not purely technical and economic, they are also social and political. Access to technology and, therefore, opportunities for movement vary not only between cultures, but also within them (see Webber, 1964). In contemporary urban/industrial society, the contacts of the professional and intellectual elites are widely dispersed since they have the means to overcome the barrier of distance. Those at the other end of the social order occupy much more restricted 'life-islands' which are territorially defined in relation to the home. Differences in life-style associated with variations in personal mobility have become more apparent as technology has advanced (see Häger-strand, 1970). Thus the cosmopolitan world of political leaders and top businessmen seems unreal when compared with the more mundane everyday existence of lesser mortals whose geographical horizons are defined by the spatial relationships between home, shops, offices and factories with occasional escapes further afield to the beaches of Blackpool or the Costa Brava. Contrasts in mobility may be much more immediate and socially relevant than those between 'jet-set' personalities and the rest of the population. For example, the vast majority of black commuters in South African and Rhodesian cities rely on public transport whilst the high level of car ownership amongst the white population permits them a quicker and more comfortable journey to work (Hardwick, 1973).

It is clear that advances in transport and communications technology have not only made the world effectively smaller, but have also created greater uniformity in living environments. Motorways and office blocks look much the same whether they are located in London or Leningrad and the identity of regional landscapes based on such features as the use of distinctive local building materials is threatened by the relative ease with which mass-produced bricks and concrete blocks may be imported from elsewhere. Nevertheless, these trends should not be over-emphasized. The vast majority of the world's population does not have access to a car, let alone the opportunity to fly on an aircraft. Man has thus a long way to go before he can escape the 'tyranny of distance' in the manner of Captain Kirk and Mr Spock; and fears that the differences between places, which make the world interesting and give the study of geography its meaning, will disappear with the breakdown of the isolation imposed by distance seem premature.

Further Reading

ADAMS, J. G. U. 1972: Life in a global village. *Environment and Planning* **4**, 381–94.

Queries the benefits of developments in transport and communications technology.

BERRY, B. J. L. 1970: The geography of the United States in the year 2000. *Institute of British Geographers, Transactions* **51**, 21–54.

Assesses the possible impact of telecommunications upon future patterns of life in the US.

BROOK, A. 1976: Spatial systems in American history. *Area* **8**, 47–52.

A retrospective assessment of the role of space-adjusting technologies in the development of the United States.

BLAINEY, G. 1969: *The tyranny of distance.* Melbourne.

An historical view of the influence of transport improvements upon the development of Australia.

ULLMAN, E. L. 1974: Space and/or time: opportunity for substitution and prediction. *Institute of British Geographers, Transactions* **63**, 125–39.

Discusses some of the complexities and implications of the interrelationship between the dimensions of space and time.

WEBBER, M. 1964: Culture, territoriality and the elastic mile. *Regional Science Association, Paper and Proceedings* **13**, 59–69.

Emphasizes social and cultural differences in mobility.

2 A Conceptual Framework

The idea, developed in chapter 1, that the world is somehow flexible in shape and size is obviously not to be taken literally. The earth may actually be shrinking as it cools and we know that the continents have moved in geological time, but such changes are not relevant to our understanding of existing patterns of settlement and land use on a human time scale. By contrast, the concept of a world which expands and contracts in the mind of man *is* important since mental images of space and location influence the decisions which are ultimately responsible for creating the distributions at the earth's surface which are the subject matter of human geography. The location of people and the artefacts such as towns, fields, factories and roads which reflect their social, economic and cultural activities may be regarded as a consequence of innumerable decisions made by individuals acting either independently or, more commonly, as members of complex groups. Thus if geographers are to explain, as well as to describe, these distributions it follows that they must be concerned with the decision-making process itself.

2.1 Decision Making – the Basic Mechanism

Decision making may be regarded as *the* basic mechanism in all of the social sciences. Human geographers are interested in this mechanism in so far as it affects the spatial distribution of man's activities. In this context, a broad distinction may be drawn between decisions which are explicitly concerned with location and those for which locational considerations are of little or no immediate significance. To focus only upon explicit or 'conscious' location decisions such as a company's choice of a site for a new factory would leave a great many obviously 'geographical' questions unanswered. For example, patterns of agricultural land use reflect the decisions of a multitude of farmers to grow wheat on one piece of land, barley on another and so on. Such decisions are normally influenced by place-to-place variations in such factors as slope, soil and climatic conditions, but it is possible to envisage situations in which land-use patterns are based on decisions that take no account of locational variables. Consider an imaginary island which is divided up into several farm holdings. Initially, all the farmers grow the same strain of rice. The availability of a new strain prompts each farmer to consider its adoption. To simplify the problem, we will assume that the farmers either totally accept or completely reject the new strain. Also we will assume that the switch takes place in a single year so that a distinction can be made between the pre- and post-decision situations. The decision of each farmer is based upon a comparative assessment of the biological properties of the two strains and their probable success given the nature of the land. The choice is not directly concerned with location, for the position in space of each farm plot is already given, but the decisions will nevertheless produce a new distribution of rice cultivation based on the distinction between those farmers who adopt the new strain and those who continue to grow the old one (Fig. 2.1).

Any meaningful interpretation of the distribution of human artefacts and activities on the surface of the earth not only requires an understanding of different kinds of decision, but also an appreciation of different kinds of decision maker.

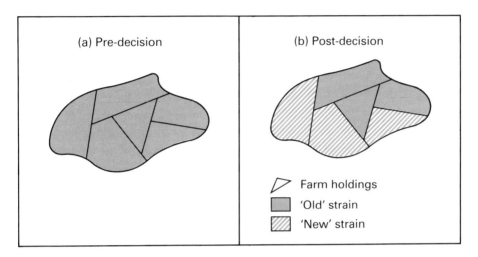

Fig. 2.1 Decision making and spatial patterns: (a) 'Pre-decision' situation; (b) 'Post-decision' situation.

Although individuals such as farmers take decisions which have important geographical consequences, so too do groups of individuals. Indeed, there is much evidence to suggest that the significance of the individual is declining in contemporary urban/industrial societies. For example, industry is dominated not by small firms owned and run by a single entrepreneur, but by major multinational corporations controlled by boards of directors responsible to shareholders. The broad distinction between decisions in which locational factors are explicitly considered and those in which locational effects may almost be regarded as incidental by-products remains valid to the actions of Shell and General Motors, but the decision-making process is much more complex in such organizations and we have to come to terms with this situation if, for example, we are to understand the distribution of modern industry.

2.2 The Spatial Context

The decisions of both individuals and groups regarding the location of activities and the use of land are not made in a vacuum, being strongly influenced by the total environment within which the decision maker operates. Location itself forms an important part of this total environment and the locational environment or *spatial context* of a decision maker derives both from the physical and human characteristics of the location itself and from the characteristics of its surrounding space. As well as content, space also has abstract qualities such as distance and direction which define its dimensions. The spatial context of decision making is therefore composed of (i) the content of space and (ii) the dimensions of space.

2.2.1 The Content of Space

Natural phenomena such as landforms, flora and fauna, and human structures such as roads and factories, make up the physical and human contents of space respectively. Taken collectively, they may be regarded as representing the world of geographical 'facts' (Kirk, 1963). However, the recognition of these facts varies between individuals (and groups) because of the influence of certain cultural and personal factors which may be conceived as filters through which the decision maker perceives his surroundings. 'Culture' extends far beyond the popular association with the arts to include the social, political and religious institutions by which a group organizes its activities as well as its prevailing level of technological achievement. Such dimensions of culture vary in space and change through time so that perceptions of environmental circumstances by decision makers are correspondingly diverse. Culture is assimilated by identification with a particular group and is therefore external to the individual. Psychological influences upon decision making are even more difficult to isolate than cultural ones because they are internal. Although an understanding of these mental processes is largely a problem for the psychologist, they are relevant to the geographer in so far as they represent a further set of variables affecting the way in which man responds to and reacts with the surrounding content of space.

Geography has traditionally attached great importance to the influence of the physical environment upon the distributions of human activities. It is obvious that elements of the physical environment such as climate, landforms and mineral deposits have been and remain important factors affecting man's use of the earth. Nevertheless, the philosophy that this use is 'determined' by the physical environment is unacceptable. For example, agriculture is possible in the most arid desert provided that water may be obtained either from underground sources or from areas experiencing adequate rainfall. The engineering works required may be expensive, but they can be installed, as schemes in the Sahara and Central Asia testify. Although such costs represent constraints upon man's range of options, they are not absolute barriers. On the other hand, the physical environment may be viewed in a positive way as providing certain opportunities through the existence of such materials as coal and oil. However, these opportunities will not necessarily be taken since they may not even be appreciated. The distribution of coal had no bearing upon the activities of early man and, given its contemporary significance, it is difficult to believe that oil was virtually unknown as a source of energy in the mid-nineteenth century.

Earth-space 'contains' not only attributes of the physical environment, but also the man-made features which comprise the human environment. These features themselves reflect earlier decisions made within the spatial context and there is a strong interrelationship between past, present and future distributions of human activities. Decisions are much influenced by past experience and by existing circumstances. For example, it has been estimated that between 60 and 80 per cent of investment in manufacturing industry in the developed countries is allocated to the expansion of existing plants (UN, 1967). This promotes the geographical concentration of economic activity and is largely due to the advantages and attractions of locating in areas which already possess the necessary infrastructure of social and economic capital in the form of housing, transport facilities and so on. This kind of development sequence underlines the significance of elements of the human environment as part of the spatial context to decision making and it is clear that 'the greatest influence on the future location of people and activities is their present location' (Morrill, 1970, 6).

2.2.2 Dimensions of Space

Although social and territorial instincts are partly responsible for the distinctive clustering of human activities, this tendency is also due to certain properties of space itself. An awareness of space, as reflected in terms such as 'near' and 'far', is a fundamental aspect of our experience. Implicit in this experience are certain basic concepts which ensure that notions of location can have meaning in a world which is devoid of the spatial variations provided by features of the physical and human environments. These concepts may be effectively demonstrated by considering a simple situation (Nystuen, 1963).

Imagine a group of pupils gathering around a teacher on the floor of a mosque. The initial location of the teacher may be random as the interior of a mosque is characterized by an expansive tiled floor lacking any obvious focal point. However, the arrangement of the pupils follows a predictable pattern. A semicircle consisting of several rows tends to develop around the teacher. The innermost row is perhaps two metres from the teacher whilst the position of the outermost row will obviously depend upon the size of the group, but will (assuming conscientious pupils!) ultimately be constrained by the teacher's ability to project his voice.

The plausibility of this scene rests upon a number of basic spatial concepts which underlie its development. Firstly, *direction* is important because the human form has a natural orientation – a front and a back – which defines a line of sight between the pupils and the teacher. Secondly, the *distance* over which the teacher's voice remains audible, given the size of the group and the accoustics of the mosque, determines the outer limit of the semicircle. Finally, the position of the entire group within the mosque is a matter of *relative location*; the arrangement of the pupils depends upon the teacher's choice of a place from which to speak. Thus the concepts of direction, distance and relative location, which are intrinsic to the dimension of space itself, ensure that the distribution of our hypothetical class reveals a definite pattern despite the fact that the featureless floor of the mosque eliminates the effect of variations in the content of space. This pattern is essentially focal in character and the concepts which underlie it are basic to the spatial organization of human activities at all scales.

The significance of our illustration lies in the implication that the intrinsic properties of space ensure that it would remain meaningful to speak of the geography of a world with a surface as featureless as a billiard ball. However, in reality, distributions cannot be explained exclusively in terms of such spatial concepts as distance, direction and relative location. Differences in the content of space associated with the uneven distribution of physical and human phenomena create a need for movement – mineral resources are available in one place but required in another; housewives live in residential areas but must shop somewhere else. Although such variations in the content of space may be regarded as 'fixed' at a point in time, their existing location may have been influenced by considerations related to the properties of the dimensions of space. Thus whereas the distribution of mineral resources is ultimately determined by geological factors, patterns of commercial exploitation are strongly influenced by the distance between a deposit and its potential market. Similarly, the location of shops may also be partially explained in terms of spatial concepts. Focal or clustered spatial arrangements help to reduce transport costs by improving the *accessibility* of these points relative to one another. The concentration of shops in the centre of towns and cities increases their accessibility relative to the consumers they serve by reducing the length of the journey which must be made to purchase a given number of items.

2.3 Spatial Pattern

Implicit in the notion of accessibility is the idea of *distance minimization*. We accept without thinking the logic of patronizing the nearer of two shops selling the same goods at identical prices. However, such behaviour has profound implications as far as the spatial arrangement of man's activities is concerned since it produces a measure of order and regularity in their distribution. Of course decision making in a spatial context is not exclusively governed by the principle of distance minimization. Other factors may influence the choice between the two shops. The farther one may have a shop assistant whose qualities justify the longer journey! If the two shops are close together, the effect of distance may be negligible and the customer may choose between them on an apparently random basis from day to day. Nevertheless, despite these complexities which often make it difficult to know how individuals will react, the principle of distance minimization is sufficiently important to influence the majority of decisions made by individual members of any group. The aggregate *spatial patterns* of human activities which emerge from such decisions are therefore frequently non-random and, to some extent, predictable.

Spatial pattern at the earth's surface is a composite of three basic geometric forms – *points*, *lines* and *areas*. The validity of this classification may not always be apparent on the ground, but is easy to appreciate when the images present on an aerial photograph are analysed. A photograph of an agricultural landscape in the Fens of East Anglia, for example, would represent farm buildings as points within a framework of areas made up of fields of differing tone, texture and colour. The buildings would be connected to the fields by linear paths and tracks. Settlements such as villages and towns would be seen to consist of concentrations of individual buildings which, when considered collectively, could be regarded as areas defined by the boundary between urban and rural land uses.

Although it is convenient to think of points, lines and areas as the elements of spatial pattern, the distinction between these forms is not absolute since it depends upon the scale at which they are viewed. Thus if a succession of photographs centred on the same locational coordinates, but taken at greater and greater heights, were considered, one set of point-like features would gradually be replaced by others which had previously appeared as areas. The individual farm buildings which could be identified on low-level photographs would be indistinguishable when seen from higher altitudes at which the towns and villages would seem to contract into points. New linear and areal elements would strike the observer as the farm tracks disappeared to be replaced by motorways and single fields merged into general areas of common land use. This process of scale change may be continued until entire continents are revealed in a single satellite picture, but, whatever level of resolution is adopted, the patterns observed may always be disaggregated into the same three basic geometric forms.

2.4 Spatial Process – Causality in Time and Space

Spatial patterns are a product of many human decisions, yet these decisions are themselves influenced by existing patterns. Although it may seem difficult to disentangle cause and effect, the distinction is largely a matter of the time scale adopted. This distinction may be best understood by considering an example. Many of the older European towns and cities have been faced with the problem of accommodating modern transport facilities, particularly the private car, within congested central areas characterized by tortuous narrow streets. Such street patterns often reflect the medieval origins of these settlements. Relative to that period, the street pattern may be regarded as a consequence or 'effect' of decisions concerning land ownership and use. However, over the much longer period extending to the present day, the street pattern may be viewed as a constraint or 'cause' influencing the daily travel and shopping decisions of the contemporary population by deterring the use of cars. The argument may also be projected forward since the problems created by the inherited street pattern may stimulate planning decisions to alter or modify it in the future. Overall, it is possible to generalize and say that in the short term decisions tend to be influenced by existing spatial patterns, whilst at the same time, these decisions create new patterns which evolve over longer periods.

The reciprocal relationships inherent in decision making in a spatial context are emphasized by the fact that such decisions generate both movement in space and change through time – a combination which makes it meaningful to speak of *spatial processes*. This term is equally valid whatever the scale at which movement occurs or the duration of the period over which change takes place. To continue the reference to urban central areas, the travel behaviour of shoppers and commuters obviously involves movement whereas redevelopment produces change in land use. Perhaps less obviously, travel habits also change through time and redevelopment leads to the movement of particular land uses from one location to another. Although journeys to shop and work may easily be visualized as spatial processes, it only requires a different time perspective to appreciate that patterns of urban land use may also conform to the Oxford dictionary definition of process as being 'a state of going on'. Therefore it is artificial, if convenient, to set spatial process apart from spatial pattern as indicated in Figure 2.2 and it is important to remember that the former is essentially concerned with 'what is happening' *over* a given time period, which may be either of long or short duration, whereas the latter relates to 'what is there' *at* a given time.

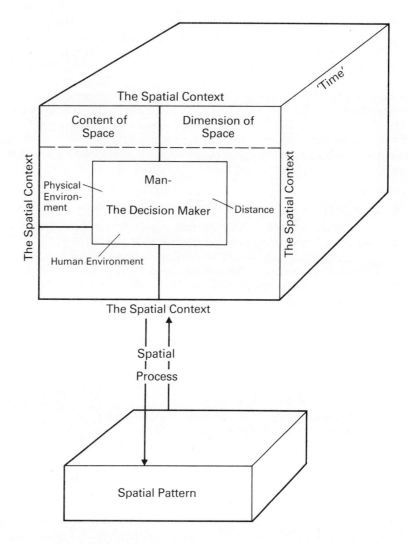

Fig. 2.2 A conceptual framework.

The diagram represents the conceptual framework to the study of human geography which will provide a structure to the remainder of this book. The next chapter considers the nature of decision making. The influence upon decision makers of the physical and human contents of space and of the dimensions of space are discussed in chapters 4, 5 and 6 respectively. Chapters 7 and 8 explore in more detail the distinction between processes operating at different time/space scales. These processes are related to spatial patterns conceived in terms of points, lines and areas in the next three chapters. Finally the major concepts developed in the book are drawn together in a conclusion which also reviews some of their potential applications in the development of policies to create a 'better' society.

Further Reading

BLAUT, J. 1961: Space and process. *Professional Geographer* **13,** 1–7.

Emphasizes that the distinction between spatial process and spatial pattern ('structure' in Blaut's terminology) is a function of the time scale over which phenomena are observed.

KIRK, W. 1963: Problems of geography. *Geography* **48,** 357–71.

Discusses the relationship between decision making and environment.

NYSTUEN, J. D. 1963: Identification of some fundamental spatial concepts. In Berry, B. J. L. and Marble, D. F. (Eds.), *Spatial analysis*, Englewood Cliffs, N.J., 35–41.

Explores the abstract properties of space and relates them to the analysis of location.

SCHUMM, S. A. and LICHTY, R. W. 1965: Time, space and causality in geomorphology. *American Journal of Science* **263,** 110–19.

The ideas contained in this analysis of time, space and causality in geomorphology are equally valid in understanding process–pattern relationships in human geography.

3 Decision Making – the Basic Mechanism

In interpreting spatial patterns as consequences of human decision making, geographers have tended to emphasize the actions of individual rather than corporate decision makers, although freedom of individual choice is often illusory. For example, agriculture is commonly seen as a stronghold of individualism in which the self-employed farmer remains his own man. This image is not unjustified and yet, at the same time, his actions are often influenced by government policy and, possibly, tied by a long-term contract to the requirements of a major food-processing corporation. Implicit here is the widening role of government and corporate organizations as decision makers in modern society. For example, it has been estimated that the assets of the 200 largest manufacturing firms in the US economy account for more than 70 per cent of the total assets held by all corporations engaged primarily in industrial production, whereas the corresponding figure in 1950 was only 46.7 per cent (Pred, 1974). On an international scale, the continuation of post-war trends suggests that multinationals will generate more than one half of the gross world product by the end of the century (Bergman, 1973). Furthermore, the largest of these organizations, General Motors, has annual sales exceeding the net national incomes of all but a dozen nation states (Bergman, 1973). Statistics such as these emphasize that whilst the individual decision maker may be 'the central elementary particle' (Hägerstrand, 1973, 75) in human geography, spatial patterns are increasingly tending to reflect the actions of corporate or collective decision makers.

The increasing scope of government intervention and the progressive concentration of economic power in the hands of very large business organizations have important repercussions upon any approach to human geography oriented towards the study of decision making in a spatial context. Decision making in government and industry is effected by an amalgam of individuals placed within an overall management structure and is therefore a more complex process than that of individuals acting independently. In the case of a small family firm, for example, the entrepreneur is both owner and manager and can directly relate policy decisions to his own goals and aspirations. By contrast, decision making within large corporations is often based on compromise between the conflicting interests of different subsidiaries and departments within the organization (Dicken, 1970). Nevertheless, corporate decision making is not different in kind from that of individuals and it is possible to identify certain basic elements within the process that are common to both the peasant farmer at one end of the scale and the multinational corporation at the other.

3.1 A Model of the Decision-Making Process

'Decision-making process' is a complex term and it is more accurate to think of a series of distinct but interdependent processes. Figure 3.1 identifies these processes within a sequence which begins with the initial choice of goals or objectives and culminates in the evaluation of alternative strategies as a prelude to the selection of a particular course of action. The general validity of this sequence may be demonstrated by analysing the peasant farmer's choice of crops to grow in the year following a very poor harvest and comparing it with an oil company's selection of a location for a refinery in a country which has previously been outside its sphere of operations.

In both cases, the first step involves identifying a *goal* or *objective* which justifies a decision being taken. It is conventional to assume that the decision maker's ultimate objective is always to maximize utility.* However, utility is an abstract measure of value or usefulness which must be converted into something more tangible. Thus the peasant farmer's objective is survival whilst that of the oil company

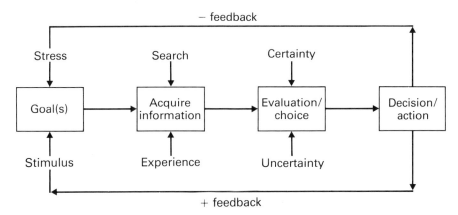

Fig. 3.1 A model of the decision-making process.

may be achieving a given share of the national market within a specified period. In so far as many decisions imply a change in the existing pattern of behaviour, the formulation of such goals is often related to external pressures. For example, the oil company's decision to break into a new market may be a response to the *stimulus* of a rapid rate of economic growth in the country concerned. On the other hand, the peasant farmer's reappraisal of the best means of achieving his basic goal of survival reflects the *stress* created by a poor harvest.

Closely related to the establishment of a general goal is its translation into a specific *criterion* or set of criteria. The oil company may seek to achieve its marketing objective with a minimum of capital investment in refining and retailing facilities. Thus its criterion is to minimize costs. Similarly, the peasant farmer may aim to produce the food necessary to ensure the survival of himself and his family while spending as little time as possible actually working his land so that he may engage in other social or ceremonial activities. In this case, the criterion is to minimize

* See glossary of terms.

the input of labour. The criterion provides the yardstick against which the decision maker attempts to assess the consequences of alternative courses of action. For example, certain crops demand more attention than others whilst the engineering costs of developing alternative sites will vary, affecting the oil company's choice of refinery location. These variables are controllable, but others may be non-controllable as far as the decision maker is concerned. The peasant farmer may be aware that a wet season favours certain crops rather than others whereas the availability of regional investment grants may be relevant to the oil company's assessment of different refinery sites. However, the peasant farmer cannot influence the climate and the oil company cannot always predict changes in government policy.

The *assembly of information* on the variables affecting the criterion is a prelude to the evaluation of alternatives. Information may be the result of a deliberate *search* or of accumulated *experience*. Practical constraints of time and money ensure that information obtained through search activities is limited and, no matter how conscientious, the decision maker must, in practice, rely upon information which is less than perfect. However, information obtained in this way will be supplemented by information derived through learning based on past experience. Although the distinction between searching and learning is blurred, their relative importance as methods of acquiring information tends to vary between decision makers. An oil company considering establishing a new refinery will probably carry out an extensive sophisticated review of alternative sites, gathering data on transport costs, labour supply, environmental restrictions and so on. The peasant farmer, on the other hand, is less geared to the systematic assembly of information and is much more likely to draw upon his own experience, rather than any formal procedure, and upon tradition, which is a form of accumulated experience, as information inputs to the *evaluation* stage.

Techniques have been developed to help the decision maker select the course of action which will either maximize or minimize the criterion that defines his objective. Unfortunately, these optimizing techniques characteristically depend upon the availability of perfect information and therefore relate to the hypothetical situation of decision making under conditions of certainty. Even the oil company will not attain this ideal and, in reality, the choice between alternatives must be made under conditions of uncertainty.

Once made, any decision becomes a matter of history, but it may have important effects upon subsequent decisions. In this respect it is convenient to distinguish between decisions which provide a stimulus to repeat an action and those which create a stress causing the decision maker to respond differently when a comparable situation occurs again. For example, high levels of demand for its products may encourage the oil company to modify its objective and attempt to obtain a greater market share than originally planned by expanding the capacity of its refinery. Conversely, a poor yield from his chosen crop can hardly change the peasant farmer's basic goal of survival, although it may, by contributing to knowledge gained through experience, influence his judgement in future years.

The model of the decision-making process represented in Figure 3.1 is used as a framework for the remainder of this chapter, which is divided into three sections concerned with (i) the formulation of goals, (ii) the assembly of information and (iii) the evaluation of information.

3.2 Goals

Several types of goal influence decision making in a spatial context and a distinction
may be drawn between those which are essentially economic in character; those
which relate to social or cultural circumstances; and finally, those which reflect
political aspirations. Although this division is convenient, it is also arbitrary and
it will become apparent that decision makers are often motivated by a combination
of goals which inevitably cut across any classification scheme. Indeed, the single-
minded pursuit of a specific goal is an exceptional form of human behaviour and
the actions of the majority of decision makers may be more realistically interpreted
in terms of the achievement of multiple objectives. The following section is divided
accordingly into a consideration of (i) economic goals, (ii) social goals, (iii) political
goals and (iv) multiple goals.

3.2.1 Economic Goals

The most important single motive upon which explanations of the location of
man's economic activities have been based is that of profit maximization. Many
of these explanations have been couched in terms of the concept of *Economic Man*.
In addition to the general objective of profit maximization, Economic Man is
assumed to possess certain other qualities which may be related to our model of
the decision-making process. He is totally rational in the sense that his actions
are governed exclusively by his attempts to maximize profit; his decisions are based
upon perfect information; his judgement is infallible as far as the evaluation of
alternative strategies is concerned. Economic Man is, therefore, an exceptional
character who has little resemblance to decision makers in the real world. Nevertheless, this contrast is the basis of the concept's usefulness since comparisons
between location patterns which may be expected to result from the actions of
Economic Man and those which reflect the decisions of the less predictable inhabitants of the real world may enhance our understanding of the distributions which
we see around us.

The concept of Economic Man has been used in this way to gain insights into
the factors responsible for patterns of urban and agricultural land use, but it has
been particularly important in the study of industrial location. The notion of profit
maximization instinctively seems appropriate in this context in view of the popular
belief that industrial firms are in business to make as much money as possible.
This assumption has certainly been incorporated into a number of theoretical
models which isolate the basic principles of industrial location. These models tend
to fall into two categories, depending upon whether they emphasize locations
which minimize production costs or locations which maximize revenues. However,
costs and revenues must obviously be considered simultaneously in any attempt
to identify the most profitable location. The greatest profit will not necessarily
be obtained at either the point of minimum production costs or the point of maximum revenues, but at the location where the difference between the two is greatest.
The implications of spatial variations in costs and revenues upon industrial location have been explored in theoretical terms by Smith (1966). Three different situations are represented in Figure 3.2. In case (a), the costs are variable in space while
demand (and therefore revenue) is constant. In case (b), the position is reversed,

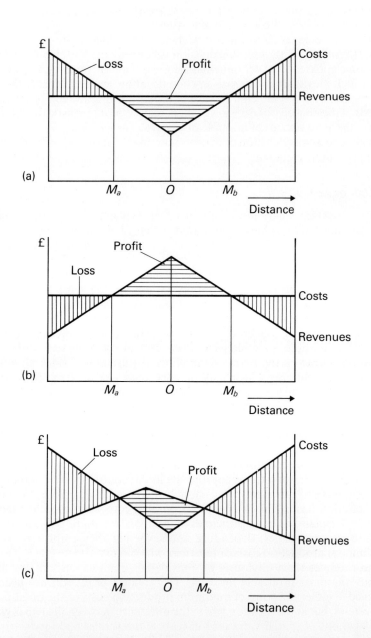

Fig. 3.2 Optimum factory location and spatial margin to profitability: (a) with variable costs; (b) with variable revenues; (c) with variable costs and revenues (after Smith, 1966, 96).

whilst case (c) indicates a more realistic situation in which cost and demand vary from place to place. Several simplifying assumptions are incorporated in the diagrams, but the important point to note is that although profits are greatest at O in each case, a location anywhere between M_a and M_b will ensure that revenues exceed costs. The distance $M_a - M_b$ on the graphs may be translated into an area around the maximum profit location at O. This area may be visualized in three-dimensional terms as a cone of profitability which slopes outwards and downwards from O to a base which defines the spatial margin beyond which an industrial plant begins to operate at a loss. Smith's notion of the spatial margin to profitability is important because it emphasizes the fact that the choice of location for an industrial plant is not tied to a single possibility. If the goal of maximum profit is replaced by the more flexible objective of 'satisfactory' profit, it is clear that decision makers have a wider range of locational choice than models which rest upon the normative* assumptions of Economic Man would imply.

Empirical studies of industrial location have underlined some of the practical difficulties associated with the concept of profit maximization. Circumstances affecting costs and revenues change rapidly, but industrial plants are, for obvious reasons, relatively immobile and their distribution at any given time is likely to be sub-optimal. For example, Milford Haven was established as the UK's major oil port during the 1960s because it was capable of receiving the new generation of oil tankers in excess of 100,000 tons dwt. By 1976, almost 25 per cent of UK refinery capacity was concentrated in the area despite the fact that it had become an obsolete location in the sense that the world's largest tankers had reached 500,000 tons dwt – well beyond the capacity of the Haven.

The lag between location patterns and changing circumstances is not the only way in which the time factor qualifies the goal of profit maximization. Business decisions are usually made within the framework of a particular time scale and the course of action adopted may differ depending upon whether the objective is to maximize profit in the short or long term. For example, a quick profit may be gained by locating an industrial plant on a rich ore field, but the life of the plant may be limited by the size of the deposit. On the other hand, the profitability of a plant located midway between several such deposits may be less spectacular in the short term, but its long-term prospects may be much better.

Case studies of individual firms have raised many doubts regarding the validity of profit maximization as a realistic goal for economic decision makers. Acceptance of 'satisfactory' profit makes it possible for non-economic considerations to influence plant location within the general area defined by the spatial margins to profitability. The literature on industrial location contains many examples of the influence of such personal factors as family ties with a particular town or city (see Smith, 1971). Furthermore, there is evidence to suggest that the importance of such factors varies with the nature of the decision-making unit (Townroe, 1969). Small firms are more likely to be influenced by non-economic factors (Eversley, 1965), although recent studies suggest that profit maximization cannot even be regarded as the dominant goal of the corporate capitalist. Long-term survival and growth are now seen as the most basic motivations governing the actions of large firms (Cyert and March, 1963). In addition, various subsidiary goals have been identified which

---

* See glossary of terms.

may conflict with the notion of profit maximization. For example, the sponsorship of cultural and sporting events by multinational corporations partly reflects their desire to promote an image of social responsibility which may not always be consistent with policies based exclusively on economic objectives.

3.2.2 Social Goals

If social factors restrain the vigour with which 'big business' pursues the profit motive, it is hardly surprising that the goals of decision makers in other fields of human activity are influenced by similar considerations. Social goals are an elusive amalgam of the beliefs of the individual and the values of the wider group to which he belongs. Since these values may be specific to the group, absolute standards or codes of behaviour which are independent of a particular cultural association are virtually impossible to establish. Despite these problems, it is feasible to identify at least two different ways in which what may be broadly termed social goals influence decision makers. First, the desire to 'get on' in life may be the principal motivation underlying the actions of an ambitious individual. Although success in this endeavour brings with it certain economic rewards, these are often seen as incidental to the principal goal of gaining the respect of others and therefore status in the community. Second, efforts to achieve desired standards in the quality of human existence rest upon the prior identification of certain social goals. For example, governments often pursue policies geared towards the attainment of specific welfare objectives such as the elimination of unemployment or gross inequalities in educational opportunities.

The scope for moving up the social pyramid varies from society to society and the status of most individuals is strongly influenced by that of the family into which they are born. It is often argued that social mobility is greater in urban/industrial societies than within agrarian or pre-industrial communities. There is no doubt that the social order is extremely rigid in many developing countries. In Latin America, for example, land ownership is an index of social status and a substantial proportion of the total area of many countries is in the hands of relatively few aristocratic families whilst most of the population remain landless (see Barraclough and Domike, 1966). This system of land tenure, which reflects the social (and political) goals of the land-owning class, has hindered agricultural development because members of this group are only rarely interested in the introduction of better farming practices and are generally content to regard the possession of land as an end in itself.

Social mobility is often associated with physical mobility. Migration decisions, for example, may be motivated by social goals. On an international scale, the new lands of the Americas have been seen by oppressed and underprivileged groups in many European countries as providing an opportunity for a fresh start and hopefully the attainment of a better position in a more fluid social order (see section 3.3.1). Similarly, residential location decisions at the urban scale often reflect a desire to move into a 'better' neighbourhood.

The nature of social goals as welfare targets is especially relevant to the formulation and implementation of public policy. The concept of the welfare state rests upon the proposition that every member of society has certain basic 'rights' such as free medical care and education. The extent to which this concept is accepted varies between countries, but there is evidence that the governments in most developed countries are assuming a growing responsibility for the living standards of their citizens. Even the US is moving towards the adoption of nationwide goals over a broad range of social policies. One of the reasons for this trend is a growing awareness of the inequalities which exist both between different sections of society and between different places. Despite the position of the US as the 'original' affluent society, 12 per cent of Americans (i.e. 26 million people) had incomes below the

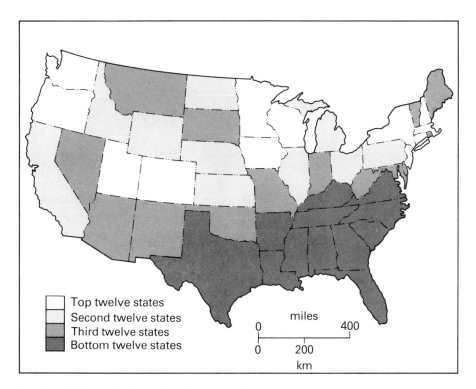

Fig. 3.3 Social well-being in the US (Smith, 1973, 89).

officially designated poverty level in 1976. Smith (1973) highlighted the spatial aspects of these inequalities in the US by mapping well-being at various scales. 'Well-being' is a composite index derived by compressing statistical data relating to such variables as income, education, health and living environment into a single measure. Distinctive patterns emerge with the southern states of the traditional cotton belt comparing unfavourably with the rest of the country when the index is plotted at a national scale (Fig. 3.3.) and a concentration of low scores around the centres of most of the major cities when it is plotted at the metropolitan scale (Fig. 3.4). These kinds of spatial variation are by no means confined to the US and similar patterns have been identified in the UK despite its smaller size and

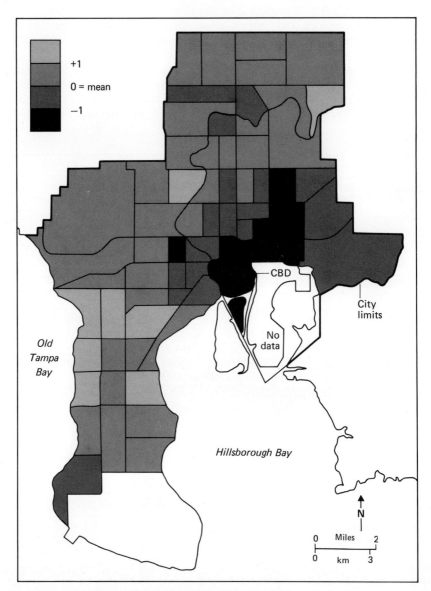

Fig. 3.4 Social well-being in Tampa, Florida (Smith, 1973, 126).

earlier acceptance of the principle of central government responsibility for welfare matters (see Coates and Rawstron, 1971; and Knox, 1974). The elimination of such inequalities is a utopian dream and the more modest objective of narrowing the differentials to generally acceptable levels is itself likely to require a very long-term commitment and hence ensure that social goals occupy an important role in central and local government decision making.

3.2.3 Political Goals

Welfare policies may be regarded as aimed as much towards achieving political as social goals since they often imply a redistribution of income in favour of the poorer sections of the community. Nevertheless, many government policies which are unambiguously political in their objectives are also clearly geographical in their effects. For example, policies of rural development have received high priority from most post-colonial African governments because of the high proportions of their populations engaged in agriculture. However, there are significant differences in approach between the various countries which may be related to the contrasting political philosophies of their governments, which in turn often reflect the views of dominant personalities. Nowhere are these contrasts more apparent than in the adjacent East African states of Kenya and Tanzania (Segal, 1967/68).

Tanzania has adopted the most radical rural development policy in Africa (see Connell, 1974). The abolition of freehold tenure was one of the first major pieces of legislation introduced following independence in 1961. In practice, this affected only a few non-African farmers by facilitating the expropriation of their land, but the legislation conformed with the political philosophy of the new government which was elected on the basis of a commitment to the principles of African socialism. These principles included notions of equity, self-reliance and communal ownership. The most important aspect of the translation of these principles into policy terms has been the establishment of cooperative village settlements. Although some of these settlements represent nothing more than a reorganization of existing villages, the majority have been entirely new creations and the policy has produced a major change in Tanzanian rural society since very few lived in villages before independence. The ideology of African socialism has been largely responsible for this transformation, but it has been reinforced by more pragmatic political considerations as officials within the villages have been able to maintain a direct link between 'grass-roots' support and the party and government hierarchy.

The approach in Kenya has been very different (see Odingo, 1971). The greatest contrast is in the emphasis placed on freehold ownership of land and individual initiative. This is, to some extent, a continuation of a policy begun in the 1950s which attempted to consolidate the fragmented holdings of the Kikuyu. These measures were accelerated following independence as a result of political pressures to resettle Africans in the White Highlands of western Kenya which had been occupied predominantly by European farmers under the colonial regime. A massive and immediate resettlement of Africans on former European land was seen as a condition of short-term political stability. Nevertheless, there is no doubt that the long-term view of Kenya's ruling elite favours a very different kind of society to that of Tanzania with a much greater commitment to the idea of individual enterprise. This contrast between the political goals of decision makers in government is reflected on the ground in the absence of fences on land surrounding Tanzanian villages compared with the division into separate plots which characterizes Kenyan settlement schemes.

Policies towards industry, as well as agriculture, are influenced by political goals. Patterns of industrial location in Eastern Europe, for example, can only be understood in the context of certain 'objective laws of socialist location' (Hamilton,

1971). These laws incorporate political objectives, such as the maintenance of national security, but they also take account of economic and social considerations such as the need to promote regional specialization in specific industries and the desirability of eliminating variations in living standards between urban and rural areas. Although officially regarded as 'objective', these 'laws', reveal inherent contradictions between different types of goal which inevitably require subjective judgements on the part of government planners as to their relative importance. Strategic arguments favoured the dispersal of heavy industry in Eastern Europe in the immediate post-war years. Since 1955, military influence on industrial-location decisions seems to have declined and the economic 'laws' have become dominant. Nevertheless, these issues are evident in a continuing debate within the Soviet hierarchy regarding the allocation of investment funds between European Russia and the eastern republics (Dienes, 1972). Per capita investment to the east of the Urals has, in recent years, been very much greater than in the more populous areas to the west. This policy offers few short-term economic benefits since the return on capital from massive projects in the east is poor. On the other hand, the exploitation of East Siberian energy resources may justifiably be regarded as a long-term investment. Even so, the debate is not solely concerned with economic issues and Soviet development policies in the east are certainly influenced by the presence of China and a desire to promote, through economic integration, the political unity of the USSR.

3.2.4 Multiple Goals

The use of examples from Eastern Europe and the Soviet Union should not be taken as an indication that political goals influence location decisions only in communist countries. A trend towards increasing government intervention in most 'western' nations is blurring the ideological distinction between communism and capitalism and contributing to the emergence of the 'mixed' economy in which both public and private decision makers are responsible for the allocation of resources. In this situation, it is becoming increasingly difficult to isolate the influence of economic, social and political goals in the formulation of policy. The controversy surrounding the future of the British steel industry following the nationalization of the major independent companies in 1967 is a good illustration of the problem. Nationalization itself was a political act resulting from the British Labour Party's commitment to public ownership. However, by creating the third-largest steel company in the non-communist world, this act provided an opportunity to create a more efficient industry, which had been impossible under the old order of fragmented commercial rivalries (Heal, 1974). Economic arguments suggested that there were too many small plants at obsolete locations and that the emphasis in future planning should be placed on large integrated works at coastal sites. However, the British Steel Corporation has found it very difficult to pursue a policy based exclusively upon economic objectives. A plan published in 1973 envisaged the partial or complete shut-down of many steel-making plants and the concentration of investment at five major locations. The social implications of closures in communities where the steelworks was the major employer provoked an angry reaction in many quarters. The issue was further complicated by the fact that shutdowns in Scotland and Wales might provide an impetus to political pressures for the break-up of the UK. Consequently, the achievement of the British Steel Corporation's economic objective of creating an efficient and internationally competitive industry has been hindered by successive government attempts to impose social and political responsibilities on the Corporation. Although the history of British Steel's attempts at rationalization suggests that conflicting objectives within government may inhibit decision making, it does underline the point that, in practice, decisions are generally aimed at achieving multiple goals or objectives. This is true of individuals, corporate bodies or governments and it is therefore naive to seek to understand decision-making behaviour in terms of a single overriding goal such as profit maximization.

3.3 Assembly of Information

The value or utility which an individual bestows on a place is a complex function of his goals and his knowledge of that place. His knowledge may be gleaned directly by visiting the place, but such visits are often impracticable, not least because of the effect of distance, and indirect sources of information may have to relied upon. 'Second-hand' impressions of places may be formed either through the casual acquisition of information by contact with others or as a result of a deliberate search. Nevertheless, constraints of time and money generally impose limits on systematic search procedures and decisions concerning the relative merits of different places typically rest upon information which is both incomplete and, when derived from secondary sources, frequently inaccurate. Some of these issues may be illustrated by reference to migration decisions at three spatial scales: (i) between continents, (ii) within countries and (iii) within cities.

3.3.1 International Migration

The mass exodus of settlers during the nineteenth and early twentieth centuries from Europe to the Americas, Africa and Australasia was one of the major migrations of mankind. The decision to leave long established homes was often prompted by negative factors such as the Irish Famine of the 1840s, but the choice between alternative destinations was influenced by positive feelings about the opportunities they offered. Sources of information were critical in the development of popular images of the 'new lands'. The fact that many of these sources were unreliable led Watson (1969) to emphasize the role of 'illusion' in the geography of pioneer settlement. These illusions reflected not only the quantity and quality of information, but also the way in which it was interpreted. Watson argues that much of the heart of the North American continent was neglected by early settlers because of the absence of trees. European experience suggested that treeless land was also infertile and so the 'Great American Desert' became reality in the minds and on the maps of the pioneers. Consequently, the Great Plains were, for a long time, seen as a barrier which the settlers must cross to reach the fertile lands of Oregon and California.

Quite apart from the psychological aspects of interpreting information, nineteenth-century emigrants often had little knowledge of the places they were going to. For example, the colony of Western Australia was established in 1829 on the basis of a favourable report following an expedition to the Swan River two years earlier. The mouth of this river is the only extensive alluvial deposit along the entire coastline of Western Australia. It covers an area of less than one hundred square miles, but favourable conclusions about the area, formed in only nine days on the mainland, were applied to a coastal plain approximately 150 miles long and 20 to 30 miles wide (Cameron, 1974). The 'stretching' of information in space was frequently accompanied by similar extrapolations through time as no account was taken of seasonal variations. Ignorance of the true nature of environmental conditions in Northern Queensland was initially fostered by the fact that most of the nineteenth-century explorers happened to arrive during the dry season. This accident of timing was partly responsible for subsequent mistakes in the agricultural development of the area around the Gulf of Carpentaria (Bauer, 1963). False impressions based on inadequate information were often reinforced by deliberate distortions on the part of promoters, who stood to gain commercially by encouraging emigrants to go to a particular place, and government officials, who sometimes used settlers as pawns in a political power game. Extravagant claims about the climate and soils of Natal were made by promoters of the British settlement between 1849 and 1851 (Christopher, 1973), and the handbook promoting the Welsh colony in Patagonia was reduced in value by the tendency of its author to select '... from what he had read that which he considered favourable to his argument' (Bowen, 1965, 17). A more subtle piece of psychology was employed by Eirik the Red who adopted the name Greenland for his discovery because, he argued, that men would be more likely to colonize a land with an attractive name (Jones, 1964)! In view of this kind of deviousness, it is not surprising that so many emigrants have had dreams of a promised land rudely shattered on arrival at some inhospitable shore.

3.3.2 Interregional Migration

Although the numbers involved are generally smaller and the time/space scales compressed, migration decisions affecting population movements within countries have important economic and social consequences. In the US, for example, most of the southern states have been net exporters of population to the Northeast and Midwest for much of the twentieth century. In the UK, the direction of movement is reversed and the 'drift south' has been a matter of concern to planners ever since the 1930s. The dominant flow in most developing countries is from rural to urban areas – very often to a single rapidly growing capital city. Persistent out-migration tends to aggravate the economic problems of underdeveloped areas as they are drained of their working population, creating an unbalanced community in which the young and the old are over-represented. Thus migration movements within a country both reflect and accentuate potentially divisive inequalities in living standards and job opportunities. These movements are obviously related to real differences in economic and social conditions, but there is evidence to suggest that even in such a small, developed country as the UK, the availability and interpretation of information about places ensure that prejudices, if not illusions, continue to exert an important influence upon migration decisions, which in turn have repercussions on patterns of regional development.

Various attempts have been made to measure attitudes about places by constructing *perception surfaces*. These surfaces are obtained by asking individuals

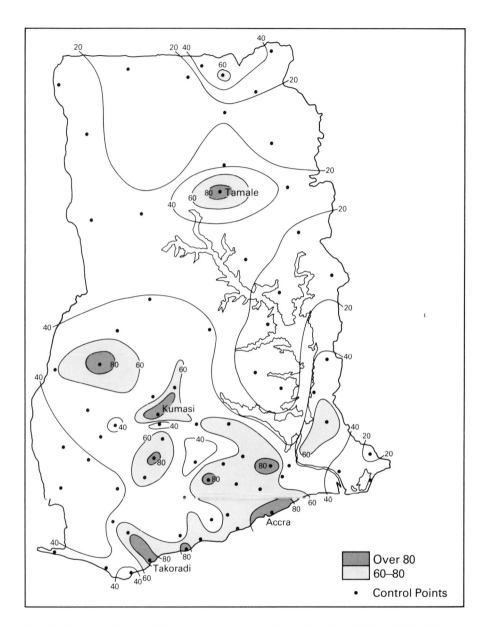

Fig. 3.5 The mental map of Ghanaian university students (Gould and White, 1974, 165).

to rank districts or regions in terms of their attractiveness as places in which to live and work. There are many technical problems attached to such questionnaires, but they do give a general index of residential desirability (see Gould, 1974). The responses of a sample of university students in Ghana provided the data for Figure 3.5. The attitudes of students are especially important because they represent the trained personnel required to promote future economic growth. The most favoured areas are indicated by the highest values and the surface was drawn by interpolating contour lines from 'spot heights' of residential desirability scores ascribed to each district. The map suggests that the urban centres are popular whereas the rural areas seem unattractive. This kind of pattern, which has been observed in other

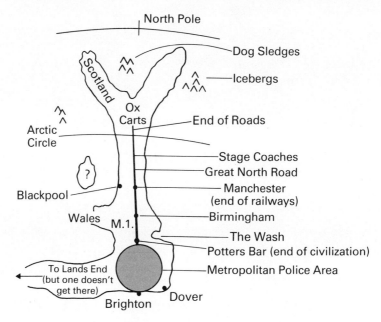

Fig. 3.6 The Londoner's view of Britain (according to the Doncaster and District Development Council) (Gould and White, 1974, 40).

developing countries (see Gould and White, 1974), supports the idea that the 'bright lights' image of the cities accelerates the exodus from rural to urban areas. It is a depressing reminder of the difficulties facing developing nations in achieving higher living standards whilst at the same time avoiding the worst problems of unbalanced growth (see section 5.2).

Whereas the growth of cities may be reinforced by over-optimistic impressions of the opportunities which they offer, declining or peripheral areas often have an unfavourable image which aggravates their problems. The map shown in Figure 3.6 was produced by a development authority in northern England as a way of drawing attention to the false impressions which many people in southeast England hold regarding the rest of the country. Although obviously tongue-in-cheek, it contains more than a grain of truth. The establishment of new industry in areas of out-migration is an important means of stemming the flow, and the movement of work to the workers has been a persistent thread running through British regional policy. However, the success of this policy ultimately depends on the location decisions of industrial firms. Studies of such decisions have suggested that the kind of prejudices represented in Figure 3.6 do affect the willingness of firms to open new plants in northern England and Scotland (see Cameron and Clark, 1966). Indeed regional and local development agencies are often established to overcome such prejudices by trying to 'sell' the qualities of their own area as a location for new industry (Hall, 1970).

3.3.3 Intra-Urban Migration

Secondary sources of information become less important as the scale of the contemplated move is reduced and more data are obtained directly through a kind of spatial learning process as individuals become most familiar with the areas around home and workplace and the route between them. Thus there tends to be a reciprocal relationship between movement patterns and images of the city. These images may be regarded as contributing to the formation by every individual of a *mental map* of his surroundings. The amount of information contained in such mental maps of a city is restricted by the movement experiences of the individual and yet these maps themselves set limits on his subsequent movement. This relationship has been tested by examining changes in residential location within cities.

Journey-to-work movements to offices located in the central area may be expected to create a linear bond of familiar territory in the mind of the commuter. Adams (1969) tested the hypothesis that this geographically constrained image of the city influences the pattern of intra-urban migration by serving as a kind of channel within which most changes of residential address will take place. He examined the distribution of moves within Minneapolis over three different time periods. The results of his work did reveal a directional bias along the axis of a line drawn from the original residence to the centre of the city. When the angle of the moves relative to this axis was plotted on a graph it was evident that the most frequently occurring values were around 0° and 180° – these two extremes representing movements along the axis inwards towards the centre and outwards towards the periphery respectively (Fig. 3.7). However, 'tunnel vision' of the city oriented towards the central area is possibly less important than Adams's work implies. The focal significance of the central area as a source of employment is tending to decline and cities do not have a simple concentric ring structure of housing quality. A study of intra-urban migration in Melbourne made the axis between the original home and workplace, whether located in the central area or not, the reference line (Whitelaw and Robinson, 1972). The results are less conclusive, but the link between spatial biases in information availability about the city and the residential location decision remains clear.

Migration decisions are not the only ones affected by quantity and quality of information. This combination is fundamental to any decision and the distinction between searching and learning in acquiring knowledge of places is also appropriate to the assembly of information required, for example, by the housewife, in choosing between different shops or by the industrial firm in selecting one location rather than another for its new plant. The significance of information and the

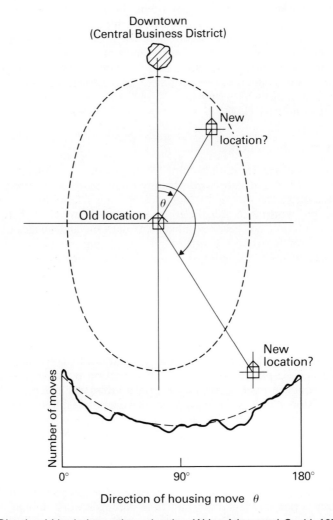

Fig. 3.7 Directional bias in intra-urban migration (Abler, Adams and Gould, 1971, 501).

factors affecting its availability to decision makers are considered further in chapter 7, but we will now examine some of the ways in which it is evaluated as a prelude to choice between alternative courses of action.

3.4 Evaluation

The final stage in the decision-making process, after establishing general objectives, translating these into specific criteria and assembling relevant information, is the evaluation of different strategies (see Kaufmann, 1968). Such evaluation may involve the formal testing of alternatives by means of analytical procedures or it may be based upon a value judgement by the decision maker. No matter if the approach to evaluation is simple or sophisticated, the choice between alternative strategies must be made in an uncertain environment. The success of the outcome, measured in terms of the initial goal(s) of the decision maker, will be strongly influenced by his ability to anticipate such uncertainties. This assertion may be supported by reference to various studies which deal with the problem of (i) uncertainty and decision making in theory and (ii) uncertainty and decision making in practice.

3.4.1 Uncertainty and Decision Making in Theory

Several studies have compared the spatial patterns which result from decision making in an uncertain real world with those created by decision making in a corresponding theoretical world of perfect information. Cox (1965) used a technique known as linear programming* to analyse patterns of inter-state movements of aluminium bars in the US in 1960. He argued that suppliers of aluminium may be expected to match the demands of consumers by adopting a pattern of flows which minimize total transport costs. The essence of this so-called 'transportation problem' is represented in Figure 3.8a, which indicates three widely separated centres of production in the Pacific Northwest, the southwest Gulf Coast and New

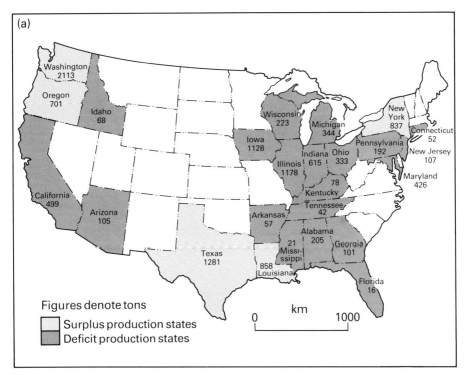

Fig. 3.8 Production and consumption of aluminium bars in the US, 1960: (a) surplus and deficit regions; (b) actual inter-state flow pattern; (c) optimum inter-state flow pattern (after Cox, 1965).

* See glossary.

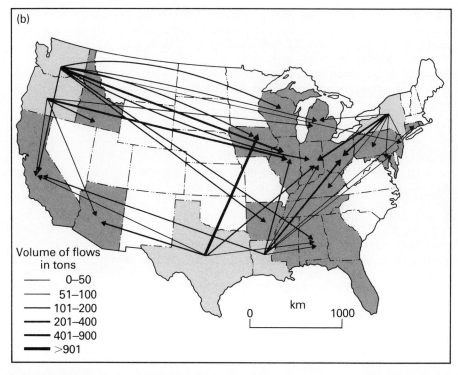

(b)

Volume of flows
in tons

—— 0–50
—— 51–100
—— 101–200
—— 201–400
—— 401–900
—— >901

km
0   1000

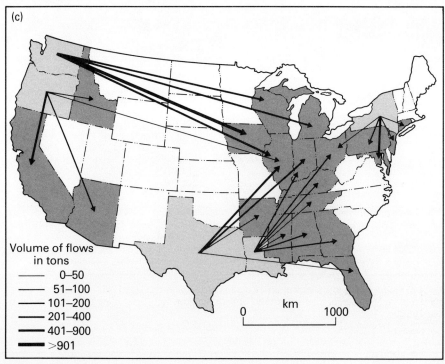

(c)

Volume of flows
in tons

—— 0–50
—— 51–100
—— 101–200
—— 201–400
—— 401–900
—— >901

km
0   1000

York state, and two principal centres of demand in California and the Midwest. Cox contrasted the actual pattern of inter-state flows (Fig. 3.8b) with a linear programming solution which minimized the total haulage distances required to match supply and demand (Fig. 3.8c). Comparison of the two maps reveals considerable differences between the complex real-world pattern and the much simpler theoretical pattern. Generally speaking, flows between distant states such as Washington and Illinois tend to be higher than the linear-programming solution whereas those between adjacent states such as Oregon and California tend to be lower. This discrepancy is not so surprising when it is remembered that transport costs per ton-mile usually decline with distance so that the cost curve is convex from the origin rather than diagonal (see section 6.1.1). Cox incorporated this relationship into a second linear-programming solution which improved the correspondence between the actual and predicted flows. Nevertheless, the correlation between them remained poor and any attempt to account for this discrepancy must take account of the difficulties facing decision makers in an uncertain world.

Cox's study is a retrospective application of linear programming. Hindsight gives many advantages, especially with regard to the availability of information. Thus, US aluminium producers could not know at any given time either the existing or the future demand situation in every state of the union. Furthermore, the linear-programming solution in Figure 3.8c is unrealistic in the sense that the freedom to switch patterns of movement would, in practice, be restricted by contractual

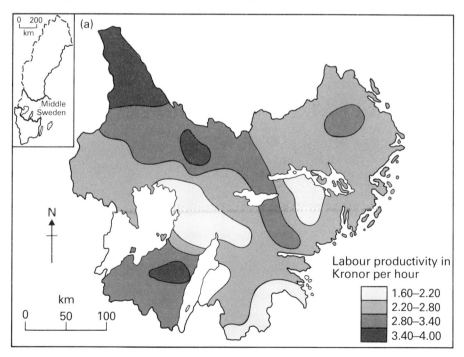

Fig. 3.9 Agricultural labour productivity in Middle Sweden, 1956–1959: (a) actual labour productivity; (b) potential labour productivity; (c) ratio of actual to potential labour productivity (after Wolpert, 1964).

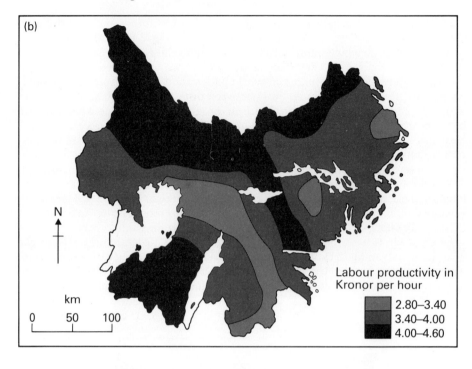

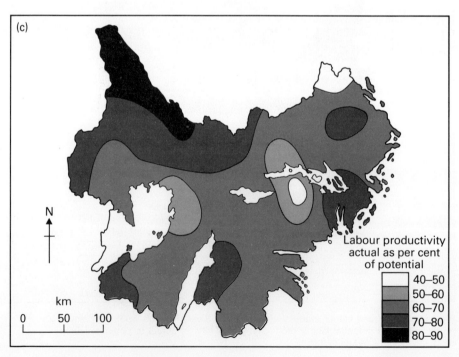

obligations and the capacity of transport facilities. Despite these qualifications, linear programming does have a place in corporate decision making, even though its value is often limited by the non-availability of information (see Rees, 1974). From an academic point of view, theoretical solutions are useful because they provide a yardstick against which reality may be measured and, as such, help us to understand the decision-making process. This property has been effectively demonstrated by Wolpert (1964) in a study of the decision-making behaviour of farmers in part of Sweden.

Wolpert carried out a sample survey of farms in Middle Sweden over the period 1956–1959 to determine their productivity in terms of the monetary return obtained for one hour's labour. Variables affecting productivity such as the size of the farms and their capital equipment were noted and linear programming was used to determine the maximum returns which could be achieved if all the farmers made the best use of their resources given 'average' environmental conditions. The results of this exercise were expressed in terms of the contrast between two maps indicating actual (Fig. 3.9a) and potential (Fig. 3.9b) labour productivity. This contrast was emphasized in a third map which combined the two distributions into a single ratio of actual to potential productivity (Fig. 3.9c). This ratio seemed to display a consistent spatial pattern with farmers in the northwest of the study area approaching 80 per cent of the theoretical optimum compared with a figure of less than 50 per cent in some eastern parts. By analysing this pattern, Wolpert was able to identify spatial variations in the factors affecting the decision-making behaviour of individual farmers. His conclusions have a bearing upon each of the three stages in our model of the decision-making process. Thus he discovered that the extent to which farmers adopted the theoretical goal of profit maximization was influenced by such factors as their age, whether they farmed as tenants or landowners and the nature of their physical environment. The availability of information upon which to base decisions was found to vary in space so that farmers close to government research institutes, for example, were more aware of new techniques than their colleagues in more isolated communities. The ability to evaluate information was influenced by similar factors, but the failure of farmers to achieve optimum labour productivity was related above all to the fact that their decisions were made without the advantages of perfect knowledge and infallible judgement which are incorporated within the linear-programming solution.

3.4.2 Uncertainty and Decision Making in Practice

All decisions are, in reality, made under conditions of uncertainty. This is partly due to practical limitations upon the assembly of information and partly due to the impossibility of accurately predicting future events. Despite employing a significant proportion of their staff in information-gathering activities such as market research, even the largest organizations restrict the resources they devote to these efforts. For example, although the choice of a location for a new factory obviously involves very large sums of money, empirical evidence suggests that such decisions are often based on surprisingly limited information (Dicken, 1971). Rapidly growing multinational corporations may make location decisions of this type at frequent intervals and it has been shown that certain US companies operating in Western Europe have developed a routine procedure for dealing with this problem (Blackbourn, 1974). But in this, they are the exception rather than the rule. However, where sophisticated evaluation exercises *are* carried out, even they cannot eliminate the uncertainty associated with future environmental states.

The spatial context is continuously evolving and successful decision makers must necessarily take account of this. Whilst distance itself has been shown in chapter 1 to be flexible through time, it is the physical and human content of space which is subject to the most rapid change. Seasonal fluctuations in weather conditions are, for example, an important element of uncertainty affecting the decisions of farmers. Similarly the success or failure of a new industrial plant may hinge upon the policies of competitors or upon the maintenance of existing economic trends, both of which are beyond the control of the firm responsible for the location decision. Temporal fluctuations in the physical environment are considered in chapter 4, but we will now look in more detail at the significance of uncertainty – firstly, in situations where decisions are directly affected by the actions of others, and secondly, in circumstances where there is disagreement regarding future economic and social conditions.

A field of study known as the *theory of games* has provided some valuable insights into the nature of interdependencies between the actions of decision makers. As the name implies, it is founded upon principles of conflict and cooperation incorporated within even the most elementary of children's games. The theory of games has been most widely used by economists and sociologists in the explanation of human behaviour, but it has also been applied to such intrinsically geographical problems as the question of industrial location (Isard and Smith, 1967). Assume that there is an island with a deposit of iron ore and that three countries are interested in building a plant to process this ore for export. The best location at which to build a plant differs for each country as a result of the orientation of three existing island ports relative to their own coastlines (Fig. 3.10). However, savings in production costs which more than offset additional transport charges may be achieved if the three countries cooperate and build a larger, more efficient processing plant at a central location. This location may be anywhere within a general area, but it is in the interests of each country to see the plant built at the point closest to its original independent choice. Isard and Smith develop a *locational game* in which these interests are resolved under alternative assumptions regarding the way the participants behave. Although the concept of a game may seem unreal, it is a valid formalization of the kind of trade-offs involved in a negotiating situation.

In some cases, the scope for compromise may be limited because the basic positions of the participants are so fundamentally different. These differences may reflect alternative views of an uncertain future. A major public debate took place in the UK during the 1960s and early 1970s over the selection of a site for a third London airport to supplement the existing ones at Heathrow and Gatwick. A Royal Commission was set up to consider the problem. Four sites were considered in detail, but the method adopted in evaluating the advantages and disadvantages of the alternative sites was heavily criticized as 'bogus accountancy' because it involved placing a monetary value on such essentially unquantifiable elements as human life itself. However, an even more basic objection questioned the terms of reference of the Commission which rested upon the assumption that a new airport was needed. The Commission's projections of the growth in air traffic indicated that the number of aircraft movements through London would triple between 1970 and 1990, resulting in the saturation of facilities at Heathrow and Gatwick by the early 1980s (Commission, 1971). By contrast, an alternative view suggested that a growth of only 50 to 80 per cent over the same period would be equally plausible if aircraft continue to increase in size as they have done in the past, thereby reducing the number of flights required to carry a given number of passengers (Whitby, 1971). Yet another critic did not regard the forecast of the Commission as necessarily inaccurate, but took it to be a self-fulfilling prophecy in the sense that the provision of a new airport would stimulate further traffic

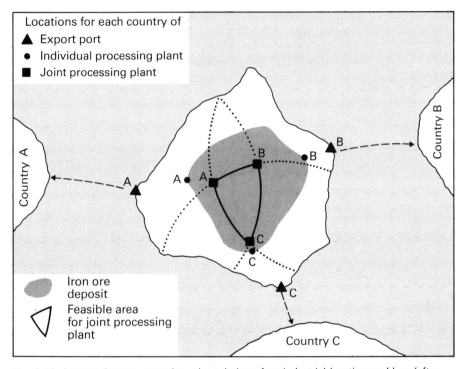

Fig. 3.10 A game theory approach to the solution of an industrial location problem (after Icard and Smith, 1067).

(Adams, 1971). These differences of opinion underline the fact that any decision to build a third London airport must be made under conditions of uncertainty. In the event, the British government eventually decided to abandon the idea altogether. This decision may be seen as a vindication of those who questioned the need in the first place, but it may also be interpreted in rather a different way.

Given the doubt surrounding the need for another airport and the enormous costs of its development, it was easier for policy-makers in Whitehall to choose the negative option of abandoning the project rather than make a positive decision in favour of a particular site. Viewed in this way, this example illustrates another aspect of the role of uncertainty in decision making. So far we have regarded the minimization of uncertainty as a prerequisite to making the best choice between alternative courses of action. However, in the case of the third London airport, it may be argued that acceptance of the status quo was itself a decision aimed at minimizing uncertainty since it avoided the risk of making a costly mistake in view of the differences of opinion regarding the need for such an airport. It is thus possible to draw a logical distinction between attempting to minimize uncertainty as part of the *evaluation* of alternative strategies and attempting to minimize uncertainty as a *goal*. Although the protracted debate over the third London airport conforms with the popular image of inertia in government, it depicts a characteristic response to uncertainty which may be seen in decision making at other levels. For example, a study of peasant farmers in Colombia revealed that their unwillingness to experiment with any new techniques or crops was a major obstacle to agricultural development (Grundig, 1970/71). Traditional methods of cultivation are, by definition, well tried and a policy of ignorant habit avoids the risks of innovation.

More obvious and direct attempts to minimize uncertainty were apparent in the decision-making behaviour of the Swedish farmers studied by Wolpert (1964). Thus the diversification of crops was seen as a safeguard against climatic variability since an analysis of production figures over the period 1921–1960 revealed little correlation between the annual yields of, say, barley and wheat. Similar strategies may be observed in corporate decision making. The emergence of so-called 'conglomerate' companies with interests in many sectors of the economy reflects the greater security of diversification, whilst policies of backward and forward integration enable large companies to control their sources of raw material and their markets respectively. In the case of large companies, these policies have international repercussions. The establishment of many pulp mills at coastal and interior locations in British Columbia since 1960, for example, reflects the attempts of firms based elsewhere in North America, Western Europe and Japan to gain security of raw material supply (Barr and Fairbairn, 1974). Paradoxically, decision making in multinational corporations may be likened to the behaviour of Colombian peasants in the sense that common solutions tend to be adopted towards recurrent problems, which may again be interpreted as a desire to minimize uncertainty (Dicken, 1971).

We have turned full circle in our discussion of the decision-making process. It is clear that uncertainty is not only a condition affecting the evaluation stage of this process, but that it also has a bearing upon the establishment of goals and objectives. Indeed, the minimization of uncertainty is a common theme which links the three stages in our model of the decision-making process: it may be regarded as a goal in its own right; it is aided by the assembly of information; and it conditions the approach to evaluation. Uncertainty has even wider implications as far as the study of human geography is concerned. The complexity of the decision-making process is such that we cannot predict human responses to real-world situations with the precision implied by such normative concepts as Economic Man. However, the nature of the relationship between the decision maker and the content and dimensions of space ensures that we can make certain generalizations about spatial behaviour at the aggregate, if not at the individual, level. Although these generalizations take the form of probability statements rather than deterministic laws, they enable us to perceive a measure of order and pattern in the spatial distribution of man's activities.

Further Reading

GOULD, P. and WHITE, R. 1974: *Mental maps.* London.

A readable account of the formation and significance of images of place.

KAUFMANN, A. 1968: *The science of decision making.* London.

Although not directly concerned with geographical applications, this book outlines the nature of the decision-making process.

VAJDA, S. 1966: *An introduction to linear programming and the theory of games* (2nd edition), London.

A simple introduction to the mathematics of linear programming and game theory.

WOLPERT, J. 1964: The decision process in a spatial context. *Association of American Geographers, Annals* **54,** 537–58.

A classic paper which demonstrates the way in which spatial patterns of human activities may be interpreted as the results of decision making.

The Content of Space

4   The Physical Environment

The idea that the properties of the physical environment control patterns of human behaviour has a pedigree extending as far back as the fifth century BC when the philosopher Hippocrates suggested that the pre-eminence of Greek civilization was somehow related to the Mediterranean climate. Very similar arguments were employed by the American geographer Huntington who postulated a link between climatic change and the rise and fall of the world's great civilizations (Huntington, 1915), but any approach to the study of human geography which emphasizes the decision-making role of man implies the need for a more flexible interpretation of human behaviour in space than the philosophy of environmental determinism permits. Nevertheless, it is clear that the properties of the physical environment do significantly affect spatial patterns of human activity. These properties may be viewed in two ways as far as their influence upon man as a decision maker is concerned. On the one hand, unfavourable climate or terrain, for example, may

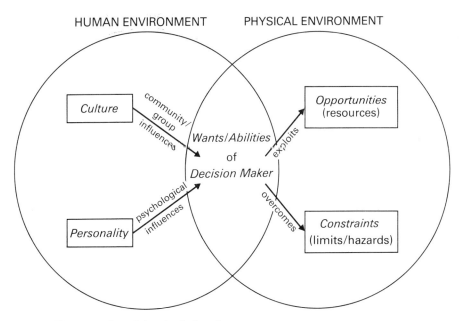

Fig. 4.1 The perception of the physical environment.

impose certain *constraints* upon the human occupation and use of land. On the other hand, especially fertile soils or rich mineral deposits may be regarded as presenting certain *opportunities*. Human responses to such constraints and opportunities are, however, 'determined' as much by the personality and cultural background of the decision maker as by the properties of the physical environment itself. Figure 4.1 provides a simple representation of these relationships and their influence upon the satisfaction of human needs. In a sense, the diagram should incorporate a third dimension reflecting the influence of time upon these relationships. Thus neither the properties of the physical environment nor the wants and abilities of man remain static. For example, changes in climate may bring about major shifts in the distribution of agricultural opportunities and constraints. Although such changes in environmental distributions may have important repercussions upon the spatial arrangement of human activities at the earth's surface, an awareness of changes in the cultural and psychological filters indicated in Figure 4.1 is even more important to an understanding of the role of (1) the physical environment as a constraint and (ii) the physical environment as an opportunity.

4.1 Physical Environment as a Constraint

In considering the role of the physical environment as a constraint upon man, it is convenient to make a distinction between (i) environmental limits and (ii) environmental hazards. The concept of environmental limits implies the existence of certain critical thresholds which man cannot afford to ignore. Environmental hazards such as floods and earthquakes are less fundamental constraints which are viewed as inconveniences rather than absolute limits. These differences in the impact of limits and hazards upon human activities reflect the time scale over which they operate. Whereas hazards may be regarded as periodic events, limits relate to more or less stable situations.

4.1.1 Environmental Limits

Environmental limits are imposed by the existing distribution of landforms, vegetation and other physical phenomena. However, such limits are specific to a particular culture and are, therefore, subject to a continuing process of human reappraisal through time. Variations in space and change through time provide a dual perspective within which human attitudes and responses towards environmental limits may be examined. These themes are considered in the following section by reference to (i) limits in space and (ii) limits through time.

Limits in Space
Spatial variations in environmental limits may be observed at various scales. Thus a farmer may be aware of certain limits to cultivation on those parts of his land which, for example, have slopes that are too steep and rocky for any kind of agricultural land use. At the other end of the scale, common sense suggests that there are certain areas of the world in which environmental conditions make human life very difficult, if not impossible. It is at this level that the significance of environmental limits is most apparent as extreme cold, aridity and the large water bodies of the oceans impose obvious restrictions upon human settlement and upon food

production (Fig. 4.2). Nevertheless, the areas which are most productive in terms of their nutritional output for human consumption are not necessarily those in which biological productivity (the rate of appearance of energy and matter as living tissue) is greatest. Comparison of Figures 4.2 and 4.3 emphasizes that some of the most important food-producing areas such as the wheatlands of North America and European Russia are found in zones of relatively low biological productivity. Although experiments in the equatorial forests have demonstrated that biological productivity is not necessarily a reliable index of agricultural potential (Harris, 1974), the discrepancies between the two maps do nevertheless suggest that a higher level of technology has enabled farmers in the temperate latitudes of North America and Europe to make effective use of environments which are less favourable to plant growth than those of the tropics.

The significance of technology in relaxing the constraints imposed by the physical environment may be illustrated by considering the possibilities for agriculture in desert areas. The productivity of the world's deserts tends to be uniformly low whether viewed from a nutritional (Fig. 4.2) or a biological (Fig. 4.3) point of view, but this situation may be transformed provided the technical and economic means are available to introduce water for irrigation. The technical possibilities for such agricultural development have been demonstrated by a recent scheme in Libya (Allan, 1976). The Kufrah project is located in the heart of the Libyan Desert. It rests upon the tapping of fossil ground-water contained in porous sandstones beneath the desert. The scheme was started in 1970 and by 1975 it consisted of 10,000 ha of fodder production for livestock breeding and fattening together with a further 5,000 ha of small farms. Despite the spectacular appearance of this man-made oasis in the middle of the desert, many problems have been experienced which place the project in perspective. The rate of ground-water depletion has been more rapid than originally predicted and the costs have escalated dramatically. Indeed, whilst Kufrah may have shown the technical feasibility of introducing agriculture into the deserts of North Africa, it has also emphasized that such schemes cannot make economic sense under present circumstances. It is significant that Libya, with its massive oil revenues, is unique amongst North African states in attempting to implement this type of scheme and the transformation of the Sahara into a green and fertile land remains little more than a dream.

Such dreams nevertheless continue to motivate plans to alter the spatial distribution of environmental limits on scales which make the Kufrah project pale into insignificance. For example, by 1975 irrigated pasture and arable land occupied more than 150,000,000 ha of former desert and steppe in Central Asia and the flow of most of the rivers in an area extending from the Caspian Sea in the west to Tashkent in the east was regulated by canals and reservoirs (Reteyum (trans. Shaw), 1976). Any undesirable side-effects such as soil salinization and a significant drop in the level of the Aral Sea are officially regarded as being more than offset by the benefits of increased agricultural production and a long-term plan for the southward diversion of water from Siberian rivers into Central Asia is under consideration. This proposal is just one of a number of massive projects including river-basin transfers, hydroelectric schemes and continental-scale shelter belts which reflect the continuing significance in Soviet policy making of attitudes originally formalized in Stalin's programme for 'The Transformation of Nature' (Gerasimov, 1976). The fact that man is able even to contemplate such schemes emphasizes

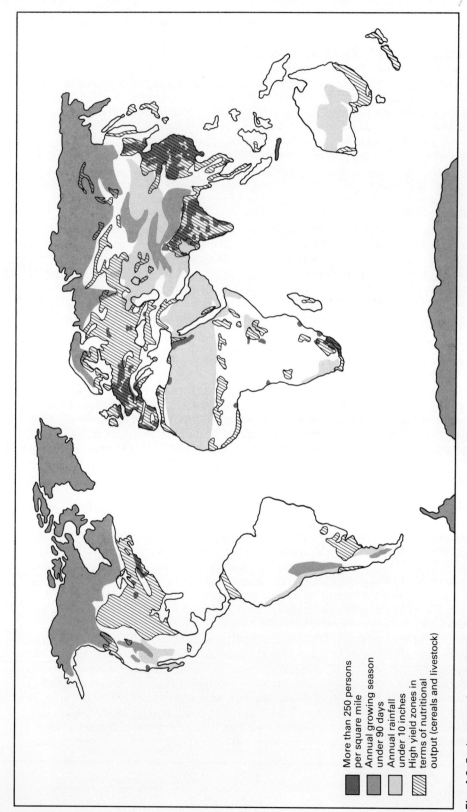

More than 250 persons
per square mile

Annual growing season
under 90 days

Annual rainfall
under 10 inches

High yield zones in
terms of nutritional
output (cereals and livestock)

Fig. 4.2 Environmental constraints, population distribution and agricultural production (after *The Times Concise Atlas of the World*, 1972, 18, 20).

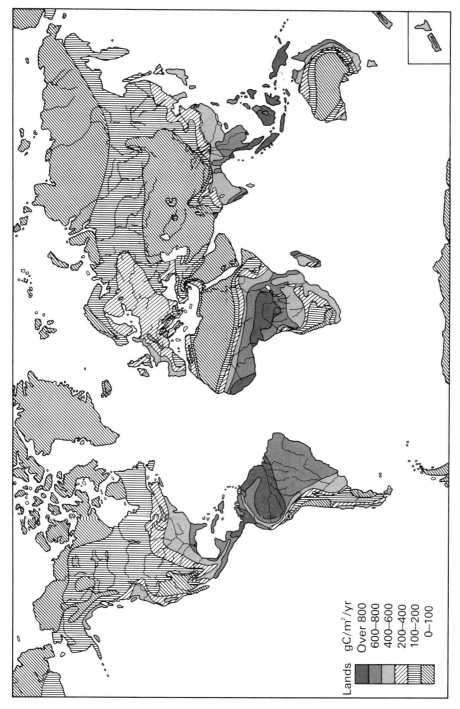

Fig. 4.3 World distribution of biological productivity expressed in grams of Carbon (after Simmons, 1974, 18).

the significance of technology in relaxing some of the constraints upon human activities imposed by the physical environment. Nevertheless, it is important to place the role of technology in perspective. The scope for extending the area of the world's cultivated land by means of irrigation is greatest in those less developed countries which, generally speaking, lack the capital to pay for such schemes. Thus political and economic constraints may reinforce physical ones. Furthermore, the consequences of environmental engineering on the scale of the Siberian river diversions for such natural systems as the hydrological cycle are little understood and such uncertainties may be related to a growing awareness within urban/industrial societies that there are indeed certain limits beyond which man should not go.

Limits through Time

Recent concern regarding the environmental implications of continued economic growth has prompted a reappraisal in Western societies of man's place in nature. The theme is an old one and many writers have reviewed the evolution of the man/ environment relationship in differing cultural situations (see Glacken, 1967; White, 1967). This relationship is typically portrayed as a sequence in which man passes from a submissive role to one of dominance over nature in accordance with advances in his technical abilities (see section 4.2.1). These advances have brought about both relative and absolute changes through time in the distribution of environmental limits. On the one hand, it may be argued that technical change has made it possible to extend areas of cultivation and settlement into different types of physical environment, the distribution of which has changed little in historic time. On the other hand, these distributions have, in certain cases, been significantly modified by man's activities.

Figure 4.4 shows the principal archaeological finds of Neolithic antiquities in England and Wales. It may be regarded as a reasonable approximation of the distribution of Neolithic population, although the southwest peninsula and East Anglia have been shown to be more important in recent work (Whittle, 1978). The map suggests a close correlation between settlement and physical environment. Neolithic agricultural implements could only cope with light soils developed on chalk, limestone, river gravels and coastal sands. The glacial boulder clays, which have subsequently become far more important in terms of agricultural output than the uplands of the Cotswolds and the Yorkshire Wolds that are so prominent in Figure 4.4, imposed clear limits on cultivation during the Neolithic.

The influence of soils upon Neolithic settlement patterns is difficult to separate from that of the forests which were themselves associated with the heavier clay lands. Thus much of Europe was once covered by dense forests that were virtually impenetrable to Neolithic Man. However, with the passage of time, these woodlands have not only been penetrated, but have also been cleared. The scale of this human modification of the physical environment is apparent in the contrast between the distribution of forest in central Europe *ca.* 900 (Fig. 4.5a) and the corresponding distribution one thousand years later (Fig. 4.5b). This clearance has been described as 'the greatest single factor in the evolution of the European landscapes' (Darby, 1956, 183). Such man-induced changes in the distribution of environmental limits are by no means restricted to Europe and it is generally agreed that the savannahs of West Africa, for example, at least partially reflect the impact of repeated burning (see Bartlett, 1956).

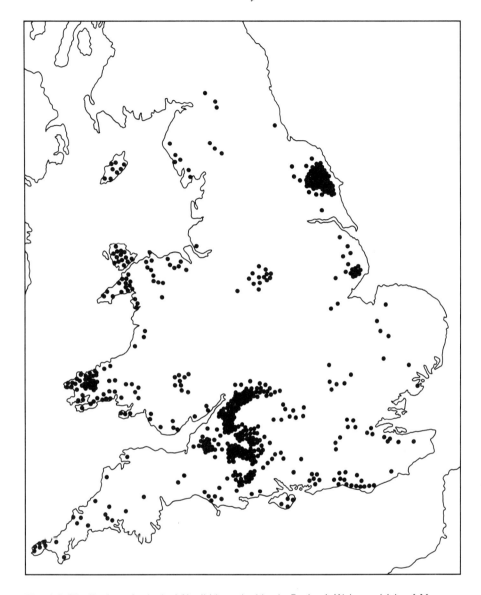

Fig. 4.4 Distribution of principal Neolithic antiquities in England, Wales and Isle of Man (Darby, 1963, 13).

As well as such evidence of human modification in the past, there is no doubt that man's impact on the physical environment is growing – partly because of advances in his technical abilities and partly because of increases in his numbers. Indeed the rapid growth in the world's population, together with a greater awareness of the limited size of the planet stemming from developments in transport and communications, lies at the heart of the debate over the 'ecological crisis'.

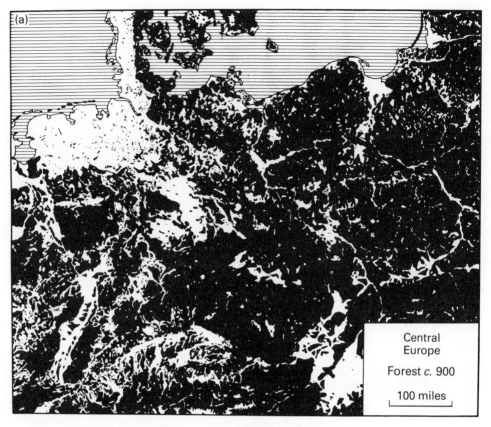

Fig. 4.5 Distribution of forest in Central Europe: (a) *ca.* 900 AD; (b) *ca.* 1900 AD (Darby (in Thomas, 1956), 202, 203).

Estimates of the world's present population are difficult to make, so it is not surprising that reconstructions of past population levels must be regarded with considerable scepticism. Nevertheless, demographers agree that whereas the total population increased from approximately 250 millions in AD 0 to 1,000 millions by 1850, it has since grown by a further 3,000 millions. Viewed in this perspective, the current 2 per cent annual growth rate is extremely rapid. Simple projections of this rate into the future produce some alarming results. The existing population of approximately 4,000 millions would double in 35 years and this doubling time would be maintained thereafter upon the basis of successively larger base levels of population. It is relatively easy to calculate that growth at this rate would create a situation of 'standing room only' by AD 2600 in which each person would be allocated a 5 sq. ft portion of the earth's land surface (Fremlin, 1964). This calculation may appear somewhat bizarre, but it serves to emphasize that the earth is finite and that, unless starships become the sailing ships of future generations of colonists, its size represents the ultimate environmental limit. Although this limit may seem hypothetical, the concept of carrying capacity is meaningful at lesser scales in interpreting, for example, the consequences of rapid population growth

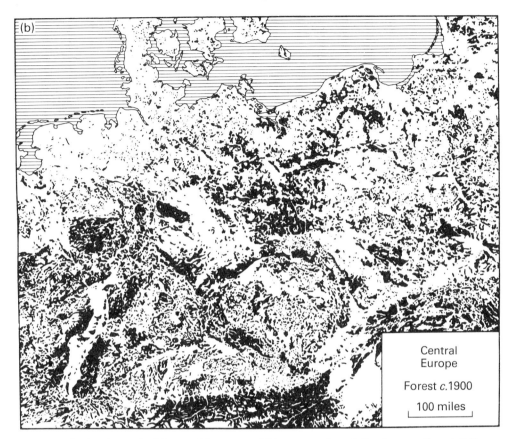

(b)

Central
Europe

Forest *c.*1900

100 miles

upon the land-use decisions of farmers within peasant societies (see section 4.2.2). At the same time, carrying capacity at both the global and local scales will depend upon prevailing levels of technology. If we postulate the ability to live on and beneath the sea, 'standing room only' may no longer be regarded as the ultimate limit to the world's population. Similarly, the introduction of new crops or methods of cultivation may have an equal effect upon notions of carrying capacity within rural communities.

4.1.2 Environmental Hazards

The term environmental hazard is a relative one in that events which are of no significance to one member of a community may have disastrous consequences for another. Farmers, for example, may be sensitive to very minor fluctuations in weather conditions which have little effect upon others. Nevertheless, certain types of natural hazard such as earthquakes are obviously negative characteristics of the physical environment from any point of view. Although such disasters somehow seem more immediate when seen through the eyes of individuals or family groups, the collective impact of these personal misfortunes may be of sufficient magnitude to have severe repercussions upon the economic life of entire countries.

For example, a combination of drought and flood has consistently resulted in the total loss of an average of 80,000 acres per year of Ceylon's paddy rice crop, resulting in a need to import basic foodstuffs and thereby aggravating the country's serious balance of payments deficit (Swan, 1967).

The time/space framework adopted in the preceding section to outline the nature and significance for man of environmental limits could also be employed to demonstrate the impact of environmental hazards upon human activities. Thus spatial variations exist in the probabilities of hazard events. For example, the countries located on the circum-Pacific 'ring of fire' are much more likely to experience earthquakes than those situated on the relatively stable 'shield' areas. Similarly, man's ability to cope with, or even control, such events improves through time as his technology advances. These arguments are essentially the same as the ones employed in the discussion of environmental limits, and a different insight into the relationship between man's activities and the negative qualities of the physical environment may be gained by focusing on the behaviour of decision makers in the face of environmental hazards. This behaviour involves (i) the perception of environmental hazards and (ii) the responses to environmental hazards. This distinction may be related to the model of the decision-making process developed in chapter 3. Thus the factors which influence the perception of hazards broadly correspond to those which affect the availability of information, whereas varying responses are a result of differences in evaluation which are in turn closely related to the problem of uncertainty. The separation of perception from response is equally valid whether applied to the decision-making behaviour of individuals or corporate groups (Kates, 1971). However, most geographical research in this field has been carried out at the level of individual decision makers. Nevertheless, it is important to appreciate the policy implications of these micro-scale studies since government agencies must make decisions which involve first the perception of the likelihood of such events as floods and earthquakes in particular areas and then the implementation of appropriate responses in the form of water-control programmes and building regulations.

Perception of Hazards
The term 'perception' was used in chapter 3 in relation to the images which people have of different places. It was shown that these images are often distortions of reality in the sense that certain features of a place tend to loom larger in the mind of the observer whereas others are suppressed or ignored altogether (see section 3.3). In much the same way, two individuals living in adjacent houses may perceive the risk of a serious flood, for example, very differently, despite the fact that their common location suggests that both will be equally affected by any such future event. Variations of this type in the perception of natural hazards may be largely explained in terms of differences in (i) the frequency of occurrence of the hazard, (ii) the availability of information to the decision maker and (iii) the psychological characteristics of the decision maker.

Frequency of Occurrence – Studies of flood hazards in the US have revealed a close correlation between the frequency of flooding and the perception of risks (see Kates, 1963). Generally speaking, where such events are regular occurrences, decision makers are more likely to be aware of the implications of flooding and take

appropriate actions to reduce damage. Figure 4.6 indicates a scale of flood frequency which was calibrated from historical data relating to flooding in 496 settlements in the US with populations greater than 1,000 in 1950. By dividing the area
under the curve into equal thirds, these settlements are divided according to the
probability of flooding. Examples of communities falling within each of these
classes are indicated in the diagram, which plots their position on the flood-fre-
quency scale. There were clear differences between the inhabitants of these communities in their perception of flood risk and in their adoptions of ameliorative
measures such as structural adjustments to buildings and the payment of insurance
premiums. In Desert Hot Springs, California, where a flood is experienced about
once a decade, the majority of householders were unaware of the possibilities of

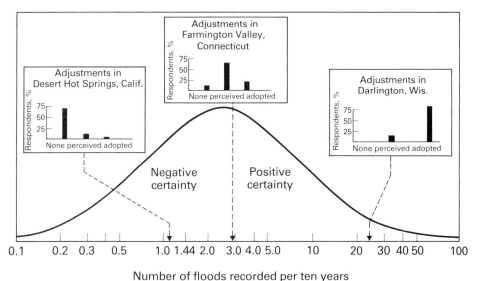

Fig. 4.6 Flood frequency and the perception of hazard (after Kates, 1963, 223).

making adjustments to minimize damage. Flooding occurs approximately three
times in 10 years at Farmington Valley, Connecticut, where awareness and adoption of ameliorative measures tended to be more variable as Figure 4.6 indicates.
The pattern of responses in Darlington, Wisconsin, was found to be almost the
reverse of that in Desert Hot Springs. This reflects the fact that the two settlements
lie at opposite ends of the certainty scale and tends to support the hypothesis that
the perception of natural hazards is strongly influenced by the frequency of their
occurrence. This conclusion is reinforced by reference to other types of environmental hazard. In countries such as Japan, where earthquakes are relatively common, many buildings are constructed to withstand strong ground vibrations. By
contrast, architects are very rarely asked to take such precautions when designing
buildings for clients in San Francisco, despite the warnings of seismologists that
the movement of the San Andreas Fault will sooner or later precipitate another
earthquake similar to that which devastated the city in 1906.

Availability of Information – Personal experience is the most important and effective source of information influencing the perception of risk. The memory of hardships endured is more likely to result in the adoption of preventive or ameliorative measures than any number of official or second-hand warnings. It follows from this that in the case of natural hazards which tend to be recurrent events in a particular area, the perception of risk is likely to be correlated with length of residence in that area. Certainly, Saarinen (1966), in his study of the perception of drought on the Great Plains, found that older farmers with considerable experience were better able to recognize and estimate the risk of dry years than colleagues who had spent shorter periods in the area. The implications of this for pioneer farming in marginal environments are obvious. The problems of the 'Okies', described so graphically by Steinbeck in *The Grapes of Wrath*, were basically a consequence of the overextension of cereal cultivation beyond 100°W into lands where the annual precipitation left no margin for farmers to withstand a succession of below-average-rainfall years such as occurred during the 1930s. Similar expansions and contractions of the agricultural frontier have taken place in Australia where patterns of land use in the 'Wheat Belt' of Western Australia may be largely explained in terms of the interaction of changing climatic and economic circumstances (Dahlke, 1975). The lessons of the 'Dust Bowl' have not yet been fully learned. Recurrent grain shortages encouraged the Soviet leadership to embark on the 'Virgin and Idle Lands Scheme' during the 1950s. This involved bringing large tracts of previously uncultivated land in western Siberia and northern Kazakhstan under the plough. The scheme has certainly enabled a higher level of overall wheat production to be achieved than would have been possible by relying upon the traditional grainlands of the Ukraine and European Russia. On the other hand, the paucity of climatic records meant that the policy decision was taken on the basis of rather limited information. Not surprisingly, crop failures have occurred and wind erosion has been a problem with the result that the total acreage under grain in Kazakhstan, which quadrupled between 1950 and 1965, has since begun to contract (Symons, 1972).

Psychological Characteristics – If availability of information is the most important factor accounting for discrepancies between objective and subjective assessments of risk, when events are rare, there is more scope for individual variations related to psychological factors. For example, storm surges resulting from tropical cyclones can produce rises in sea level of 3–4 m above predicted tides along the Queensland coast, but the necessary combination of circumstances is likely to occur only once in 50 to 100 years at any given location (Oliver, 1975). Probabilities of this order of magnitude may deter the more cautious from investing in a holiday home by the sea, but recent tourist developments along the Queensland coast suggest that the majority are prepared to take the chance. This conclusion is consistent with the findings of other studies (see Saarinen, 1966) which suggest that there is often a human tendency to err on the side of optimism when assessing hazard risks. It seems that we seek to reassure ourselves by minimizing the danger of events over which we have little control. This psychological characteristic is epitomized in questionnaire responses which either deny the existence of a hazard ('It can't happen here') or transfer the uncertainty to a higher authority ('The government is taking care of it') (Burton and Kates, 1964). Despite their apparent naivety, such statements underline the point that many decisions which have had profound consequences upon spatial patterns of human activity in difficult physical environments are better regarded as misplaced acts of faith than as the objective evaluations of rational men.

Responses to Hazards

Immediate reactions to major disasters represent the most obvious human responses to natural hazards. However, the role of the physical environment as a constraint is best illustrated in adjustments which are subsequently made to cope with any repetition of a hazard event. These adjustments may involve (i) modifying the pattern of human activities and (ii) modifying the hazard.

Modifying Human Activities – Farmers are probably more familiar with the difficulties involved in anticipating environmental hazards than any other section of the community. The problem is common to both the commercial and the subsistence farmer: in one case the penalty for failure is measured in financial terms; in the other case it may literally be a matter of life and death. The nature of this problem has been clarified by Gould (1963) in relation to the land-use decisions of farmers located in a village in the Middle Belt of Ghana which is subject to very variable rainfall. Gould formulates the problem in terms of game theory. It is assumed that the farmers may grow five crops – yams, cassava, maize, millet and hill rice. To simplify the problem, rainfall variability is compressed into two extremes – wet years and dry years. The relationship between crop yields and climatic conditions is expressed in Table 4.1 where it can be seen that certain crops

Table 4.1 Crop-Choice Payoff Matrix

	Environmental states	
	Wet years	Dry years
Yams	82	11
Maize	61	49
Cassava	12	38
Millet	43	32
Hill rice	30	81

(After Gould, 1963)

do better in wet years whereas others are more suited to dry conditions. In the terminology of game theory, Table 4.1 is a *payoff matrix*. The units in each cell of the matrix may be regarded as indicating the food value of the various crops to the farmer. The optimal strategy, based on the information contained in Table 4.1, may be identified graphically (Fig. 4.7). If two scales from 0 to 100 are drawn and the yields of each crop in wet and dry years are plotted on alternate axes and then joined up, the intersection that forms the lowest point on the upper boundary will indicate which crops the farmer should grow – in this example, hill rice and maize. The next stage involves deciding the amount of land to place under each crop. Maize does best in wet years and hill rice in dry years, but given the rainfall variability, some kind of 'mixed' strategy is clearly desirable to minimize annual

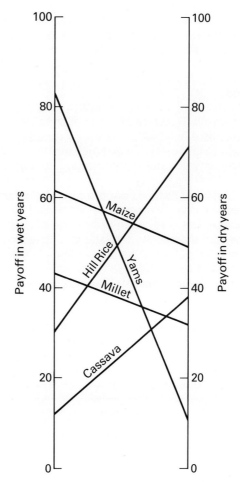

Fig. 4.7 Graphical solution to crop-combination problem (Gould, 1963, 292).

fluctuations in food production. Since maize is most tolerant of rainfall variations, it is not surprising to find that the 'best' solution is achieved by devoting approximately three-quarters of the land to this crop and the remainder to hill rice. This solution may be interpreted in another way. Thus by exclusively growing maize 77.4 per cent of the time and hill rice for the remaining 22.6 per cent, the farmers can also expect to achieve maximum food output in the long run.* However, the long-term approach is scarcely relevant to the subsistence farmer who has to survive from one year to the next and attempts to minimize the potentially damaging effects of an uncertain environment may be seen in the seasonal land-use strategies of farmers in a wide variety of cultural situations.

Diversification offers some insurance against the total failure of a particular crop

---

* These proportions are derived by applying the mathematical rules of game theory. See Gould (1963) and Vajda (1966) for a full explanation.

due to either climatic conditions or, perhaps, the effects of disease. Evidence of such a policy was found by Wolpert (1964) in his study of the decision-making behaviour of farmers in Middle Sweden (see section 3.4.1). The diversification of holdings rather than crops represents a variation on this theme. Holdings in many parts of Southeast Asia are often divided into several non-contiguous plots. Despite the inefficiencies of this system in terms of movement between fields, ownership of land at different elevations enables the farmer to salvage at least something from years which produce the climatic extremes of drought or flood. In wet years, fields on sandy sloping land do well, and in dry years, a crop is assured from fields in low-lying alluvial areas (Demaine and Dixon, 1972). A similar policy is adopted by commercial grain farmers at the northern margins of continuous cultivation in Alberta (Hayter, 1975). The intensity and, more important, the occurrence of frost tend to vary locally as a result of differences in elevation. This variation is a problem which the farmer must take into account when allocating crops to his fields. Generally speaking, barley is grown in the 'frost hollows' and wheat, which requires a greater number of frost-free days to reach maturity, is grown on the higher land.

The impact of natural hazards upon agriculture is frequently related more to the timing than to the spatial distribution of events. An early frost may be disastrous for the fruit grower and the interruption of harvesting may mean the difference between a good and a bad year for many farmers. Similarly, in subsistence agricultural communities the arrival of the first rains marking the start of the growing season is often anxiously awaited. Farmers may respond in various ways to these problems which are essentially temporal rather than spatial. Farm operations are normally organized in such a way as to smooth out some of the irregularities resulting from seasonal changes in climatic conditions. Curry (1963) has examined the concept of climatic programming in relation to the activities of sheep farmers in New Zealand. For example, the transhumance practised on high country sheep stations flanking the Southern Alps enables larger flocks to be supported on a given area of land. The 'summer country' comprises the higher, colder ground and shaded slopes whereas the sunny faces and lower areas form the 'winter country'. Storage is often critical in the effective transfer of resources between different climatic periods. Grain silos and cold stores perform an important regulatory function in matching the seasonal flow of products from the farms with the more stable pattern of demand, thereby reducing fluctuations in market prices. Food storage is even more vital in subsistence economies, especially where the growing season is short. The rains last for only three months at the northern boundary of the Sahel in West Africa and survival depends upon the ability to carry supplies over from one season to the next.

Modifying the Hazard – The responses to natural hazards so far described have basically involved adaptations in either the spatial or temporal organization of human activity. The modification of the hazard itself is an alternative approach. For example, attempts to induce precipitation by 'cloud-seeding' have been practised on a commercial scale in parts of the US for many years (see Dennis and Kreige, 1966). However, the results of such activities are often inconclusive and 'weather modification is still at an embryo stage' (Sewell, 1966, 16). Similarly, despite much research, the timing of earthquakes remains a mystery even if their spatial distribution can be predicted in general terms. In these situations, human responses are, to a greater or lesser extent, conditioned by a feeling of helplessness epitomized in the acceptance of events as 'Acts of God' or in appeals to supernatural powers through the medium of such practices as rain dances.

The kind of river-basin and irrigation schemes described in section 4.1.1 illustrate the fact that man does have the ability to divert the spatial and/or temporal distribution of natural events to his advantage. Nevertheless, technical solutions may be impractical in economic terms. Attitudes within developing countries towards natural disasters are typically fatalistic in the absence of the financial resources required to modify their impact. An estimated 300,000 deaths caused by floods in coastal Bangladesh in November 1970 have resulted in no long-term preventive measures. By contrast, the loss of 1,800 lives in floods in the winter of 1953 were sufficient to encourage the Dutch to embark upon the construction of a massive system of dams and surge barriers across the mouth of the Scheldt. Although the scale and cost of the Delta Plan are exceptional, the scheme, which is due for final completion in 1985, is typical of attempts to modify natural hazards in developed countries in the sense that it reflects decisions taken at government level. The great irony of man's attempts to modify the hazards presented by nature is that the more he spends, the more costly annual losses seem to become (Dury, 1977). This paradox, because it arises from a tendency for modifications made in natural systems to encourage development in areas formerly regarded as too hazardous for the location of homes and factories, underlines the point that the impact of many natural hazards is closely related to human use of the land.

4.2 Physical Environment as an Opportunity

The distribution of many human activities may be regarded as consequences of man's attempts to take advantage of the opportunities afforded to him by the physical environment. The growth of major industrial concentrations such as the Ruhr may, for example, be related to the occurrence of potentially useful materials such as coal and iron ore. On a rather different scale, the desire to obtain a 'house with a view' is an aspiration which only has meaning in relation to differences perceived in the aesthetic qualities of the physical environment in one location as compared with another. Although ultimately based upon environmental attributes, such opportunities are essentially man-made. Coal and iron ore only acquire value when the appropriate technology is available and a 'view' implies a human interpretation of an intrinsically neutral assemblage of landscape features. Thus it is meaningful to speak of the *resource process* – the means by which certain elements of the physical environment become potentially useful to man and are therefore recognized as *natural resources*. The variables involved in this process are subject to change through time, but, even if these variables are held constant, the uneven spatial distribution of natural resources will favour some places rather than others and will also affect the way in which these resources are exploited. The following section therefore discusses (i) natural resources through time and (ii) natural resources in space.

4.2.1 Natural Resources through Time

Natural resources have been termed cultural appraisals (Zimmerman, 1964). The difficulty of defining 'culture' was noted in section 2.2.1, but it is clear that many aspects of the concept are dynamic – they change through time. Technology is obviously important in enabling man both to perceive the utility of a substance such as petroleum and also to overcome the resistances to its exploitation associated with the fact that it is usually found at great geological depths. Even if exploitation is technically possible, the decision to develop a known oil deposit into a producing field will be influenced by economic assessments which themselves respond to fluctuations in supply and demand. Whilst changing technological and economic circumstances may be the major influence upon patterns of oil exploitation, they are not the only factors. The level of oil production in the US, for example, is boosted by the output of wells which are uneconomical in world terms, but which are justified on the basis of a political desire to minimize the country's dependence upon imports. In this context, political considerations represent just one element in a complex of cultural factors, other than technical and economic variables, which have a bearing upon the perception and utilization of natural resources. These dimensions of the notion of resources as cultural appraisals are explored below by reference to the relationships between (i) technology and resources, (ii) economics and resources and (iii) other cultural factors and resources.

Technology
Knowledge is the key to the resource process. It is applied to two interrelated problems. On the one hand, the existence of a *technology to use* a material may be critical in its perception as a resource. On the other hand, the existence of a *technology to exploit* a material will determine its availability and price. A further important influence upon resource availability is exerted by the existence of a *technology to find* which provides a link between the perception and exploitation of a substance. Increasingly sophisticated search procedures are employed by large corporate organizations in their attempts to meet the growing demands of urban/industrial society for raw materials. These organizations operate on an international scale and the popular image of the lone prospector reflects a period in history rather than the contemporary situation.

If knowledge is itself regarded as a resource, it is unique in the sense that its quantity, quality and availability all tend to increase through time. This character-istic has an important bearing upon man's evolving relationship with the physical environment. Although it is unsatisfactory to regard advances in technology as separate from broader socio-political changes in the organization of human society, certain general stages may be identified in the utilization of natural resources which parallel man's level of technical achievements in general and his control and application of energy in particular (Zobler, 1962). In pre-industrial societies man's use of the physical environment is geared mainly towards the exploitation of its biotic elements and his own physical strength is the principal source of energy. Hunter-fisher-gatherer communities are the first rung on the development ladder and it is estimated that such groups now form as little as 0.001 per cent of world population (Simmons, 1974). At this stage, natural resources are scarce because technology is poorly developed. With the introduction of sedentary agriculture, man not only achieved more direct control over his food supply, but also gained a new source of energy in the form of domesticated animals. The technology of the Industrial Revolution encouraged the view that the natural resources of the earth were limitless and these advances certainly transformed the pre-industrial position by creating a situation of apparent abundance. This stage has been and still is characterized by a massive dependence upon fossil fuels. Differences of opinion regarding the future consequences of this dependence, apparent in the debate over the reality of 'Limits to Growth' (cf. Meadows *et al.*, 1972; Cole *et al.*, 1973), simply underline the fact that resource definitions reflect prevailing levels of technology and therefore change through time.

Economics and Resources
Economic factors are an integral part of the resource process. Even if the technology exists to utilize and to exploit a particular material, the costs may outweigh the anticipated returns. In most cases, reserve estimates for resources such as oil and coal are expressed in terms of what is economically recoverable rather than in terms of what is physically available. Furthermore, the definition of what constitutes an 'economically recoverable' deposit tends to change through the operation of the laws of supply and demand. In simple terms, scarcity creates pressure on supplies which induces a rise in price. This in turn makes the exploitation of poorer quality deposits an economic proposition, or encourages the substitution of one material for another.

The Brazilian 'rubber boom' of the nineteenth century was ultimately based upon a combination of technical change, which created a demand, and a unique resource endowment, which meant that the Amazon region had a virtual monopoly over world supply. The discovery of the vulcanizing process in 1839 increased the utility of rubber by making it possible to prevent it from becoming sticky in hot weather and brittle in cold. The significance of this breakthrough was reinforced by the manufacture during the nineteenth century of various mechanical and electrical devices in which rubber was an essential component. A spiralling world demand provided the opportunity for great fortunes to be amassed. The ultimate symbol of this period is the famous opera house in Manaos which epitomizes the wealth gained through the exploitation of this lucrative natural resource. The Brazilian monopoly was undermined when some seeds of *Hevea Braziliensis* were smuggled out of the country and successfully germinated in the botanical gardens at Kew. From this beginning, the British and Dutch were able, by the early twentieth century, to establish plantations in Malaya and Sumatra which produced better quality rubber at a fraction of the cost of the rather haphazard Brazilian system of production which relied upon tapping scattered wild trees. In the face of this competition, the Brazilian rubber industry collapsed as quickly as it had grown, so that in the 20 years from 1905 to 1925 the contribution of the Amazon region to world production declined from about 100 per cent to virtually nothing. Attempts to introduce the plantation system during the inter-war years were unsuccessful and the story of Brazilian rubber exemplifies the way in which changing economic circumstances may destroy resource-based activities long before the physical exhaustion of the resource itself.

The Cornish tin-mining industry demonstrates that the economic forces which may eliminate a resource are not irreversible. This small area of southwest England was a leading producer of tin in the last century, but production fell away from a peak in 1871 as the deep Cornish mines were unable to compete with the lower costs of working the richer veins of Bolivia and the alluvial deposits of Malaya and Indonesia. The numerous workings existing at the industry's peak were eventually reduced to only two as one after another failed. However, at the beginning of the 1960s, world consumption of tin began consistently to exceed production. Although buffer stocks of the metal were drawn upon, an inevitable increase in price occurred. This trend, which has continued into the 1970s, has stimulated a revival of commercial interest in Cornish tin. Consequently, the South Crofty and Geevor mines, which remained in production throughout the nadir of the industry, have since been joined by new workings at Wheal Jane and Pendarves which opened in 1971 and 1973 respectively.* Although these events have by no means restored tin to its former importance in Cornwall, they emphasize that resources may be surprisingly durable when measured in economic terms.

Cultural Factors and Resources

Economic principles do not always provide the most appropriate criteria for regulating resource use. The most serious limitation stems from the fact that price cannot necessarily be equated with value. The desire to reopen a number of Cornish tin mines has, for example, created a conflict between business and amenity interests. Many of the old mines happen to be located on or near the coast, which is also one of the most attractive in England. Even if it were possible to estimate correctly the financial gains to be made from opening a mine, how could this be set against the aesthetic loss of an unspoilt coastline? Such problems resulting from the adoption of an essentially economic approach to resource evaluation underline the broader aspects of the resource process. Although technical and economic variables have been the greatest influence upon man's perception of natural resources, such factors represent only part of the totality of 'culture' within which the concept of a natural resource has meaning (see Spoehr, 1956). This may be demonstrated by reference to contrasting situations in which cultural factors may encourage or inhibit the exploitation of a resource.

Strategic and political considerations may be regarded as falling within any broad definition of what represents a cultural influence upon resource use. The implications of relying upon other countries for vital raw materials have encouraged exploration and development activities within the frontiers of both of the major world powers. In the US, the domestic oil and gas industry has long received favourable tax treatment to encourage the exploitation of reserves that would be uneconomic upon the world market and similar policies have been adopted for other minerals during the 1970s as dependence upon foreign sources of supply has increased (see Prestwich, 1975). Similar politically motivated encouragement of mineral production has been a feature of Soviet economic policy since the 1920s. Indeed the emphasis placed upon mineral development in early communist planning has probably contributed much to the USSR's present position as a leading producer of most of the major minerals, although this has only

* Another slump in world tin prices, which began in the mid-1970s, brought about the closure of Wheal Jane in 1978.

been achieved by allowing political objectives to override economic considerations (Warren, 1973).

Cultural factors may inhibit as well as promote resource use. In chapter 3 (section 3.3), it was argued that the notion of the Great American Desert was largely a result of the cultural background of European settlers. In this case, the agricultural opportunities presented by the treeless prairies were not recognized because such environments were beyond the realms of the emigrants' previous experience. Even when objective evidence of the potential benefits to be gained by utilizing a particular material has been assembled, such evidence may be irrelevant in the face of powerful social and institutional prejudices. Food taboos in many societies are an apparently irrational obstacle to the improvement of nutritional standards. The unwillingness of Muslims and Jews to eat pork and the Hindu attitude towards beef together affect a significant proportion of the world's population. The complex interrelationships between economic activities and social structures may also prevent the 'best' use of resources. For example, agricultural development in parts of East Africa has been seriously hindered by the unwillingness of the Masai and other cattle-raising peoples to reduce their herds despite serious over-grazing. This failure to recognize the depletion of grassland resources reflects the significance attached to the possession of cattle as an index of status within the community and underlines the fact that resource problems may, in certain situations, be overcome only by changing the cultural milieu in which the relevant decisions are made.

4.2.2 Natural Resources in Space

Although the perception and utilization of natural resources change through time, spatial variations in their availability ensure that certain places may have 'built-in' advantages over others. Further, the location of resources relative to existing patterns of settlement and economic activity has an important bearing on their utility, which is often reflected in the manner of their exploitation. These different, but interrelated, spatial aspects of the resource process are considered by reference to (i) patterns of resource availability and (ii) patterns of resource exploitation.

Patterns of Resource Availability
Just as the global distribution of population may be inversely related to negative features of the physical environment such as extreme cold and aridity (see section 4.1.1), so the occurrence of positive attributes such as mineral deposits often serves as a focus for human activities. A corollary of this is the fact that certain locations or areas may be disadvantaged by virtue of relatively poor resource endowments. A distinction between 'haves' and 'have nots' in resource terms may apply at a variety of spatial scales and the issue may be explored by reference to the relationship between (i) resources and national economic development and (ii) resources and population in agricultural communities.

Resources and National Economic Development – The significance of the availability of natural resources as an explanatory variable accounting for observed differences in levels of economic development between countries has been examined by Ginsburg (1957). Several problems make it difficult to test this relationship. On the one hand, there is no agreement upon what constitutes an acceptable measure of economic development, although per capita national product is probably the best indicator. On the other hand, it is virtually impossible to derive any single common denominator to represent resource endowment, even assuming the existence of satisfactory resource inventories on a country-by-country basis. A further complication stems from the fact that most developed countries have attained their present position not only by using indigenous resources, but also by importing materials from elsewhere. Consequently, a simple correlation between a country's existing economic situation and its internal availability of resources is not valid. Nevertheless, certain general statements can be made and it seems reasonable to postulate that, *ceteris paribus*, a country possessing an extensive resource base is better placed for economic development. Historical evidence suggests that most of the developed countries were well endowed with natural resources at the critical stage in their economic development when they were transformed from pre-industrial to industrial societies. The UK, for example, not only had abundant energy supplies in the form of coal, but was also in a favourable position for iron ore, tin and several other resources vital to industrialization. At the same time, it is not difficult to think of other European countries which now outrank the UK in terms of per capita national product in spite of comparatively meagre resource endowments. Thus states such as the Netherlands overcame this disadvantage by establishing colonial empires geared to the supply of raw materials to the mother country. Others, such as Switzerland, have relied upon the application of technology to create wealth by adding value to imported goods.

The success of certain countries in achieving high levels of economic development, despite limited indigenous resources, emphasizes the importance of cultural factors. A fairly catholic view of resources, incorporating both physical and cultural attributes, is required to provide any reasonable interpretation of spatial variations in levels of economic development. Figure 4.8 is a cartographic representation of such a view which attempts to combine a measure of physical resource availability with an estimate of technological abilities in different parts of the world (Zelinsky, 1966). The resulting fourfold classification is very crude, but it does emphasize the contrast between such 'haves' as the US, which are well off in both physical and technical terms, and such 'have nots' as India in which the ratio of natural resources to population is low and indigenous technology is poorly developed.

Overall, it is clear that no simple relationship exists at the international scale between physical resource endowment and economic development. The possession of resources may certainly provide the opportunity to acquire capital and 'know-how' to initiate the development process. The industrialization of South Africa was set in motion in this way, and more recently, oil-producing states such as Iran and Venezuela are using export revenues to finance broader-based development programmes. At the same time, countries such as Brazil seem to have failed to capitalize upon the opportunities presented by generous resource endowments. The superlatives used by outside observers to describe the economic potential of Brazil since the eighteenth century are testimony to a long history of unfulfilled promise (see Henshall and Momsen, Jnr, 1974) and it is only in relatively recent years that a concerted effort has been made to utilize the country's abundant resource base.

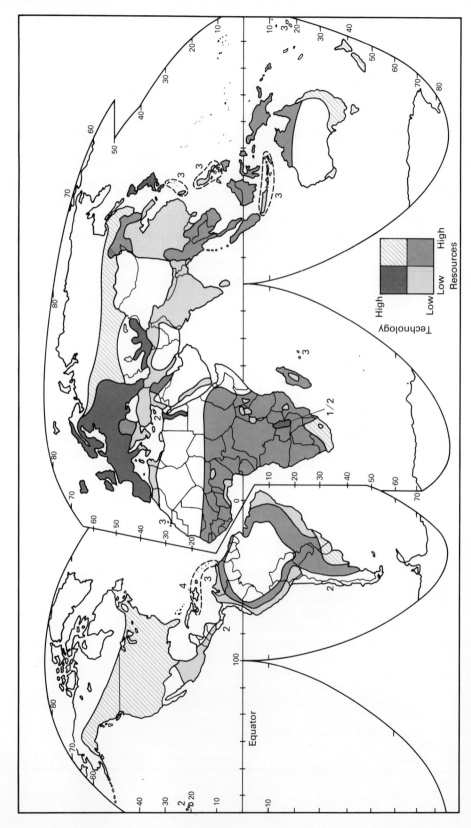

Fig. 4.8 Technology/resource regions of the world (Abler, Adams and Gould, 1971, 344).

Resources and Population in Agricultural Communities – Unequal resource endowments may also be observed at regional and local scales. The implications of such differences are also similar. Just as the economic development of a country may be accelerated by the possession of a valuable resource, so the agricultural development of a community may be assisted by a favourable allocation of different types of land within its boundaries. The significance of uneven resource distributions at this level has been examined by Hamilton (1977) with reference to the central Andes of Peru. The study focused on the departments of Junin and Pasco which contain a variety of land types ranging from the High Andean plateaux (*puna*) above 4,000 m, through the extremely steep-sided river valleys of the north and east to the relatively large Tarma and Huancayo basins (Fig. 4.9a). One of the objectives of the study was to identify population pressure within these different physical environments by translating agricultural output in a number of sampled communities into the achievement of specified income levels. The concept of population pressure serves to emphasize the complementary nature of the distinction between the positive and negative qualities of the environment in the sense that its presence may crudely be regarded as reflecting a resource deficit (i.e. a constraint) and its absence may be viewed as an indication of a resource surplus (i.e. an opportunity).

The essential features of Hamilton's study are summarized in Figure 4.9b, c and d. Each map shows the productivity that would have to be achieved in each community to enable a family of average size to obtain each of three levels of annual income. These incomes represent a series of dietary norms which essentially describe differing degrees of survival rather than define qualities of life acceptable in a developed country. Five productivity classes are identified. 'Low' estimates reflect the levels which typically prevail throughout the study area; 'medium' estimates are derived from the experience of the most efficient communities; 'high' estimates are based on the results of agricultural experiments within the central Andes; 'super high' estimates represent a theoretical target that might be achieved if traditional fallowing practices were abandoned; the 'unattainable' classification refers to communities which could not achieve the specified income level under any of these productivity assumptions. Comparison of Figures 4.9b, c and d reveals significant spatial variations in the required productivity levels which may themselves be explained largely in terms of the different resource endowments of the various communities. The most obvious contrast exists between the communities of the *puna* and those located in the Huancayo Basin. The former must rely almost exclusively upon extensive pastoralism on the bleak and windswept plateaux whereas the latter are able to produce a wide range of crops from irrigated fields. The northern and eastern valleys fare better than the *puna*, but, because their steep sides limit the scope for irrigation, cannot match the potential of the southern basins. Although these differences partly reflect organizational factors such as the distinction between Indian and *hacienda* agricultural systems, they nevertheless underline the point that the availability of resources in space is not uniform and that the environmental opportunities (and constraints) influencing human activities vary from place to place.

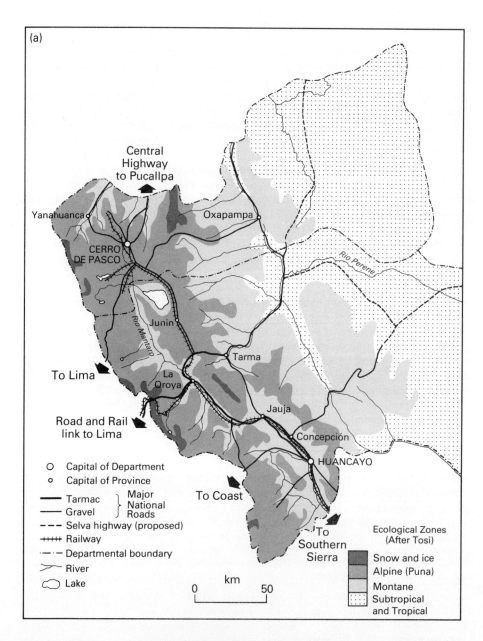

Fig. 4.9 Population, physical environment and agricultural productivity in the High Andes of Peru: (a) study area; (b) productivity levels required to attain annual income of 4,000 soles; (c) productivity levels required to attain annual income of 18,000 soles; (d) productivity levels required to attain annual income of 30,000 soles (Hamilton, 1977).

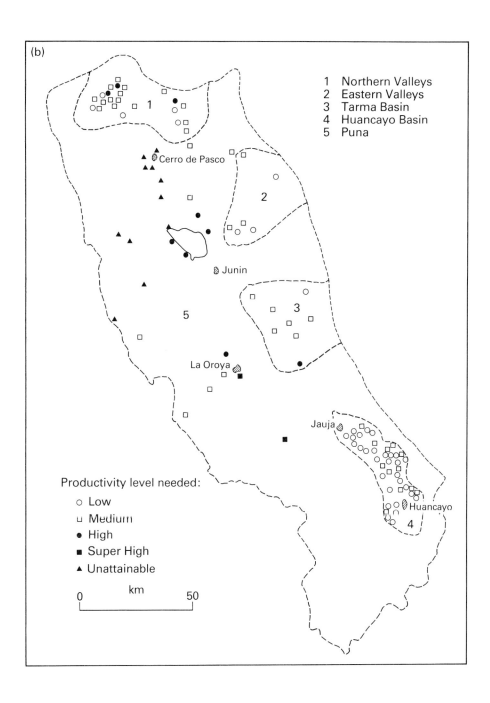

(b)

1 Northern Valleys
2 Eastern Valleys
3 Tarma Basin
4 Huancayo Basin
5 Puna

Cerro de Pasco

Junin

La Oroya

Jauja

Huancayo

Productivity level needed:

○ Low
□ Medium
● High
■ Super High
▲ Unattainable

km

0   50

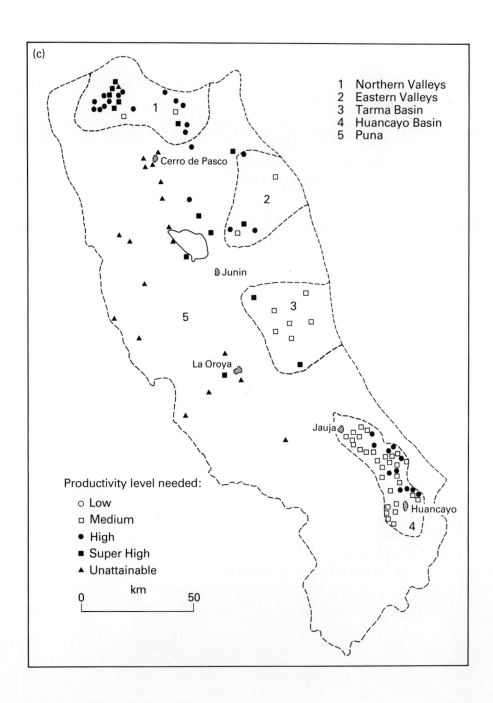

(c)

1 Northern Valleys
2 Eastern Valleys
3 Tarma Basin
4 Huancayo Basin
5 Puna

Cerro de Pasco

Junin

La Oroya

Jauja

Huancayo

Productivity level needed:

○ Low
□ Medium
● High
■ Super High
▲ Unattainable

km
0   50

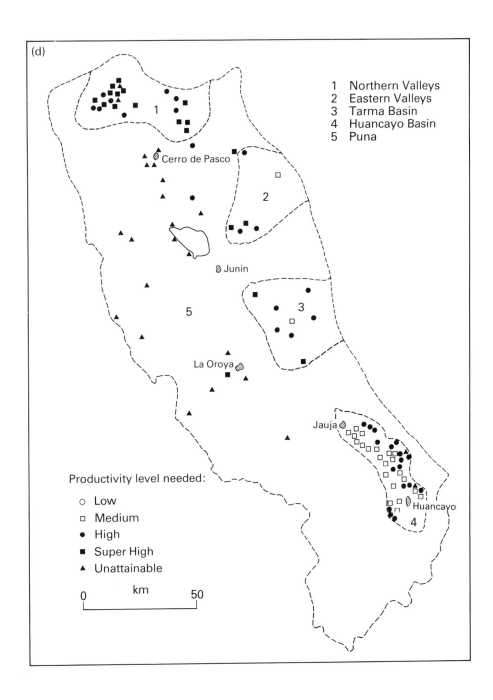

(d)

1 Northern Valleys
2 Eastern Valleys
3 Tarma Basin
4 Huancayo Basin
5 Puna

Cerro de Pasco

Junin

La Oroya

Jauja

Huancayo

Productivity level needed:

- ○ Low
- □ Medium
- ● High
- ■ Super High
- ▲ Unattainable

0   km   50

Patterns of Resource Exploitation

The known occurrence of a particular natural substance such as a mineral deposit does not guarantee its exploitation by man. Even if it has 'become' a resource from a technical point of view (section 4.2.1), it may remain inaccessible in economic terms. Thus although the availability of natural resources is determined by such essentially physical factors as geological circumstances, patterns of human exploitation in space and time are largely a function of the relative costs of tapping one deposit rather than another. These costs are of two types. Firstly, costs of production related to the quality of a deposit, and secondly, costs of transport related to its location. Production costs are affected by several factors including

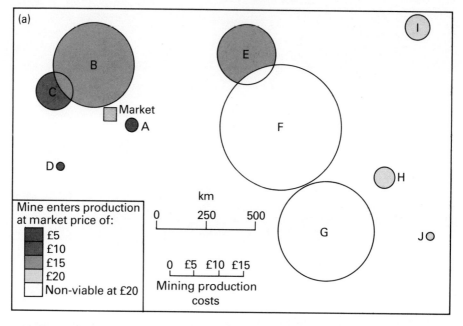

Fig. 4.10 Transport and production costs in the exploitation of mineral deposits (after Hay, 1976, 68).

the mineral content of a deposit, its size and such geological conditions of its occurrence as its depth below the surface. The interplay of these factors alone may be very complex so that the disadvantages associated with working a small deposit may, for example, be offset if it is extremely rich in mineral content. The situation is further complicated when transport costs are introduced. Whilst production costs are largely determined by physical circumstances, transport costs mainly reflect the location of a deposit relative to such elements of the human environment as factories and transport facilities.

Some of the implications for spatial patterns of mineral exploitation of the inter-relationship between production and transport costs are represented in Figure 4.10 (Hay, 1976). The location of several deposits relative to a market is given. Production costs are assumed to vary and the geographical pattern of these variations

(Fig. 4.10a) are plotted as vertical bars of differing heights in Figure 4.10b. The intersection of the bars with the base line defines the distance of each deposit from the market. By making the initial assumption that a freight rate of 1 pence (p) per tonne km is charged, total transport costs rise in a simple linear fashion as distance from the market increases. The cost of transport must be deducted from the prevailing market price to yield a net price at the mine which therefore declines

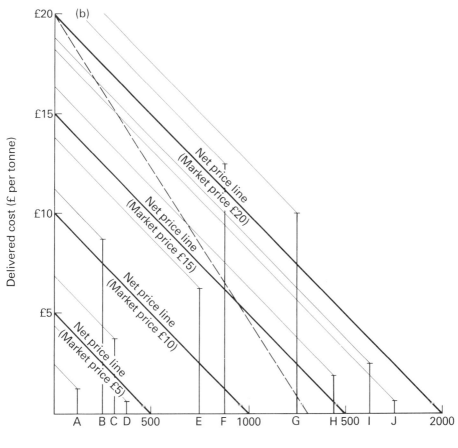

Distance from market (in km)

with distance at the rate of 1p per km or £1 per 100 km. If the initial market price is £5 per tonne there will be a net price which declines to zero at 500 km from the market. This outer margin of viability extends successively to 1,000 km, 1,500 km and 2,000 km as the market price rises in £5 steps to £20 (Fig. 4.10b). At each stage only those mines at which the production costs lie below the net price line will be worth exploiting. It is apparent that mines which lie within the spatial margin of viability defined by each rise in the market price will not necessarily come into production. Thus at a price of £5 only mines A and D are economic whilst the higher production costs of B and C ensure that they remain untouched despite the fact that they are less than 500 km from the market. Similarly, mines F and G are still uneconomic at the much higher price of £20 per tonne although they are much closer to the market than several other mines whose locational disadvantage is more than offset by lower production costs. A further complication is introduced if the freight rate is changed. The dotted line on the graph indicates what happens at a fixed market price of £20 per tonne if transport costs are raised from 1p to 1.5p per tonne. The steeper slope of the transport cost line leads to a contraction of the outer margin of viability whereas a shallower line resulting from lower freight rates would obviously have the reverse effect.

The situation depicted in Figure 4.10 incorporates several simplifying assumptions such as a linear increase in transport costs with distance, the homogeneity of products from different mines and a rather naive view of the relationship between supply and demand at different price levels. Nevertheless, the essential ideas implicit in this model may be validated by reference to examples at two different levels of resolution: (i) the international pattern of iron ore supply and (ii) regional patterns of mineral exploitation.

International Pattern of Iron Ore Supply – Iron Ore is one of the most important resources upon which the operation of the modern industrial economy is based. The availability of this raw material was a critical factor promoting the early development of iron and steel making which was in turn so important in the economic transformation associated with the Industrial Revolution in countries such as the UK and France. As the scale of operations increased, so individual steelworks tended to outstrip local supplies of iron ore and it became necessary to look further and further afield. By the end of World War II, only the US and the USSR of

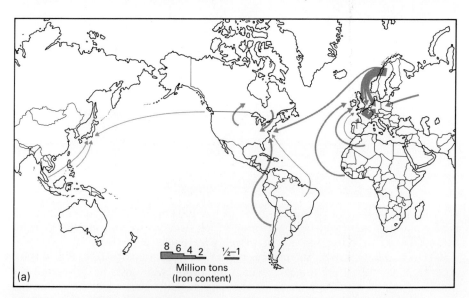

Fig. 4.11 International trade in iron ore in: (a) 1950; (b) 1964; (c) 1980 (projected) (Manners, 1971, 247, 276 and 318).

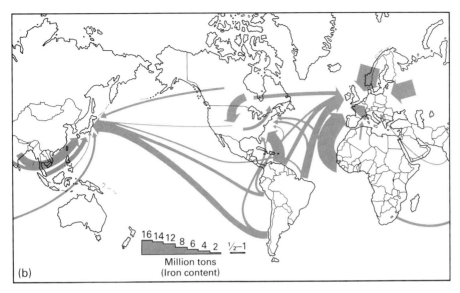

(b)

Million tons
(Iron content)

the major world steel producers were largely self-sufficient. Figure 4.11a indicates
the volume and direction of international trade in iron ore in 1950. The most important movements took place within Western Europe as the mines of northern
Sweden and the Lorraine in northeast France supplied the steel industries of the
UK, West Germany and the Benelux countries. Despite these important international movements in 1950, a comparison between Figure 4.11a and 4.11b underlines the massive expansion which took place during the next 15 years. Not only
did the tonnages increase in absolute terms, but also the directional complexity
of the trade was much greater by 1964 as steelmakers in the US, Western Europe

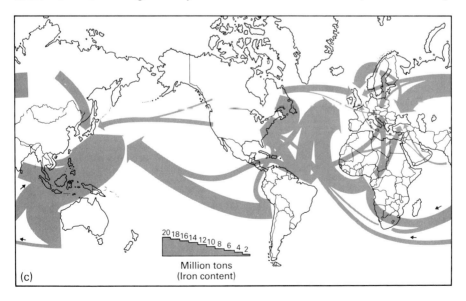

(c)

Million tons
(Iron content)

and particularly Japan obtained their supplies from a wider range of more distant sources. Thus the average length of haul for iron ore consumed within the six original member countries of the EEC increased from 3,850 km in 1957 to 5,300 km in 1971 whilst the corresponding figures for Japan rose from 8,700 km to 11,350 km (Manners, 1971). Since the iron-ore trade had become a truly international one by the mid-1960s, the opportunities for further increases in these distances are limited and forecasts for 1980 (Fig. 4.11c) suggest that the average length of haul to Japan, for example, will actually fall as a result of the opening of new mines in Australia.

Although Australian mines are relatively close to the Japanese market, postwar changes in the international iron-ore trade have been based upon the commencement of mining operations in areas more and more remote from the major consuming centres. The growth of iron-ore production in West Africa, Latin America and Southeast Asia may be explained in terms of the variables incorporated in the model represented in Figure 4.10 – a combination of price increases, declining transport costs and differential production costs. A general upward trend in iron-ore prices throughout the 1950s had the effect of encouraging the search for new sources of supply rather than resulting in the opening up of more expensive, but already known deposits, as indicated in the model. Exploration undertaken during the 1950s was so successful that there has been a tendency for supplies to exceed demand with a consequent fall in iron-ore prices from the peak reached in 1959. This downward movement has not seriously affected the position of the newer mines because the gap between their generally low production costs and the corresponding costs in Western Europe and the US has widened as it has become necessary to operate in progressively more difficult geological conditions in these older mining areas. Furthermore, changes in the shipping industry, notably the introduction of very large bulk-ore carriers, began to reduce freight rates in the 1960s (Manners, 1967). In terms of our model, this implies a shallower gradient to the transport-cost line, thereby pushing the margin of viability farther away from the market and so enhancing the competitiveness of remote deposits.

Regional Patterns of Mineral Exploitation – Patterns of resource exploitation at the regional level, within an individual coalfield for example, may be regarded as a non-issue in the sense that extractive industries are, by definition, located at their source of raw material. However, the manner in which such deposits are exploited is determined by the same interrelationships between production and transport costs which affect the choice between alternative deposits at the macro-scale so that while 'The discovery of a great mine continues to be a largely fortuitous event' subsequent exploitation tends to be 'a more ordered investigation with generally predictable returns' (Aschmann, 1970, 172).

Figure 4.12 identifies stages in the development of a hypothetical coalfield (Wilson, 1968). A single continuous seam outcropping in the west and dipping gently eastwards is postulated together with a single market or distribution centre. Production costs are assumed to increase as mining progresses down the dip of the seam and transport costs are directly proportional to the distance from the market. Early developments take the form of tunnel or adit mines where the seam outcrops near the market. In the second phase some shaft mines are sunk on the downslope

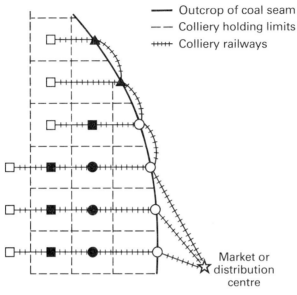

DEVELOPMENT OF
HYPOTHETICAL COAL FIELD

—— Outcrop of coal seam
—— Colliery holding limits
++++ Colliery railways

Market or
☆ distribution
centre

○ Tunnel mines-1st phase
▲ Tunnel mines -2nd phase
● Shaft mines -2nd phase
▦ Shaft mines -3rd phase
□ Shaft mines -later phases

Fig. 4.12 Stages in the development of a hypothetical coalfield (Wilson, 1968, 79).

of the seam whilst more distant adits are able to compete by substituting lower production costs for their transport-cost disadvantage. Further development of the coalfield follows similar lines with additional tiers of pits operating at still greater depths and attempting to compensate for this depth by working first those sections of the coalfield remaining for exploitation in closest proximity to the shipping point and probably also by operating at a larger scale. This least-cost model was originally tested in relation to the evolution of the Maitland, Newcastle and Illawarra fields in New South Wales. The development of these fields accorded fairly closely to the pattern indicated in the model, although geological circumstances in the Illawarra district provided no opportunity for second or third-tier mines. Nevertheless, the existence of a dipping seam is not uncommon and the down-dip migration of mineworkings through time has occurred, for example, in the Durham coalfield of northeast England and in the Ruhr coalfield. The assumption of a single shipping point is, however, less realistic and the interplay of production and transport costs is usually much more complex than the model suggests.

Surface patterns of exploitation are often easy to appreciate in the case of coal because they partially reflect sequential changes in underground conditions. However, the distribution of many resources is discontinuous and irregular even at the regional scale. In these circumstances, the effect upon spatial patterns of development of the interrelationship between production and transport costs may be less apparent. Nevertheless, the same principles operate. The Chinese entrepreneurs responsible for the exploitation of the alluvial tin deposits on the island of Bangka off the coast of Sumatra during the eighteenth century were well aware of these principles (see Jackson, 1969). At its peak in the 1760s, Bangka was producing the equivalent of contemporary Cornish mines. By employing a 'skim and shift' technique, the Chinese kept production costs to a minimum, but at the same time left behind large quantities of untouched material. Similarly, since deposits were so abundant, it was possible to minimize transport costs by ignoring the interior of the island and always remaining close to the coast from which refined metal was exported to China.

Oilfields provide another example of a discontinuous resource distribution. Although oil production is concentrated in relatively few areas when viewed at the world scale, oilfields may be conceived of as point distributions at the regional level since the production costs of individual fields *within* these areas are often highly variable. Thus a large productive field may be located in close proximity to a small, non-commercial deposit with the result that spatial patterns of oilfield development may seem random. Nevertheless, decisions to exploit one field rather than another may again be related to the interplay of production and transport costs. For example the problems of maintaining a supply link between the interior and the coast has strongly influenced the phasing into production of successive Iranian oilfields (see Melamid, 1959). The North Sea presents a mirror image of this in the sense that distance from the coastline is also important in affecting the viability of different offshore fields (see Chapman, 1976). Most of the fields are located in the middle of the North Sea, a situation which increases their costs of development, which in turn tends to reduce the commercial prospects of the smaller oil deposits.

The relationship between man as a decision maker and the properties of the physical environment are very complex and the distinction, adopted in this chapter, between the environment viewed as a constraint and as an opportunity is an over-simplification. Not only do human attitudes towards the physical environment change *through time*, they may also vary between individuals and groups within a community at any given moment *in time*. The concept of resources as cultural appraisals emphasizes the dynamic nature of the relationship between man and the physical environment, as yesterday's constraints may become today's opportunities. For example, the European Alps were transformed with changes in landscape tastes during the nineteenth century from hostile and forbidding peaks to places of great beauty and attraction. Controversies surrounding proposals for industrial development within rural areas are often based on differing perceptions of the qualities of the physical environment. During the mid-1970s, the deep-water lochs of western Scotland were regarded by the oil industry and its contractors as offering excellent opportunities as construction sites for the fabrication of concrete production platforms to be used in the exploitation of North Sea oil and gas. Not surprisingly, amenity and conservation groups took a very different view of the qualities of the Highland coastline. But despite the importance of such cultural appraisals it would be foolish to deny the importance of the physical environment as part of the spatial context to decision making.

Further Reading

GOULD, P. R. 1963: Man against his environment: a game theoretic framework. *Association of American Geographers, Annals* **53,** 290–7.

An application of game theory to the problem of subsistence farmers' land-use decisions in the face of climatic uncertainty.

HAYTER, R. 1975: Farmers' crop decisions and the frost hazard in east-central Alberta. *Tijdschrift voor Economische en Sociale Geografie* **66,** 93–102.

Considers similar issues to those discussed by Gould, but in a different cultural context.

KATES, R. W. 1963: Perceptual regions and regional perception in flood plain management. *Regional Science Association, Papers and Proceedings* **11,** 217–27.

A good summary of early work in the US on the perception of flood hazard.

SCIENTIFIC AMERICAN 1980: Economic development. *Scientific American* **243** (September).

A special issue which contains several articles concerned with the role of key resources in future patterns of economic development both at a global scale and at the level of individual countries.

SIMMONS, I. G. 1974: *The ecology of natural resources.* London.

A comprehensive assessment of natural resources from an ecological perspective.

THOMAS, W. L. (ed.). 1956: *Man's role in changing the face of the earth.* Chicago.

A dated, but nevertheless valuable, collection of papers which discusses the impact of man's activities on the physical environment.

WHITE, G. F. (ed.) 1974: *Natural hazards: local, national, global.* London.

Contains many case studies of human responses to natural hazards.

WILSON, M. G. A. 1968: Changing patterns of pit location on the New South Wales Coalfields. *Association of American Geographers, Annals* **58,** 78–90.

Examines the significance of the interrelationship between transport and production costs for the spatial pattern of coalfield development.

5 The Human Environment

The impact of man's activities is apparent in such tangible features of the human environment as roads, factories and fields, which form part of the spatial context within which decisions are made. Not only do they reflect past decisions: they are also an important influence upon future decisions. In chapter 2, for example, we noted the influence upon contemporary movement patterns within certain European cities of street plans inherited from the Middle Ages. Similarly, the freedom of choice of every individual with respect to such important decisions as where to live and where to work is constrained, to a greater or lesser extent, by the existing location of residential areas and employment opportunities. Rather than attempt the impossible task of undertaking a comprehensive survey of the various types of situation in which past, present and future spatial patterns of human activity are linked through the mechanism of decision making, the following chapter relates this theme explicitly to a basic characteristic of the spatial organization of human society – unbalanced economic growth.

Economic development is unevenly distributed whatever the scale at which it is viewed. On an international level, the various disparities between 'rich' and 'poor' countries is one of the most divisive aspects of the world order. At a continental scale, supranational organizations such as the EEC face similar problems in reconciling differences in living standards between peripheral and core areas. Within individual countries, the existence of a 'regional problem' often stimulates policy measures which seek to achieve a more even geographical spread of economic growth. Although the universality of unbalanced growth may almost seem to elevate it into a basic principle of spatial organization, there are great difficulties in explaining why development should occur in one place rather than another. The initial stimulus may be provided by the availability of a particular resource, but it may also be based upon less obvious advantages of location or, indeed, upon chance factors. Whatever the reasons for its origin, economic development, once set in motion, exerts a powerful influence upon the spatial pattern of subsequent development and 'concentration becomes the important geographical fact' (Ullman, 1958, 180) since such concentrations are often self-perpetuating as their existing attributes reinforce their attractiveness to new economic activities. In considering this process, a distinction may be drawn between (i) the nature of unbalanced growth and (ii) the consequences of unbalanced growth. This distinction is somewhat artificial in the sense that it is very difficult to isolate causes from effects because unbalanced growth is based upon a positive-feedback situation in which the effects themselves sustain the process. Nevertheless, it is necessary to break into this process at some stage and the first half of the chapter focuses on the mechanisms responsible for unbalanced growth whereas the second half attempts to place these mechanisms more explicitly within a spatial framework by examining the relationships between growing and declining areas.

5.1 The Nature of Unbalanced Growth

The model of the decision-making process outlined in chapter 3 incorporated a feedback loop whereby goals may be modified in the light of experience (Fig. 3.1). Thus stimulus and stress represent positive and negative influences respectively. Feedback mechanisms affecting the actions of decisions makers are also central to the phenomenon of unbalanced growth, but these mechanisms predominantly operate in a positive direction as a chain-reaction of separate, but interdependent, decisions through time promotes the concentration of development in space.

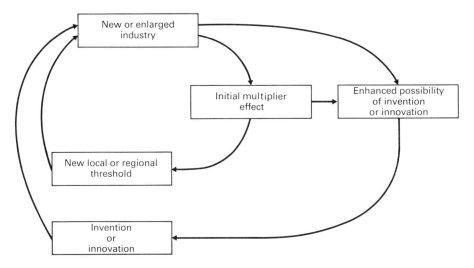

Fig. 5.1 A model of urban/industrial growth (Pred, 1966, 25).

Attempts have been made to understand this complex process of circular and cumulative causation by isolating its component parts with the aid of various simplifying models (see Keeble, 1967). Figure 5.1 indicates the essential features of just one of these models. It was developed following a detailed study (Pred, 1966) of the changes which occurred in the US between 1860 and 1914 as the nation's economy was transformed from a predominantly commercial orientation based on the distribution of imported goods to an industrial one dominated by manufacturing. Despite its North American derivation, there is no reason to suppose that the processes which the model identifies are specific to that continent. Pred's ideas have received some empirical support from an historical analysis of urban growth in the UK (Robson, 1973) and they also have some relevance for an understanding of recent events in many countries of the developing world which are currently experiencing similar economic transformations to those which occurred in North America and Western Europe during the last century.

The initial impetus to development in Pred's model is provided by the introduction of a new or enlarged industrial plant into an area. This event precipitates two circular chains of reaction which are indicated as inner and outer feedback loops in Figure 5.1. The inner loop is itself a composite of two quite separate concepts which are, nevertheless, inextricably linked in time and space. The *multiplier* is largely self-explanatory. It rests upon the idea that new industrial investment in an area will generate a set of local demands. These demands will in turn generate further investment in other economic activities, but only when the minimum levels of demand or *thresholds* required to support these activities are attained. For these later developments, the location of the initial industrial plant obviously represents a critical component of the human environment. Furthermore, these developments in turn will generate their own multiplier effects, thereby ensuring the perpetuation of the inner feedback loop in the model. The outer loop, which Pred termed the invention/innovation cycle, rests upon the notion that the communication of the various new ideas and techniques necessary to maintain the impetus of economic development is encouraged by the spatial concentration of population within rapidly growing areas. Although the kinds of improvement in communications technology described in chapter 1 have reduced the geographical significance of the invention/innovation cycle, the continuing importance of certain psychological factors, associated with the availability of information to decision makers, in maintaining the momentum of a growing centre emphasizes that the influence of the human environment upon decision making is not restricted to the tangible contents of space. These issues associated with the various elements of the model represented in Figure 5.1 are discussed in relation to the significance of (i) multiplier effects, (ii) threshold and market factors and (iii) psychological factors.

5.1.1 Multiplier Effects and Unbalanced Growth

The multiplier effect has been extensively studied by economists in their efforts to understand the operation of economic systems. The geographical significance of the multiplier lies in the spatial distribution of its effects, and its relevance to the process of unbalanced growth hinges upon the proposition that these effects are typically concentrated in specific areas. In order to examine this proposition, it is necessary to consider the role of (i) linkage and (ii) leakage within economic systems.

Linkage
Economic activity involves the transformation of inputs into outputs, which implies the existence of linkages between different stages in the productive process. These linkages may be in the form of movements of materials such as steel sheets between a rolling mill and shipyard. Exchanges of information may also be regarded as linkages since the smooth running of any economic system depends upon communication between, for example, buyers and sellers. The role of information flows in the spatial organization of society is considered in chapter 7 and it is material linkages which are normally identified as critical factors contributing to the typically concentrated or agglomerated distribution of industry. The signifi-

cance of such linkages in promoting unbalanced growth is related to the advantages gained, in terms of reduced transport costs, by the adjacent location of inter-dependent economic activities.

Although most research into the geographical significance of linkages has been concerned with the location of modern manufacturing industry (Wood, 1969), the same advantages of agglomeration may be observed in the location of artisan acti-vities in pre-industrial societies. The clustering of particular crafts and merchant activities in certain quarters and streets was a characteristic feature of medieval towns and cities (see Sjoberg, 1960), and was ultimately based upon the difficulties of internal movement as geographical concentration made it easier for producers, consumers and middlemen to transact their business. Craft quarters have largely disappeared in most modern cities as workshop techniques have been superseded by mass-production methods. Nevertheless, these techniques remain important in certain cultures and Bray (1969) has examined the nature of such quarters in the Nigerian town of Iseyin. The town has a population of approximately 60,000 and was established in pre-colonial times by the Yoruba, one of Nigeria's principal tribal groups. Despite its size, Iseyin remains an essentially pre-industrial settle-ment with no factories, little service employment and few amenities. One of its most distinctive features is the existence of a well-developed craft-textile industry which is highly localized within the town. Thus in certain quarters virtually all of the compounds are engaged in weaving whereas in others this activity is almost completely absent. Furthermore, functional linkages between related stages in the chain of textile production have emphasized this areal specialization so that spin-ning and dyeing activities, for example, are also found in close proximity to weav-ing. However, this clustered distribution is reinforced by the operation of social factors as traditional skills are passed down from father to son and carried on within the organizational framework of the extended family compound. Indeed the influence of the social structure of the Yoruba upon the location of their eco-nomic activities may be regarded as illustrating the impact of another dimension of the human environment upon spatial organization.

Clusters of economic activity based upon material linkages between inter-dependent production units still exist within modern cities. However, concentra-tions such as the clothing industry in Manhattan and furniture manufacture in parts of inner London are exceptional and the post-war fragmentation of Birming-ham's jewellery quarter as a consequence of urban redevelopment is more typical. Nevertheless, functional linkages may still be important at the conurbation scale. For example, a high proportion of manufacturing employment in the West Mid-lands is engaged in a wide range of metal-working industries and linkages between different establishments appear to offer the most obvious explanation for their spectacular concentration in the 'Black Country' between Birmingham and Wolverhampton. A detailed analysis of linkage patterns in the area has provided broad support for this argument, but has also suggested important differences between large and small firms (Taylor and Wood, 1973). Thus the linkages of smaller businesses are much more local than those of larger organizations, which have input-output links that extend far beyond the conurbation. If this connection between size of firm and geographical range of linkage patterns is applied to other situations, it has important consequences for the relationship between the mul-tiplier effect, industrial linkage and agglomeration. As the organizations which control manufacturing industry increase in size (see chapter 3), it follows that the multiplier effects generated by a new plant may not be concentrated in the surrounding area as implied in Pred's model, but may 'leak' elsewhere and thereby present opportunities for the dispersal of development away from rapidly growing centres.

Leakage

Despite this possibility, leakage often operates to the disadvantage of peripheral areas as newly established industrial plants fail to generate the anticipated levels of investment and employment growth in related activities. These anticipated effects are based upon the hope that backward linkages may attract industries supplying inputs to the plant whilst forward linkages may provide opportunities for the establishment of operations based on its outputs. This type of thinking certainly influenced the UK government in its attempts during the early 1960s to promote the dispersal of the car industry away from its traditional centre in the West Midlands into areas of high unemployment on Merseyside and in Scotland. Experience in Scotland has not matched official expectations, partly because local firms have failed to take advantage of the opportunities presented by the new plants and partly because the car firms have remained loyal to long-established suppliers located in the West Midlands (James, 1964). Any transport-cost penalties incurred by such loyalty are probably not very great anyway in view of the evidence that distance is little deterrent to the maintenance of industrial linkages in modern economies with well-developed transport systems (see Keeble, 1969).

The location requirements of interdependent economic activities may be different so that savings in transport costs achieved by their adjacent location may be less significant than advantages gained by their separation. The petrochemical industry provides one of the most spectacular examples of the way in which linkages may promote agglomeration and, at the same time, illustrates the dangers of assuming an automatic geographic association between linked activities (see Chapman, 1973). Many of the materials involved in the early stages of petrochemical manufacture are difficult and expensive to transport and the characteristic agglomeration of interdependent plants in oil-based industrial complexes is based on this simple fact (Fig. 5.2). Despite the impressive appearance of such complexes, the range of products manufactured in them is normally limited to what may be termed basic intermediates. The plastic buckets, synthetic fibres and so on which are ultimately derived from these intermediates tend to be produced elsewhere and the local multiplier effect of petrochemical complexes is correspondingly reduced, much to the disappointment of regional planners who have regarded such complexes as catalysts of economic development in remote or declining regions. The oil refinery/petrochemical complex at Grangemouth in central Scotland was officially designated as a growth centre in 1963, but there has been little diversification into downstream activities such as plastic fabrication (Chapman, 1974). The risks and high costs associated with movement of gases in the early stages of production no longer apply in these downstream stages, by which time most of the materials have been transformed into solid or liquid form. Consequently, location relative to customers becomes a more important consideration than proximity to sources of supply and, seen from the planners' point of view, jobs 'leak' back to the markets which are already the major centres of economic activity.

Even if direct linkages fail to generate anticipated levels of development, the introduction of a new plant may produce a chain-reaction of successive multipliers. Thus wages paid to employees in a new factory may increase the turnover of local shops, thereby encouraging retailers to expand their facilities, which may in turn provide business for building contractors, who may employ painters, and so on. The practical problems involved in actually measuring such a sequence of events are immense and wide variations have been described in the size of the local multiplier effect associated with major industrial developments (see Lever, 1974). In-

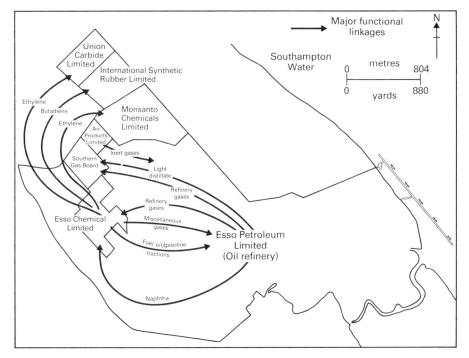

Fig. 5.2 Technical linkages within an oil refinery/petrochemical complex, Fawley, UK (Chapman, 1970, 169).

deed, in certain circumstances, investments which are expected to stimulate a regional economy may, in fact, have the reverse effect. It has been shown, for example, that expenditure in local shops actually declined following the establishment of a new aluminium smelter at Holyhead on Anglesey as increased levels of car ownership made possible regular trips to the larger centre of Bangor on the mainland (Sadler, 1974). Similar changes in consumption patterns are partly responsible for increasing food imports into many African countries as rising incomes associated with economic development have encouraged a shift in tastes away from indigenous foodstuffs (see Mabogunje, 1973), thereby causing leakage on an international scale.

5.1.2 Threshold and Market Factors in Unbalanced Growth

Although the operation of the multiplier does not *necessarily* promote agglomeration, it is nevertheless an important factor contributing to the uneven distribution of economic growth. The translation of linkages of various kinds into further development is based upon the interrelationship between (i) demand thresholds and (ii) market size.

Demand Thresholds
The idea that critical demand thresholds exist for different economic activities is easy to grasp in principle, but such thresholds are difficult to identify in practice. Research into this problem has mainly been concerned with the service functions of settlements. The widely observed positive correlation between the size of a settlement and the number and diversity of its service functions provides circumstantial evidence in support of the threshold concept (Fig. 5.3). It appears that as the population of a settlement increases, the critical thresholds of different functions are successively passed, although the curvilinear nature of the relationship suggests that fewer

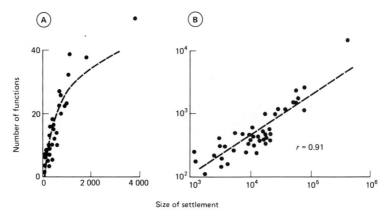

Fig. 5.3 Settlement size and number of functions in: (a) southern Illinois (arithmetic axes); (b) southern Ceylon (logarithmic axes) (Haggett *et al.*, 1977, 140).

functions are added per increment of population increase. Further insight into this relationship may be gained by examining the frequency of occurrence of various functions within settlements of differing size. The curves in Figure 5.4 were derived by plotting the number of establishments providing each function against the population size of 33 settlements in Snohomish County, Washington (Berry and Garrison, 1958). They are, in effect, the lines which provide the best fit through the scatter of points. The intersection point between the dotted line and the curves defines the threshold population required to support each function. These results are, of course, specific to a particular cultural situation and the threshold population of 426 for a dentist could scarcely be regarded as a universal standard! The method also relies upon inference rather than the direct measurement either of financial receipts or number of customers. Nevertheless, evidence from this and numerous

similar studies does confirm the importance of the threshold concept in determining the occurrence of service functions. These functions are not only of the retail
type and threshold factors are important influences upon the location of public
facilities such as schools and hospitals (see section 11.1.2). Specialized commercial
services such as insurance, banking and advertising also have their own thresholds
which tend to reinforce the economic advantages of the large urban centre.

Comparatively little attention has been devoted towards identifying the demand
thresholds of industrial plants, but a general trend in manufacturing towards progressively larger individual production units implies that demand thresholds have
increased through time. In industries where the increase in the optimum size of

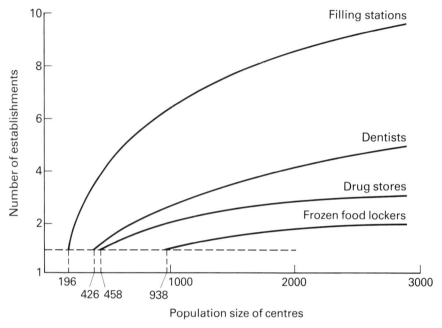

Fig. 5.4 Threshold populations of central-place functions in Snohomish County, Washington
(after Berry and Garrison, 1958).

plant has outstripped the overall growth of the market, it follows that production
must be concentrated in fewer locations thereby accentuating the uneven distribution of economic activity. Factory closures, often following takeover bids, have
become more frequent occurrences in recent years (see Watts, 1974). For example,
the disappearance during the 1970s of many of the UK's regional breweries, which
has been a source of much dismay to connoisseurs of the beverage, has been accompanied by the concentration of the industry in fewer commercial hands and in
fewer locations (Watts, 1977) (see section 10.1.3). A less obvious consequence of
economies of scale in manufacturing is that they tend to reduce the viability of
development away from existing centres of production. This has the effect, on an
international scale, of making it difficult for developing countries to establish
manufacturing industries. In Africa, countries such as Liberia, Sierra Leone,

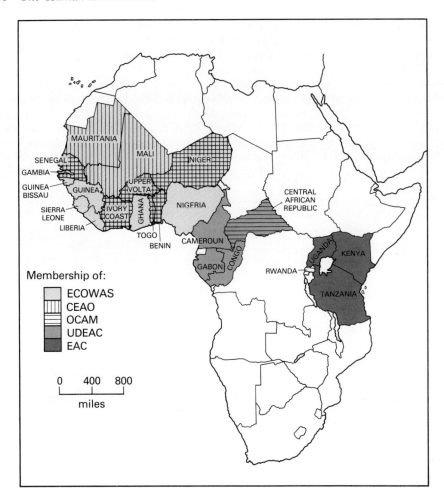

Fig. 5.5 International economic groupings in Africa, 1977. (*Note:*
CEAO – Communauté Économique de l'Afrique de l'Ouest;
EAC – East African Community;
ECOWAS – Economic Community of West African States;
OCAM – Organisation Commune Africaine et Mauricienne;
UDEAC – Union Douanière et Économique de l'Afrique Centrale.)

Guinea and Mauretania which have major deposits of iron ore cannot use these
resources to establish indigenous iron and steel industries because their domestic
markets fall below the threshold required to support even the smallest plant, and
export opportunities are stifled by the fact that the major consuming countries
have their own steelmaking capacity (Mabogunje, 1973). One of the few ways
around this problem for the developing world seems to lie in the organization of
international economic groupings aimed at the creation of much larger common

markets (Fig. 5.5). In theory, such groupings enable member countries to specialize in particular types of economic activity and, by serving an enlarged market, these activities may operate at levels which take full advantage of potential scale economies. In practice, experience in Latin America and Africa has generally been disappointing and it may be noted that one of the most significant components of the human environment for the less developed countries is the very existence of the developed world.

Market Size

The significance of the threshold concept and market size in the context of the phenomenon of unbalanced growth ultimately rests upon the assumption that the costs of transporting products to their markets is an important factor affecting the location of economic activities. The complex linkages which are characteristic of modern economies ensure that for many factories the 'market' is not the domestic household but another factory, as the outputs of one become the inputs of the other. Thus at any point in time, existing concentrations of industry are likely to be the greatest attraction to new investment. This in turn will generate multiplier effects which will tend to increase the size of the market still further, thereby attracting yet more development as new thresholds are passed.

An attempt to demonstrate the implications of this kind of sequence for the future pattern of development in Western Europe has been made by mapping *economic potential* (Clark, Wilson and Bradley, 1969). This index is an extension of the concept of *market potential* which is derived as follows:

$$MP_i = \sum_{j=1}^{n} \frac{M_j}{d_{ij}}$$

where
MP_i is the market potential at i,
M_j is the measure of the size of market at j,
d_{ij} is the distance between i and j.

The value obtained is a measure of the accessibility of point i to a known distribution of markets j. Economic potential is calculated in much the same way, although income levels are used as an indicator of demand and distance is replaced by various direct measures of transport costs. Such calculations rest upon many simplifying assumptions. Fixed routes between the various markets must be specified and even the most sophisticated computer program cannot hope to incorporate all the variables which influence transport costs within an area as large as the EEC. Nevertheless, there is no doubt that the map indicated in Figure 5.6 does provide a valid general impression of the relative attractiveness to industrialists of the different parts of the Community. The map not only describes the existing pattern of development, with the highest values centred upon the Benelux countries and the Ruhr, but may also be regarded as predictive in the sense that these areas may be expected to accentuate their economic dominance over peripheral areas of the UK, Eire and Italy by obtaining a high proportion of future investment. This inference may be supported by reference to the location policies of US companies which have played an important role in the economic recovery of Western Europe

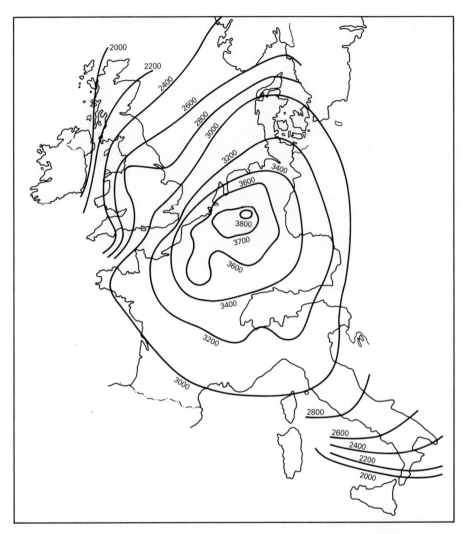

Fig. 5.6 Economic potential in the EEC (assuming Norwegian membership) (Clark *et al.*, 1969, 205).

since 1945. Although the common-language heritage gave the UK an initial advantage in attracting US firms, recent evidence suggests that American companies have been concentrating more and more of their European investment in the economic core identified in Figure 5.6 (see Hamilton, 1976). This trend is not surprising in view of the fact that a survey of US companies with European operations revealed that two-thirds of the respondents rated market size as the decisive factor in choosing between different countries (Blackbourn, 1974). Similar results emphasizing the importance of the market have been obtained from numerous studies of the decision-making process at the level of the individual firm (see Krumme, 1969). These conclusions may be interpreted as confirmation of the proposition that the attractiveness of market locations is based upon the desire to minimize distribution costs. However, the achievement of this objective provides only a partial explanation for the concentration of development in areas of high economic potential and the benefits gained by location in such areas are not always quantifiable in terms of reduced costs and increased revenues.

5.1.3 Psychological Factors in Unbalanced Growth

The uneven distribution of economic development is often reinforced by various intangible factors which contribute to a general atmosphere of economic optimism in growing centres. In many cases, these factors may be traced back to the significance of information availability and risk minimization in decision making (see chapter 3).

Although information is more mobile in the twentieth-century world of mass communication than in the nineteenth-century period to which Pred's invention/ innovation cycle relates, perception studies have underlined the continuing significance of spatial bias in information availability. It was shown in chapter 3 that attitudes based on ignorance can have important repercussions upon patterns of economic growth in both developed and developing countries (see section 3.3.2). The most important single effect of such attitudes is to polarize development upon existing centres. The 'bright lights' syndrome not only applies to the migration of people, but is also apparent in the behaviour of firms. For example, a desire to be associated with a prestige metropolitan centre has probably contributed to the massive expenditure on office blocks in capital cities such as London and Paris. By its very nature, this kind of decision-making behaviour tends to be self-perpetuating. Major centres acquire a growth momentum which accentuates discrepancies in the availability of information relating to locations in the core as compared with the periphery, thereby reinforcing the circle of cumulative causation.

The concentration of investment in existing centres is not simply related to ignorance of opportunities in alternative areas. It may also be interpreted as a consequence of many independent decisions with the common goal of minimizing uncertainty (see section 3.4.2). Rapidly growing areas often represent the 'safest' location for new investment. An untried product is most likely to succeed in the largest market and a new firm will also be able to take advantage of already established fixed capital in the form of roads, railways and other aspects of the infrastructure. The role of Greater London as an innovation centre has been identified as an important factor contributing to its dominant position within the UK economy (Keeble, 1972). Thus London has not only led the way in the creation or adoption of British-made industrial innovations, but has also frequently provided the initial centre through which imported technology has been channelled. The advantages of capital cities are often further reinforced by the significance for economic decision makers of access to the 'corridors of power' and the highly centralized and bureaucratic administrations typical of most Latin American countries, for example, have been held partly responsible for the continent's problems of unbalanced growth (see Gilbert, 1974).

Repetitive and imitative behaviour are closely associated with the minimization of risk in contributing to unbalanced growth. It may be argued on probability grounds that a firm which has accumulated funds for investment will already be

associated with a rapidly growing centre. In this situation, not only will its information be biased in favour of that centre, but there will also be a strong impulse
to repeat a previously successful pattern of behaviour by expanding operations
at its existing location. Where *in situ* expansion is impracticable or a firm is setting
up its business for the first time, the imitation of others may be an important influence upon plant location. This kind of behaviour is yet another approach to the
minimization of uncertainty since it amounts to the input of 'second-hand' experience into the decision-making process.

The contribution of what may be broadly termed psychological factors to unbalanced growth is difficult to evaluate and evidence of their influence is largely
circumstantial. For example, a recent study has suggested that the highly concentrated distributions of the ironfounding industry in the West Midlands and
East Lancashire cannot simply be explained in terms of economic advantages
gained through the existence of local linkage networks, but are related to 'psychic'
return obtained from agglomeration (Taylor, 1973). On an international scale, a
similar phenomenon has been observed to influence the location decisions of multinational corporations. De Smidt (1966) noted a tendency for foreign-owned
plants in the Netherlands to cluster in specific areas according to their country
of origin. Blackbourn (1972) explored the idea further by reference to the location
of factories established by overseas companies in the Republic of Ireland between
1955 and 1969. An analysis of the distribution of plants set up by British, West
German and US companies suggested that the latter tend to congregate in particular areas for no obvious economic reasons. This type of psychological agglomeration is important in a country which has made a conscious attempt to encourage
foreign investment as a means of improving its economic performance and Irish
efforts to stimulate development in the west of the country away from Dublin are
paralleled by similar policies in a wide variety of cultural situations which seek
to redress some of the inequalities associated with unbalanced growth.

5.2 The Consequences of Unbalanced Growth

In discussing the nature of unbalanced growth the emphasis has been placed upon
internal mechanisms which create a positive feedback system. Despite the self-
generating momentum which is implicit in such a system, a growing centre cannot
be divorced from the wider area in which it is placed. Several attempts have been
made to understand the nature and the consequences of these external relationships. Pred's ideas bear a close resemblance to an earlier model postulated by
Myrdal (1957) who was explicitly concerned with the problem of explaining the
spatial pattern of economic development within countries. He argued that the
mechanisms of cumulative causation inevitably tend to accentuate economic inequalities between regions leading to the emergence of a dynamic *core* surrounded
by a stagnant or declining *periphery*. The early work of Friedmann (1966) provides
a more optimistic interpretation. He maintained that national economies pass
through a series of stages in the transition from pre-industrial to post-industrial
societies and that each of these stages is characterized by a distinctive spatial
structure (Fig. 5.7). The model implies a progression towards ultimate convergence. Friedmann (1972) later acknowledged that this equilibrium situation
represents an ideal which is extremely difficult to achieve in practice for reasons

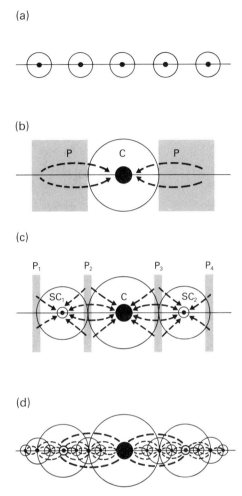

Fig. 5.7 Spatial structure and stage of development: (a) pre-industrial; (b) incipient industrialization; (c) industrial maturity; (d) post-industrial (after Friedmann, 1966, 36).

outlined in the following section, which examines (i) the nature of core/periphery relationships and (ii) the policy implications of core/periphery relationships.

5.2.1 The Nature of Core/Periphery Relationships

Myrdal coined the terms *spread* and *backwash* to describe the various economic and social effects associated with unbalanced growth. He regarded spread effects as beneficial to the periphery and backwash effects as detrimental. The relative strengths and spatial distribution of these effects determine whether the gap between core and periphery is widening or narrowing. A distinction may be drawn between the operation of (i) spread/backwash effects in theory and (ii) spread/backwash effects in practice.

Spread/Backwash Effects in Theory

Theoretical arguments identify a wide range of spread effects which together provide the mechanism whereby growth is transmitted from core to periphery (see Parr, 1973). Growth at the core may be expected to generate demands for the products of the periphery. Increased levels of food consumption represent one of the most obvious beneficial effects of a growing core upon an agricultural periphery, although subsistence farmers will not necessarily respond to commercial opportunities. Similarly, expansion at the core in processing industries dependent upon raw materials from the periphery may result in return transfers of money which may be used to promote development. Finally, linkages based on the supply of certain goods and services to the core may reinforce the effects of the financial multiplier in the periphery.

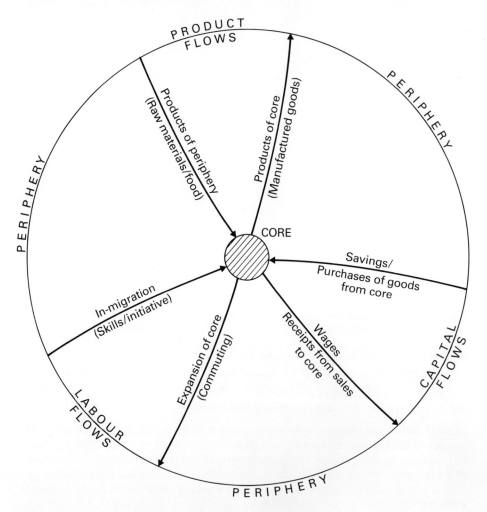

Fig. 5.8 The nature of spread and backwash effects.

Job opportunities in the core may stimulate commuting from the surrounding area. Wages gained in this way may be regarded as another contribution to the general redistribution of capital away from the core. This process of outward spread may be supported by migration over longer distances which may also absorb surplus labour in the periphery. This may, it is argued, relieve pressure on land and raise the per capita incomes of the remaining population by enabling agriculture to be conducted on a more efficient basis.

Backwash may, in certain respects, be regarded as a mirror image of the forces encouraging dispersal (Fig. 5.8). Indeed it is possible to show that the various mechanisms by which growth is thought to be transmitted to the periphery may also operate in exactly the opposite way by focusing growth at the core. Thus increasing levels of demand at the centre will not necessarily have a commensurate effect upon economic activity in the periphery. Primary commodities such as raw materials and agricultural products are the principal outputs of the peripheral areas. Demand for such products is often inelastic – it grows less rapidly than the corresponding rise in incomes. This reflects the fact that much of the additional wealth created at the centre is spent on consumer goods which are either manufactured within the core region itself or imported from external sources. Furthermore, much of the capital transferred to the periphery in return for its products 'leaks' back to the core because it is spent on goods which the periphery cannot provide. In addition, the supposed benefits of out-migration from the periphery to the core are usually based upon the assumption of rural overpopulation. Even if this is accepted, continued rural–urban migration can have adverse affects on the periphery. Migration tends to be selective in the sense that it is the young and enterprising who are most likely to leave. The remaining population is therefore less willing and less able to make the social and economic changes necessary for development.

Spread/Backwash Effects in Practice
The ambiguity of economic theory with regard to the relative strength of spread and backwash effects makes it important to test these arguments against reality. Attempts to measure spread and backwash effects have usually concentrated upon the former by analysing the distribution of various indices of development around a core region. These indices are usually based upon published statistics relating to such diverse parameters as levels of literacy, number of telephones per head of population, birth rates and all kinds of other variables which may be loosely regarded as being indicative of economic development. Multivariate techniques make it possible to compress large sets of data into single measures of development. The distribution of these values around a core and therefore, by inference, the impact of spread effects, may be visualized as a surface, the height of which is directly proportional to the level of development. Theoretically, it should also be possible to devise a similar representation of backwash effects and, by superimposing one surface upon the other, to obtain a composite view of their relative strengths. In practice, however, official statistics tend to be more comprehensive when it comes to indicating such positive aspects of government policy as the spread of infrastructure and services to rural areas and more reticent about such potentially adverse consequences of polarized growth as the effects of selective migration upon agricultural productivity. Weinand (1973) has argued that this

problem may be overcome by devising surfaces which measure the spread and
backwash effects independently. He demonstrated the argument in a case-study in
which he assembled various measures of economic development relating to the
provinces of Nigeria. The data were analysed using a technique known as principal-
components analysis* which reduces complex data sets to manageable proportions
by extracting a relatively small number of factors or components which account
for a large amount of the variability among the original criteria. Thus Weinand
found that data describing the availability of health services, primary education
and the density of roads were apparently highly interrelated whereas five indices

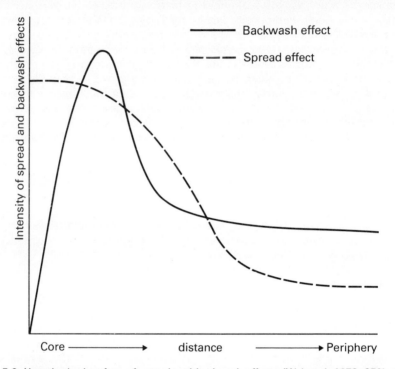

Fig. 5.9 Hypothesized surface of spread and backwash effects (Weinand, 1973, 250).

expressing in per capita terms the number of motor vehicles, telephone lines, banks,
wholesale/retail establishments and the level of traditional market activity seemed
to vary in a consistent fashion. He interpreted the first factor as a measure of the
provision of infrastructure which he regarded as evidence of the spread effect. He
suggested that the second factor was closely associated with the society's ability
to consume and the volume of entrepreneurial activity which, he argued, would
be absent or poorly represented in areas where backwash effects are dominant.
Weinand postulated certain hypotheses concerning the anticipated distribution of
spread and backwash effects. He maintained that because of the difficulties of transport and communication in developing countries, backwash effects would be most
pronounced near to the core areas. Overflow of wealth would ensure that spread

* See glossary.

effects were also strongest in the immediate vicinity of the core, but attempts to disperse economic activities might be expected to produce a more uniform distribution of spread effects elsewhere. These hypotheses are expressed diagrammatically in Figure 5.9.

The factor scores* are plotted as isopleth maps in Figure 5.10. They are expressed in terms of standard-deviation units above or below their respective means.† The predominant trend for the infrastructure or spread factor is from high in the south to low in the north (Fig. 5.10a). The pattern generally conforms to the initial hypothesis, but there is a noticeable outlier of higher values in central Nigeria. This is matched in Figure 5.10b by a similar, but more extensive, feature indicating limited backwash. In the south, the scores on the backwash factor are more complicated than those describing the spread effect. Nevertheless, backwash does appear to be most intense in the vicinity of the major urban cores of Ibadan and Lagos. The Niger Delta is characterized by low scores apart from peaks centred upon Port Harcourt and Calabar.

In relating these patterns to his initial hypothesis (Fig. 5.9), Weinand concluded that some modifications were necessary. Firstly, with the exception of isolated peaks in the vicinity of secondary cores, spread effects seemed to fall away much more rapidly than expected. Secondly, although the configuration of the backwash curve was more or less as anticipated over short and medium distances, it began to rise rather than level off beyond 110 km. Figure 5.11a expresses these modifications in graphical terms and Figure 5.11b represents their spatial implications in the form of a generalized economic landscape of Nigeria. Spread and backwash effects decline in parallel throughout the 'hinterland' as distance from the core increases. The 'economic frontier' represents a secondary core area beyond which lies an extensive 'underdeveloped periphery' which not only lacks modern economic activity, but which is also unable to provide the infrastructure necessary to attract such activities.

Weinand's conclusions that spread effects are limited to the vicinity of core areas and that much of the periphery is virtually immune to development impulses have been supported by the findings of other studies (see Robinson and Salih, 1971; Gilbert, 1975). The weight of empirical evidence suggests that Friedmann's initial belief in the ultimate integration of core and periphery was misplaced. The reality of the situation in many developing countries is recognized in a later publication in which Friedmann (1972) argues that certain social and political obstacles are preventing the achievement of spatial equilibrium through the operation of economic forces. Thus whilst backwash effects continue unchecked, spread effects are deliberately suppressed by vested interests wishing to retain power and influence at the core. The highly centralized administrative systems which are characteristic of the developing world are less likely to heed 'voices from the periphery' demanding a more equitable distribution of the national wealth (see Brookfield, 1975). In these circumstances, the core/periphery dualism expressed in economic terms is simply a reflection of a more deep-seated problem which rests upon the maintenance of political authority/dependence relationships, a problem which is not necessarily confined to developing countries (see Holland, 1974).

* See glossary (factor analysis).
† See glossary.

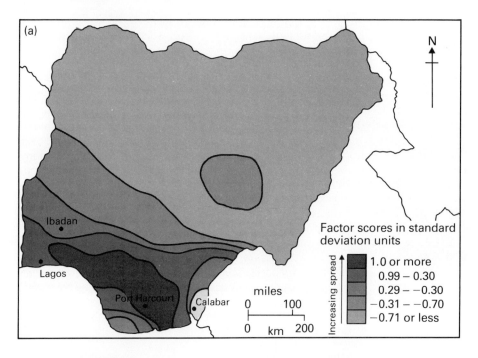

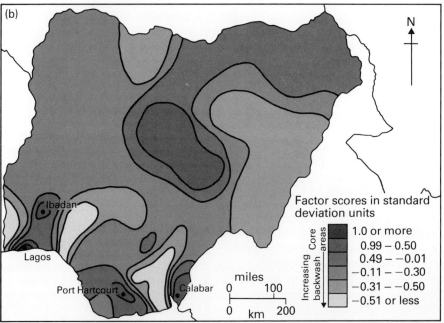

Fig. 5.10 Nigeria, distribution of: (a) spread effects; (b) backwash effects (Weinand, 1973, 256 and 258).

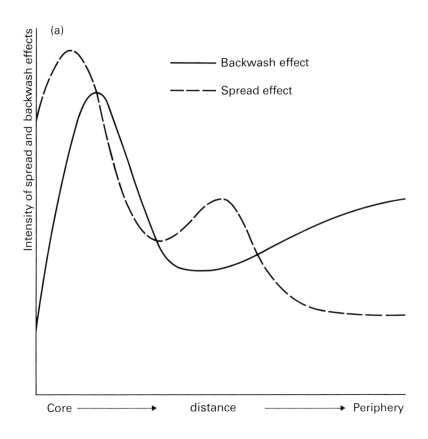

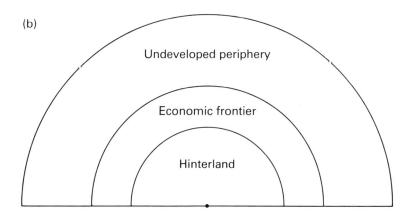

Fig. 5.11 Spread/backwash effects in Nigeria: (a) modified spread/backwash surface; (b) generalized economic landscape (Weinand, 1973).

5.2.2 Policy Implications of Core/Periphery Relationships

Contrasts between core and periphery are often very pronounced in former colonies in which economic activities have been geared towards the supply of raw materials to a mother-country. This kind of relationship tends to generate an unbalanced spatial structure, frequently oriented towards a dominant coastal centre which is unsuitable as a focus for the integrated development of an independent state. Although each case is unique, the core/periphery model provides a unifying framework upon which to base an analysis of patterns of development within different countries and some of the practical consequences and policy implications of unbalanced growth may be appreciated by reference to the experiences of (i) Australia, (ii) Venezuela and (iii) South Africa.

Australia
Well over 80 per cent of Australia's population live in towns and cities, making it one of the most highly urbanized nations in the world. Almost half this number are concentrated in the metropolitan areas of Sydney and Melbourne with the result that a substantial proportion of the country's total population is clustered in its southeast corner, which is backed by a vast underdeveloped periphery. The origins of this pattern may be traced back to the establishment of the first convict settlements towards the end of the eighteenth century. The desire to separate these settlements for reasons of internal security together with the need to avoid the 'contamination' of the rest of the population encouraged the dispersal of early settlements. Leaving aside the inhospitality of the interior, the coastal location of these settlements was determined, to a large extent, by strategic considerations and Blainey (1968, 96) maintains that 'Britain claimed the whole continent simply in order to claim a few isolated harbours astride trade routes'. The initial advantage gained by these early settlements was reinforced as Australia became something more than just a convenient exile for British convicts. By virtue of their coastal locations, they served as entry points for imported manufactured goods and as the export centres through which gold, wool and other resources were channelled to the mother-country. The exploitation of these resources did not lead to the growth of major new urban centres, partly because of the ephemeral nature of the 'gold rush' and partly because of the importance of wool. The advent of the railways accentuated the dominance of the original settlements by extending their hinterlands and so inhibiting the development of new inland centres.

　　Although the introduction at the beginning of the twentieth century of a federal system of political organization has prevented the extreme polarization upon a single city which is characteristic of many less developed countries, it has certainly reinforced the position of each metropolitan centre within its own administrative area and there is much evidence that, whether viewed at national or state level, the continued growth of these centres is producing a wide range of undesirable consequences. Various reports have emphasized the discrepancies between urban and rural population in terms of income levels, employment opportunities and access to public services (see Logan, 1975). Furthermore, these inequalities seem to be increasing. For example, a study of unemployment rates over the period 1955 to 1970 revealed significant contrasts in the experience of rural and urban areas as the most rapidly growing types of activity become more concentrated in the major metropolitan centres whilst stagnant or declining sectors were dominant elsewhere (Jeffrey, 1975). This imbalance imposes numerous economic and social costs such as increased public expenditure on unemployment benefits and the inflationary pressures created by shortages of labour in the cities.

Studies such as Jeffrey's emphasize the need to introduce policies aimed at counteracting the adverse consequences of the uneven distribution of economic development in Australia. Although various measures have been introduced, they have generally been ineffective and it has been argued that their impact has been more than offset by various actions which have promoted further centralization in existing state capitals (Stillwell and Hardwick, 1973). For example, the effectiveness of dispersal policies is reduced when industry is able to play off one state against another by arguing that it will invest elsewhere rather than be pushed away from metropolitan areas by planning controls. Public administration is one of Australia's major growth industries and attempts have been made to decentralize various government departments, but these policies have not been coordinated and opportunities to establish viable alternative centres of population and employment growth have been lost (see Langdale, 1976). Despite periodic demands for the creation of new towns and cities (Neutze, 1974), little has been achieved in bringing about any fundamental change in a spatial pattern of development which ultimately reflects decisions taken by colonial authorities in the eighteenth century. Indeed, the Australian experience seems to underline the strength of the forces responsible for unbalanced growth and the difficulties involved in breaking out of the cycle of circular and cumulative causation which these forces create.

Venezuela

Venezuela was a second-rank Spanish colony which was by-passed economically because it failed to yield the precious metals that were the principal objective of the Conquistadores. It developed primarily as an agricultural colony based on the production of hides, cacao and indigo. Although most of the principal Spanish settlements were established on or near the Caribbean coast, the contemporary dominance of the capital city of Caracas is a product of the twentieth century. It is ironic that in their search for gold and silver, the Conquistadores were unaware of the existence and potentialities of the resource which has made Venezuela the wealthiest state in Latin America and 'enabled it to enjoy one of the highest, sustained rates of economic growth of any nation, in modern history' (Robinson, 1971, 236). Venezuela's oil boom began in the early 1920s at a time when approximately 80 per cent of the country's population lived in rural areas. Forty years later, 60 per cent resided in urban areas and more than half of these were concentrated in the Caracas metropolitan region with a substantial proportion of the remainder in the second city of Maracaibo which developed in conjunction with the country's oil industry. Thus whilst the exploitation of this resource increased the national wealth, it also resulted in a very unbalanced pattern of economic development. Nevertheless, the accumulation of oil revenues has made it possible for Venezuela to undertake a massive and costly project to try and overcome this imbalance by establishing a new core of economic activity in the interior of the country.

The project, in which Friedmann was closely involved, officially began in 1960 with the setting up of a public corporation responsible for devising a development strategy centred on a new city called Ciudad Guayana to be built on the site of a small existing settlement at the confluence of the Orinoco and Caroni rivers (Rodwin, 1970). This site seemed to offer considerable scope for development based on the exploitation of various resources in an area that was remote from the influence of Caracas. Iron-ore mining had begun during the 1950s and prospects were considered good for a wide range of other minerals including manganese, nickel, chromium and gold. Known deposits of oil and natural gas further reinforced the attractions of the area and abundant energy for heavy industry could be generated by harnessing the hydroelectric potential of the Caroni River. The planners have attempted to take full advantage of the economic opportunities presented by the area's resource base by promoting the establishment of complexes of interrelated activities. The project has required massive injections of both public and private capital and has been sustained by a continuing political commitment on the part of successive Venezuelan governments. The results of these efforts are apparent in the increase in the population of Ciudad Guayana from 4,000 in 1950 to 130,000 by the mid-1970s and an anticipated 300,000 by 1980.

Not surprisingly, the scheme has encountered many problems. Despite rapid population growth, the market thresholds of many consumer goods have not been attained and much of the income generated in the area is spent on imports from Caracas or abroad (see Stohr, 1975). Backwash effects have been more powerful than spread effects within the vicinity of Ciudad Guayana as the city draws resources from the surrounding areas. For example, the smaller centre of Ciudad Bolivar, 100 km up the Orinoco River, has lost certain of its regional functions to the new city. Nevertheless, local backwash effects may be temporary and the emphasis of recent policies upon agricultural development in the Orinoco Delta is partly aimed at overcoming this problem. Viewed on a national scale, however, there is no doubt that the Ciudad Guayana project has transformed a remote peripheral area into an integral part of the national economy. This suggests that, provided sufficient funds are made available, it is possible to produce an environment in which the feedback mechanisms responsible for unbalanced growth may be controlled and directed towards solving some of the problems they create.

South Africa

Core/periphery concepts may be applied to the development of the South African economy where the situation is complicated by the political, economic and social implications of apartheid. An attempt has been made to compare the evolving spatial pattern of economic development in South Africa with Friedmann's core/periphery model (Browett, 1976). Browett distinguishes three phases in the evolution of this pattern corresponding to Friedmann's pre-industrial, transitional and industrial stages (Fig. 5.7). In the first phase before 1870, Cape Town and Durban stood out as the principal core areas (Fig. 5.12a). Contact between these and lesser centres was very limited and the situation closely matched Friedmann's pre-industrial structure of independent local centres. The period between 1870 and 1911 witnessed the consolidation of the two coastal core areas and the rapid emergence of Johannesburg to a position of equal significance in the interior (Fig. 5.12b). The discovery of mineral resources was not only responsible for the growth of Johannesburg, but also stimulated development at the lesser centres of Kimberley and Bloemfontein. These developments were superimposed upon a semi-subsistence agricultural economy which was incompatible with the new mining activities. Consequently, spread effects were limited and the South African economy in 1911 was characterized by the existence of an urban oligarchy rather than the primate core hypothesized in Friedmann's transitional stage. Subsequent development has largely confirmed the 1911 patterns, although the interior core focused on Johannesburg has been superseded by the more extensive metropolitan region of the

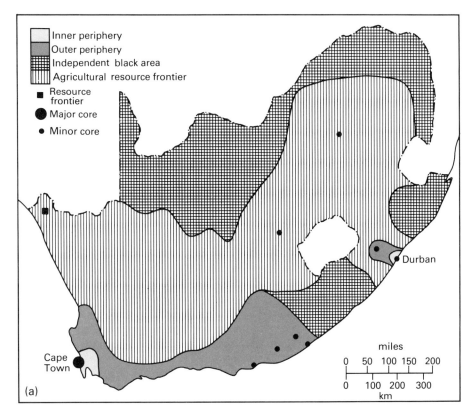

Fig. 5.12 A core/periphery interpretation of the South African economy: (a) pre-industrial period (pre-1870); (b) transitional period (incipient industrialization, 1870–1911); (c) industrial period (1911–) (after Browett, 1976, 119, 121 and 126).

Witwatersrand (Fig. 5.12c). Spread effects have gradually extended outwards from the three principal core areas, but South Africa is far from attaining the kind of national economic integration postulated in the final stage of Friedmann's model. Indeed, if the triple centres of the Witwatersrand, Cape Town and Durban are regarded as a single non-contiguous core, there is abundant evidence that backwash effects are stronger than spread effects and that the dominance of these centres over the rest of the South African economy is increasing (see Fair, 1976).

Various measures designed to offset this polarization have been introduced.

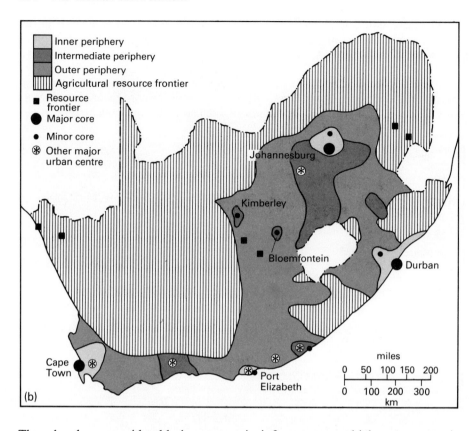

Legend:
- Inner periphery
- Intermediate periphery
- Outer periphery
- Agricultural resource frontier
- ■ Resource frontier
- ● Major core
- • Minor core
- ⊛ Other major urban centre

Johannesburg
Kimberley
Bloemfontein
Durban
Cape Town
Port Elizabeth

miles
0　50　100 150　200
0　100　200　300
km

(b)

There has been considerable investment in infrastructure which may attract industry to peripheral areas. At the same time, efforts have been made to direct new industrial investment away from the core areas. These have not been very successful (see Rogerson, 1975) and policies to restrict the physical expansion of urban areas appear, at first sight, to be the most rigorous approach to the problem of unbalanced growth. In fact, the containment of urbanization by controls upon land use, population movement and rights of residence is not so much geared towards achieving economic objectives as a desire to retain the political authority/dependence relationships which are central to South Africa's policies of apartheid or 'separate development' (see Fair and Schmidt, 1974). The country's growth rests upon the continuing supply of Black labour to support economic activities controlled by the White minority. Controls upon urban expansion which are not accompanied by a corresponding decentralization of employment opportunities imply an accentuation of the backwash effects engendered by the migrant-labour system (see Board, 1976). In their desire to reduce the feelings of insecurity engendered by a rapidly growing Black population in the major cities of South Africa, the Republic's policy-makers are negating their own efforts to disperse economic activity since prospects for growth in the periphery are hindered by the withdrawal of its labour resources. Thus the core/periphery structure of the South African economy is not simply a reflection of the polarizing economic forces which

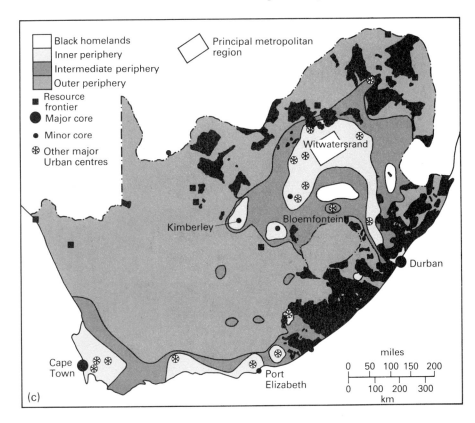

Black homelands
Inner periphery
Intermediate periphery
Outer periphery
■ Resource frontier
● Major core
• Minor core
⊛ Other major Urban centres
◇ Principal metropolitan region

Witwatersrand
Kimberley
Bloemfontein
Durban
Cape Town
Port Elizabeth

miles
0 50 100 150 200
0 100 200 300
km

(c)

operate elsewhere, but is maintained and reinforced by the political philosophy of 'separate development'.

The difficulties involved in reversing the forces encouraging the geographical concentration of economic activities suggest that it is the human rather than the physical environment which is the most powerful influence upon the actions of decision makers. It requires a major policy commitment, such as that undertaken by the Venezuelan authorities, to bring about any significant change in the core/periphery structure which is a characteristic feature of the spatial organization of so many countries. Such an effort essentially involves modifying the human content of space in the hope that the circular and cumulative process of economic growth will be initiated. This process rests upon the complex interrelationships between past, present and future decisions which are transmitted through the medium of evolving spatial patterns of human activity.

Further Reading

BROOKFIELD, H. 1975: *Interdependent development*. London.

A stimulating review of the international 'development problem'. Chapter 4 is particularly relevant.

CLARK, C., WILSON, F. and BRADLEY, J. 1963: Industrial location and economic potential in western Europe. *Regional Studies* **3,** 197–212.

Outlines a model-based approach to the assessment of the relative attractiveness of different areas to industrial investment.

FRIEDMANN, J. 1966: *Regional development policy: a case study of Venezuela.* Cambridge, Mass.

An interesting illustration of the translation of theoretical propositions into policy recommendations.

PARR, J. B. 1973: Growth poles, regional development and central place theory. *Papers of the Regional Science Association* **31,** 173–212.

An excellent summary of ideas concerning the nature of unbalanced growth. Relates the phenomenon to several themes which are introduced later in this book.

PRED, A. R. 1969: *The spatial dynamics of US urban-industrial growth 1800–1914.* Cambridge, Mass.

A collection of essays which provides a historical perspective on the spatial implications of circular and cumulative causation.

The Dimension of Space

6 Distance

Physical and human resources are unevenly distributed: movements are therefore essential to the functioning of human societies. These movements are not random. If plotted on a graph, in which the vertical axis relates to their volume or significance and the horizontal axis indicates the distance between origins and destinations, those movements are represented by a downward sloping line which describes a consistent *distance-decay* effect (see section 8.1.2). This effect rests upon the fact that the abstract dimensions of space itself impose certain restrictions upon human activity in the sense that distance represents a barrier to movement. Man tends to respond to this property, often referred to as the *friction of distance*, in a predictable fashion which may be explained in terms of his adherence to the *principle of least effort*.

An American sociologist has asserted that 'an individual's entire behaviour is subject to the minimizing of effort' (Zipf, 1949, 6). In an important and original work, Zipf applied this philosophy to an interpretation of many aspects of human behaviour including movement. Zipf's concept of the 'economy of geography' is essentially based upon the interrelationship between the principle of least effort and the effect of distance as a barrier to movement. The empirically observed regularities in movement patterns reflected in various distance-decay relationships are ultimately based upon the fact that decision makers generally attempt to minimize the effort involved in overcoming this barrier. It requires little imagination to appreciate that, in many situations, minimizing the effort expended in movement is achieved by minimizing the distance travelled. A perfect coincidence between effort and distance is a characteristic of an *isotropic surface* which may be conceived of as a flat, featureless plain upon which movements are not restricted to specific routes or channels. The effects of variations in the content of space are thus eliminated and 'the most basic spatial concept [is that] the shortest distance between two points is a straight line' (Bunge, 1962, 178).* Although great advances have been made in our understanding of the factors influencing the distribution of, for example, industry and settlement by deducing patterns of location upon an isotropic surface (see sections 6.1 and 10.2.1), it is obvious that such a surface is far removed from reality. In practice, movement effort is rarely independent of direction, and variations in the human and physical content of space ensure that paths of least effort and minimum distance do not converge in the straight-line

---

* It is worth noting that this apparently obvious assertion is not always true. For example, the spherical shape of the earth ensures that the shortest distance between two points is not, strictly speaking, a straight line, but a curved one.

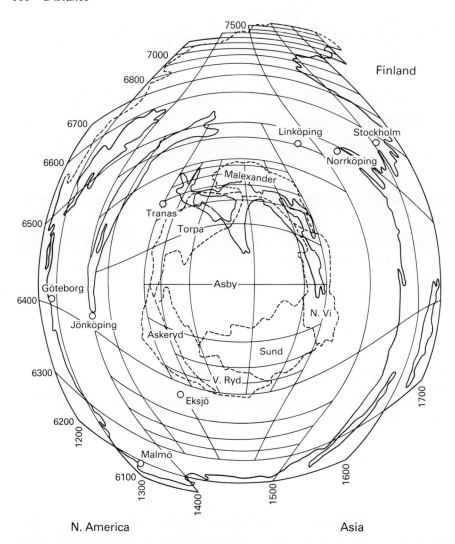

Fig. 6.1 Asby in information space (Hägerstrand, 1957, 73).

point-to-point connections of location theory. A mountain range separating two towns may mean that a long detour involves less effort than a direct route, bearing in mind the costs of building and maintaining a high-level road. Similarly, it may be easier to get from one side of a major city to the other by travelling on an outer ring-road rather than risk the delays involved in a traverse across the heart of the urban area.

Directional differences in ease of movement ensure that least effort is not necessarily synonymous with the minimization of distances travelled in the real world. Furthermore, the actions of decision makers are based not upon objective assessments of places, but upon subjective images (see section 3.3). These images may not only incorporate distorted ideas about the content of space, as illustrated in the Londoner's alleged view of the rest of Britain (Fig. 3.6), but may also involve false impressions regarding the nature of distance. In a pioneering study of migration to and from the district of Asby in central Sweden, Hägerstrand (1957) found that despite consistent underestimation of distances to the northern part of the country, migrants remained ignorant of living conditions in this area by comparison with their knowledge of nearby places. Hägerstrand recognized that in explaining the behaviour of migrants, their impressions were more important than the distances of absolute space. Figure 6.1 is an attempt to express these impressions

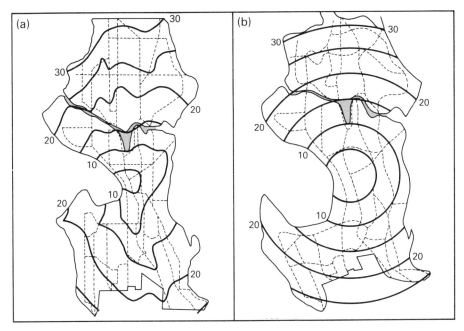

Fig. 6.2 Travel time in Seattle: (a) isochrones in absolute space; (b) in time–space (Bunge, 1966, 55).

in cartographic form. In effect, the map makes Asby the centre of a world defined in terms of *information space*. The projection exaggerates the significance of nearby places, with which the residents of Asby were more familiar, whilst, at the same time, it tends to shrink the distances to peripheral areas.

How long it takes to get from one place to another is often a more important consideration than the straight-line distance between them. This is certainly true of movements within cities. Different approaches to the problem of cartographically representing *time-distance* are indicated in Figure 6.2. In 6.2a, lines are drawn joining all points at equal time-distances from the centre of Seattle, Washington, during the city's rush-hour. These *isochrones* are redrawn as concentric circles in 6.2b and the shape of the city itself is transformed into *time-space*.

Despite their unfamiliar appearance, cartographic transformations of absolute space underline the point that man organizes his various activities within very different kinds of space. Recognition of this does not invalidate our initial proposition that human behaviour in space may be interpreted as a consistent attempt to minimize the effort involved in overcoming the friction of distance. It simply means that such conventional units of absolute distance as kilometres and miles are not necessarily the most appropriate for measuring this. Some of the implications of this for the spatial organization of society are discussed below by reference to the nature of (i) cost-distance, (ii) time-distance and (iii) social distance.

6.1 Cost-Distance

Freight rates charged by carriers such as railway companies and shipping lines provide a direct measure of the costs of overcoming distance. These costs are important influences upon the location of economic activity. For example, it has been demonstrated theoretically that the most efficient location for any industrial plant is the point at which the combined costs of assembling raw materials and distributing finished products are at a minimum (Weber, 1909, trans. Friedrich, 1929). To take the simplest case, Weber considered the problem of finding the least-cost location for an industrial plant which required two types of raw material obtained from different sources and which sold its product in a single market. This situation may be expressed in diagrammatic form as a *locational triangle* (Fig. 6.3), the edges of which define the range of feasible plant locations. Isolines indicating the costs of transporting each of the raw materials and the finished product are then drawn around the apexes of the triangle (Fig. 6.3a). These *isotims* are concentric circles because Weber assumed the existence of an isotropic surface. However, the spacing of the circles differs according to the relative costs of movement. The closer spacing around S_1 suggests that this raw material is more expensive to transport than either the raw material from S_2 or the finished product. Alternatively, since isotims reflect transport costs per unit weight of product, large quantities of S_1 may be required to produce one unit of output. The final stage in the solution of Weber's location problem involves the construction of *isodapanes*. These lines connect points of equal total transport cost. Thus a plant located at R (Fig. 6.3b) would incur charges of 44 in assembling enough of raw material S_1 to produce one unit of output, of 28 in obtaining the necessary quantity of S_2 and of 12 in transporting the product to the market at M – a total transport bill of 84. The configuration of isodapanes in Figure 6.3b indicates that the least-cost location is drawn away from the midpoint of the locational triangle towards S_1 as a result of the closer spacing of the isotims around this focus. In effect, S_1 is exerting a greater relative 'pull'. Indeed an alternative to the graphical solution to Weber's location problem indicated in Figure 6.3 would be to construct a mechanical model in which the transport costs associated with moving the various inputs and outputs were translated into differential weights passing through pulleys attached at each corner of the triangle. The equilibrium position of the resulting forces would correspond to the least-cost location at X in Figure 6.3b.

A basic assumption of Weber's model is the existence of a simple arithmetic relationship between the costs of movement and distance travelled so that it costs twice as much to travel twice as far. This is apparent in the concentric spacing

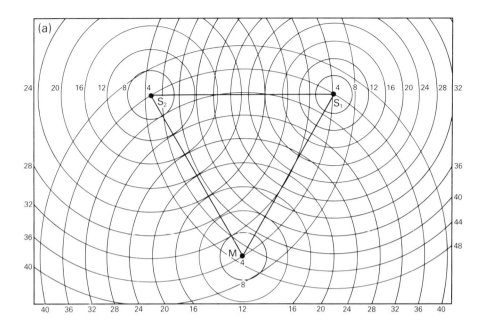

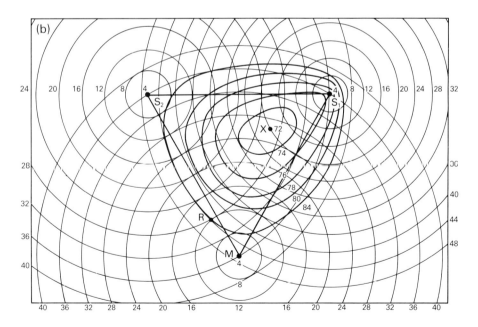

Fig. 6.3 Solution to Weber's location problem involving the construction of: (a) isotims; (b) isodapanes.

of isotims, which underlines the point that absolute or geographical distance and cost-distance are synonymous in Weber's model. Reality is not so simple and Paterson (1972, 96) observes that 'if we substituted cost-distance for geographical distance in world commodity movements, then we should require a separate globe for each commodity, and that globe would be distorted out of all recognition ... The quays of Liverpool or Bristol would suddenly become as broad as the Atlantic Ocean, because the per-ton cost of unloading a cargo across them was as great as carrying it from New York to the dockside.' This illustration underlines the importance of the expense involved in transferring a shipment from one mode of transport to another, but the characteristics of cost-space are largely determined by the structure of freight rates which, by the adoption of (i) tapering rates and (ii) zonal pricing, introduce significant departures from the straight-line relationship between costs and distance which forms the basis of Weber's model. Decision makers concerned with the location of economic activities must take account of such departures in their evaluation of alternative strategies.

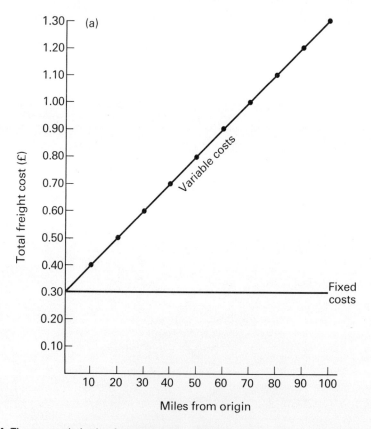

Fig. 6.4 The economic basis of tapered freight rates: (a) fixed and variable transport costs; (b) per-mile transport costs (after Taaffe and Gauthier, 1973, 39, 40).

6.1.1 Tapering Rates

Generally speaking, freight rates are tapered so that total transport charges increase with distance, but at a declining rate. Expressed in terms of costs per unit it is therefore cheaper to travel long distances than short distances. This characteristic ensures that widely separated places tend to be drawn together in cost-space whereas nearby places tend to be pulled further apart. Tapered freight rates reflect differences in the relative contributions of the fixed and variable components to total costs over long and short distances. Before any journey can be made, substantial investments are required in all kinds of equipment, including terminal facilities and the means of transport itself. Such overheads represent *fixed costs* which are independent of the distance travelled and which cannot be allocated to any specific user. *Variable costs* include such items of expenditure as fuel and wage bills which are incurred during a particular journey. These costs do increase with distance. Figure 6.4a shows a hypothetical example in which the fixed cost for one ton of a particular commodity is 30 pence and the variable cost is 10 pence per mile. The total per-mile cost will then decline with distance since the 30 pence fixed cost will be spread over a larger number of mile units (Fig. 6.4b).

Tapered freight rates are not confined to any particular mode of transport. However, the relative importance of fixed and variable costs differs between, for example, canal and road transport. Once on the move, the costs of operating a

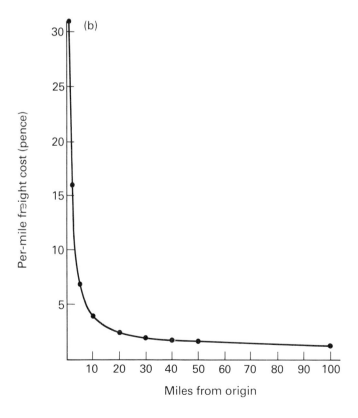

barge increase only gradually with distance. Fixed costs, on the other hand, are high because of the expenditures involved in constructing and maintaining canals and associated port facilities. The situation is reversed for road transport; variable costs rise more steeply whereas fixed costs tend to be lower. These differences in the structure of transport costs ensure that the various modes possess cost advantages over differing distance ranges (Fig. 6.5).

6.1.2 Zonal Pricing

The curvilinear form of the cost/distance relationship indicated in Figure 6.4b implies a continuously variable freight charge per unit weight depending upon the

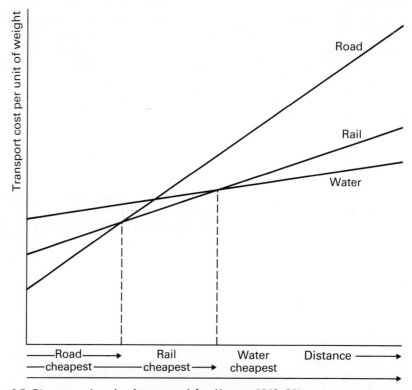

Fig. 6.5 Distance and mode of transport (after Hoover, 1948, 20).

length of haul. Such a pricing system is, however, difficult for the carrier to administer and difficult for the customer to understand. Consequently, it is common practice to impose blanket rates in which a different uniform charge is adopted in different zones. The extent to which zonal pricing distorts the simple cost/distance relationship is determined by the size of the zones and their orientation relative to the origin of the journey. Figure 6.6 indicates that the haulage rates charged by an Aberdeen-based supplier of agricultural goods such as fertilizers and animal feedstuffs are stepped so that they relate to distance zones of differing size. Although the width of the zones increases progressively from 5- to 50-mile bands for distances over 150 miles from Aberdeen, the size of each individual step is somewhat irregular for reasons best known to the supplier. Figure 6.6 also emphasizes that size of load is an important variable influencing transport charges. Rates per ton-mile are higher for small loads because the costs of operating a truck over a specified distance remain much the same whether or not it is fully loaded. Furthermore, the tapering principle is evident only in the delivery charges for larger customers which represent a more attractive type of business for the supplier. In this example, the supplier operates largely within a 100-mile radius of his depot. The rates are fairly sensitive to changes in distance and, since the price zones are defined

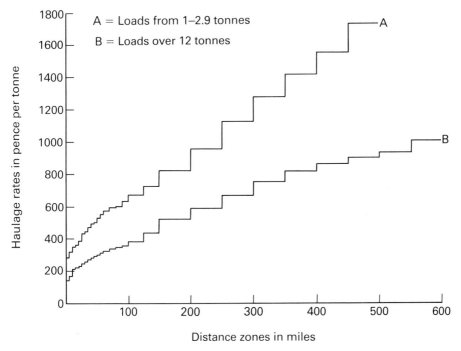

Fig. 6.6 Delivery charges of an Aberdeen-based supplier of agricultural goods.

by circles centred on Aberdeen, they do not vary with direction from the basing-point. Essentially, they represent a pragmatic adjustment of the curvilinear cost/distance relationship indicated in Figure 6.4b to overcome the need for separate quotations for each shipment.

Zonal pricing may involve much more significant distortions of this relationship (Alexander *et al.*, 1958). In particular, the zones may be of uneven size and shape so that it may be cheaper to move a given distance from a point of origin in one direction rather than another. Figure 6.7 shows the areal distribution of charges for shipping lumber from the Pacific Northwest to other parts of the US. The configuration of the zones is such that the amount paid for a shipment of fixed size increases with distance from the origin zone. However, a circle of 2,000-mile radius centred on Seattle passes through four different price zones so that a customer on the Gulf Coast of Texas pays transport charges of 139 cents per 100 lb whilst buyers located on the circumference of the same circle as it passes through Mississippi, Kentucky and Indiana pay 141, 150 and 148 cents respectively. The most obvious anomalies occur at the boundaries of price zones where the width of a road may make all the difference between paying a lower or a higher rate.

The most extreme form of zonal pricing is the so-called postage-stamp rate. The name derives from the fact that the charge for delivering a letter is usually the same whether it is delivered next door or to an address at the other end of the country. Distance becomes irrelevant as far as the cost of transport is concerned

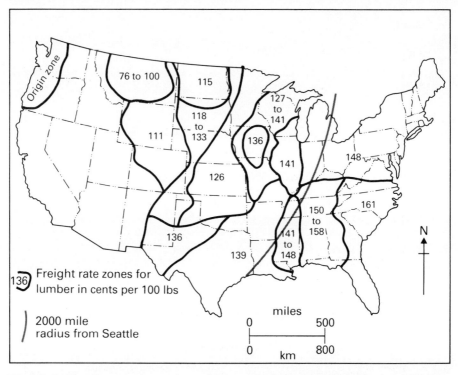

Fig. 6.7 Freight-rate zones from western Oregon and Washington (after Sampson, 1961, 45).

and cost-space shrinks to a point. This can have important effects upon patterns of economic activity. One of the primary aims of the Milk Marketing Board in the UK is to reduce the costs of transporting milk from the farms to the consumer. Part of this strategy involves defining a number of regions for England and Wales within which producers pay a standard collection charge to the Board, irrespective of their distance from the nearest dairy. This policy amounts to a transport subsidy for the more remote farms. In addition to the adoption of uniform transport charges *within* regions, the Board has also attempted to standardize charges *between* regions. In 1970, the maximum difference in regional charge amounted to 1.7 per cent of the producer milk price. This transformation of cost-space has largely removed the locational advantage of farmers close to the centres of demand

and has resulted, since the policy was introduced in the 1930s, in the expansion of dairying in comparatively isolated parts of England and Wales where climatic conditions favour pasture rather than arable (Morgan and Munton, 1971).

It has so far been assumed that the price charged for a transport service bears some relation to the cost of running it, which is in turn related to the distance travelled. However, as the size of uniform-rate zones increases, the validity of this assumption is called into question and divergences between the nature of cost- and absolute-distance are accentuated. The principle of charging 'what the commodity will bear' is widely adopted by carriers and this ensures that high-value goods, for which the cost of transport will add proportionately less to total costs, usually pay more to move a given distance whereas goods of low unit value may be charged rates which do not even cover the costs involved. Some of the most significant distortions of absolute space are associated with discriminatory pricing policies. For example, artificial 'break-of-bulk' charges are often imposed upon carriers crossing international frontiers. Thus the notional costs of unloading and reloading the lorry or railway waggon at the frontier are added to the total cost despite the fact that the vehicle passes straight through to its ultimate destination. It is this type of practice restricting international movement which groupings such as the EEC are designed to overcome. Nevertheless, the EEC is not without its own discriminatory practices affecting the costs of moving industrial goods. For example, a system of charges for steel products is employed which is a refinement of the notorious 'Pittsburgh Plus' operated by the steel barons in the US between 1900 and 1924. This system is a good example of a deliberate attempt to reinforce and maintain a situation of unbalanced economic development since it was designed to ensure the continued dominance of the Pittsburgh area as the major iron and steel centre of the US. All steel had to be sold at the Pittsburgh price plus the freight charge from that centre, no matter where the steel was actually produced. Consequently, there was no incentive for new steel centres to develop since cost advantages conferred in local markets by distance from Pittsburgh were nullified by the obligation to charge 'Pittsburgh Plus' prices. In the EEC, several centres are nominated for the calculation of freight charges on steel products. These *basing-points* introduce similar distortions in the costs of movement through space to those associated with 'Pittsburgh Plus'. For example, the basing-point for steel billets in the UK is Sheffield, so that a rolling mill at Cardiff, which obtains virtually all of its input of billets from an adjacent works of the British Steel Corporation, pays a notional transport charge from Sheffield.

The dimensions of cost-distance are not defined exclusively by freight rates. Recent studies have emphasized that the quality and reliability of a transport service are often more important to the industrialist than the payments made for it (see Bayliss and Edwards, 1968; Wallace, 1974). Consignments which fail to turn up on time impose indirect costs by interrupting production schedules. Indeed, in certain industries the time factor is critical. Cost of transport is no object in the oil industry when a spare part is needed to keep an offshore drilling rig in operation. In these circumstances, time becomes the parameter by which the friction of distance is measured.

6.2 Time-Distance

Time-distance may be regarded as an aspect of cost-distance in the sense of the businessman's cliche that time is money. However, in many situations the duration of a journey is a more important consideration than its cost. The journey to work in (i) agricultural societies, and (ii) urban/industrial societies, is a good example. In the former, the journey to work involves outward movement from a central focus such as a farm or village to surrounding fields. In the latter, the flow is reversed and commuting is predominantly an inward movement from peripheral residential areas to offices and factories which tend to be located in the urban core. Despite these differences in the direction of movement, the friction of distance is largely measured in terms of time rather than cost both by rural farmworkers and by urban commuters. Some of the consequences of this view of distance for patterns of agricultural land use and for the form and internal structure of cities are considered below.

6.2.1 Journey to Work in Agricultural Societies

Farming has been described as 'a system of movements articulated around farm-steads' (Baker, 1973, 259). These movements include the distribution of inputs such as fertilizers and manure, the harvesting and gathering in of the crops themselves and the daily journey to work in the fields. Although they may be expressed in terms of transport costs, it is the time spent in making such movements which is of primary concern in many agricultural societies (see Chisholm, 1962). In rudimentary market economies, rates for transport and labour may have no meaning as these tasks are performed by the farmer himself. Also the value of time spent travelling may be difficult to translate into monetary equivalents. Social and leisure activities may be regarded more highly than the possibility of additional production and it is the value placed on these other uses of time which provide a measure of the true costs involved in overcoming distance.

Two basic types of spatial relationship between home and workplace may be postulated in agricultural communities. Firstly, the location of the farmhouse or village relative to the surrounding fields may be regarded as fixed. Secondly, the origin of daily movement may shift over time. Some of the consequences of time-distance for the organization of life within agricultural communities may be examined by reference to situations of (i) fixed-settlement location and (ii) variable-settlement location.

Fixed-Settlement Location
If variations in the physical characteristics of the land are ignored, we may expect two different types of adjustment in agricultural practices resulting from the increase in the time which must be spent travelling to more distant fields. On the one hand, the same crop may be farmed less intensively by reducing the input of labour; on the other hand, beyond certain critical distances crops which require less attention may be grown. The latter strategy will be more readily observable since it implies a concentric zoning of land-use patterns around a farm or village. Many attempts have been made to identify such adjustments to distance (see Chisholm, 1962; Found, 1971) and the results of a study of the spatial organization

of agriculture in some north Indian villages are typical of those obtained in many other cultural situations (Blaikie, 1971).

The village of Daiikera is located near the town of Jodphur in western Rajasthan. Several factors ensure that commuting time is an important influence upon agricultural practices in this part of India. The monsoon rains are meagre in quantity and unreliable in occurrence. Rain may fall in one part of a village's lands, but not in another. Farmers therefore tend to cultivate a wide scatter of fields to minimize the risk of total crop failure. This strategy clearly increases the amount of time spent in travelling from field to field and the most remote plots may be as much as 10 km away from the farmer's residence. Although a seasonal migration to the fields takes place at the beginning of the monsoon, a highly nucleated settlement pattern ensures that movements during the rest of the year originate in the villages, thereby increasing the proportion of the working day spent in travel. In this situation, Blaikie argues that distance from the village may be expected to influence both the type of crops which are grown and also the manner in which they are cultivated.

In the case of Daiikera, Blaikie uses information obtained from a questionnaire survey of farms to calculate the effect of increasing distance from the village upon the total production costs of different crops. The transport component of these costs was obtained by relating current seasonal rates of hire for human or draught-animal labour to the number of journeys needed to carry out such operations as sowing and weeding for the different crops. This calculation made it possible to derive an anticipated sequence of crops around the village related to differences in their total transport requirements. Expressed in terms of the input of labour, Blaikie found that with each 1,000-yard increase in the distance from the cultivators' homes, the amount of extra time spent travelling in one year was as follows:

Wheat	28.3 man/days
Chifter	16.2 man/days
Jowar	12.6 man/days
Bajra	10.9 man/days

Thus wheat may be expected to be grown in greater quantities nearer the village and an inverse relationship to be maintained between the transport inputs of the remaining crops and their distance from Daiikera. Detailed fieldwork confirmed the existence of a land-use pattern which more or less corresponds to this sequence (Fig 6.8)

The land-use zones were not exclusively devoted to the crops specified in Figure 6.8 and the next stage in the analysis was aimed at identifying any changes associated with distance from the village in the method of cultivating a single crop. Detailed fieldwork again made it possible to express annual inputs of labour in terms of standard-deviation units* about the mean for that crop. The results for barani (Fig. 6.9) are typical of those obtained for other crops and show a marked decline in the amount of time spent in the fields as distance from the village increases. Blaikie carried out a principal-component analysis† incorporating several variables describing the agricultural system of Daiikera. Figure 6.10 plots the distribution of factor scores† on the first component, which accounts for 47 per cent of

---

* See glossary.
† See glossary (factor analysis).

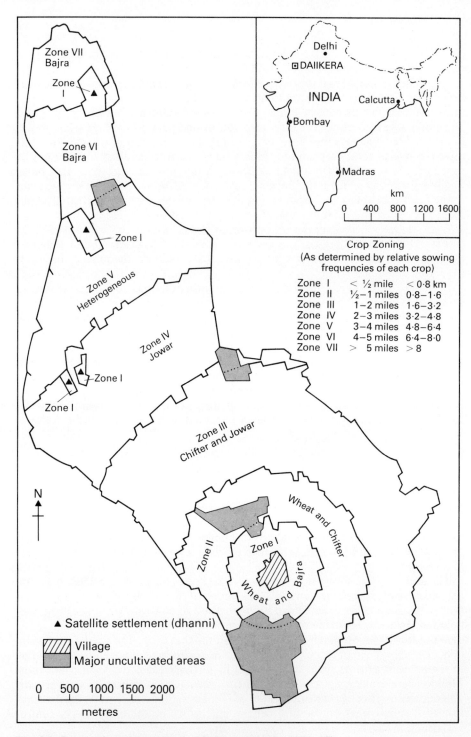

Fig. 6.8 Crop zoning around village of Daiikera (Blaikie, 1971, 15).

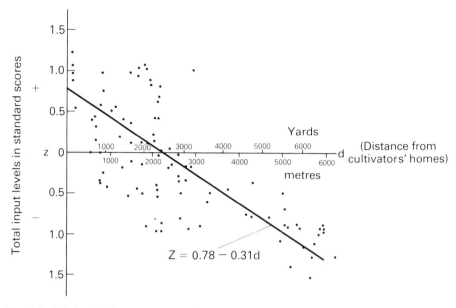

Fig. 6.9 Relationship between inputs of labour and distance from village for Barani, Daiikera (Blaikie, 1971, 18).

the total variation. It may be interpreted as a representation of intensity of cultivation for all crops. As expected, the surface declines in height away from the village. However, two outliers of positive scores are apparent. These correspond to the location of satellite settlements (*dhannis*) which, as noted earlier, are occupied on a seasonal basis. The striking effect of these settlements upon the intensity of cultivation underlines the fact that the time spent on unproductive travelling within agricultural societies may be reduced not only by modifying land-use patterns and cropping practices relative to a fixed-settlement location, but also by periodically shifting the origin of daily movement.

Variable-Settlement Location
A more complicated system of satellite rural settlements designed to reduce the daily journey to work of the farmer has been studied in the territory of the Yoruba people in southwest Nigeria (see Ojo, 1973). Traditionally, the Yoruba have been the most urban-oriented of all African ethnic groups and yet, at the same time, farming remains the most important occupation. The combination of these two characteristics results in a daily pulsing of population out to the fields and back to the town. The distances travelled are often increased by the tendency to retain a forest belt around Yoruba towns and by the need to ensure that cultivated plots are well beyond the reach of domestic animals that are never penned. The exhaustion of nearby land is another factor which promotes expansion of the cultivated area around Yoruba towns. In the case of the town of Idanre, Ojo has observed that distances of over 30 miles between family residence and fields are not uncommon. Since walking is the dominant method of transport in Yorubaland, it is obvious that the agricultural hinterland of Idanre extends well beyond the range

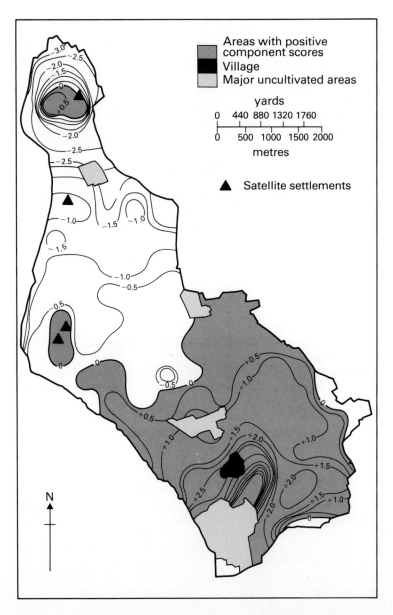

Fig. 6.10 Surface representing intensity of cultivation around Daiikera (Blaikie, 1971, 21).

of feasible daily commuting. In order to overcome this problem, periodic commuting patterns based upon farm huts and villages scattered around the principal focus of Idanre are superimposed upon daily movements. A 14-day cycle is dominant in Idanre, although the periodicity differs between towns throughout Yorubaland. Economic, social and cultural factors such as the frequency of markets or festivals influence the duration of these cycles, but distance, largely measured in terms of time, is the major control. Generally speaking, the more extensive the agricultural hinterland of a town, the longer the stay in satellite farm huts or villages. The significance of periodic commuting as a means of minimizing the time spent in overcoming the friction of distance is related to the growth of population. As they expand, the towns gradually encroach upon formerly cultivated land and it becomes necessary to bring more distant areas into use to avoid reducing soil fertility.

A permanent shift in the origin of daily movement by the creation of a new settlement is an alternative approach to the problems imposed by time-distance in primitive agricultural societies. The practice of shifting cultivation, which involves the periodic migration of an entire community to a new village site, is generally regarded as a response to declining yields resulting from deterioration of the soil. Although this interpretation is basically correct, time-distance is also important in the sense that lands nearest the village or farmstead tend to be exhausted first so that it becomes necessary to move further afield. Eventually a point is reached at which removal of the household to a new site becomes worth while by virtue of a reduction in the amount of daily travelling. Brown and Brookfield (1967) have examined the relationship between distance from fields and shifts in settlement amongst the Chimbu of New Guinea. By analysing the spatial relationship between individual households and their gardens through time, they concluded that it is possible to think in terms of a 'tolerable distance' beyond which cultivation becomes impracticable. In the area studied, this distance was estimated to be about 5,000 yards, although more than three-quarters of any family's garden area normally lay within 1,500 yards of the place of residence – a distance corresponding to a walking radius of approximately half an hour. Brown and Brookfield emphasize the importance of time spent on other activities such as ceremonial functions in the life-style of the Chimbu, but there is no doubt that distance, measured in terms of time, exerts a significant influence upon the relationship between settlement and agriculture in this society.

6.2.2 Journey to Work in Cities

With the separation of the place of residence and employment, the journey to work has become an important factor influencing the choice of residential location. Studies have shown that there is often no attempt on the part of house-buyers to evaluate the relative journey to work costs of different locations within an urban area and the ultimate constraint appears to be the amount of time that an individual is prepared to spend in commuting (see O'Farrell and Markham, 1975). It therefore follows that improvements in urban transport have, by modifying time/distance relationships within the city, provided greater freedom in the choice of residential location. This in turn has had important repercussions upon the spatial form of towns and cities since houses are the most important single component of urban land use in terms of area occupied (see Boal, 1968).

It is possible to develop a simple model which illustrates the significance of trans-formations of time-distance for the size and shape of urban areas. Two simplifying assumptions are made. Firstly, the influence of physical variations in site condi-tions is eliminated. Secondly, employment opportunities are clustered at the centre of the city. Under these circumstances, a series of stages may be identified in the evolution of the city. These stages reflect the characteristics of the prevailing mode of intra-urban transport. Figure 6.11 represents the shape of the city in plan at

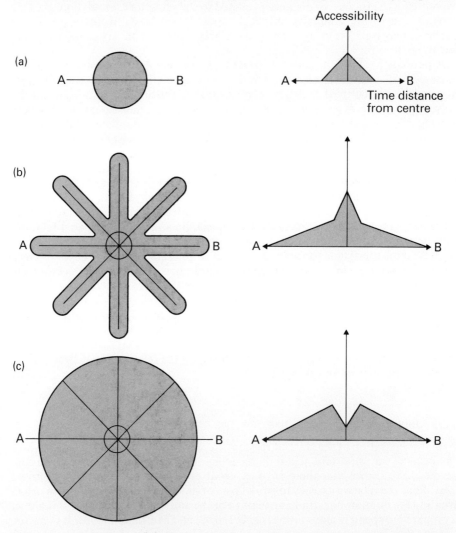

Fig. 6.11 A model of the relationship between transport technology, accessibility and urban form: (a) the 'walking' city; (b) the 'tracked' city; (c) the 'rubber' city; (d) the 'motorway' city.

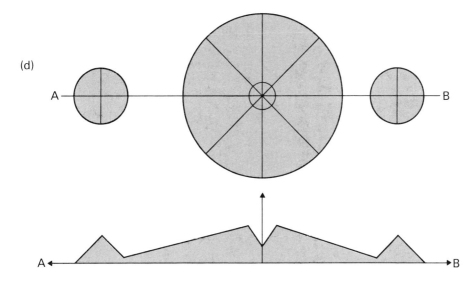

(d)

each stage and also takes a hypothetical cross-section through the urban area in an attempt to provide an indication of changes in accessibility. Accessibility is defined as the degree of interconnection between the central point of the city and all other points in the urban area and is measured in terms of the time taken in overcoming the friction of distance. There is abundant empirical evidence in support of the evolutionary model outlined in Figure 6.11. Some of this evidence may be incorporated in a review of the principal characteristics of each stage.

The 'walking city' (Schaeffer and Sclar, 1975) was relatively small in area (Fig. 6.11a). Growth of population was accommodated, as far as possible, by increasing the density of the built-up area. The spatial arrangement of land uses was designed to minimize the need for movement by the agglomeration of interdependent activities (see section 5.1.1). The distribution of social classes partly reflected differences in accessibility to the centre, and the upper echelons of society were usually concentrated at the heart of the city in close proximity to the ecclesiastical and public buildings which represented the seats of political and economic power (Sjoberg, 1960). A parallel situation was often found in some of the urban creations of the Industrial Revolution. The mill and the pit replaced the cathedral and the palace as the focal points around which housing was arranged, but the outer limits of the built-up area were still restricted by the dependence upon walking as the means of getting from one place to another.

The 'tracked city' emerged with the introduction of various forms of public transport (Fig. 6.11b). These had a dramatic, but spatially restricted effect upon time/distance relationships between the urban core, towards which routes typically converged, and the areas along the lines or tracks which extended outwards in a radial pattern. Several forms of mass public transport displayed these characteristics. Initially, horse-drawn and electric trolley-buses and then electric trams were introduced. Later, more exaggerated effects were produced as suburban railways of various types pushed further and further into the surrounding countryside. The dates of introduction varied from city to city, but the effects were more or less the same as urban development followed the new lines of communication. Virtually all of the major cities of the UK experienced a tentacular spread of residential development linked to the provision of public transport in the late nineteenth and early twentieth centuries (Fig. 6.12) (Hall *et al.*, 1973). Numerous examples may be quoted of suburbs which were 'created' in this way. Suburban railways have combined with physical constraints to produce the elongated horse-shoe plan of Norway's capital at the head of Oslofjord (see Braekhüs, 1976). The effects of public transport upon urban form are even more clearly seen in the development

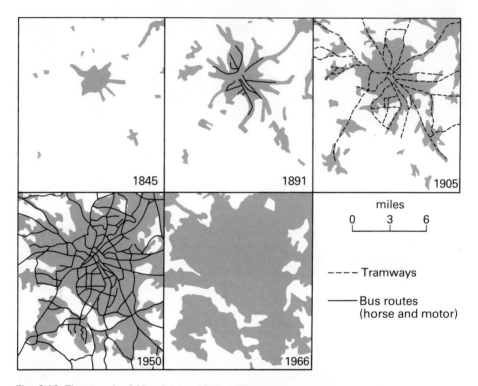

Fig. 6.12 The growth of Manchester, 1845–1966 (Hall *et al.*, 1973).

of Buenos Aires, where a relatively flat site minimizes the complicating influence of the physical environment (see Sargent Jnr, 1972). Thus trolley corridors created in the first decade of the century opened up a vast area of new land to permanent settlement as compared with the much more limited impact of the earlier horse-trams. Although it seems unlikely that public transport will ever regain its former importance in intra-urban movement, the provision of such facilities can still affect residential development by modifying time/distance relationships. For example, Davies (1976) has shown how a new link added to Toronto's underground-railway network between 1949 and 1954 has promoted residential growth in the vicinity of the line.

Stage three of our model may be characterized as representing the 'rubber city'

(Fig. 6.11c). The wider availability of the private car relaxed the constraints imposed by the narrowly defined corridors of improved accessibility of the public transport era. Consequently, the wedges of undeveloped land between the corridors came onto the housing market. In the US particularly, the car caught on rapidly and the supply of urban land rose dramatically without a proportionate expansion in demand (see Adams, 1970). This situation prompted the extravagant use of land through the construction of low-density suburbs. Such developments were a characteristic of the inter-war period in the US, but came later to Western Europe where car ownership is less universal.

The great paradox of the motor car is that increased individual mobility is achieved at the expense of a collective decline in accessibility to the city centre. Accessibility is therefore often highest along the line of an inner ring road because traffic congestion and parking restrictions inhibit further penetration to the centre (Fig. 6.11c). The adverse effects of the motor car upon city roads are partly responsible for the emergence of the urban motorway systems incorporated in the final stage of our model (Fig. 6.11d). Although such motorways are designed to facilitate intra-urban movement, they also have an effect beyond the built-up area similar to that of the tramways and suburban railways of an earlier period. Access to motorways is limited in the same way that trains can only be boarded at stations. Thus motorway interchanges represent points of greater accessibility relative to the centre of the conurbation. Since the time penalties incurred by the motorist away from these points are not so severe as those imposed on the railway traveller who has to walk to the station, motorway suburbs are more diffuse than those 'created' by public transport. Nevertheless, the principle remains the same even if the scale over which it operates differs. Indeed it is noticeable that the characteristics of the different stages in the model tend to repeat themselves through time. The sharply delineated movement networks in stages two and four tend to promote 'leapfrogging' development as settlement patterns respond to the intricacies of time/distance relationships. By contrast, in stages one and three, accessibility is independent of direction and urban growth is more evenly distributed.

These changes in urban transport have been accompanied by a general increase in the length of the journey to work. For example, in 1921 the percentage of the working population who lived in one local authority area in England and Wales but worked in another was 21 compared with a corresponding figure of 34 per cent in 1966 (Royal Commission (Vol. 3), 1969, 25). On the whole, these increases in journey length have been achieved with a less than commensurate increase in their duration. Nevertheless, these trends have important repercussions upon land-use patterns within urban areas. A basic assumption of our model is that residential areas are arranged around a central focus of employment opportunities with the result that the journey to work takes the form of a simple inward flow in the morning which is reversed in the evening. This remains a valid generalization of the situation in UK cities where new office jobs are highly clustered in the central areas and the dispersal of manufacturing has lagged far behind the outward shift of population to peripheral suburbs. Nevertheless, there is evidence, particularly in North American cities, of the emergence of more complex movement patterns between home and workplace within urban areas (see Logan, 1968). The freeway systems of the major US cities have not only encouraged an outward movement of population, but have also been responsible for a corresponding change in the intra-urban distribution of jobs as outer ring routes become attractive locations for industry (Hughes and James, 1975). Initially, this seems to be an improvement on the progressive separation of home and workplace in the UK. However, it is mainly upper- and middle-income groups that are moving out. The economic factors which make it difficult for the poorer sections of the community to buy housing on the urban fringe are often reinforced by planning restrictions and discriminatory legislation (see Harvey, 1973). The benefits of the freeways such as easy access to city-centre offices and proximity to peripheral factories tend to be enjoyed by the better-off. Low-income families, on the other hand, suffer because the exodus of factories to the freeways makes it necessary for them to undertake expensive and time-consuming 'inside-out' commuting whilst inner-city authorities are deprived of tax income from industry. These kinds of problem emphasize that our model of the effects of transport technology upon time/distance relationships within urban areas obscures significant variations in the nature of these effects as between different sections of the population. Recognition of these differences may be linked to the concept of social distance.

6.3 Social Distance

Social distance differs from cost- and time-distance in the sense that it cannot readily be defined on the basis of any standard units of measurement. Essentially it is a structural concept used by sociologists to locate individuals within an abstract dimension defined in terms of such personal characteristics as their income, occupation and educational background. Although this dimension is aspatial, there are, nevertheless, many situations in which decisions which have important spatial consequences, such as the purchase of a house, can only be understood by reference to notions of social distance. The concept was originally defined exclusively in terms of differentiation between individuals upon the basis of their socio-economic characteristics. However, other criteria may be employed to identify sub-groups within any society. Thus ethnic and cultural differences may be equally important variables affecting the perception of space and distance. Adopting this wider interpretation of social distance, we will examine some of the implications of (i) socio-economic groups, (ii) ethnic groups, and (iii) cultural groups, for patterns of spatial behaviour within cities.

6.3.1 Socio-Economic Groups

Generally speaking, we choose to communicate with people with whom we can identify. Thus, apart from contacts with relatives linked by family ties, social interaction tends to take place between individuals who perceive themselves as being close together on a social-distance scale calibrated in terms of common values and attitudes. These values and attitudes are often related to socio-economic status.

Although absolute distance is a constraint upon social interaction, most people do not restrict their choice of friends to immediate neighbours. Conversely, geographical proximity is no guarantee of friendship. Generally speaking, the spatial range of social interaction is positively correlated with socio-economic status. Stutz (1973) examined the social travel habits (i.e. the visits to friends and relatives) of the inhabitants of four different socio-economic areas within San Diego, California. Figure 6.13 plots the orientation and distance of social trips generated by the sampled population within each area during the study period. These contact patterns cannot be related to any single explanatory variable. However, it is noticeable that a more dispersed pattern emanates from the upper-income area of San Carlos as compared with Bird Rock and East San Diego where median housing values are lower by factors of one-third and one-half respectively. College Heights, with intermediate housing values, displays an equally dispersed pattern to San

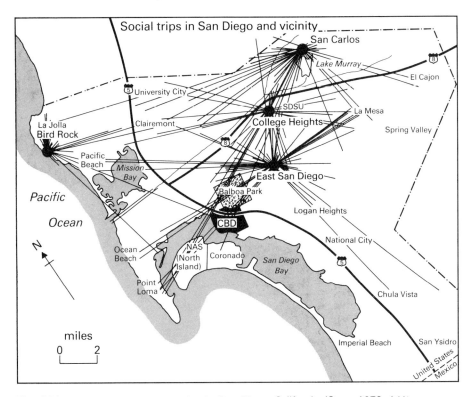

Fig. 6.13 Patterns of social interaction in San Diego, California (Stutz, 1973, 140).

Carlos. Thus it appears that the personal relationships of the inhabitants of the wealthier suburbs are less constrained by absolute distance at the city scale than are those of the residents of lower-income areas. This conclusion is not surprising in view of the time and cost penalties imposed by distance. The significance of these penalties is, to a large extent, inversely related to socio-economic status since families dependent upon public transport find intra-urban movement more difficult than car-owning households. These economic implications of the friction of distance tend to reinforce the agglomerative effect of social affinities and the operation of the housing market in promoting the development within cities of distinctive residential areas composed particularly of lower-income groups and other underprivileged sections of the community.

6.3.2 Ethnic Groups

The need to gather together with similar people is most strongly felt in an unfamiliar environment and some of the most distinctive social areas within cities are created by immigrant communities. Although post-war immigration from Commonwealth countries into the UK has declined to a comparative trickle since reaching its peak in 1961–1962, this influx has affected residential land-use patterns within virtually all of the major British cities. Figure 6.14 plots the distribution of coloured immigrants in Birmingham, which is second only to London in terms of the numbers received, at two time periods. The highly clustered pattern is typical of that found in other cities, as is the association, particularly apparent by 1966,

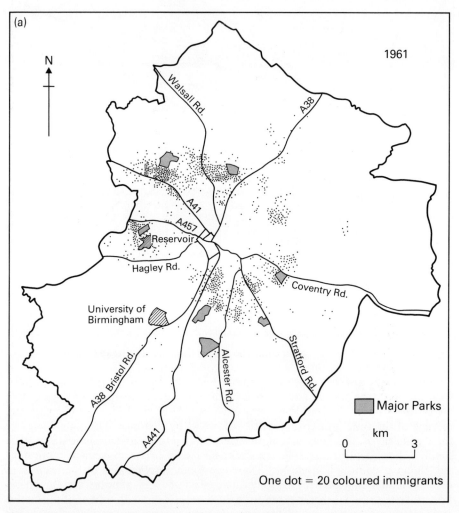

Fig. 6.14 Distribution of coloured immigrants in Birmingham in: (a) 1961; (b) 1966 (Jones, 1970, 204–5).

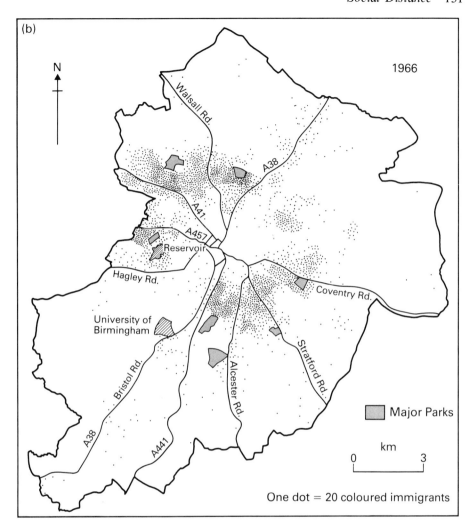

(b)

N

1966

Walsall Rd.

A38

A41

A457

Reservoir

Hagley Rd.

Coventry Rd.

University of
Birmingham

Bristol Rd.

Alcester Rd.

Stratford Rd.

A38

A441

Major Parks

km

0   3

One dot = 20 coloured immigrants

with a concentric zone of late nineteenth-century housing lying between the slum-
clearance areas in the city centre and the more recent outer suburbs. Analysis of
the patterns depicted in Figure 6.14 has suggested that despite the physical expansion of the reception areas between 1961 and 1966, the density of immigrants within
them increased (Jones, 1970). Part of the reason for this 'intensification' lies in
the nature of the migration process itself. New arrivals are encouraged by the
reports of earlier migrants and they naturally gravitate towards existing concentrations of their own people. This chain-like mechanism tends to perpetuate and reinforce the distinctiveness of immigrant areas. Within the overall distribution of
coloured immigrants in Birmingham, it is possible to identify significant clusters
of different groups by country of origin, such as the Pakistani community in parts
of Highgate. Extreme forms of this desire to retain a traditional geographical
identity may be seen in the distribution of West Indians in London where residen-

tial clusters may be traced back to associations with particular islands in the Caribbean. Jamaicans, for instance, are mainly concentrated in boroughs south of the
Thames such as Lambeth and Lewisham.

This type of spatial separation based on traditional loyalties and cultural associations is partly voluntary, but patterns of residential segregation initially based upon
the conscious decisions of different groups to live apart may be maintained and
reinforced by economic and political institutions. The immigrant areas of British
cities owe much of their distinctiveness to the relatively low economic status of
their inhabitants, most of whom would gladly exchange their ethnic identity for
a better paid job and the opportunity to move away from their existing
environment. The black ghettos found in the inner areas of most of the major
US cities represent some of the most extreme forms of residential segregation. The
development of these areas is ultimately a reflection of the social distance between
the black and white sections of the population and repellent forces based on mutual
suspicion are absorbed within the organization of the housing market. Consequently, a negro family wishing to move into a white area is faced with all kinds
of obstacles such as excessive price quotations, demands for unfair down-payments
and the reluctance of banks or savings institutions to provide financial support
(Morrill, 1965). In so far as 'housing markets simply mirror the value systems of
the larger society' (Rose, 1972, 54), these devices represent adjustments by economic institutions to the reality of racial prejudice. Political power may also be

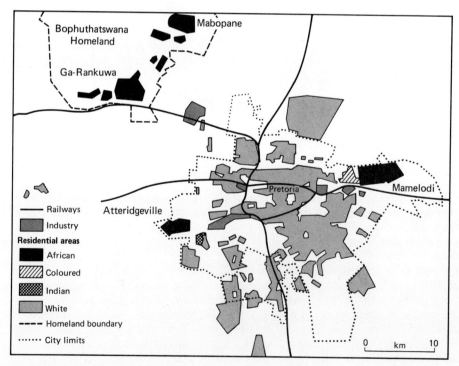

Fig. 6.15 Residential areas and race in Pretoria (Smith, 1977, 244).

used to create a spatial order which reflects such sentiments. South Africa provides the most striking, but not the only example (see Hill, 1973) of the utilization of the concept of social distance in the political organization of space. Apartheid policies have, by enforced population movements (see Baldwin, 1975), ensured rigid geographical separation along racial lines (see Smith, 1977). This is apparent at the urban scale in the allocation of specific areas on the basis of skin-colour (Fig. 6.15).

6.3.3 Cultural Groups

In many situations it is difficult, and perhaps futile, to try and separate the ethnic and cultural dimensions of social distance. The search for mutual support which

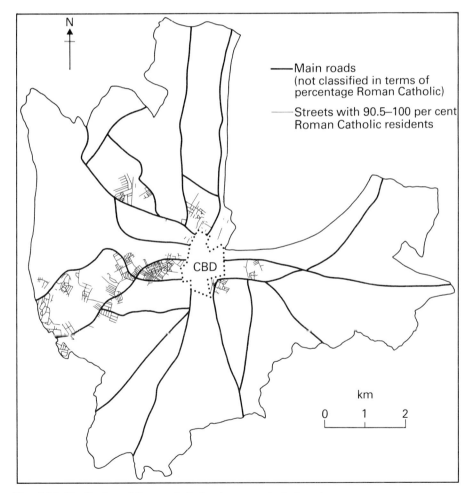

N

——Main roads
(not classified in terms of
percentage Roman Catholic)

——Streets with 90.5–100 per cent
Roman Catholic residents

CBD

km

0   1   2

Fig. 6.16 Distribution of Roman Catholics by streets in Belfast County Borough, mid-1969 (Poole and Boal, 1973, 16).

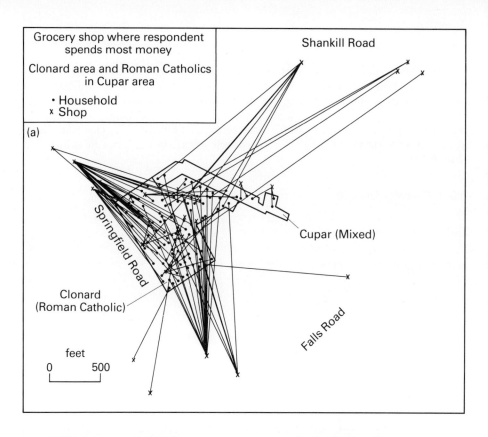

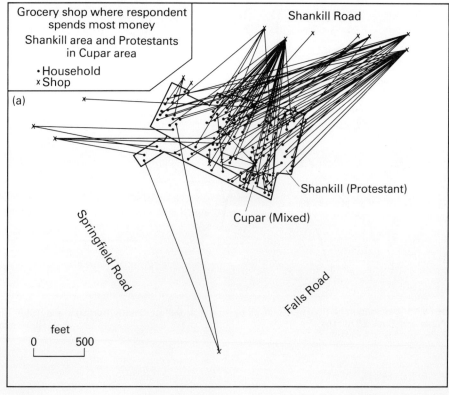

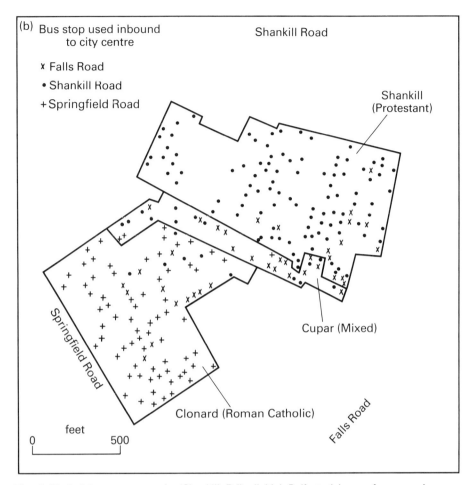

Fig. 6.17 Activity patterns on the 'Shankill–Falls divide', Belfast: (a) use of grocery shops; (b) use of bus stops; (c) visits to friends and relatives (Boal, 1969, 39–44).

encourages immigrants of the same race to group together in cities may also provide the basis for segregation on cultural grounds. Segregation as a kind of defence mechanism may be observed in many of the towns of West Africa which have traditionally contained a 'strangers' quarter' reserved for immigrants from non-local tribal groups. For example, a long-standing trading link whereby livestock from northern Nigeria are exchanged for kola nuts from the southwest of that country has been maintained by traders from the Hausa tribe in the north living as 'strangers' in Yoruba towns in the south. Although they normally occupy houses within the town walls and are therefore an integral part of the urban area, they retain a separate cultural identity (see Ojo, 1968). Contacts between the immigrant Hausa and the indigenous Yoruba population are strictly confined to commercial relationships and, despite their physical proximity, they are still as far apart in cultural terms as if they had remained at opposite ends of Nigeria. This lack of

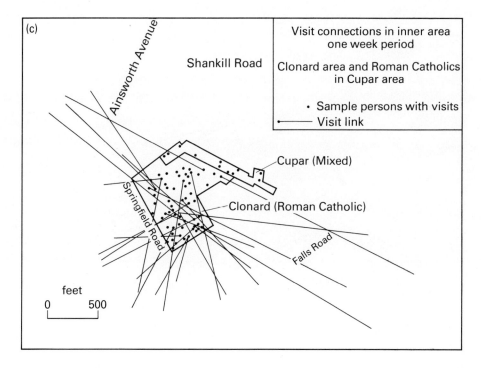

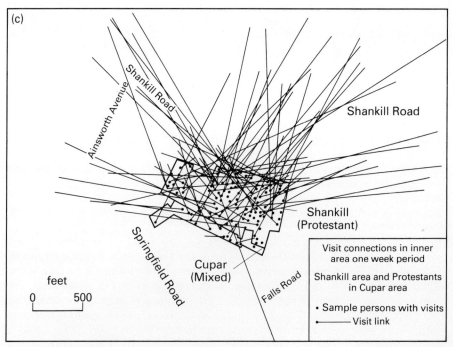

social interaction has fairly obvious implications during times of political unrest when 'strangers' quarters' acquire a special significance. The upheavals associated with the Nigerian civil war resulted in the abandonment of such 'quarters' in towns throughout the country as individuals living more or less permanently as 'strangers' amongst another tribal group felt obliged to return to their homelands.

The ability of the Hausa to live together with the Yoruba in physical space and yet apart in social space is paralleled, to some extent, by the position of Roman Catholics in the predominantly Protestant city of Belfast. Residential segregation by religious affiliation, which is a cultural rather than a socio-economic or racial attribute, is a characteristic of this city and areas may be identified that are almost exclusively Roman Catholic (Fig. 6.16). Although the boundaries separating Roman Catholic and Protestant areas have periodically found physical expression as barricades, there are few obvious differences between these areas apart from the sentiments of the wall slogans and the colours of the flags displayed to commemorate key events in their respective calendars. In those parts of west Belfast which have suffered most since the latest period of unrest began in 1969, both sections of the community live in equally poor housing conditions. Despite their shared misfortunes in this respect and the fact that the boundary line between a Roman Catholic and a Protestant area may be no more than the width of a narrow street, they maintain a degree of separation in social terms which is difficult for an outsider to comprehend. This polarization has been demonstrated in a study of activity patterns within an area which straddles the 'divide' between the residential sectors along the Protestant Shankill Road and the Roman Catholic Falls Road (Boal, 1969). The religious composition of the northern (Shankill) and southern (Clonard) halves of the study area was found to be almost entirely Protestant and Roman Catholic respectively and a narrow transition zone (Cupar) in which there was a two-to-one Protestant majority was identified along the axis of a single street. There was virtually no overlap between the everyday lives of the two sections of the community in spite of their 'cheek by jowl' existence. Figure 6.17 illustrates differing aspects of this cultural separation. The activity patterns are oriented towards either the Falls Road in the case of the Roman Catholics or the Shankill Road in the case of the Protestants. In situations where the principle of least effort implies the adoption of a minimum-distance route, such as in the choice of shops for grocery purchases (Fig. 6.17a) or in the selection of a bus stop from which to make the inward journey to the city centre (Fig. 6.17b), there are significant exceptions where individuals are prepared to travel further to use the facilities appropriate to their religious affiliation. This behaviour may appear illogical when distance is measured in terms of cost or time, but it is consistent with the distance between the two communities, apparent in their totally different contact patterns with friends and relatives (Fig. 6.17c), within the dimension of social space.

Geography has been described as a 'discipline in distance' (Watson, 1955). The brevity of this belies the complexity of the concept. Distance is perceived in very different ways. In order to explain patterns of human behaviour in space, it is necessary to recognize these differences and to think of distance in the appropriate terms – relative to units of cost, time or some index of social differentiation.

Further Reading

ADAMS, J. S. 1970: Residential structure of mid-western cities. *Association of American Geographers, Annals* **60**, 37–62.

Examines the impact of changes in transport technology upon urban form.

ALEXANDER, J. W., BROWN, S. E. and DAHLBERG, R. E. 1958: Freight rates: selected aspects of uniform and nodal regions. *Economic Geography* **34**, 1–18.

A good discussion of the way in which freight-rate practices influence the costs of movement.

BAKER, A. R. H. 1973: Adjustments to distance between farmstead and field: some findings from the southwestern Paris Basin in the 19th century. *Canadian Geographer* **17**, 259–73.

An effective study of the influence of time- and cost-distance upon farming practices.

BOAL, F. W. 1969: Territoriality on the Shankill–Falls divide, Belfast. *Irish Geography* **6**, 30–50.

A case-study of the influence of religious affiliation upon social behaviour.

ROSE, H. M. 1972: The spatial development of black residential subsystems. *Economic Geography* **48**, 43–65.

Relates the ethnic dimension of social distance to the formation of black ghettos in US cities.

WATSON, J. W. 1955: Geography: a discipline in distance. *Scottish Geographical Magazine* **51**, 1–13.

An early paper which draws attention to the significance of relative distance.

Spatial Process

7   Diffusion

The significance of the dimension of space as an influence upon human behaviour was stressed in the last chapter. However, it is obvious that spatial patterns are rarely static and an understanding of existing distributions must necessarily involve an awareness of their evolution through the dimension of time. Furthermore, time is not only important in relation to the interpretation of contemporary patterns, but is also implicit in the attempts of planners to predict and direct future patterns.

Recognition of the time dimension in geography is not new. Historical geography is by definition concerned with the relationship between space and time. Nevertheless, not all studies within this branch of the subject have succeeded in or even aimed at elucidating the nature of this relationship. Many have sought only to describe the geography of the past by taking cross-sections at different points *in time*. The 'Domesday Geographies' of the British Isles are good examples (Darby *et al.*, —). 'Vertical' studies which trace the development of specific features or areas *through time* either by working backwards from the present (see Prince, 1964) or forwards from a base-date (see Broek, 1932) come closer to tackling the complexities of space/time relationships. Much of this work has focused on the spread of culture traits and Sauer's (1952) study of the origins of agriculture is widely regarded as a classic of its type. The approach is essentially descriptive, building up a picture of the diffusion of the techniques of sedentary agriculture from a limited number of source areas or 'hearths' in Central America, West Africa and Southeast Asia, by the painstaking assembly of archaeological and documentary evidence. The emphasis in recent work, stimulated mainly by the early work of Hägerstrand (1952), has shifted towards the analysis of the decision-making processes that lie behind the kind of patterns which Sauer and others were content to describe. This philosophy has been applied in studies of the evolution of a wide variety of distributions. These distributions may involve permanent alterations in the physical appearance of the landscape as evidenced in the spread of settlement (see Morrill, 1963) or they may relate to essentially transient events such as the passage of an influenza epidemic through a population (see Hunter and Young, 1971). The spread of less tangible phenomena such as technical innovations (see Hägerstrand, 1967) and political ideologies (see Huff and Lutz, 1974) has also fallen within the scope of spatial-diffusion studies.

The interrelationship of space and time within the process of *spatial diffusion* is, therefore, fundamental to an understanding of the distribution of a wide range of phenomena over the surface of the earth. Despite the variety of these phenomena, the patterns which they create tend to evolve in one of two basic ways (Fig.

7.1). On the one hand, the phenomena themselves may move from one location to another through time. Migration is a good example of such *relocation diffusion* since nobody can literally be in two places at once. On the other hand, the phenomena may spread outwards from an initial focus which nevertheless retains the feature in question. The spread of information about a new crop through a farming community would fall into this category, which is termed *expansion diffusion*.

Although the distinction between relocation and expansion diffusion is useful in classifying the forms which the diffusion process takes, this simple division tells us nothing about the mechanisms responsible for the creation of these forms. To

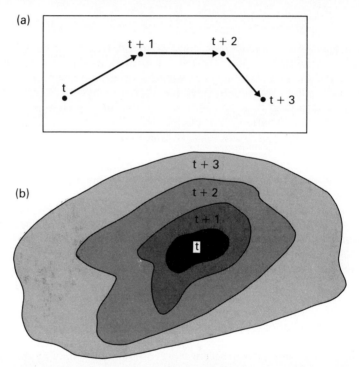

Fig. 7.1 Forms of diffusion pattern: (a) re-location diffusion; (b) expansion diffusion.

regard migration as an example of relocation diffusion does not explain the forces underlying the individual decisions to move. Similarly, to say that the adoption of a new crop by successive farmers is an illustration of expansion diffusion does not help us to understand why certain individuals are quicker than others in trying it out. However, in analysing these and other cases of diffusion at the aggregate level, two recurring themes may be identified – the role of distance and the influence of hierarchical structures. With regard to the diffusion of a new crop, we find that the evolving pattern of adoption through time may be largely explained in terms of the location of the farmers relative to one another and their position in a hierarchy of farm-size.* Thus the crop may be grown first by a farmer with a large

* There is much evidence from empirical studies to support the proposition that large farmers are more willing to experiment than their colleagues with smaller holdings.

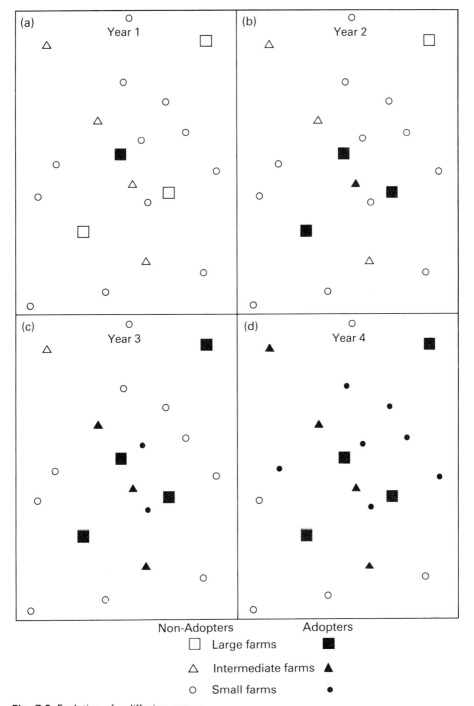

Fig. 7.2 Evolution of a diffusion pattern.

holding (Fig. 7.2a). In the following year, the distribution is 'patchy' as one or two others with the resources and the inclination to take a risk copy the innovator (Fig. 7.2b). By the third year, the crop is grown on all the large farms and on those of intermediate and small size located near the big holdings (Fig. 7.2c). Finally, by the fourth year there are only a few small farms in an area remote from the bigger estates that have not decided to cultivate the crop (Fig. 7.2d). In this example, the diffusion pattern is a composite of a 'spreading out' in space and a 'trickling down' through a farming hierarchy. Although the illustration is much simplified, most diffusion patterns reflect the operation of these horizontal and vertical components. This is mirrored in the organization of the following chapter, which considers separately the relationship between (i) distance and diffusion and (ii) hierarchy and diffusion, before applying these ideas to an interpretation of a contemporary illustration of diffusion, (iii) the spread of modernization in developing countries.

7.1 Distance and Diffusion

Diffusion implies movement. The direction and speed of movement, and hence the form of the diffusion pattern, are affected by the existence of barriers. Distance itself inhibits movement, but its effect may be modified by an amalgam of physical, cultural and psychological constraints. It is therefore possible to distinguish between (i) spatial barriers and (ii) non-spatial barriers.

7.1.1 Spatial Barriers

Distance influences diffusion patterns in several ways. Diffusion may require direct physical contact between a carrier and a receiver. The spread of certain types of disease falls into this category. Similarly, patterns which reflect the exchange of information by word of mouth tend to spread in centrifugal fashion from a point of origin. The time and cost penalties imposed by distance may also be important. The physical expansion of a town or city, which may also be regarded as an example of a diffusion pattern, was considered in some detail in chapter 6. We will now look at the role of distance in the context of the diffusion of (i) disease and (ii) innovations.

Disease

The world's principal endemic focus of cholera is thought to lie in the delta of the Ganges and Brahmaputra rivers in eastern India and Bangladesh. Diseases differ from many other cases of diffusion in the sense that they are often recurrent rather than one-off events (see Haggett, 1975). Cholera is no exception and it has broken out of its source area in a succession of global pandemics, the first of which began in 1817. The infection is transmitted by person-to-person contact, either directly or indirectly by such means as articles of clothing or shared sanitation facilities. In these circumstances, the disease may be expected to diffuse fairly evenly over space with the timing of its occurrence depending upon the distance from its point of origin. This hypothesis was tested by Pyle (1969) in an analysis of three epidemics which took place in the US during the last century. The first of these in 1832 probably entered North America carried by travellers from Europe passing through the common port of Quebec and Montreal at Gross Ile on the St Lawrence. In addition to this Canadian origin, New York served as another, slightly later, entry-point. Water transport was the dominant form of movement in the US at this time and this is reflected in the diffusion of the 1832 epidemic. By plotting the dates that the disease was first reported in various towns and cities, Pyle identified the principal lines of movement – along the Hudson–Mohawk valleys from the Canadian origin whilst the New York strain spread down the Eastern seaboard as a result of contacts maintained by the coasting trade and penetrated inland via the Erie and Ohio canals before turning southwards down the Ohio and Mississippi rivers (Fig. 7.3a). When dates of occurrence are plotted against distance from the points of origin, the 1832 epidemic reveals a fairly consistent and regular outward spread from these foci (Fig. 7.3b). However, a similar analysis of the 1849 epidemic, when New York and New Orleans were the starting-points (Fig. 7.3a), proved less satisfactory and the incidence of the disease appears to be more strongly correlated with the size of a settlement than with its distance from either of the ports of entry (Fig. 7.3b). This trend was even more apparent in the 1866 epidemic. Although the lines of movement were similar to those of 1832 with the Ohio–Mississippi system again an important control (Fig. 7.3a), the dates of occurrence were more irregular with, for example, over a month separating outbreaks in the adjacent cities of New Orleans and Baton Rouge. These differences between the spread of the 1832 epidemic, which seemed to display the distance-related pattern expected for a disease transmitted largely by person-to-person contact, and that of the 1866 epidemic, which seemed to 'trickle down' the urban hierarchy (Fig. 7.3d), may be related to the development of the US transport system in the intervening period. By 1866, movement between urban centres had become much easier as a result of the construction of the railways which linked virtually all of the major cities in the eastern US. Consequently, the disease seemed to jump from one city to another rather than diffuse gradually in the fairly continuous fashion characteristic of the 1832 epidemic. The hierarchy effect was thus the dominant control at the national scale, although the distance factor operated at a regional level as each city became the centre of its own 'cholera field'.

Cholera is no longer a problem in North America and Western Europe, but it remains a serious threat to human life in much of the developing world. For example, the disease swept through fifteen West African states between August 1970, when it first appeared in Guinea, and the end of the following year. A study of these events (Kwofie, 1976), has emphasized that in practice spatial diffusion rarely takes the form of the distance-determined outward spread from an origin that might be expected on an isotropic surface. Movements are normally channelled along specific routes. Probabilities of contacts are highest along these routes and this in turn ensures that there is often a directional component apparent in diffusion patterns. Kwofie identifies two such components in the case of the West African cholera outbreak. Firstly, the activities of coastal fishermen promoted a west–east movement along the Gulf of Guinea. Secondly, a north–south trend was encouraged by the traditional movements of cattle-traders and reinforced by an unprecedented migration of people fleeing from the drought-stricken areas of the Sahel.

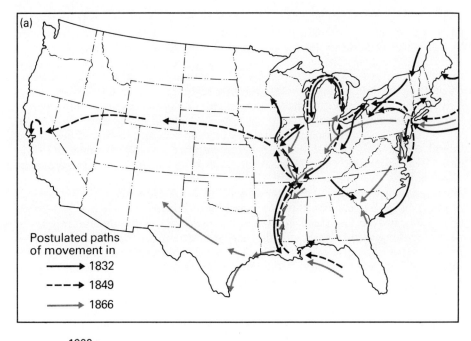

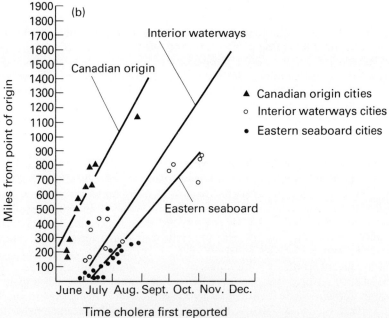

Fig. 7.3 Diffusion of cholera epidemics in North America, 1832, 1849 and 1866:
(a) postulated paths of movement; (b) date of outbreak and distance from origin, 1832;
(c) date of outbreak and city size, 1849; (d) date of outbreak and city size, 1866 (after
Pyle, 1969).

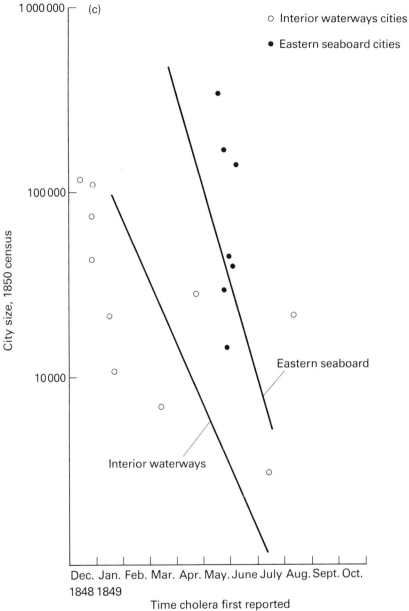

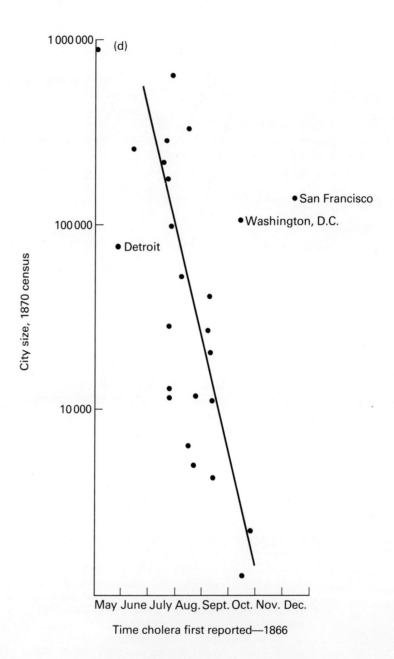

(d)

City size, 1870 census

1 000 000

100 000

10 000

• San Francisco

• Washington, D.C.

• Detroit

May June July Aug. Sept. Oct. Nov. Dec.

Time cholera first reported—1866

Innovations

The spread of innovations – new ideas, concepts and techniques – has been an important focus of concern in the study of spatial diffusion. Apparently intangible movements of this type may be very significant in human terms. Figure 7.4 represents the situation in 1974 of what is arguably the most important contemporary example of innovation diffusion – the spread of nuclear technology. As recently as 1959, only four countries possessed nuclear weapons – the US, USSR, UK and France. China has definitely joined this group, whilst India and Israel are also rumoured to have manufactured explosive nuclear devices. Although the number of countries with the capability of waging an intercontinental nuclear war remains small, many more states operate nuclear reactors either for the commercial generation of electricity or for research purposes. All of these reactors produce plutonium, which is the essential raw material for the production of a nuclear bomb. The risk that an increasing number of these countries may be tempted to exploit this possibility has prompted an attempt to restrict the further diffusion of nuclear weapons by the provisions of the Non-Proliferation Treaty. Although this treaty is primarily concerned with the destructive aspects of nuclear technology, this same technology may also be utilized for peaceful purposes and it is not difficult to appreciate that the diffusion of innovations is closely related to the the incidence of economic development. This in itself makes an understanding of the factors affecting innovation diffusion of concern to policy makers, but the interest of geographers in the problem is largely due to the influence of Hägerstrand's (1967) pioneering work.

Hägerstrand initially focused his attention upon the diffusion of innovations within a farming community in southern Sweden. He selected six different innovations and examined the spatial pattern of their adoption throughout a relatively small study area (Fig. 7.5). One of these innovations related to the attempts of the Swedish government to persuade the farming community to abandon the custom of allowing its cattle to graze in the open woodlands during the summer months. This practice damaged young trees and seedlings and a subsidy was offered in the late 1920s to encourage all farmers to fence and generally improve their pasture lands. As a first step, Hägerstrand plotted the location of farmers taking advantage of this offer in a series of maps showing the cumulative pattern of adoption between 1928 and 1933. Figure 7.5 indicates these distributions in a generalized form in which the number of farmers adopting pasture improvement is recorded by grid squares and isolines are drawn enclosing areas where 20 and 40 per cent of the total farm population had adopted the innovation by 1933. Reference to Figure 7.5 reveals an early concentration of adopters in the western part of the study area and a secondary focus in the northeast. As the pattern develops, these initial clusters seem to intensify and also provide the momentum for a gradual outward spread towards the central part of the study area. Hägerstrand was struck by the regularity of these patterns through time and he developed a model which attempted to replicate them upon the basis of certain assumptions designed to simulate the processes responsible for their creation.

Hägerstrand initially postulated the existence of an isotropic surface upon which the location of the first innovator was given. He assumed that information about the subsidy was passed from one farmer to another when they met. The critical assumption relates to the frequency of such meetings. Essentially, the likelihood

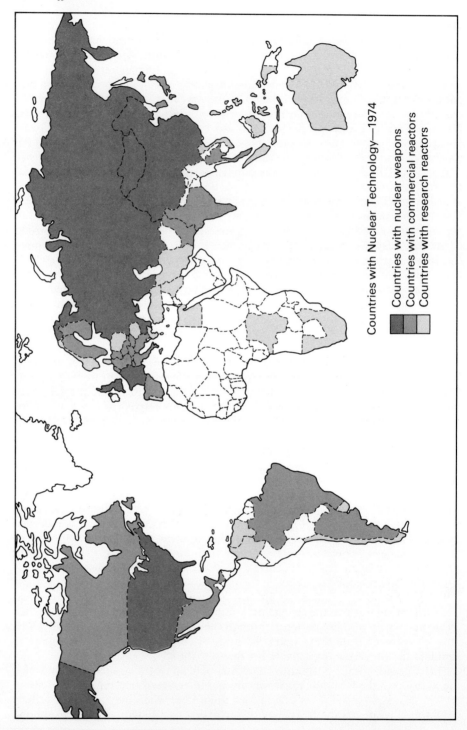

Fig. 7.4 Countries with nuclear technology, 1974 (compiled from data in Stockholm International Peace Research Institute, *Preventing nuclear-weapon proliferation*, Stockholm, 1975).

of a farmer who has adopted the subsidy meeting a colleague who has not is assumed to be a function of the distance between them. Hägerstrand believed that distance inhibited such communication and was therefore indirectly responsible for the nature of the outward spread apparent in the diffusion of pasture improvements. Intuitively, this assumption of a 'neighbourhood effect' seems reasonable. Our ability to communicate with others does depend upon our ability to overcome the friction of distance. Each of us stands at the centre of a *personal communication field*. This field may be viewed as a cone having three properties: a height which is proportional to the general probability of communicating with someone nearby as opposed to someone further away; sloping sides which indicate the rate at which our personal contacts decline with distance; and a base, the diameter of which provides a measure of our ability to overcome distance, either through personal mobility or the use of communication devices. Although the concept of a personal communication field is easy to grasp, it is clear that its dimensions will vary depending upon such attributes as the age, occupation and cultural background of the individual. This makes it difficult to formulate a model of general applicability. However, Hägerstrand suggested that it was possible to think in terms of a *mean information field* that defined the effect of distance upon the contact patterns of the 'average' farmer in his study area. It is worth noting that this proposition has a significance that extends far beyond the specific problem with which Hägerstrand was concerned. The use of probability concepts has made it possible to reconcile the uniqueness of individual decision makers with the existence of regularities in the behaviour of groups of individuals such as Hägerstrand's farming community.

In order to translate his assumptions into an operational model, Hägerstrand conceived of the mean information field as a square grid composed of 25 cells, the size of which corresponds to a grid superimposed on the maps of the study area. Each cell of this grid is given a value which represents the probability of communication (Fig. 7.6). The probability values decline with distance away from the central cell, in which the individual is assumed to be located, and are therefore lowest in the four corners where there are only 96 chances in 10,000 that a meeting will take place with another farmer located in these cells. The derivation of these values is, of course, basic to the model. Ideally they should be obtained by a comprehensive survey of the day-to-day personal contacts of the population within which diffusion is occurring. In practice, more readily available data which are assumed to provide an indirect measure of such contacts are normally used. Hägerstrand employed local migration statistics to calibrate his mean information field whilst others, in differing contexts, have used the distances between the former addresses of marriage partners (Morrill and Pitts, 1967) and information obtained from daily travel diaries compiled by urban commuters (Marble and Nystuen, 1963).

The simulation process is set in motion by centring the grid over the location of the initial adopter. A series of random numbers are then generated, perhaps by a computer. If the first number lies within the range 0–95, it is assumed that information about the innovation is passed to somebody located in the top left corner of the grid. If the second number is between 9,903 and 9,999, contact is made with somebody in the opposite corner whilst any number from 2,784–7,214 implies communication with a neighbour within the central cell. The probability of contact is obviously determined by the range of numbers allocated to each cell

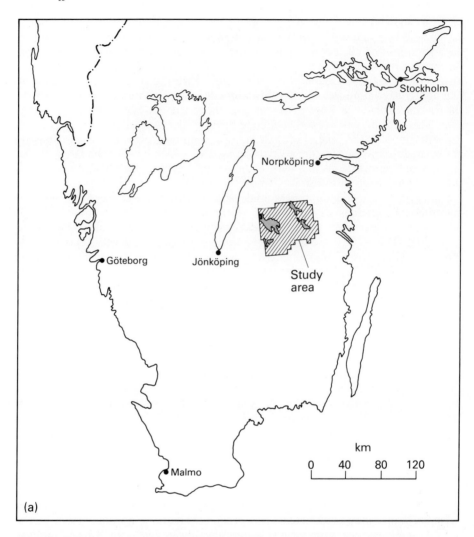

Fig. 7.5 Adoption of pasture improvement subsidies in part of southern Östergötland, Sweden: (a) study area; (b) 1928–1929; (c) 1928–1930; (d) 1928–1931; (e) 1928–1933 (after Hägerstrand (trans. Pred), 1967).

and is highest at the centre of the grid. A diffusion pattern is gradually built up by passing the grid over the entire area and generating the contacts of adopters at different time periods.

The success of the model is ultimately judged in terms of the degree of correspondence between the simulated and the actual pattern. How close these patterns must be for the researcher to feel confident about the validity of the parameters included in his model raises certain thorny methodological and statistical problems (see Brown and Moore, 1969). Notwithstanding these difficulties, a straightforward visual comparison remains acceptable in reaching preliminary conclusions. The

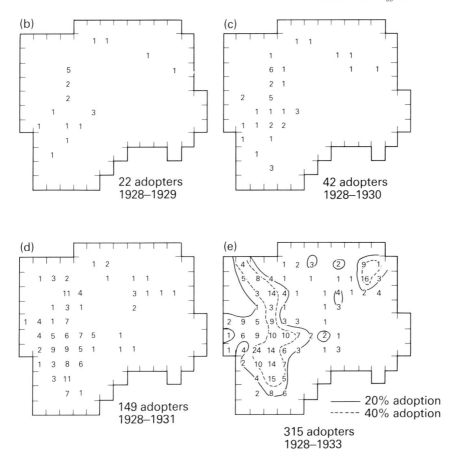

(b) 22 adopters 1928–1929

(c) 42 adopters 1928–1930

(d) 149 adopters 1928–1931

(e) 315 adopters 1928–1933

——— 20% adoption
------ 40% adoption

similarity between the actual (Fig. 7.5) and the simulated (Fig. 7.7) patterns is evident, with a clear distinction between the major cluster in the west and the smaller outlier in the east. Figure 7.7 represents the 'best fit' simulation and was actually obtained by adjusting the distance-determined probability values in the mean information field to take account of the combined effects upon communication between farmers of physical barriers such as lakes (see section 7.1.2) and an uneven population distribution. Despite these modifications, the neighbourhood effect of the mean information field remains at the heart of the model. The apparent significance of this effect in the context of a Swedish farming community is interesting, but it is important to know whether it also operates in other situations. Remembering that exchange of information by person-to-person contact provides the presumed explanation for the neighbourhood effect, the application of Hägerstrand-type models in other agricultural communities, where this assumption seemed reasonable, has produced two main strands of criticism.

Firstly, just as the transmission of diseases tends to follow specific routes, so information is channelled in the same way. Various studies have noted the effect of new or improved roads in rural areas in stimulating change in agriculture. This

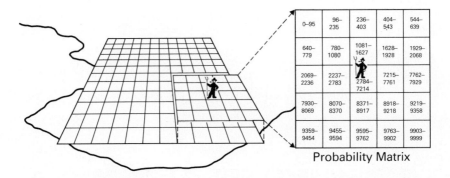

Probability Matrix

Fig. 7.6 Probability matrix and mean information field (after Hägerstrand (trans. Pred), 1967).

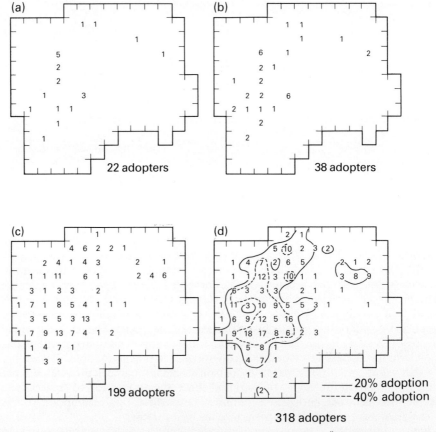

Fig. 7.7 Simulated adoption of pasture improvement in part of southern Östergötland, Sweden: (a) 1928–1929; (b) 1928–1930; (c) 1928–1931; (d) 1928–1933 (after Hägerstrand (trans. Pred), 1967).

may obviously be as much a response to improved accessibility to a market as to access to information. However, attempts to isolate these two components have suggested that the latter is often more important. This was certainly true of Wilbanks's (1972) study of the rate at which certain villages in Uttar Pradesh, India, adopted the various innovations introduced by extension officers responsible for executing the central government's Community Development Programme at grassroots level. Evidence assembled by Leinbach (1976) relating to the impact of feederroad upgrading and construction in three rural areas of peninsular Malaysia was less conclusive. Nevertheless, he emphasized the positive effect of improved physical mobility upon information flows as increased travel between villages and urban centres promoted contact between traditional and modern economic systems. The significance of these studies for Hägerstrand's model is that they underline the point that diffusion does not take place on an isotropic surface. Directional differences in the friction of distance affect the probabilities of communication and the mean information field cannot be conceived of as assuming the convenient shape of a square.

Secondly, it is often more realistic to think of information as passing through a network of social contacts rather than spreading out over space. An individual is more likely to communicate his experience of a new piece of machinery to a friend or relative located some distance away than to a neighbour with whom he is not on speaking terms. In essence, this involves thinking of the mean information field as existing within social rather than physical space. For example, Tarrant (1975) has shown that the spread of maize as a commercial crop throughout most of southern England since its introduction in 1970 has been facilitated by interpersonal contacts between farmers living up to 160 km apart. Another study in rural India sought to identify the principal communication networks, such as kinship ties and marketing activities, through which information relevant to agricultural change may be expected to pass (Mayfield and Yapa, 1974). In a North American context, Johansen (1971) argued that centres of community activity such as churches and local markets are likely to play an important role in the exchange of information within a rural area. This view was supported by the results of an attempt to simulate the diffusion between 1933 and 1967 of strip-cropping (i.e. contour ploughing) in part of southwest Wisconsin. The Hägerstrand model was tried first of all, but better results were obtained with a modified version which effectively accelerated the diffusion process in the vicinity of county seats to take account of their presumed function as centres of information exchange.

7.1.2 Non-Spatial Barriers

Patterns of spatial diffusion are not simply a response to the friction of distance and it is convenient to distinguish between the influence of (i) psychological barriers and (ii) other barriers. The former exist in the minds of the potential adopters of an innovation whereas the latter are introduced by abandoning the simplifying assumption that diffusion takes place on an isotropic surface.

Psychological Barriers
In his early experiments Hägerstrand assumed that adoption was instantaneous in the sense that a single meeting was sufficient for any farmer who had taken

advantage of the pasture subsidy to persuade a colleague who was unaware of it to do the same. This assumption tended to result in an erratic simulated pattern rather than a steady outward spread because it exaggerated the effect of isolated adopters. A further consequence of instant adoption was that the simulated diffusion pattern developed too quickly by comparison with the real one. This is not surprising in view of the obvious differences between individuals when it comes to responding to new ideas. These differences may be ascribed to such socio-economic attributes as age, income and education or they may simply reflect

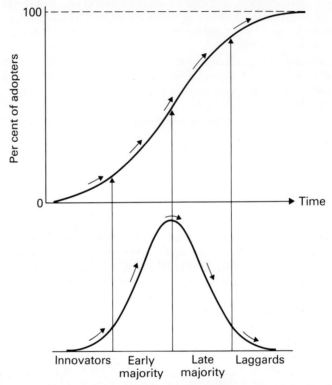

Fig. 7.8 Psychological barriers to adoption and the logistic curve (Abler, Adams and Gould, 1971, 405).

personality traits implied by our use of adjectives such as cautious or adventurous to label the behaviour patterns of individuals. Whatever the reasons for these differences, it is possible to classify members of a society into an arbitrary number of groups depending upon their resistance to innovations. Thus Hägerstrand's farming community may be viewed as containing a small number of early *innovators*. Having set the example, these were followed by the *early majority*. These in turn were copied by the *late majority*, with the *laggards* responding belatedly. Such differences in levels of resistance ensure that the diffusion of innovations tends to adopt a characteristic form in time. If the distribution of the resistance classes within a population is regarded as normal* in the statistical sense, a cumulative

* See glossary.

plot of the proportions adopting a given innovation should reveal an S-shaped or logistic curve through time (Fig. 7.8). The early section of the curve is shallow because the number of innovators is relatively small. The steeper mid-section reflects the impact of early and late majority adopters, whilst the upper inflexion occurs when the remaining laggards 'take the plunge'. Numerous empirical studies (see Brown and Cox, 1971) have confirmed that the adoption of innovations follows this course through time, although the point of inflexion cannot always be seen unless the entire population of potential adopters is reached.

Distance and psychological barriers affecting communication of information and adoption decisions respectively combine to produce characteristic 'waves' of

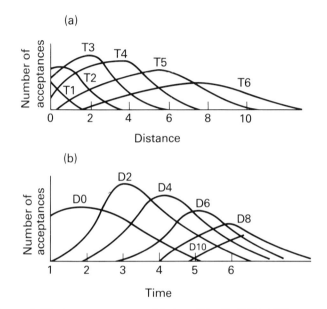

Fig. 7.9 Waves of diffusion in: (a) space; (b) time (Morrill, 1970, 265).

diffusion in both time and space. Morrill (1970) attempted to clarify the nature of these waves by analysing information relating to several examples of diffusion, including Hägerstrand's original Swedish data. Figure 7.9a indicates that during the first time period (T1), the number of adopters is highest nearest the origin of the innovation. As the innovators in this area are copied by the early and late majority, the number of acceptances must inevitably decline so that by time period 5 (T5) even the laggards have adopted the innovation. This kind of logic accounts for the gradual outward displacement of the crest of most active change. Figure 7.9b shows what Morrill regards as the typical form of the diffusion wave in time. The curves in space and time are not symmetrical and it appears that 'there is less variation in the time period of maximum change at various distances [Fig. 7.9a] than there is in the distance at which change is maximum during various time periods [Fig. 7.9b], simply because the entire diffusion process begins slowly, accelerates and later slows' (Morrill, 1970, 261). Theoretically, an expanding circle

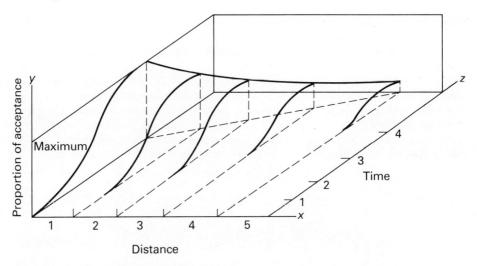

Fig. 7.10 Waves of diffusion in space and time.

of innovation may be expected to spread outwards indefinitely, but in practice the waves gradually die out either because they are only appropriate in a limited area (pasture subsidies would be irrelevant in arable districts) or because they meet a competing wave from another origin.

Figure 7.10 is an attempt to combine the ideas separately represented in Figures 7.9a and b. The diagram has three axes relating to time, distance and proportion of acceptances. At time 1 in distance-band 1, diffusion is at the first point of inflexion on the logistic curve. Simultaneously, in distance-band 2, there are some early adopters, but the wave has not yet reached distance-bands 3 or 4. By time 3, the innovation has reached saturation levels in distance-band 1, the wave is cresting in band 3, is incipient in band 4 and has not yet entered band 5.

Other Barriers

Figure 7.10 implies that the wave of diffusion is uninterrupted. Thus its height declines with increasing distance from the point of origin much as the ripples created by a stone tossed into a pool gradually fade away. We have already seen that even where diffusion depends either upon physical contact or upon face-to-face communication, the spread from the origin rarely takes the form of concentric circles due to the influence of lines of communication, in both absolute and social space, upon the probabilities of contact (see section 7.1.1). Further modifications to the stone-in-the-pool analogy are required when the assumption of the existence of an isotropic surface is relaxed to incorporate the influence of various types of barrier. These barriers may be classified in two ways. Firstly by reference to their effect upon patterns of diffusion, and secondly by considering the forms which they may take.

The effects of barriers may be expressed in terms of their influence upon the energy needed to sustain the wave motion (Morrill, 1968). An *absorptive* barrier halts the process of diffusion completely. A *reflective* barrier generally absorbs some of the energy, but causes the diminished wave to be deflected in another direction. Finally, a *permeable* barrier absorbs and/or reflects part of the energy, but allows the remainder to pass through. Pure absorbing and reflecting barriers are rare and the majority are of the permeable type which result in a slowing down of the diffusion wave in their lee.

The significance for spatial diffusion of barriers is probably easier to appreciate by considering their forms rather than their properties. Physical features such as mountains, rivers and swamps obviously hinder the movement of people, goods and information. For example, Hägerstrand recognized that the existence of several elongated lakes within his study area reduced the probability of contact between farmers on opposite shores and he modified the values in his mean information field accordingly. Thinking of urban growth as a diffusion process, there must be few cities which have not had their expansion constrained in some way by the effects of steep slopes, rivers or some other 'barrier' imposed by the physical environment. Such barriers tend to possess both reflective and permeable properties. The westward shift of settlement in North America was certainly delayed by the Appalachians, but this barrier did not prevent the more enterprising from penetrating the interior either by passes such as Cumberland Gap or by moving around the southern edge of the mountain chain.

The extreme case of total absorption is probably approached more closely by cultural barriers, based on religious, linguistic and political differences, than by obstacles imposed by the physical environment. Churchill originally coined the phrase 'Iron Curtain', but it has become common usage because it so aptly conveys the impression of an almost impenetrable ideological barrier dividing Europe into East and West. The role of religious beliefs in inhibiting the introduction of birth control and dietary changes in certain countries is another example of a powerful cultural barrier which has important policy implications. The differential permeability of such barriers is well illustrated by the contrast between the northern and southern frontiers of the US. Despite Canadian sensitivities regarding the influence of its more powerful neighbour, there is no doubt that the diffusion of various aspects of US folk culture takes place more readily across the 49th parallel than across the border with Mexico. A common language (to a large extent) and a similar settlement history have meant that Canada is generally more receptive to cultural influences from the US than is Mexico.

7.2 Hierarchy and Diffusion

Despite the complicating influence of the various types of barrier, there are good *a priori* reasons for expecting distance-controlled diffusion processes to display a more or less continuous outward spread through time in the resulting distributions. By contrast, diffusion patterns associated with the operation of hierarchical controls are typically 'patchy' as the appearance of the phenomenon at different points in time 'jumps' from one location to another. Diffusion processes operate through many different kinds of hierarchy, including organizational structures such as big companies, but the urban hierarchy, extending from the largest metropolitan cities to the smallest hamlets, is one of the most significant in terms of its influence upon a wide range of phenomena with important social, economic and political consequences. Migration, for example, which is a form of relocation diffusion, is often step-like in character as individuals move up the hierarchy to

successively larger urban areas. Innovation diffusion, which is closely correlated
with the process of economic growth, is frequently channelled in the reverse direction as new techniques, products and cultural phenomena filter down the hierarchy.
This spatio-temporal sequence is a result of the interplay of what may be termed
(i) information factors and (ii) market factors.

7.2.1 Information Factors

Urban centres serve as magnets encouraging the concentration of information and
as switching-points for the exchange of information. It is therefore not difficult
to appreciate their significance in the transmission of economic growth when it
is remembered that 'all theories of innovation diffusion stress the role of communication defined ... in terms of the passage of information' (Brown and Cox, 1971,
557). It is possible to distinguish between information flows that take place via
(i) inter-urban communication networks and (ii) corporate structures, as determinants of hierarchical patterns of innovation diffusion.

Inter-Urban Information Flows
Cities may be expected to be centres of innovation simply because of the higher
probability that an entrepreneur will be found within a major concentration of
population rather than a small one. However, it is the adopters who transform
an isolated event or discovery into a spatial diffusion pattern. Generally speaking,
the more information people have about an innovation, the more likely they are
to adopt it. Such information is usually more readily available in towns and cities
than in smaller centres. Flows of information are positively correlated with settlement size, as various studies of telephone traffic have emphasized (see section
8.2.1). Indeed the interrelationship between telephone links, information flows and
innovation diffusion is a good illustration of the concept of positive feedback described in chapter 5. As a centre grows in size, its telephone links with other places
tend to be improved; this promotes the inter-urban exchange of information which
in turn improves the chances of further growth-inducing innovations being
adopted, thereby completing the circle of cumulative causation.

   The significance of inter-urban information flows in the process of economic
development has been demonstrated by Pred (1971) in the context of the US.
Through a careful analysis of the contents of newspapers produced in different
towns and cities to the east of the Mississippi during the late eighteenth and early
nineteenth centuries, Pred was able to identify the way in which non-local information passed through the urban system before the advent of electronic means of
communication. At this time, newspapers had fairly limited areas of circulation
and served the hinterlands of individual settlements. A definite sequence of contacts existed as newspapers in smaller towns conveyed information gleaned from
the pages of journals serving larger centres. Information from Europe was particularly important in view of the significance of trans-Atlantic trading links in the
national economy. New York, as the major port of entry, was usually first to receive
news of events in Europe and this information gradually filtered through the urban
system. As a result of improvements in transportation, the time-lag between publication in New York and receipt elsewhere gradually declined and this is reflected
in the expansion of the area enclosed by the 10-day isoline at different dates in

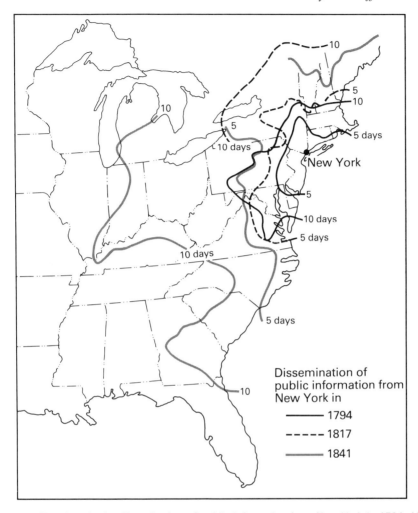

Fig. 7.11 Time-lags in the dissemination of public information from New York in 1794, 1817 and 1841 (after Pred, 1971).

Figure 7.11. However, the benefits of these improvements were nearly always first experienced in New York, which was therefore able to maintain and even reinforce its relative information advantage over competing commercial centres. This ensured that New York was usually first to hear about and first to adopt new innovations – a situation which, Pred argues, has helped the city to retain its position as the largest metropolitan complex in the US through the operation of a positive-feedback mechanism.

Although spatial variations in information availability may have been significant in initiating unbalanced growth, their influence upon contemporary patterns of economic activity might have been expected to decline in an age of electronic communications. Nevertheless, there is evidence that the role of cities as switching-points for the exchange of information has, if anything, increased in importance.

One of the features of the modern economy is the growing proportion of the total labour force that is employed in service as opposed to manufacturing occupations. Within the general category of service employment, the most dynamic growth has been experienced in the so-called quaternary sector of the economy, which includes such activities as banking, publishing and administration, all of which are essentially concerned with the handling and management of information. The fact that these are just the kind of activities that occupy the multi-storey office blocks that have become the hallmark of the modern metropolis suggests that a city-centre location possesses certain attractions for information-oriented activities. Research in Sweden (see Tornqvist, 1968, 1970; Thorngren, 1970) and the UK (see Goddard, 1971) has shown that these attractions are based upon the continuing importance of face-to-face meetings in the execution of business. The agglomeration of offices facilitates such meetings, but tends to aggravate commuting and congestion problems. The growth of city-centre office employment has reached such proportions that official policies designed to encourage job dispersal have been introduced in many countries. The limited success of these policies in the Netherlands, for example, is typical of experiences elsewhere and it underlines the magnitude of the information advantages which Amsterdam, Rotterdam and The Hague possess over the rest of the country (see Dietvorst and Wever, 1977). The difficulties involved in reversing these polarizing forces suggest that spatial variations in access to information continue to exercise an important influence upon patterns of economic development (see Tornqvist, 1973; Westaway, 1974).

Corporate Information Flow

Many of the office blocks within major cities are the headquarters of private-enterprise organizations which operate plants dispersed throughout the country or, in the case of multinational companies, throughout the world. The economic power of such organizations has been steadily growing whatever criterion is used to measure their influence and whatever scale of view is adopted (see chapter 3). The significance of these trends for innovation diffusion is related to the research and development activities of big companies. The commercial survival of these corporations to a large extent depends upon their success in developing (and selling) new products and methods of production. The promotion of innovation diffusion is therefore a necessary aspect of the functioning of private-enterprise corporations.

The spatial consequences of innovations that are internal to a corporation, such as the introduction of a new process in its factories, can only be understood by reference to the location of its facilities, which does not necessarily reflect the urban hierarchy. The head offices of big companies, which represent the ultimate centre of corporate decision-making responsibility, are usually, but not always, located in the great metropolitan cities (see section 5.1.3). Figure 7.12 indicates that more than a quarter of the 'top 1,000' US manufacturing corporations in 1972 had their principal office in New York. However, several cities of much lesser population size serve as the headquarters location of firms from this elite. For example, over 20 are based in the Minneapolis–St Paul metropolitan complex which ranked 16th in terms of population in 1970, and there is evidence of a decline in the dominance of New York and the contributions of Pittsburgh, Philadelphia, St Louis and other traditional 'manufacturing belt' centres (Pred, 1974). In Western Europe, London,

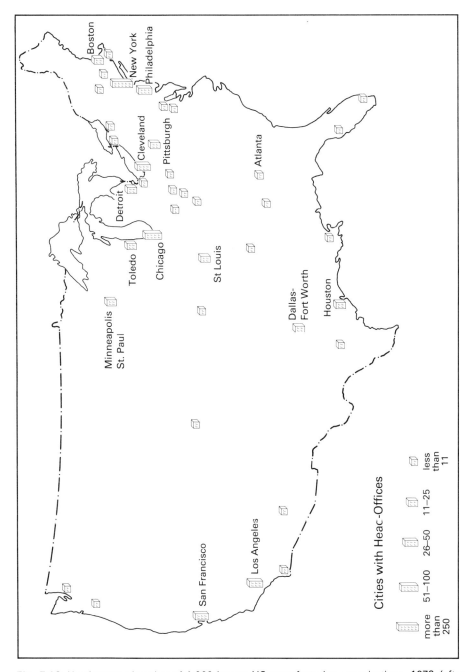

Fig. 7.12 Headquarters location of 1,000 largest US manufacturing organizations, 1972 (after Pred, 1974, 19).

Paris and the Ruhr conurbation are the principal headquarters locations, although there is a fairly extensive scatter in lesser centres. The fact that head offices are not automatically located in the city at the top of the urban hierarchy means that the effects of decisions to adopt innovations do not necessarily 'trickle down' from larger to smaller centres in the traditionally accepted sense. The situation is further complicated by the fact that a head office will often be neither the site at which

Fig. 7.13 The location of the chemical business of the 'Shell' group of companies, 1976.

the innovation is made nor the location at which it is first introduced, but will nevertheless be responsible for its diffusion throughout the organization. For example, with reference to the chemical business of the Shell group (Fig. 7.13), an innovation may be made at the Delft laboratory, the decision to introduce it on a commercial scale would probably be taken at head office in the Hague and the trial may actually be carried out in Bombay. The distribution indicated in Figure 7.13 is, of course, unique to the Shell group and it would be necessary to produce different maps to show the geographical spread of the activities of other

multinational companies. Thus, if it is accepted that major corporations are an important source of innovations, such maps would be essential to an understanding of the spatial diffusion of corporate innovations for which the hierarchy concept has validity only in an organizational rather than a locational sense (see Pred, 1976).

7.2.2 Market Factors

The influence of hierarchical structures upon the diffusion of innovations is not simply related to the channelling of information flows. It has already been suggested that corporate organizations may have a vested interest in stimulating innovation diffusion. The link between profitability and market size ensures that the promotion of this self-interest is often consistent with the idea that diffusion filters down the urban hierarchy. In the case of certain types of innovation, market size is important in defining a minimum population threshold necessary to justify adoption. Although technical advances often lead to a gradual reduction through time in the threshold of economic viability, the existence of such a criterion obviously encourages adoption in larger population centres before smaller ones. This 'trickle down' effect is accentuated by the risk and competitive elements involved in the adoption of most entrepreneurial innovations. Generally speaking, the financial returns are potentially higher and the risks correspondingly reduced the greater the margin between the actual population and the minimum threshold. Furthermore, a single adoption in a given town may effectively block the introduction of similar establishments which are therefore 'diverted' to a lesser centre.

These ideas may be illustrated by reference to the introduction of gas works in English towns in the first half of the last century (see Robson, 1973). The development of town gas works and associated street lighting must have been one of the most obvious visual impacts of the Industrial Revolution upon the urban landscape. The spread of these utilities took place very rapidly. The first company – the London Gas Light and Coke Company – was founded in 1812 and the vast majority of towns with populations exceeding a critical threshold of 2,500 had their own companies by the middle of the century. Figure 7.14 relates the proportions of towns with their own gas works at three points in time to their positions in a ranked hierarchy of population size. The close correlation between the date of adoption and town rank is striking. By the end of 1820, all but two of the ten largest English towns had gas works and, ten years later, there was not a single town in the top thirty without a gas works. Much the same kind of sequence is apparent in the smaller towns, and the speed with which the gas works became a symbol of urban status in Victorian England makes it more appropriate to speak of a diffusion pattern which 'cascaded' rather than 'trickled' down the settlement hierarchy.

The influence of corporate decision makers upon innovation diffusion is not restricted to phenomena such as gas works which are adopted by representative bodies on behalf of a wider community of individuals. Consumer goods such as motor cars and refrigerators, for example, are adopted at the household level, but their availability is determined by the policies of the organizations responsible for their manufacture. Even if an individual is keen to buy a new product there may be a limit to the distance he is prepared to travel to get it. Retail and agency outlets

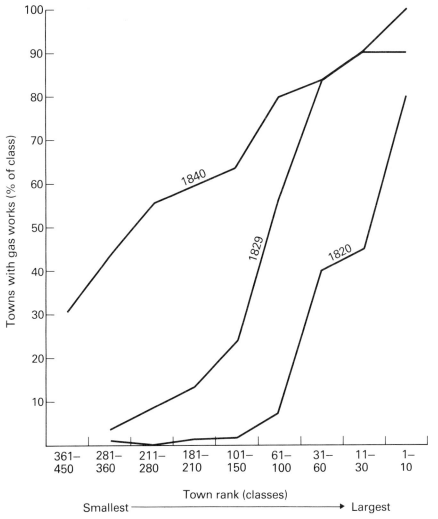

Fig. 7.14 Hierarchical diffusion of gasworks in English towns, 1812–1840 (after Robson, 1973, 179).
Note: Towns are ranked by their populations in 1821, 1831 and 1841 respectively.

normally appear first of all in the biggest population centres which are then followed by those lower down the hierarchy. The market factor is therefore important in this context not so much in defining a rigid threshold as in determining a set of distribution priorities. Once these have been established, however, the nature of such innovations is such that a distance-related diffusion pattern may be expected as communication between individuals, epitomized in the 'Keeping up with the Joneses' syndrome, promotes an outward spread from specific regional centres of adoption.

In certain cases, the adoption of an innovation at community level is a prerequisite to the adoption of a related innovation at household level. For example, Berry (1972) has examined the link between the spread of television transmitting stations in the US between 1940 and 1968 and the purchase of receiving sets. The relationship between the size of a centre and the date that its television station was opened is very similar to that described by Robson in relation to gas works in nineteenth-century England. The first adopters on the eve of US entry into the Second World War were the cities of New York, Chicago and Philadelphia. Figure 7.15 indicates a clear correlation between the size of a city and the date it first acquired a television

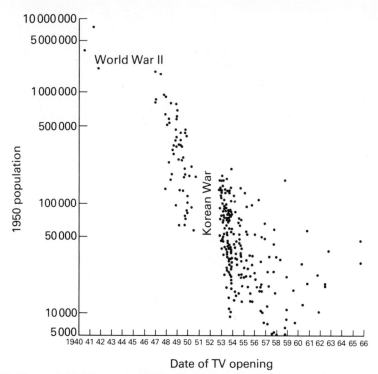

Fig. 7.15 Hierarchical diffusion of television stations in the United States, 1940–1965 (Berry, 1972, 116).

station, although many urban centres which might have been expected to possess their own television stations on the basis of this observed relationship are not represented because of the competitive nature of the television business in the US. For example, reception from the nearby cities of New York and Boston has inhibited the introduction of stations in several relatively large urban centres in Massachusetts, Connecticut and Rhode Island. Although the diffusion of television stations is best understood in terms of the graph in Figure 7.15, the impact of these events upon television ownership is most effectively represented cartographically. Reference to Figure 7.16 suggests that household purchases of television sets spread steadily outwards from the nodes initially created by the early broadcasting stations and the isolated peaks apparent in 1953 had coalesced into an almost continuous distribution by 1965.

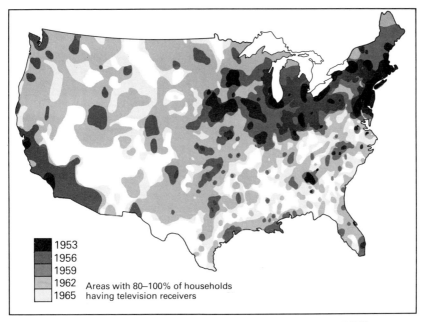

1953
1956
1959
1962   Areas with 80–100% of households
1965   having television receivers

Fig. 7.16 Diffusion of television receivers in US, 1953–1965 (after Berry, 1972).

7.3 The Spread of Modernization

Research into the principles of spatial diffusion has largely been based upon the experiences of countries that are normally regarded as developed. However, the kind of examples we have used to demonstrate these principles have obvious contemporary parallels in the developing world. The way in which Swedish farmers respond to government subsidies may offer lessons for the organization of agricultural extension services. The factors affecting the early development of the town gas industry in the UK may be relevant in the formulation of strategies for the location of public utilities. Thus a clear link exists between the spatial dimensions of the development process and the diffusion of innovations. The core/periphery model discussed in chapter 5 implicitly assumed the existence of such a link, but we are now in a position to clarify this.

The conceptual framework provided by earlier research into the nature of innovation diffusion has been used by several geographers as a basis for various studies of 'modernization' in developing countries. The term modernization is generally accepted to mean a process of change involving the abandonment of traditional social, economic and political systems and their replacement by the equivalent institutions and life-styles typical of 'Western' urban/industrial society. Colonialism has played an important role in this process by 'exporting' Western culture to many parts of the world and thereby promoting contact between widely differing ways of life. These themes are explored in the remaining part of this chapter which (i) examines the nature of modernization as innovation diffusion, and (ii) outlines the relationship between innovation diffusion and development strategy.

7.3.1 Modernization as Innovation Diffusion

Some studies of modernization in developing countries have traced the diffusion of specific institutions such as banks (Engberg and Hance, 1969) and agricultural cooperatives (Harvey and Greenberg, 1972). Others have adopted an integrated approach by seeking to describe the spread of development in terms of some composite index of modernization. Soja's (1968) analysis of Kenya was one of the first so-called geographies of modernization. The book examines the spatial dimensions of the changes brought about by the breakdown of a fragmented society with very limited inter-tribal contact between the various ethnic groups which occupied their

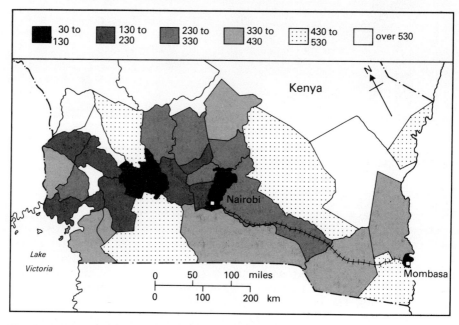

Fig. 7.17 Scores on factor 1 – 'development' Soja, 1968, 79).

own spatially restricted territories. At the heart of Soja's study was his attempt to synthesize by means of principal-components analysis* the interdependence of factors contributing to the phenomenon of modernization. He used a data set of 25 variables representing demographic characteristics, educational provision, quality of communications and economic circumstances in each of the 35 Administrative Districts established by the British. This selection was partly determined by practical considerations of data availability and reliability, but implicit in the choice of variables is the author's definition of what constitutes modernization. The intercorrelations between the variables was such that principal-components analysis revealed a single dimension of 'development' which accounted for 63 per cent of the total variance. The compression of so many variables into a single factor or component tends to support the contention that modernization involves the

* See glossary.

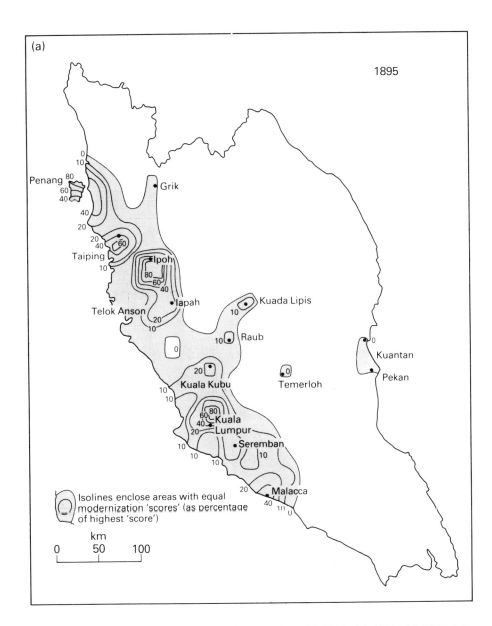

Isolines enclose areas with equal modernization 'scores' (as percentage of highest 'score')

km
0   50   100

Fig. 7.18 Modernization surface in Malaya in: (a) 1895; (b) 1911; (c) 1931; (d) 1969 (after Leinbach, 1972, 267, 269, 271 and 275).

simultaneous occurrence of a large number of interrelated events. The position of specific areas on this continuum of 'development' was identified by plotting factor scores.* The results of this operation are indicated in Figure 7.17 where low scores are associated with high levels of development and vice versa. Not surprisingly, 'development' is greatest in the principal areas of European settlement such as Nairobi and the White Highlands, although there is also a tendency for favourable

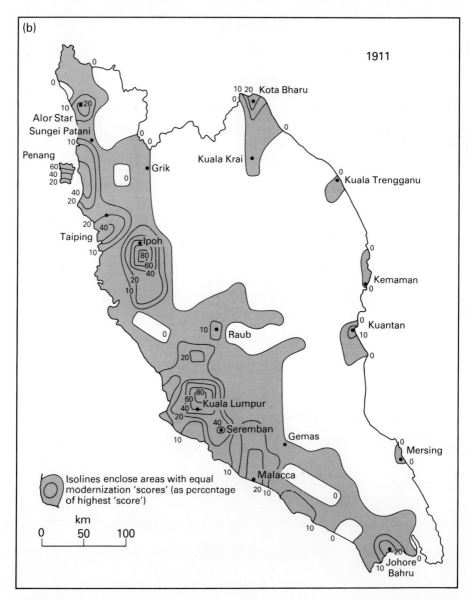

(b)   1911

Isolines enclose areas with equal modernization 'scores' (as percentage of highest 'score')

* See glossary.

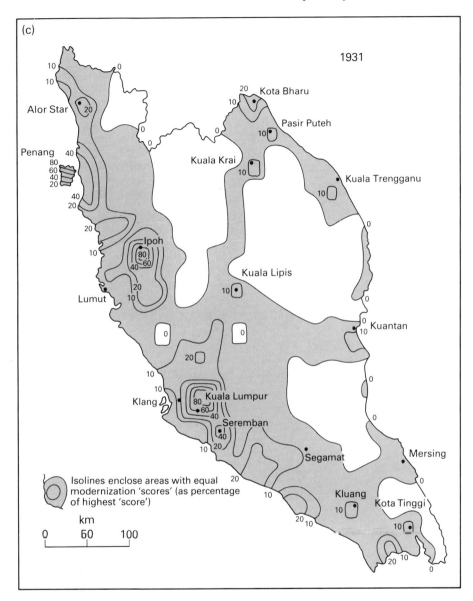

(c)

1931

Alor Star

Kota Bharu

Pasir Puteh

Penang

Kuala Krai

Kuala Trengganu

Ipoh

Kuala Lipis

Lumut

Kuantan

Klang

Kuala Lumpur

Seremban

Segamat

Mersing

Isolines enclose areas with equal modernization 'scores' (as percentage of highest 'score')

Kluang

Kota Tinggi

km

0   50   100

factor scores along the axis of the railway line between the port of Mombasa and the interior.

Soja's analysis is static in the sense that it is based on data relating to the early 1960s and therefore describes the situation in Kenya at a point in time. The nature of modernization as a process of spatial diffusion can only be inferred by postulating that the geographical clustering of the more developed areas suggests the operation of a spread effect away from the centres of European settlement and the main lines of communication linking Mombasa and Nairobi. However, attempts have

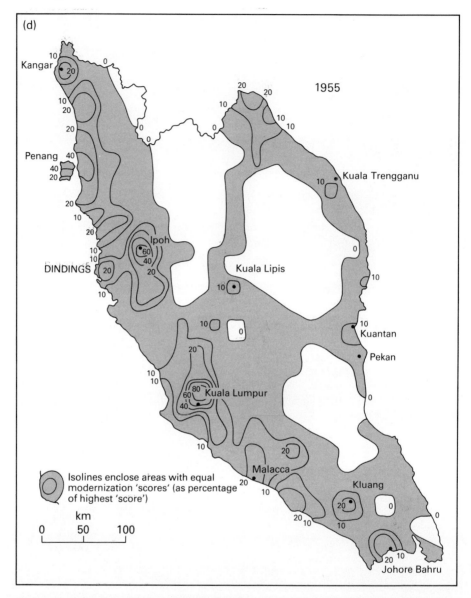

been made in the cases of Tanzania (Gould, 1970) and Malaysia (Leinbach, 1972) to apply the kind of techniques used by Soja to plot the distribution of scores on some composite index of modernization at successive time periods, thereby examining more directly the nature of development as a diffusion process.

Figure 7.18 summarizes the results of Leinbach's study of the spread of modernization in Malaya between 1895 and 1969. Similar data to those employed by Soja were obtained for each time period and allocated to a basic spatial framework of uniform hexagonal cells superimposed over the country. A dimension of

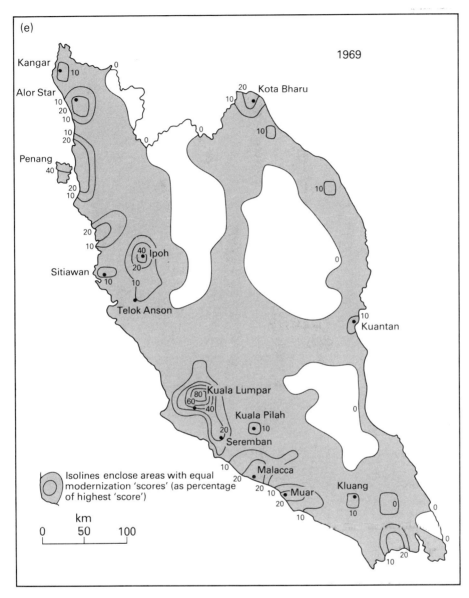

(e)

1969

Kangar

Alor Star

Penang

Sitiawan

Telok Anson

Ipoh

Kota Bharu

Kuantan

Kuala Lumpar

Kuala Pilah

Seremban

Malacca

Muar

Kluang

Isolines enclose areas with equal modernization 'scores' (as percentage of highest 'score')

km
0   50   100

modernization was derived using principal-components analysis* and translated into factor scores for each cell. These were expressed as percentages relative to the most 'developed' cell which therefore had a value of 100. The results of this operation make it possible to think in terms of a surface, the contours of which provide an index of modernization. The evolution of this surface in Peninsular Malaysia is represented in Figure 7.18. The significance of lines of communication as agents of change is suggested by the existence at every stage of connecting ridges between

* See glossary.

high-points on the surface. Nevertheless, the results are, to some extent, contradictory. Whilst the blank areas, within which modernization has no impact, are gradually eroded, the peak around Kuala Lumpur is accentuated. Thus a veneer of modernization, in the form of such aspects of rural development as the increased availability of electricity, had reached most of the country by 1969, but the relative dominance of the capital city was more pronounced than ever. This accords with the arguments outlined in chapter 5, regarding the circular and cumulative nature of the development process. At the same time, in viewing economic development as a diffusion process, it becomes possible both to understand better some of the factors which affect its spatial distribution and also to frame more effective national policies to minimize regional imbalance.

7.3.2 Innovation Diffusion and Development Strategy

One of the main objectives in studying innovation diffusion is to help find ways in which the process may be accelerated in time and guided in space. Certain lessons may be drawn from studies of spontaneous innovation diffusion that are relevant to policy makers seeking to induce or promote economic growth (see Pedersen, 1969). A recurrent theme of studies such as those carried out by Soja and Leinbach is the critical importance of transport and communications in the development process. By providing links between one place and another, transport and communications systems perform a dual role in the diffusion of innovations. On the one hand, they serve as channels for flows of information and therefore promote the spread and exchange of new ideas. On the other hand, they reduce the costs of movement which may itself be a prerequisite to the adoption of a particular innovation. For example, the changeover from subsistence to commercial agriculture can only be achieved if the output can be transported to a market at a cost which permits a satisfactory return to the farmer. The market, as far as the farmer is concerned, may not necessarily be the point of final consumption, but rather the location of some kind of intermediate storage or processing facility. Thus rural development strategies aimed at encouraging the diffusion of new crops and new agricultural practices often rest upon the establishment of government-sponsored centres which serve both as sources of information and as collection points from a surrounding hinterland to which links are strengthened by associated investment in transport facilities (see Garst, 1974).

Transport and communications are not the only aspects of infrastructure that are important in facilitating the diffusion of innovations. The existence of an electricity distribution system may, for example, be a requirement for the introduction of a new industrial plant to an area. Entrepreneurial innovations may also be encouraged by attempts to reduce the risks associated with capital projects. Government-backed guarantees, loans, subsidies and tax concessions for projects in certain areas are all fairly common devices which fall into this category. At the household level, education, in the broadest sense, is synonymous with the diffusion of innovations. For example, the family-planning programme in India is essentially concerned with educating the country not only in the techniques of contraception, but also in the consequences of excessive population growth.

Many authors concerned with the development process have stressed the need for an urban hierarchy of interdependent centres ranging from large cities at the upper levels to small villages at the other end of the spectrum of population size (see Berry, 1961). One of the major roles of the urban hierarchy in this respect is to provide a mechanism for the diffusion of innovations through the operation of the 'trickle-down' effect. The existence of such a hierarchy is taken for granted in developed countries, but in many parts of the world the orientation of society away from a predominantly rural emphasis towards life in towns and cities is a comparatively recent change. The principal findings of a study of the structure and functions of towns in Tanzania underline the problems facing many developing countries (Hirst, 1973). The majority of the 16 settlements defined as towns in the Tanzanian census can trace their origins back no further than 1890. In 1967, only 5.5 per cent of the country's population were classed as residents of these towns compared with corresponding figures of between 60 and 80 per cent urban dwellers in most developed nations. Analysis of their employment structures revealed very little functional differentiation between the towns, which largely act as service centres for their respective agricultural hinterlands. Consequently, inter-urban linkages, which are essential to the operation of the 'trickle-down' effect, are poorly developed. The dominating influence of Dar es Salaam, which has a population four times the size of the second largest town, further inhibits the downward transmission of growth impulses through the urban system as a result of the negative effects of the kind of polarizing forces discussed in chapter 5. In so far as the situation in Tanzania may be regarded as typical of that in other developing countries, the conclusions of Hirst's study suggest that the creation of an integrated hierarchy of urban centres should be the cornerstone of any planning strategy aimed at promoting the diffusion of modernizing influences throughout a nation's territory. Certain countries, for example Chile (Berry, 1969), have expressed a commitment to such a policy, but the obstacles to implementation are immense and the prospects of achieving success often fall short of the ideals expressed in political rhetoric.

Consideration of the planning problems of the developing countries underlines the validity of the distinction made in the opening section of this chapter between distance and hierarchy effects in the evolution of spatial patterns. Thus urban nodes and transport links play an important role in the development process – the former serving as isolated centres of innovation, the latter helping to foster outward spread from these regional centres. Development problems are essentially concerned with the location of facilities in space and the occurrence of events in time. The concept of spatial diffusion provides a useful framework for the analysis of these or any other problems which require explicit reference to the interrelationship between change through time and movement in space.

Further Reading

BROWN, L. A. and COX, K. R. 1971: Empirical regularities in the diffusion of innovations. *Association of American Geographers, Annals* **61**, 551–9.

A good review of the various factors affecting the diffusion of innovations.

BROWN, L. A. 1981: *Innovation diffusion*. London.

The concluding chapters of this book use specific examples to explore the relationship between innovation diffusion and the development process.

HÄGERSTRAND, T. 1967: *Innovation diffusion as a spatial process*. Translated by A. R. Pred, Chicago.

A translation of a pioneering work on spatial diffusion.

MORRILL, R. L. 1970: The shape of diffusion in space and time. *Economic Geography* **46,** 259–68.

Provides a clear insight into the nature of diffusion waves.

PRED, A. R. 1977: *City-systems in advanced economies*. London.

Discusses the role of urban and corporate hierarchies in the diffusion process.

SARRE, P. 1978: The diffusion of Dutch elm disease. *Area* **10,** 81–5.

Uses a Hägerstrand-type diffusion model to demonstrate the role of long distance transport of logs in promoting the spread of the disease.

SOJA, W. E. 1968: *The geography of modernization in Kenya: a spatial analysis of social, economic and political change*. Syracuse Geographical Series No. 2, Syracuse, New York.

The first of a series of 'geographies of modernization' which interpret the development process as spatial diffusion.

8 Interaction

Whereas spatial diffusion tends to be a one-way, one-off movement, spatial inter-action is associated with reciprocal and continuing flows. The most fundamental distinction, however, is determined by the relationship between these movements and the spatial systems within which they take place. Spatial diffusion processes bring about changes, such as those associated with the spread of modernization in developing countries, in the state of the system. By contrast, spatial interaction processes are necessary to maintain the system in its existing state. The day-to-day functioning of spatial systems depends upon interaction between their component parts. The extent of this dependence tends to increase with the sophistication of the system. Modern urban/industrial society is characterized by a complex network of linkages between the various activities which comprise the economic system. Fragmentation of functions is accompanied by their physical separation in space. Thus spatial interaction is fundamental to the operation of any economic system whether it occurs in the form of transfers between plants in an individual factory at one end of the scale or in the form of trade between countries at the other. The necessity for and the nature of such movements are examined in the following chapter by reference to (i) the bases for interaction and (ii) the analysis of commodity flows.

8.1 Bases for Interaction

It is important to appreciate that the term spatial interaction is not restricted in its applicability to the movement of commodities. For example, the journey to work of commuters and the shopping habits of housewives are short-term two-way flows which cannot therefore be regarded as examples of diffusion. The same kind of argument may also be applied to certain types of information flow. Thus, telephone calls are reciprocal exchanges of information which also conform with our definition of spatial interaction. This process is not, therefore, specific to the movement of commodities. Nevertheless this narrow view of the process is adopted in much of the following chapter, partly because movements of people and infor-mation have already been discussed at some length and partly because most re-search concerned with spatial interaction has concentrated upon the analysis of trading relationships at various scales. In a study of interregional trade in the US, Ullman (1956) identified three 'bases for interaction' which he termed (i) comple-mentarity, (ii) transferability and (iii) intervening opportunity. Complementarity and transferability are necessary conditions for movements to be initiated between one place and another, whilst intervening opportunity is often a modifying influence upon the orientation and volume of the resulting flows.

8.1.1 Complementarity

The notion of complementarity is closely tied to the existence of the kinds of variation in the content of space that were discussed in chapters 4 and 5. In the case of the physical content of space, these variations reflect natural distributions which ensure that, for example, important minerals are found at few locations, but are required as industrial raw materials in many manufacturing centres. Even if physical variations were eliminated by postulating the existence of an isotropic surface, the operation of certain economic forces would create opportunities for trade. In particular, the economic concept of the division of labour would encourage specialization in particular types of activity because theoretical arguments and practical experience suggest that higher levels of productivity may be achieved by attempting to do a few things well rather than by trying to be a jack-of-all-trades. Variations between people and places based on this elementary economic principle are often further reinforced by the whole complex of forces promoting unbalanced growth (see chapter 5). When these forces are combined with spatial variations in such natural phenomena as climate and soils, they give rise to situations in which people in certain places may be more efficient producers of one commodity whilst others may be better at making a different item. The benefits of such comparative advantages can only be gained if exchange occurs. Thus geographical variations in production create *potential complementarities* which only become *specific complementarities* when supplies in one location are matched by a corresponding demand somewhere else.

Although the role of these spatial variations could be illustrated at a variety of scales, their significance is perhaps most readily appreciated in the context of international trade. Such trade is not necessarily restricted to societies which use money. Couper (1968) has described the complex trading chains which operated within and between the archipelagos of Fiji, Tonga and Samoa long before the arrival of the first Europeans in the Central Pacific. Most of these early patterns of trade exploited geographical variations based both upon natural distributions and upon cultural specializations. Thus some of the most important links appear to have been between rich food-growing islands and less fertile areas which provided craft goods in return. Trade was to some extent seen as an insurance against natural disasters such as hurricanes and droughts, and the ethics of inter-island trade meant that a community was under a moral obligation to trade with any other which required its products. Highly localized village skills and crafts seem to have been deliberately preserved in order to increase the range of specific complementarities and, thereby, the opportunities for trade.

The indigenous trading relationships of the Pacific islands clearly illustrate Ullman's notion of complementarity, but the exchanges involved were insignificant by comparison with the scale of contemporary trade between countries. The volume of international trade has increased steadily since 1945. This trend has been encouraged by technological advances which have improved the economics of sea transport and therefore reduced the friction of distance. Even more important has been the implementation of international agreements which have brought about a gradual liberalization of trading relationships through the elimination of tariff barriers. Although every commodity entering world trade displays a unique pattern of flows between origins and destinations, it is possible to identify certain characteristic orientations (see Johnston, 1976). Although exchanges between industrialized nations account for a major proportion of total world trade, the reciprocal relationship between the developing and the developed world, such that the raw-material exports of the former are exchanged for manufactured goods from the latter, is an important feature of the global pattern. To some extent, this situation reflects geographical complementarities. For example, the temperate countries of Western Europe and North America are obviously unable to meet their own requirements for tropical produce such as bananas and cocoa. However, the pattern is also related to historical factors in the sense that many developing countries have been unable to break out of a system of trading relationships established during the colonial period. Certain countries remain almost entirely dependent upon a single export commodity to earn their foreign currency. The oil-producing states of the Middle East are perhaps the most obvious example. Since the early 1970s these countries have managed to bring about a fundamental shift in the balance of trade between themselves and the major oil consumers. However, the political leverage associated with control of a substantial proportion of the world's oil reserves is not necessarily available to suppliers of less vital raw materials and their economic fortunes are often tied to fluctuations in the international price of a single commodity.

Whether trade is viewed on an international scale or at a spatially much more restricted level, the translation of 'specific complementarities' into 'operating complementarities', where exchange actually takes place, depends upon the influence of two other factors. These are the cost of transport or transferability of the commodity and the relative location of sources of supply and centres of demand which together determine the intervening opportunities to trade.

8.1.2 transferability

The effect of distance as a constraint upon movement was discussed in chapter 6 where it was shown that, because of the nature of freight rates, cost-space and absolute space are rarely isomorphic. Although virtually all forms of interaction display the distance/decay effect whereby the volume of movement falls off with increasing distance from the point of origin, the rate of decline shows considerable variation. The downward slope of the line on such graphs may be defined by a distance/decay function which is derived from the following equation:

$$Q_{ij} = \frac{1}{d_{ij}^{e}}$$

where Q_{ij} represents the quantity transported between place i and place j,
d_{ij} represents the distance between place i and place j, and e is a distance/decay function.

The equation may obviously be solved for e if the values of Q_{ij} and d_{ij} are known. Figure 8.1 illustrates the effect on the slope of the curve of substituting different values for *e* in the equation. The larger the value of *e*, the steeper is the curve and the more rapidly it falls away. Conversely, the smaller the value of *e*, the less pronounced is the distance/decay effect. The size of *e* is therefore directly related to the influence of distance upon interaction. This influence is itself subject to two sources of variation. On the one hand, it varies between places, depending upon differences in the quality of transport facilities linking them. On the other hand, it varies between commodities, depending upon the ease or difficulty with which they may be transported. In this latter respect, the distance/decay function *e* is an index of transferability. The derivation of the exponents indicated in Figure

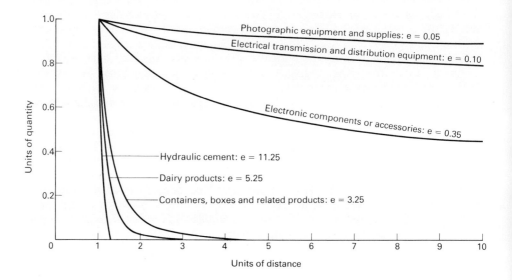

Fig. 8.1 Distance exponents of different commodities entering US interregional trade, 1967 (compiled from data in Black, 1972, 112).

8.1 provides evidence in support of this interpretation. They were calculated on the basis of a study of 1967 census data relating to the interregional movement of various commodities in the US (Black, 1972). Exponents were obtained for 80 different commodity groups of which those shown in Figure 8.1 are a representative sample. It is noticeable that high *e* values are associated with goods that are heavy and of low value (cement), perishable (dairy products) or bulky (containers and boxes). The exponent is characteristically low when the product is valuable (electronic components), small (photographic supplies) and highly specialized (electrical transmission equipment).

Not only does the value of *e* vary between places and commodities but it also changes through time as technical developments in transport improve the transfer-

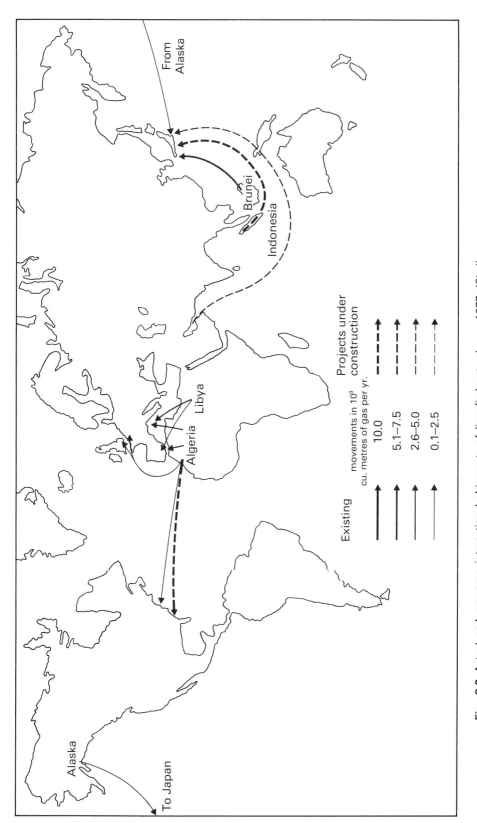

Fig. 8.2 Actual and proposed international shipments of liquefied natural gas, 1977 (Shell, 1977, 4–5).

ability of specific items. These advances may either bring about a gradual decline in the relative costs of movement or they may make it possible to carry a commodity that was previously considered non-transportable. Examples of both situations may be drawn from the petroleum industry – the first by reference to postwar trends in the economics of operating oil tankers; the second by reference to the use of specially designed vessels to transport liquefied natural gas. The oil tanker has rapidly established itself as the largest type of ship on the world's oceans (see Couper, 1972). Whereas a 20,000-ton vessel was considered large in 1950, carriers of 400,000 tons were not unusual by the mid-1970s and the composition of the international tanker fleet has changed radically since 1945 as owners have attempted to take advantage of the economies of scale associated with operation of bigger ships. Whereas the increasing size of oil tankers has effectively reduced the friction of distance with regard to the movement of petroleum, the introduction of refrigerated ships has meant that distance has recently become a surmountable obstacle rather than an impenetrable barrier as far as the marine transport of natural gas is concerned. Consequently, the specific complementarities between the gas supplies of North Africa, the Middle East and Southeast Asia and the energy demands of North America, Western Europe and Japan are being translated into operating complementarities as new international movements are initiated (Fig. 8.2). This contemporary illustration of the significance of refrigerated transport has obvious historical parallels such as the development in the late nineteenth century of a corresponding technology for the storage of meat, which was vital to the agricultural export prospects of countries such as Argentina and New Zealand.

Indirect evidence of the effects of technological change upon transferability is provided by a general decline in the contribution of transport costs to the overall costs of production. This proportion amounted to only 3 per cent in the case of total primary and secondary economic activities in Great Britain in 1968 (Dawson, 1977). In relation to manufacturing, the proportion was highest for those industries, such as oil-refining, brick-production and cement-making, which utilize bulky, low-value raw materials. Even in these industries, transport did not account for more than 20 per cent of total costs whilst in others transport was an insignificant element in their cost structure. Although this situation cannot be ascribed solely to the relative ease of movement in a highly developed economy, it is indicative of the 'shrinking world' syndrome and it is not unreasonable to suggest that the distance/decay function relating to the transfer of any commodity within the UK will have become smaller and the distance over which interaction takes place will have increased through time.

8.1.3 Intervening Opportunity

The third of Ullman's bases for interaction is concerned with relative location and therefore hinges upon the geometry of spatial arrangements rather than the characteristics of commodities. The essential idea behind intervening opportunity is very simple. Consider two islands divided into four regions (Fig. 8.3). In both cases, regions A and D have a surplus of a particular commodity which is demanded by regions B and C. Common sense suggests that interactions will take place between adjacent regions. Thus in the case of the elliptical island (Fig. 8.3a), A will trade with B and D will trade with C. In Ullman's terminology, C represents an intervening opportunity between D and B whilst B represents an intervening opportunity between A and C. However, the different spatial arrangement on the circular island ensures that the complementary surplus and deficit regions all share common frontiers so there is no 'natural' pattern of interaction between them. The argument so far is based upon the convenient but unrealistic assumption of an isotropic surface. If this assumption is relaxed it is not difficult to visualize situations in which the apparently obvious trading links postulated for the elliptical island may be modified. For some historical reason, transport links may be much better developed from the west of the island so that region C is nearer to A than to D in terms of time- or cost-distance. Alternatively a mountain range may separate D from the rest of the island, again affecting its proximity to C in relative space.

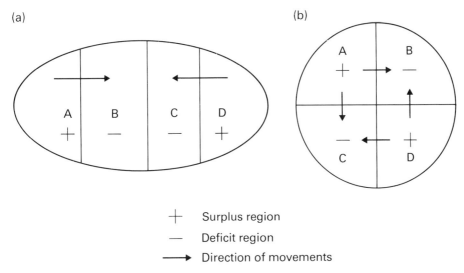

+   Surplus region

—   Deficit region

⟶   Direction of movements

Fig. 8.3 Relative location and interaction in: (a) elliptical island; (b) circular island.

Despite the simplicity of the concept, the effect of intervening opportunity upon spatial interaction is very difficult to measure in practice. For example, the argument that the attractions of France may divert German tourists who would otherwise make the longer journey to holiday in the Iberian Peninsula is plausible, but it is virtually impossible to say what proportion of the potential interaction between Spanish beaches and German cities is frustrated in this way (see Williams and Zelinsky, 1970). It is also worth noting that whilst intervening opportunities may be regarded as negative influences upon movement in the short term, such proximate trading may have the long-term effect of promoting interaction between distant places. Thus by making intermediate transport links profitable, a sequence of such opportunities may eventually result in connections being established between widely separated but complementary places. Transcontinental links often develop in this way as trade builds up gradually over short distances and thereby contributes towards meeting some of the fixed costs of the total route.

Although Ullman originally conceived intervening opportunity specifically in terms of the relative location of complementary places, the notion may be extended to incorporate the effect upon interaction of variations in transport modes. In this sense, the Atlantic Ocean as an intervening obstacle may theoretically be regarded as having a similar negative effect upon trade between Europe and North America as if a prosperous Atlantis were to emerge from the depths to present an intervening opportunity! Similarly, topographical features have a bearing upon the economics of land transport. Roads may be constructed on inclines of one in four, but the tolerance of railways to slopes is much more limited. The various modes of transport all display different characteristics as far as their speed, suitability for different types of commodity and cost to the user are concerned. In so far as the configuration of the earth's surface affects the feasibility of using alternative modes of transport, it exercises an influence upon the intensity of interaction between one place and another.

8.2 Analysis of Commodity Flows

It has been argued that Ullman's bases for interaction are relevant to an understanding of both the reasons for and the characteristics of movement, but the validity of this assertion can only be tested by relating the concepts of complementarity, transferability and intervening opportunity to the findings of empirical studies of movement. Most of these studies have been concerned with the analysis of commodity flows rather than other forms of spatial interaction and they tend to fall into two broad categories – descriptive and predictive. In examples of the former approach, the objective is to identify the principal characteristics of the flow patterns under study. In examples of the latter approach, attempts are made either to replicate existing or to forecast future flows by the use of models incorporating the appropriate explanatory variables. This methodological distinction forms the basis for the subsequent division of this chapter which considers (i) the interpretation of flows as matrices, and (ii) the application of the gravity model, in studies of spatial interaction.

8.2.1 Flows as Matrices

Spatial interaction within a system of places is probably most conveniently represented in quantitative terms by means of a commodity-flow data matrix (see Smith, 1970). Such a matrix takes the form of a square table in which the rows indicate the origins of movements and the columns represent their destinations (Table 8.1). The numerical values in the cells of the matrix measure the volume of movement between a particular origin and a specific destination. This measure may relate to the number of items involved or it may be expressed in units of weight, but where several commodities are involved in a composite flow, financial value may serve as the only meaningful common yardstick. In Table 8.1, the diagonal cells of the matrix are blank because a place cannot interact with itself.

Individual row and column totals do not necessarily balance. For example, place D sends only 12 units to the other places in the system, but it receives 17 units in return. However, the system represented by Table 8.1 is assumed to be closed and internal equilibrium is maintained by ensuring that outflows (rows) are matched by inflows (columns) and hence the overall summation of 56 units in the bottom right-hand cell of the matrix. The nature of the 'places' in Table 8.1 is undefined, but, depending upon the scale of study, they may be conceived of as points such as towns or factories or as areas such as administrative or political units.

In itself a commodity-flow matrix is little more than an accounting framework. However, it provides a useful starting-point in the analysis of such flows and is particularly helpful in identifying (i) the intensity (or volume) of interaction, and

Table 8.1 A Hypothetical Commodity-Flow Data Matrix

From	To A	B	C	D	Total Outflows
A		10	3	2	15
B	9		1	4	14
C	2	2		11	15
D	3	1	8		12
Total inflows	14	13	12	17	56

(ii) the structure of interaction, between the places specified in the rows and columns. Thus in Table 8.1, the larger numbers within the cells clearly reveal those places which seem to interact most intensively with one another. Furthermore the distribution of these numbers within the matrix tells us something about the structure of interaction within our hypothetical system of four places. The high values in the top-left quadrant of the matrix suggest that A and B are closely linked in a functional sense whilst those in the bottom right indicate that C and D are bound together in a similar fashion. This hypothetical example is obviously absurdly simple and we will now try to pursue these themes by looking at more complex and realistic situations.

Intensity of Interaction

The use of matrices to represent flows was pioneered by certain economists who were interested not so much in interaction between *places* as in interaction between the sectors of specialized functions or activities into which any economic system may be divided. The basic configuration of such input–output tables is the same as the commodity-flow data matrix represented in Table 8.1. The only fundamental difference lies in the labelling of the rows and columns. The former indicate the outputs or sales of individual sectors and the latter relate to their inputs or purchases. The number of rows and columns ultimately depends upon the objective of the investigator and the availability of suitable data. The US economy, for example, has been divided into as many as 450 sectors for the purposes of representing its internal structure in the form of an input–output table consisting of over 200,000 cells (see Evans and Hoffenberg, 1952).

No matter what level of sectoral disaggregation is adopted, such tables remain essentially non-spatial in the sense that they reveal nothing about the pattern of interaction between places. This limitation has been partially overcome by the development of interregional input–output tables which enable linkages both between sectors and places to be represented in a single matrix. Table 8.2 outlines the structure of an interregional input–output table in which an economy is divided into four sectors and four sub-regions. This kind of table is organized on the same

Table 8.2 A Hypothetical Inter-Regional Input–Output Table

From \ To		NORTH				SOUTH				EAST				WEST				Total Out
		A	B	C	D	A	B	C	D	A	B	C	D	A	B	C	D	
NORTH	A																	
	B																	
	C																	
	D																	
SOUTH	A																	
	B																	
	C																	
	D																	
EAST	A																	
	B																	
	C																	
	D																	
WEST	A																	
	B																	
	C																	
	D																	
TOTAL IN																		

basic principles as a conventional input–output matrix with the rows and columns corresponding to the sales and purchases respectively of a particular sector. However, these transactions are also broken down into geographical origins and destinations. Thus, referring to Table 8.2, it is possible by reading along the first row to identify not only the way in which sector A in region 'North' distributes its products to other sectors *within* the region, but also the relative importance of sales *outside* the region. By highlighting the sectoral and spatial interdependencies which exist within any economic system, interregional input–output tables have important practical as well as academic implications. For example, once the relationships between sectors and regions have been quantified within the framework of such a table, it may be feasible to predict how a major change in one part of the system, such as the opening of a new iron and steel plant, will affect other parts of the system through the operation of the multiplier (see section 5.1.1). Interregional input–output tables are also useful in demonstrating imbalances in trading relationships. The consequences of a balance-of-payments deficit are fairly well known in the context of international trade, but the policy implications of such a situation at the regional scale are less widely appreciated. Morawski (1967) attempted to explore some of these issues with reference to Poland by means of an analysis of interregional rail movements of various commodities. Data for 1962 in tonnage form were converted into Polish currency units (zlotys) and a distinction was drawn between 'surplus' regions, in which the value of outflows exceeded the value of inflows, and 'deficit' regions, in which the trade balance was reversed. These regions are plotted in Figure 8.4 and, not surprisingly, the distribution reflects the pattern of economic activity with the heavy industrial centres of the south and west enjoying a surplus relative to the less developed parts of the country in the north and east. The favourable position of the southern regions (voivodships) is largely based upon the wealth created by exploiting the resources of the Silesian coalfield.

The efficiency of commodity flows is another aspect of the question of interregional equilibrium. The nature of the 'transportation problem', which is concerned with the derivation of a minimum-distance solution to the matching of supply and demand at a number of geographically separated points of production and consumption, was discussed in chapter 3 (section 3.4.1) by reference to interstate flows of aluminium bars in the US. Similar studies have been undertaken in relation to various other examples of interregional commodity movements including wheat in India (Dickason and Wheeler, 1967) and wool in Australia (Dent, 1966). Comparison between the actual and the optimal flows makes it possible to identify those which are 'more than expected' and those which are 'less than expected'. This type of study serves as a link between interregional input–output tables, which provide rather coarse information about the spatial dimension of commodity flows, and the analyses of transport networks which actually identify the routes by which surplus and deficit regions are connected. This latter problem is considered in the next chapter, although another intermediate step between the limited spatial information contained in interregional input–output tables and the specific concern with this dimension implicit in the analysis of transport network, is provided by those studies of the structure of interaction patterns which enable general statements to be made concerning the spatial orientation of various flows.

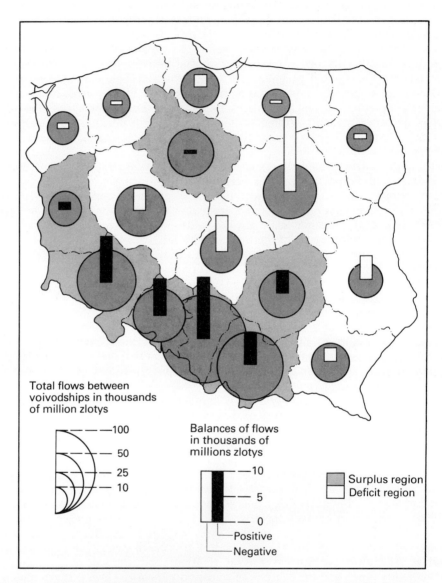

Fig. 8.4 Surplus and deficit regions in Poland based on balances of commodity flows by railways, 1962 (Morawski, 1967, 37).

Structure of Interaction

Analyses of the structure of commodity flows try to identify, within a total system, sub-sets of places that are functionally bound together by a high degree of spatial interaction. Although it was easy to isolate the dominant links between A and B and between C and D within the four-place system represented in Table 8.1, such interdependent clusters of origins and destinations may not be so obvious in larger matrices. Two approaches have been used to identify this type of structural interdependence within a flow matrix. Firstly, consideration of major flows alone may reveal a distinct hierarchy of interaction with certain places dominating others. Secondly, more sophisticated multivariate techniques may be used to extract the principal associations of origins and destinations and to reject 'redundant' information relating to minor connections.

(a)

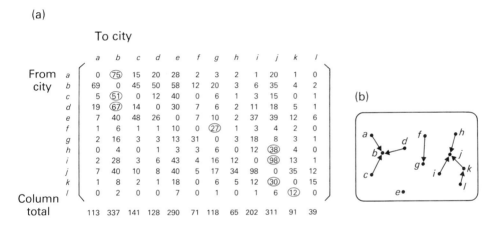

To city

		a	b	c	d	e	f	g	h	i	j	k	l
From	a	0	⑦⑤	15	20	28	2	3	2	1	20	1	0
city	b	69	0	45	50	58	12	20	3	6	35	4	2
	c	5	㉕①	0	12	40	0	6	1	3	15	0	1
	d	19	㉖⑦	14	0	30	7	6	2	11	18	5	1
	e	7	40	48	26	0	7	10	2	37	39	12	6
	f	1	6	1	1	10	0	㉗	1	3	4	2	0
	g	2	16	3	3	13	31	0	3	18	8	3	1
	h	0	4	0	1	3	3	6	0	12	㊳	4	0
	i	2	28	3	6	43	4	16	12	0	㊘⑧	13	1
	j	7	40	10	8	40	5	17	34	98	0	35	12
	k	1	8	2	1	18	0	6	5	12	㉚	0	15
	l	0	2	0	0	7	0	1	0	1	6	⑫	0
Column total		113	337	141	128	290	71	118	65	202	311	91	39

(b)

Fig. 8.5 Hypothetical telephone calls between 12 cities represented as: (a) flow matrix; (b) graph (Nystuen and Dacey, 1961, 35).

The recognition of dominance/dependence flow relationships was pioneered by Nystuen and Dacey (1961) in a study of telephone traffic between settlements in the state of Washington. The technique is simple and may be understood by reference to a hypothetical example. Figure 8.5a is a matrix indicating the number of direct calls made between 12 different cities (*a* to *l*) during a specified time period. The circled values represent the largest flow from an origin to a particular destination. Thus the greatest single number of calls from *a* (75) is made to *b* whereas the largest flow from *h* (38) is to *j*. No values are circled along the rows representing outgoing calls from *b*, *e*, *g* and *j*. This is because the largest flow from each of these cities is to a centre which receives fewer incoming calls (*cf.* column totals). Although *b* sends more calls to *a* than to any other centre, overall it is the destination for a greater number of calls than is *a* (*cf.* 337 and 113) and is therefore regarded as a terminal node. These relationships are shown in diagrammatic form in Figure 8.5b. The 12-centre system has been partitioned into four sub-systems. Cities *b* and *j* appear as the foci of flows from constellations of lesser centres whilst *f* and *g* interact with one another independently of these clusters and *e* stands out in functional isolation.

(a)

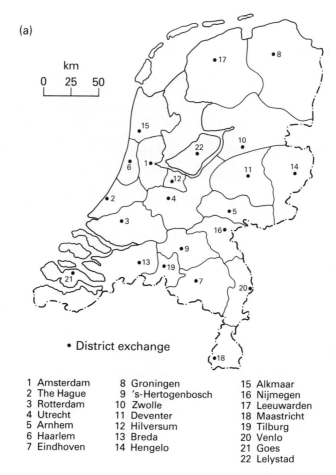

• District exchange

1 Amsterdam	8 Groningen	15 Alkmaar
2 The Hague	9 's-Hertogenbosch	16 Nijmegen
3 Rotterdam	10 Zwolle	17 Leeuwarden
4 Utrecht	11 Deventer	18 Maastricht
5 Arnhem	12 Hilversum	19 Tilburg
6 Haarlem	13 Breda	20 Venlo
7 Eindhoven	14 Hengelo	21 Goes
		22 Lelystad

Fig. 8.6 Telephone traffic in the Netherlands, 1967–1974: (a) telephone exchange districts; (b) nodal and dominant flows, 1967; (c) nodal and dominant flows, 1974 (after Dietvorst and Wever, 1977, 74 and 76).

Dietvorst and Wever (1977) have applied the dominance/dependence technique in a study of changes in the pattern of telephone traffic in the Netherlands. All calls are channelled through district exchanges which are generally located in the largest town or city, in each of the 22 telephone areas into which the country is divided (Fig. 8.6a). Information was collected on the volume of traffic passing through these exchanges at specified time intervals during successive years from 1967 to 1974. Flow matrices containing values representing the summation of out-going (rows) and incoming (columns) traffic for each district (except Lelystad) were assembled. Figure 8.6b and c indicates the structure of the dominant flows between these districts in 1967 and 1974 respectively. Two major sub-systems focused on Amsterdam and The Hague/Rotterdam are identified with a much smaller inde-pendent cluster of northern provinces centred upon Groningen emerging in 1974. Further analysis of the relationships shown in Figure 8.6 suggests that the tech-

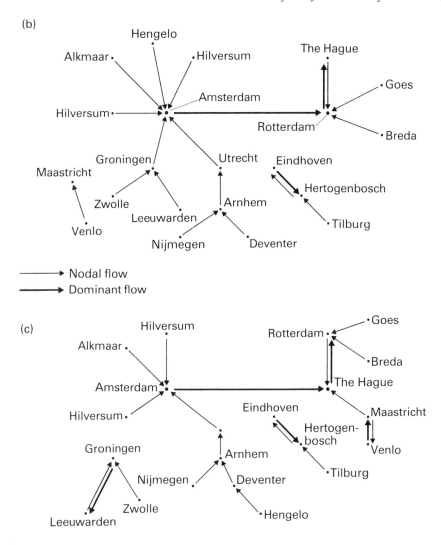

(b)

Nodal flow
Dominant flow

nique of plotting dominant flows can be misleading. Despite the impression of increasing isolation created by the separation of Groningen, Leuwarden and Zwolle into a distinct cluster in 1974 (Fig. 8.6c), the volume of traffic between these exchanges and the two major nodes actually increased over the 8-year period and in this sense they were effectively drawn closer to the rest of the country. Nevertheless, the technique remains a useful preliminary to more sophisticated multivariate analyses of flow structures.

Figure 8.7a to g indicates the direction of the dominant outflows for various forms of movement from each of the Australian states and territories (Holsman, 1975). Although very simple, the diagrams clearly reveal the basic elements of interstate interaction within Australia in the early 1970s. With the exception of airpassenger traffic (Fig. 8.7b) New South Wales is the destination of the major out-

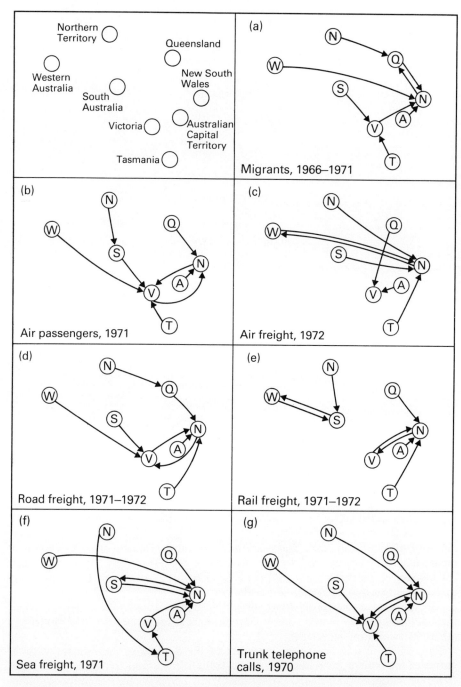

Fig. 8.7 Interstate interaction patterns in Australia—largest outflows of: (a) migrants, 1966–1971; (b) air passengers, 1971; (c) air freight, 1972; (d) road freight, 1971–1972; (e) rail freight, 1971–1972; (f) sea freight, 1971; (g) trunk telephone calls, 1970 (Holsman, 1975, 45).

flow from at least half of the states despite the fact that the great distances within the continent might be expected to encourage interaction between adjacent states. Only in the case of rail freight (Fig. 8.7e) do the three central and western states form their own sub-system, thereby underlining the 'lopsided' nature of the Australian economy due to the concentration of population in the southeast corner. The pattern of sea movement (Fig. 8.7f) suggests the operation of Ullman's complementarity effect as raw materials are drawn from source areas in other states towards the industrial centres of New South Wales. The validity of the general patterns indicated in Figure 8.7 was largely confirmed by Holsman's subsequent use of more complicated techniques. However, this is not surprising given the relative simplicity of the flow matrix, both in terms of its limited size (8×8, representing the seven states plus Australian Capital Territory) and also in terms of the dominating influence exerted by New South Wales.

Interregional flow structures are not always as straightforward as the Australian case. The potential of the by now familiar technique of principal-components analysis* in dealing with more complex situations has been demonstrated by Berry (1966) in a study of interregional flows in India. Census data were available in the form of 36×36 flow matrices describing movements between the states comprising the federal union of India plus additional origin/destination nodes for major ports such as Bombay, Calcutta and Madras. Separate matrices were provided for 63 commodities with widely differing regional distributions and transferability characteristics. For example, coal and coke production is highly concentrated in the northeastern states of West Bengal, Bihar and Orissa whereas certain agricultural products such as cattle and ghee (clarified butter) are available throughout much of the sub-continent. Berry applied factor-analytic techniques to the matrices in order to 'explore similarities in flow patterns, group origins and destinations into functional regions on the basis of these similarities, and reveal the basic anatomy of the flows' (Berry, 1966, 155). The results of this exercise may be divided into two categories. Firstly, an overall view was obtained by grouping all 63 commodities into composite matrices indicating total interregional flows measured by value and quantity. Secondly, individual matrices were analysed to see if any common features could be identified in the movement of different commodities.

The basic structure of interregional flows in India is represented in Figure 8.8 in which the principal producing areas (origins) are connected to the major consuming centres (destinations) by straight lines. The metropolitan orientation of the pattern towards Madras, Calcutta and Bombay is apparent whether the flows are measured by quantity or value, although it is noticeable that, because of the correlation with transferability, the nodal regions tend to be more extensive when value is used as the criterion. The dominating position of these port cities is partly a reflection of a colonial past in which import/export requirements were the principal determinants of commodity movements. The virtual independence of these nodes from one another suggested by Figure 8.8 is indicative of the poorly developed north–south transport link which represents a serious problem for planners seeking to integrate the regional components of the Indian economy (see Lakshmanan, 1972).

The individual elements of the total pattern of interaction, together with the

* See glossary.

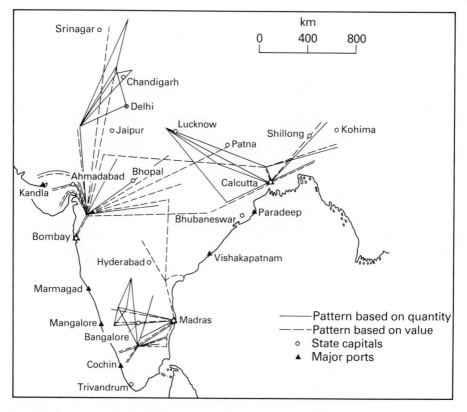

Fig. 8.8 Orientation of principal commodity flows in India, 1960–1961 (after Lakshmanan, 1972, 64).

specific contributions of particular groups of commodities, are summarized in Figure 8.9a to e. Factor 1(a) records the northward and eastward flows of products such as tobacco and vegetable oils which are associated with the Bombay and Madras regions. Factor 2(b) picks out the eastward and southerly movement of commodities originating in the northwestern states. The role of Calcutta in the distribution of coffee, sugar, tea and various other items is highlighted by factor 3(c). The apparent complexity of factor 4(d) may be resolved by reference to the relationships between the manganese-producing areas in north-central India and the exporting ports of Bombay, Madras and Calcutta. Finally factor 5(e) shows the extent of shipments between Delhi and Bombay of agricultural products from western and northern India.

8.2.2 The Gravity Model

Despite the sophistication of the techniques employed, Berry's study is essentially descriptive. An alternative approach to the problem of understanding the nature of spatial interaction is provided by the use of models which seek to clarify the relationship between the variables influencing the process. These variables have

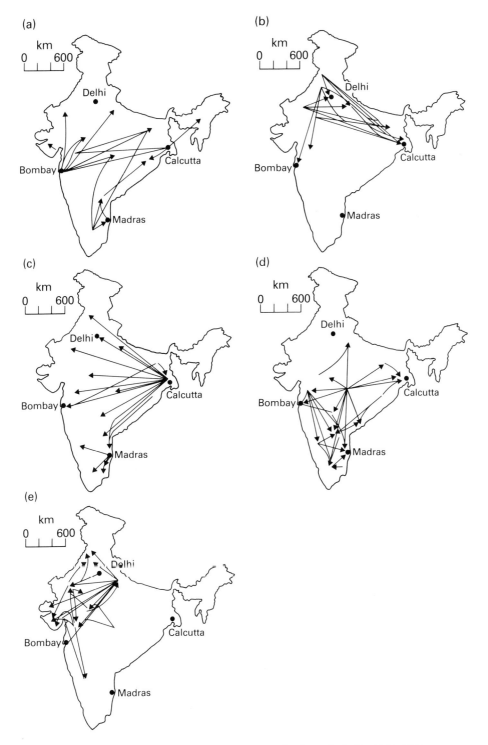

Fig. 8.9 Principal components contributing to commodity flows in India, 1960–1961:
(a) factor 1; (b) factor 2; (c) factor 3; (d) factor 4; (e) factor 4; (f) factor 5 (Berry,
1966, 240, 242, 244, 246 and 248).

already been identified within the framework of Ullman's bases for interaction and we will now examine the way in which the notions of complementarity, transferability and intervening opportunity have been incorporated within a model-based approach to the analysis of spatial interaction by reference to (i) the derivation of the 'gravity model' and (ii) the application of the 'gravity model'.

Derivation of the Model

We have already seen how the concept of economic potential is based upon a gravity formulation (see section 5.1.2) and it is more accurate to regard the term 'gravity model' as referring to a family of such models (Wilson, 1971). In its basic form, the model may be represented as

$$I_{ij} = \frac{P_i P_j}{d_{ij}^e}$$

where I_{ij} represents interaction between place i and place j,
  P_i represents the population of place i,
  P_j represents the population of place j,
  d_{ij} represents the distance between place i and place j, and
  e is a distance-decay function.

In verbal terms, the formula implies that the amount of interaction between any two places will be directly proportional to the products of their populations and inversely proportional to some power of the distance between them. Thus referring to the system of cities represented in Figure 8.10a and assuming a distance/decay factor of 2 (see section 8.1.2), application of the gravity model results in the pattern indicated in Figure 8.10b. Despite their equal size, B and C experience different levels of interaction with A because C is nearer to A. Similarly B and D are equidistant from A, but flows are greater from B because of its larger size. The analogy between this type of reasoning and basic physical concepts of mass and distance is obvious, hence the label 'gravity model' (see Carrothers, 1969).

The terms in the model may be intuitively related to the three bases for interaction if these are condensed into two factors – one encouraging movement, the other inhibiting it. The numerator represents the complementarities between places that generate interaction. The denominator relates to the frictional effect of distance – an effect which is defined by the value of the exponent e which may itself be regarded as a composite measure of the influence upon movement between two places of transferability and intervening opportunity. One of the most attractive features of the gravity formulation is its simplicity. However, the economy of the model in this respect is achieved at the expense of some ambiguities in the precise meaning of the terms in the expression.

Population is not necessarily the most appropriate representation of mass and better results may be achieved if other indices of complementarity are used. For example, whereas interaction between two places in the form of telephone traffic may be closely related to their respective population sizes, the volume of trade in basic commodities may be more accurately predicted by substituting appropriate production and consumption figures for P_i and P_j. For example, a more accurate prediction of the anticipated level of trade in steel bars between two centres is likely to be achieved by replacing the population terms by output and demand

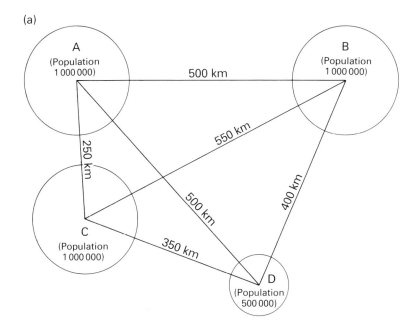

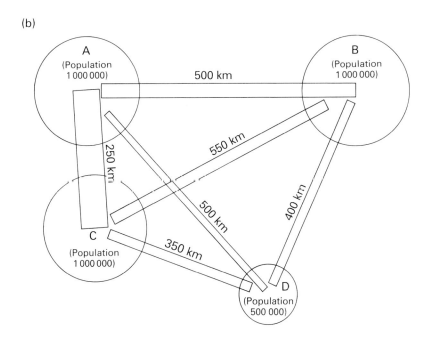

Fig. 8.10 Estimation of flows using the gravity model: (a) size/distance relationships in a four-city system; (b) predicted flows.

figures for the producing and consuming centres respectively. Even if population seems a reasonable index, it has been suggested that the propensity for interaction between two places may not be a simple function of their size (Stewart, 1947). Thus the interaction between a pair of Indian cities would probably be less intensive than that between a corresponding pair located the same distance apart in the US because of the differing cultural environments in which they are placed. Similarly, differences in purchasing power between cities or regions *within* a country may also be expected to affect the level of interaction between them. Recognition of such variations does not invalidate the model, but it does mean that P_i and P_j may need to be weighted in much the same way as distance by the application of exponents.

With regard to the denominator in the gravity formula, the problems of measuring distance were discussed in chapter 6. No matter whether time, cost or some other units are used, it is the value of the exponent which defines the impact of distance upon interaction. We have already seen how this may be linked to the concept of transferability (see section 8.1.2). However, the strength of the distance/decay effect is also influenced by the spatial arrangement of the system within which movement occurs. For example, if a commodity which is a necessity for life in other places is produced at only one location, the exponent will be low because interaction must take place throughout the system regardless of the distances involved. On the other hand, if several sources of supply exist, it is reasonable to assume that the average length of haul will decline, thereby suggesting a more pronounced distance/decay effect. Essentially, the introduction of alternative sources creates an intervening opportunity between the original supplier and its more distant customers. Although it is easy to appreciate on a conceptual level the role of transferability and intervening opportunity in the derivation of the distance exponent, it is much more difficult to quantify their respective contributions in real world situations.

Application of the Model
Basic and refined versions of the gravity model have been used in the analysis of widely differing forms of interaction ranging from the movement of customers to a shopping centre (see Department of Town and Country Planning, University of Manchester, 1966) at one end of the scale to patterns of international trade (see Linnemann, 1966) at the other. No matter what type of interaction is studied and what level of resolution is adopted, it is possible to distinguish between two kinds of approach in the application of gravity models. On the one hand, attempts may be made to replicate existing flows in the hope that comparisons between actual and predicted movements will enable a better understanding of the factors affecting interaction to be achieved. On the other hand, the gravity model may be used to forecast future movements between specified origins and destinations. It is the comparative success of the former approach which has inspired confidence in the gravity model as a predictive tool upon which to base policy decisions relating, for example, to the provision of public transport facilities and new roads within urban areas (see Ridley and Tresidder, 1970). Despite the obvious practical relevance of such applications, further insights into the role of complementarity, transferability and intervening opportunity as variables influencing spatial interaction may be gained by focusing upon two studies – one of interregional commodity

flows in the US and one of similar flows in the UK – which have used the gravity model for comparative rather than predictive purposes.

California makes a major contribution to the agricultural and manufacturing output of the US and it exports commodities to every other state in the union. Utilizing statistics for 1957, Abler *et al.* (1971) employed the gravity model to replicate these shipments expressed in terms of the number of railcar lots involved. This was done by obtaining data for each state on the actual number of shipments from California, the total personal income (as a measure of potential demand for Californian products) and the average length of rail haul from California (as a measure of distance). Substituting these values in the gravity formula, it was

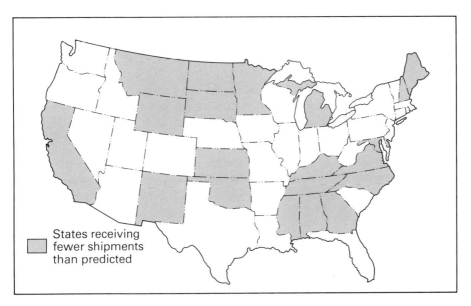

Fig. 8.11 States receiving fewer commodity rail shipments from California in 1957 than expected on the basis of gravity model prediction (Abler, Adams and Gould, 1971, 226).

possible to derive an exponent of 1.88 which defined the magnitude of the distance/ decay effect upon California's trade with *all* other states in 1957. However, when this exponent was used in the gravity model to forecast the level of trade with *individual* states, it was found to under-predict in certain cases and over-predict in others. Although these discrepancies were generally slight, their spatial distribution suggests a basic weakness in this example of the use of the gravity model in that, by concentrating upon the relationship between a single source of supply and many centres of demand, it fails to take account of the influence of intervening opportunities between California and its potential customers. Figure 8.11 plots the distribution of states receiving fewer rail shipments than predicted by the gravity model. Two principal clusters may be identified – one composed of the north mid-western states of Minnesota, Montana, Wyoming and the Dakotas, the other in the south and southeast. In the absence of further research, the significance of these deviations can only be guessed at, but it may be that in the first case industrial goods from California face stiff competition from the manufacturing belt of the northeast whereas fruit and vegetables from nearby Florida reduce California's share of the food market in the southeast. Just as the pattern of negative residuals (i.e. over-predicted cases) in Figure 8.11 may be tentatively related to the concept of intervening opportunity, so some of the positive residuals may be interpreted by reference to the notion of transferability. Thus the corridor of under-predicted states running diagonally from California to New York more or less follows the line of the major transcontinental railways. It may be argued that the friction of distance between these states is reduced because of their position on these routes.

Further insights into the significance of commodity characteristics and relative location as influences upon transferability were provided by Chisholm and O'Sullivan's (1973) analysis of the movement by road of 11 commodities between 78 traffic zones in Great Britain. Unlike the Californian example, which focused on a single origin and many destinations, the British study involved the simultaneous consideration of movements within the 78×78 system of places. The gravity model was used in two different ways. Firstly as a means of demonstrating variations in distance exponents between commodities, and secondly to highlight corresponding variations between places. With regard to the first objective, e values were obtained which displayed similar rankings to those established by Black (1972) in the US (see section 8.1.2), although the range between the highest (building materials) and the lowest (steel) was very much narrower. When the total flow originating and ending in each traffic zone was tested against the gravity model, it became apparent that significant variations existed in their respective patterns of interaction which were reflected in distance exponents that ranged from an upper limit of 4.8 for northern Scotland to a minimum of 1.3 for central London. These e values are plotted in Figure 8.12 as standard-deviation units* about the national mean of 2.4. Low values, indicating a less pronounced distance/decay effect, appear to be associated with four main regions of England – the Northeast, the Northwest, the Midlands and the London area. In terms of both the tonnage and the value of flows, these represent the principal supplying and receiving centres in Great Britain and the provision of better transport facilities may be expected to reduce the costs of movement on major routes as compared with less important ones. The location of traffic zones with respect to one another also seems to exert an influence upon the size of the distance exponent. Thus, apart from East Anglia, high values tend to be associated with areas such as southwest England, Wales and Scotland which are peripheral to the dominant centres of economic activity in the UK. This suggests that the remoter areas try to compensate for their peripherality by attempting to maintain higher levels of regional self-sufficiency which in turn implies that their pattern of freight movements will be more spatially restricted than those of the core areas.

Throughout our discussion of interaction as a spatial process the emphasis has been placed upon attempting to identify, within the conceptual framework provided by Ullman's notions of complementarity, transferability and intervening opportunity, the factors which stimulate and constrain movement. However, the spatial patterns associated with such movement have only been considered on a

* See glossary (standard deviation).

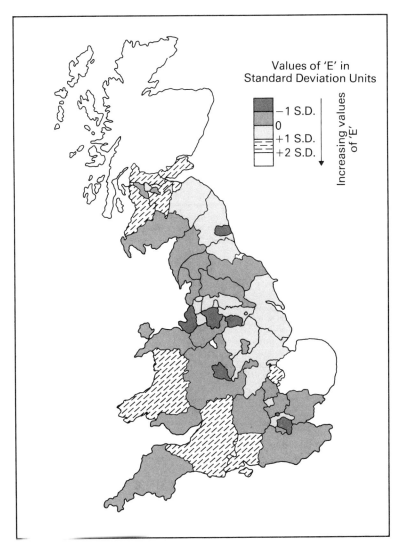

Fig. 8.12 Distribution of 'E' values for traffic zones in the UK, 1964 (after Chisholm and O'Sullivan, 1973, 73).

very generalized level by reference to various analyses of the structure of inter-action. These studies are useful in defining such broad characteristics of movements as their magnitude and direction, but they say little about the routes which channel flows between specific origins and destinations. In order to appreciate *how* things move as opposed to *why* they move, it is necessary to focus attention upon these routes and the linear patterns which they create in the landscape.

Further Reading

OLSSON, G. 1965: Distance and human interaction: a review and bibliography. *Regional Science Research Institute, Bibliography Series*, **2.**
Contains many useful references as well as a review of the literature.

SMITH, R. H. T. 1970: Concepts and methods in commodity flow analysis. *Economic Geography* **46,** 405–16.
Another, more recent review article which is a valuable source of further references.

TAAFFE, E. J. and GAUTHIER, H. L. 1973: *Geography of transportation.* Englewood Cliffs, N.J.
An exclusively US-oriented, but useful textbook.

ULLMAN, E. L. 1956: The role of transportation and the bases for interaction. In Thomas, W. L. (Ed.), *Man's role in changing the face of the Earth*, Chicago, 862–80.
A seminal paper in the development of ideas concerning the nature of spatial interaction.

Spatial Pattern

9 Lines

Most types of movement are restricted to some sort of channel. The channels may be apparent as physical structures, such as roads and railway lines, or they may be organizational arrangements, such as internationally agreed airline flight paths. An individual channel linking two points in space forms a *route*. The points, upon which movements are focused, may themselves be described as *nodes*. The combination of several routes into a more or less integrated structure permitting movement between many nodes is termed a *network*. In so far as individual routes normally form part of a wider network, their location can often only be explained by reference to the structure as a whole. Consequently, attempts to understand the nature and significance of movement channels are likely to be more productive if networks rather than routes are made the object of study.

When viewed as spatial structures within a temporal context, networks may be regarded either as static features at a point in time or as dynamic phenomena which are subject to change through time. Both approaches are equally valid, providing differing but complementary insights. Static representations enable comparisons to be made between networks in different places and are also useful in the solution of problems which involve either making the best use of an existing network or designing a new one to link a given set of nodes. The dynamic view of networks effectively demonstrates the complex reciprocal relationship between the movement processes described in chapters 7 and 8 and the spatial patterns which are discussed in the remainder of this book. This distinction between networks as static and dynamic structures provides the basic framework for the organization of the following chapter which discusses (i) the properties of networks* and (ii) the evolution of networks.

9.1 Properties of Networks

Two different representations of the network of 'A' roads in Anglesey are provided in Figure 9.1. In (a), the network is portrayed as the familiar scaled-down version of absolute space provided by a conventional topographic map. This shows the general orientation and some of the detailed sinuosities of the links in the network as well as giving some indication of the relative size of the various settlements. In (b), the network is generalized into a series of straight-line links between points. Figure 9.1b is a *topological* representation in which places are located in terms

---

* It might be argued that change through time is itself a property of networks.

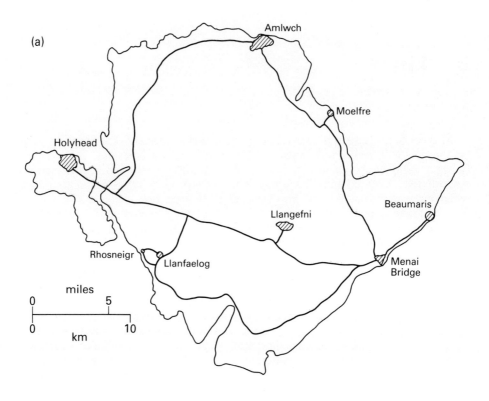

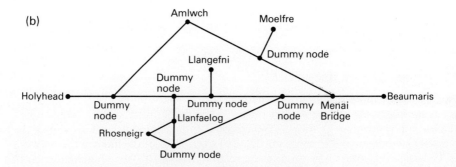

Fig. 9.1 The primary road network of Anglesey represented as: (a) a topographic map; (b) a graph.

of their position on the network rather than with respect to their position in absolute space. At first sight, there seems nothing to be gained by adopting this simplistic view of reality. However, such a level of abstraction is often helpful in revealing structural similarities between complex networks which initially appear to have little in common (Haggett and Chorley, 1969). Thus a fuller understanding of the properties of the road network of Anglesey or indeed of any other network may be obtained by regarding it both as (i) a topologic structure and (ii) a geometric structure.

9.1.1 Topologic Structures

Topology is a branch of geometry which is concerned only with the nature of the connections between the points of a figure. Furthermore, topological views of networks are not totally unfamiliar, for example, the map of the London underground system. Since the traveller is interested only in the sequence-order of stations, detail relating to the true position and curvature of individual lines has been eliminated (see Fig. 9.5).

Graph theory is a branch of topology which is concerned with the analysis of abstract configurations consisting of points and lines.* In the terminology of this field of study, Figure 9.1b is a *graph* in which individual links are described as *edges* and the nodes are referred to as *vertices*. On the basis of such abstractions, indices may be derived which describe (i) connectivity and (ii) accessibility. These two properties are closely interrelated. Connectivity expresses the degree to which a network permits direct movement between its various nodes and is therefore a single aggregate measure relating to the structure as a whole. Accessibility, on the other hand, is specific to individual nodes, which are differentiated in terms of their location relative to one another.

Connectivity

The significance of network connectivity becomes apparent when we relate Zipf's (1949, 6) proposition that 'an individual's entire behaviour is subject to the minimizing of effort' and Bunge's (1962, 178) statement of the obvious but important property that 'the shortest distance between two points is a straight line' (see section 6.1). The principle of least effort implies that the ideal situation as far as the user of a network is concerned is that it should directly connect any two points between which he wishes to travel. For example, the divergence between the official network of paths on a university campus and the unofficial routeways of the students may reflect badly upon the planners responsible for the design of the campus, but it is possible that the addition of new buildings has created entirely different patterns of movement from those which existed when the paths were first laid out. Networks which frustrate rather than aid movement by virtue of poor connectivity between important origins and destinations tend to be modified. There was little need for direct flights between Aberdeen and Stavanger before they became the centres of North Sea oil operations in Scotland and Norway respectively. However, the complaints of oilmen faced with a tedious journey via London and Oslo quickly

---

* An application of the concepts of graph theory was introduced in chapter 8 (section 8.2.1) where hierarchical relationships between cities were identified by plotting the principal flows of telephone traffic as straight lines joining the various nodes.

resulted in the introduction of a direct service which added a further link to and therefore improved the connectivity of the airline network in northwest Europe.

Various indices have been developed describing the extent to which a network approaches maximum connectivity, which requires the existence of a direct link between each node (Kansky, 1963). These indices are all based upon the relationship between the number of edges and vertices in a network which is regarded as a topological graph. Thus

$$\beta = \frac{e}{v} . \qquad\qquad\qquad\qquad\qquad\qquad\qquad (1)$$

$$\gamma = \frac{e}{3(v-2)} \times \frac{100}{1} . \qquad\qquad\qquad\qquad\qquad (2)$$

$$\alpha = \frac{e-v+1}{2v-5} \times \frac{100}{1} . \qquad\qquad\qquad\qquad\qquad (3)$$

where *e* is the number of links (edges) in the network (graph), and
         v is the number of nodes (vertices) in the network (graph).

The beta index (1) is the simplest. It expresses the number of edges present in relation to the number of vertices to be connected and therefore may be regarded as indicating the average number of links leading into or out of each node. This average is clearly higher in Figure 9.2b ($\beta = 1.3$) than in Figure 9.2a ($\beta = 0.8$). The gamma index (2) is the ratio of the number of edges in a network to the maximum which may exist between a specified number of vertices. The denominator in the expression reflects the fact that the addition of a single vertex necessarily increases the number of possible edges by 3.* Referring again to Figure 9.2, network (b) scores better (66 per cent) than the more rudimentary network (a) which achieves only 42 per cent of maximum connectivity. The alpha index (3) is closely related to the gamma index, but is a ratio based on the number of circuits in a network rather than the number of edges. A *circuit* is defined as a path through a network which begins and ends at the same node without passing over any edge more than once. A little thought and experimentation will confirm that the numerator in formula (3) corresponds to the actual number of circuits in a network containing *e* edges and *v* vertices whilst the denominator is the maximum number of circuits in any network linking *v* vertices.† In practice, the higher this ratio, the greater the number of additional or alternative paths in a network. Thus a traveller faced with network (a) ($\alpha = 0$ per cent) in Figure 9.2 can only proceed along a single path between any pair of nodes whereas several options exist in the case of network (b) ($\alpha = 43$ per cent).

Evidence on the ability of the three indices to discriminate between networks of differing complexity is contradictory. Werner (1968a) maintains that alpha is the most sensitive despite the fact that any branching network (i.e. with no circuits) must always have an alpha index of zero per cent as Figure 9.2a suggests. In so

---

* To take the simplest case, three edges are required to join three vertices, but six edges may be drawn when a fourth vertex is added. Any attempt to construct more than six edges will produce intersections which are automatically defined as vertices applying the assumptions of *planar* graph theory. An alternative set of rules is applied to the analysis of *non-planar* graphs which are visualized as existing in three rather than two dimensions so that edges may cross without creating a node. An airline network is a good example.

† A fuller explanation of the alpha and gamma indices is provided by Taafe and Gauthier, 1973, 102–5.

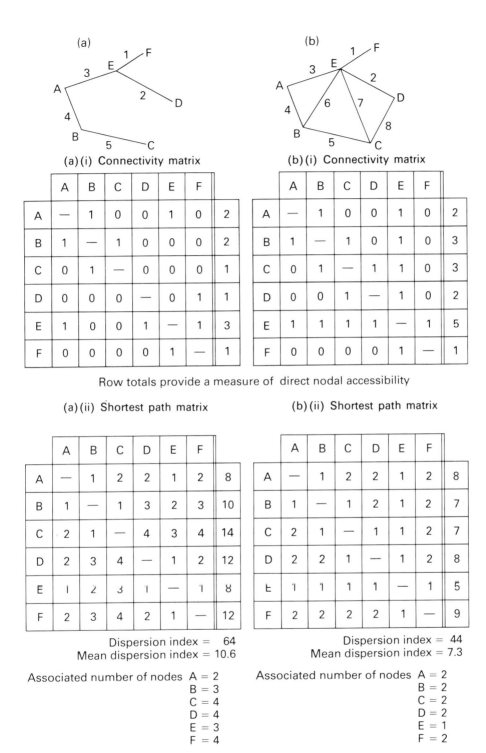

Fig. 9.2 Graph and matrix representations of alternative network structures.

(a)(iii) Relative importance of edges

Edge	No. of shortest paths
1	5
2	5
3	9
4	8
5	5

(b)(iii) Relative importance of edges

Edge	No. of shortest paths
1	5
2	4
3	4
4	2
5	3
6	3
7	3
8	2

(a) Connectivity indices

(b) Connectivity indices

$$\beta = \frac{e}{v} = \frac{5}{6} = 0.8$$

$$\beta = \frac{e}{v} = \frac{8}{6} = 1.3$$

$$\gamma = \frac{e}{3(v-2)} \times \frac{100}{1} = \frac{5}{3(6.2)} \times \frac{100}{1} = 42\%$$

$$\gamma = \frac{3}{3(v-2)} \times \frac{100}{1} = \frac{8}{3(6.2)} \times \frac{100}{1} = 66\%$$

$$\alpha = \frac{e-v+1}{2v-5} \times \frac{100}{1} = \frac{5-6+1}{7} \times \frac{100}{1} = 0\%$$

$$\alpha = \frac{e-v+1}{2v-5} \times \frac{100}{1} = \frac{8-6+1}{7} \times \frac{100}{1} = 43\%$$

far as the indices only serve to confirm the obvious in Figure 9.2 that network
(b) is better connected than network (a), they may appear to be of little value.
However, visual impressions may be less reliable in the case of more complex networks and, despite the ambiguities involved in their interpretation, indices based
on graph-theoretic concepts have proved effective in comparative studies. For
example, the analysis of transport networks in various countries has revealed a
strong correlation between levels of economic development (measured in terms
of per capita energy consumption) and topological connectivity indices (Kansky,
1963). Thus the rail networks of European countries tend to have higher indices
than those of countries in the developing world (Fig. 9.3). The impact of the extension of the US inter-state highway system upon connectivity between cities and
upon internal movement within cities has also been explored using these indices.
In the former case it was shown that certain places benefited more than others
as a result of changes in connectivity at the regional scale (Garrison, 1960). Similarly, a comparison of the effect of federally funded highway projects upon
Indianapolis and Columbus (Ohio) between 1954 and 1964 suggested that more
radical changes occurred in Indianapolis (Muraco, 1972). In particular, isolated
segments were linked up to form a ring-road which has created new opportunities

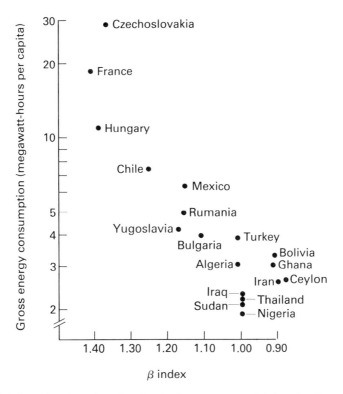

Fig. 9.3 β-index values for selected national railway systems related to development levels (Kansky, 1963, 42).

for the kind of peripheral industrial development that has become a characteristic of many North American cities in the motorway era (see section 6.2.2).

Accessibility

Connectivity indices provide useful aggregate measures of the spatial structure of a network. However, there are many situations in which interest is focused on the accessibility of individual nodes relative to the network as a whole and also on the consequences of adding or removing a particular link. These consequences can often be best understood by regarding any network or graph as a matrix. We have already noted the value of matrices in representing flows of commodities or information between origins and destinations (see section 8.2.1). However, they also have applications in analysing the structure of the networks through which such movements are channelled. Networks (a) and (b) in Figure 9.2 may be transformed into *binary connectivity matrices* (Figure 9.2(a)(i) and (b)(i)) which indicate the presence or absence of direct links between individual nodes by recording a 1 or 0 respectively in the appropriate cell. Such matrices are symmetrical, as indicated in Figure 9.2(a)(i) and (b)(i), provided that no one-way routes are present in the network. The immediate value of binary-connectivity matrices may appear limited, but their usefulness increases dramatically when it is realized that they may be used to identify indirect paths between nodes. Applying the rules of matrix algebra, it is possible to raise a matrix to successive powers, the values in the cells of a matrix indicating the number of two-step, three-step, etc., connections between nodes according to whether the matrix has been squared, cubed and so on (see Taaffe and Gauthier, 1973). By isolating alternative paths between particular nodes, this type of manipulation is useful, for example, in the context of airline bookings where a passenger who cannot get on a direct flight to his destination may be offered an indirect route which involves changing from one airline to another at an intermediate stop.

Notwithstanding these situations in which knowledge about *alternative* paths between two points is useful, adherence to the principle of least effort ensures that the user of a network is, more often than not, interested in finding the *shortest* path between them. Several indices have been developed which express the accessibility of individual nodes in terms of the shortest path to every other node rather than in terms of the range of alternative paths. This minimum-distance path is measured topologically by counting the number of edges (links) to be traversed. Figure 9.2(a)(ii) and (b)(ii) are the *shortest-path matrices* for the networks represented in Figure 9.2. Thus the cell describing the journey between C and D in network (a) indicates that four edges must be traversed, whereas the corresponding value in Figure 9.2(b)(ii) shows the existence of a direct link between the two nodes in the second network. Several indices may be derived from the information contained in a shortest-path matrix. The sum of the row or column totals (identical in a symmetrical matrix) is an indication of the compactness or dispersion of a network. This value may itself be divided by the number of nodes to indicate the average number of links that have to be traversed from any one node to all other nodes in the network. The better connected structure of network (b) as compared with network (a) is confirmed by its lower total and mean *dispersion indices*. As well as this aggregate measure of accessibility, it is possible to evaluate the relative position of a specific node by separately considering the appropriate row or column total. Thus A and E have identical *accessibility indices* in network (a), but E is clearly in the most favoured position in network (b). The *associated number*, which measures the topological distance from a single node to the node which is most remote from it, involves scanning each row or column in a shortest-path matrix and isolating the highest entry rather than summing the entries as with the accessibility index. Referring again to network (a), the associated number differentiates A and E despite their identical accessibility indices.

An alternative approach to the measurement of accessibility involves focusing attention upon the links rather than the nodes. Certain edges within a network contribute more to general accessibility than others because they form part of a large number of minimum-distance paths. The relative importance of edges may be measured by counting the number of times a particular link is used in the paths represented in the shortest-path matrix (Figure 9.2(a)(iii) and (b)(iii). The critical link in network (a) is the one that joins A and E since it is the only connection between the cluster of nodes comprising A, B and C and that made up of D, E and F. A similar analysis of network (b) reveals that the link between E and F is the most important. This is due to the fact that all the other nodes have at least two separate links leading from them whereas F would be completely isolated if its connection with E were severed. It follows that if topological indices can help

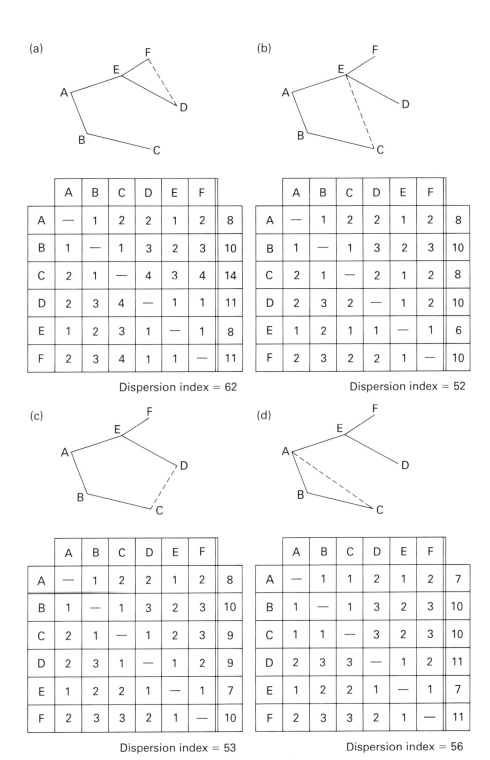

Fig. 9.4 Effect of new links in a network upon accessibility.

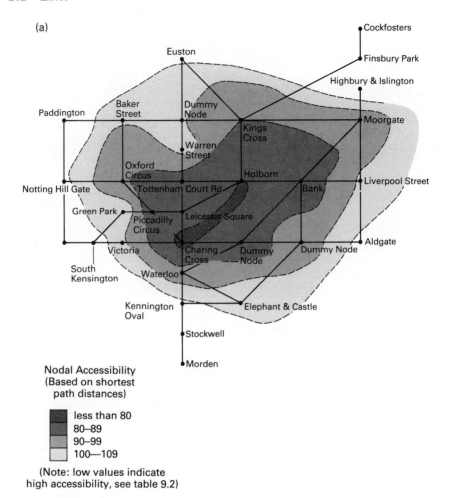

(a)

Nodal Accessibility
(Based on shortest
path distances)

less than 80
80–89
90–99
100—109

(Note: low values indicate
high accessibility, see table 9.2)

Fig. 9.5 Effect of Victoria Line upon part of London underground network: (a) accessibility surface pre-Victoria Line; (b) accessibility surface post-Victoria Line; (c) percentage change in accessibility. (*Note:* Only stations which permit interchange between lines or which are directly affected by the Victoria line are included. Three dummy nodes are included to create a planar graph.)

to highlight the consequences of eliminating links, they may also be used to consider the implications of adding new ones. Four different additions to network (a) are shown in Figure 9.4 together with the respective dispersion indices for the modified networks. The influence of these additions upon overall accessibility differs in each case and the connection of C to E produces the greatest improvement. In reality, investment decisions will, of course, take account of factors other than the relationship between network structure and accessibility. Nevertheless, Burton (1963) has demonstrated the potential of topological measures in establish-

(b)

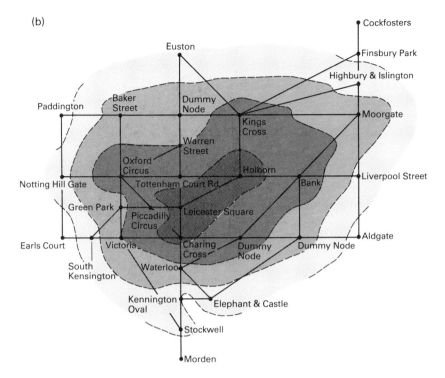

ing road-investment priorities in part of northern Ontario and there is no doubt that this kind of approach is implicit in decisions affecting the construction and operation of many different types of network.

Figure 9.5 provides a topological representation of accessibility changes in the London underground system resulting from the opening of the Victoria Line in 1969. Although the accessibility indices take no account of the inconvenience caused by the need to change, for example, from the Central Line to the Victoria Line to travel from Bank to Victoria, such a topological view of the system is not so far removed from reality. Station frequency in central London is such that the traveller tends to measure distance in terms of the number of intervening stations rather than in terms of absolute units such as miles or kilometres. Similarly, the expression of individual links as straight lines is not unreasonable since deviations from this do not significantly affect the duration or cost of a journey on one stretch of line relative to another. Comparison of (a) and (b) in Figure 9.5 suggests that the Victoria Line brought little change in the overall pattern of accessibility with the highest values remaining focused on a triangle of stations made up of Charing Cross, Holborn and Leicester Square. However, when the accessibility index of each station after the opening of the line is expressed as a percentage of the corresponding value before it was added to the network, certain trends became apparent (Fig. 9.5c). The greatest changes have occurred at the extremities of the line because its diagonal orientation across the grain of the old system has meant that stations

(c)

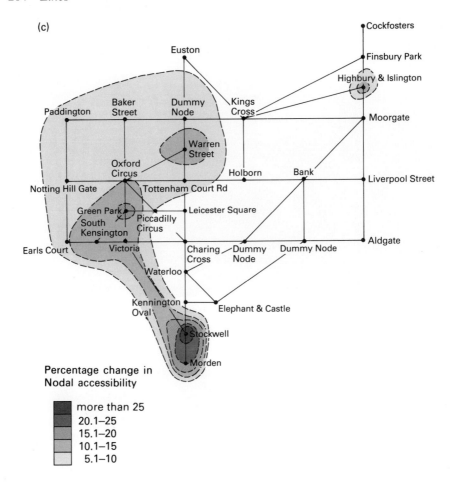

Percentage change in
Nodal accessibility

- more than 25
- 20.1–25
- 15.1–20
- 10.1–15
- 5.1–10

such as Stockwell in the south and Highbury and Islington in the north are no longer situated on isolated branches, but have become part of a circuit. The other main feature of Figure 9.5c is the general improvement in accessibility in the western half of the system where the Victoria Line has provided an additional south–north route across central London.

An underground system is an unusual example of a transport network in the sense that the traveller pays little attention to such properties of individual links as their straightness and their width. These characteristics are often important to the user of other types of transport network. Concern for wear and tear on his vehicles may cause a road haulier, for example, to opt for an indirect motorway route between two places in preference to a shorter route along minor roads. Various attempts have been made to reconcile differences in link 'quality' with the topological approach to network analysis by devising weighted connectivity matrices in which the cell entries measure distance in terms other than the number of edges between two places. This kind of modification involves no change in the basic structural relationships of the network, but it does provide a more refined measure of nodal accessibility. The manner in which the weighted values are derived obviously determines the validity of any analysis subsequently based upon them. Gauthier (1968) and Kissling (1969) have nevertheless demonstrated the feasibility of this type of operation in studies of road networks in parts of Brazil and Canada respectively. Thus they were able to incorporate within connectivity matrices information on such aspects of road 'quality' as the nature of the surface, the severity of gradients and the width of the carriageway.

9.1.2 Geometric Structures

Attempts to take account of differences in the 'quality' of individual links represent a move away from a strictly topological view of networks towards a concern with more familiar properties such as (i) the orientation of individual links and (ii) the density of these links within the area which they serve.

Orientation of Links
The generalization of individual links into straight lines is one of the most obvious discrepancies between the topological representation of a network and its appearance in reality. Although a road or railway line may occasionally be observed stretching away across the landscape in a dead-straight line, such situations are the exception rather than the rule. Most routes are more circuitous. One way of measuring the sinuosity of individual links is by calculating the *route factor*. This is the ratio of the actual link-distance between any two points to the straight-line distance between them – the larger the ratio, the less direct the route. This type of calculation was carried out by Timbers (1967) for journeys between 780 pairs of towns in the UK. The average route factor was found to be 1.17. It is interesting to compare this result with corresponding figures derived for road distances between urban centres in three West African countries (Hay, 1971). These ranged from 1.33 for 45 pairs in Ghana, through 1.35 for 55 pairs in Ivory Coast, to 1.52 for 276 pairs in Nigeria. The route factors calculated by Hay cannot simply be interpreted as meaning that West African roads have more bends than their British counterparts. The higher values also reflect the fact that fewer pairs of towns in West Africa are linked by direct routes than in the UK, an inference which supports the previously noted correlation between economic development and network connectivity.

   The deviations from straight-line links that are indicated by high route factors are not necessarily inconsistent with the principle of least effort as an influence upon human behaviour. Such deviations are often a response to various types of barrier which tend to deflect routes along alternative minimum-distance paths in cost- or time-space (see sections 6.1 and 6.2). Physical obstacles have the most apparent effect upon route alignments. For example, many of the early canals in England and Wales wound through the countryside in tortuous paths which closely followed the contours of the land in an attempt to minimize gradients and therefore the need for the construction of expensive locks. A similar kind of approach is often adopted by airline navigators in selecting transatlantic routes (Warntz, 1961).

Figure 9.6 shows the trajectories selected by two scheduled flights between Copenhagen and New York on 1 September, 1960. Considerable deviations may be seen about the minimum-distance great-circle route. These are a result of attempts to minimize flight-times by taking advantage of high-altitude tail-winds. This technique of 'pressure-pattern navigation' tends to result in a southward deflection of eastbound routes and a northward deflection of westbound routes. Airline flight paths may also be used to illustrate the effects upon route orientation of barriers which are essentially human creations rather than natural ones. Restrictions on commercial over-flying are imposed by many countries for various political and strategic reasons. For example, flights between Western Europe and South Africa are forced around the western coastline of the African continent because many

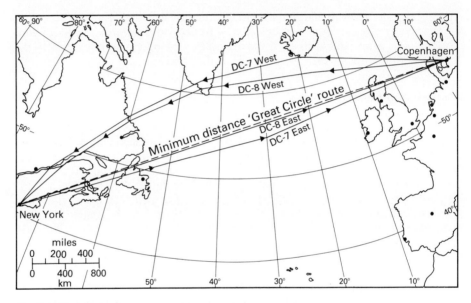

Fig. 9.6 Flight-plans of DC-7 and DC-8 jets between Copenhagen and New York (Warntz, 1961, 193).

countries on the alignment of a direct north–south route have chosen to demonstrate their objections to 'apartheid' policies by banning aircraft flying to and from South African destinations from entering their air-space. On a more limited scale, the adoption of the township-and-range system of land division in much of the American Midwest has tended to create high route factors for rural roads by producing a gridiron network which often makes it necessary to travel along two sides of a triangle to get from one point to another (Thrower, 1966).

Deviations from straight-line routes are not only a consequence of the effects of barriers. Historical studies of the actions of decision makers responsible for route selection have emphasized that numerous variables may influence their choice. In many cases, apparently obvious 'natural' routeways are not taken, as Appleton (1963) has shown with reference to railway developments across the Great Australian Divide. Meinig (1962) has argued, on the basis of a study of the evolution of railway networks in the Columbia Basin of the western US and in South Australia, that positive factors affecting revenues as well as negative factors affecting costs may be responsible for the deviation of specific routes away from minimum-distance paths. The operation of such influences may be explained by considering the nature of a hypothetical route-selection problem in an area containing eight towns. The towns differ in terms of the traffic and, therefore, the

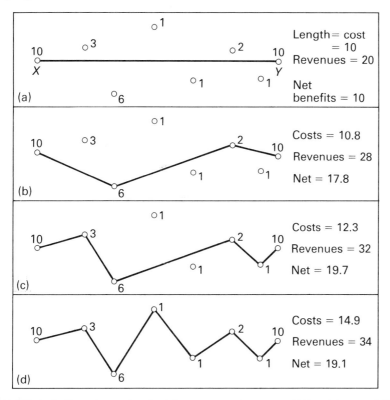

Fig. 9.7 Effect of alternative route orientations upon net revenues (Abler, Adams and Gould, 1971, 275).

revenues they are expected to generate (Fig. 9.7). The connection between the major centres of X and Y is the principal objective, but deviations from this route clearly raise the prospect of additional revenues by exploiting the traffic potential of the intervening towns. However, by increasing the length of the route, such deviations imply greater construction costs which must be set against any improvement in revenues. The results of this calculation are indicated in Figure 9.7, which suggests that net receipts are maximized by an alignment which by-passes two of the smaller centres.

Network Density
In discussing the properties of networks we have so far regarded them as one-dimensional linear structures. However, it is obvious that the separation of these

structures from the two-dimensional areas in which they are placed is artificial. Networks are not only designed to link nodes, but are also built to serve areas. Just as a great river system drains its catchment areas through a complex system of successively smaller tributaries, so any transport network consists of a corresponding hierarchy of individual links. At one level of resolution, a road map may show only the principal arterial links between major cities, but the dependence of these trunk routes upon secondary and lesser roads becomes apparent as the scale and detail of the map is increased.

Topological indices of connectivity and accessibility are based upon the assumption that the 'ideal' network should provide a direct straight-line link between any two nodes. Such a structure is obviously most convenient from the point of view of the user, but it implies a very dense and, therefore, a very expensive network. Consequently, for any given set of nodes, we may recognize two different 'ideal' solutions to the problem of linking them – one which minimizes the user's travel costs and one which minimizes the builder's construction costs (Fig. 9.8). It is understandable for the frustrated motorist stuck in a city-centre traffic jam to reflect upon the advantages of a personal road between his home and workplace.

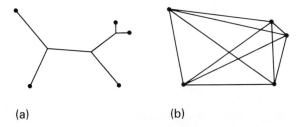

(a)   (b)

Fig. 9.8 Least-cost network designs for: (a) builder; (b) user (Bunge, 1966, 187 and 189).

However, apart from the obvious practical difficulties, such an arrangement would not make economic sense because the use of the road would not justify the cost of building and maintaining it. In practice, most networks represent a compromise between the demands of individual users and the costs of construction (Werner, 1968b). Barbour (1977) has attempted to quantify this compromise by measuring the difference between the minimum (builders' solution) and maximum (users' solution) road lengths necessary to link individual farms to market towns in north-east Ulster. Despite an apparently dense network of rural roads, he concluded that the need for economy in public expenditure, rather than the minimization of the farmers' operating costs, has been the primary determinant of the pattern.

The relationship between transport networks and the areas they serve was graphically portrayed by Jefferson (1928) in a series of maps of the various continents. Areas within 10 miles of a railway line were superimposed as white corridors on a black background. This representation ensured that whereas the background was eliminated entirely over much of Western Europe and the eastern half of the US, it was scratched by relatively few white traceries in Africa, Asia, Latin America and Australasia. The 10-mile limit was taken to be a reasonable estimate of the outer margin of accessibility to the 'civilizing rails'. The validity of this estimate will obviously vary with the nature of the intervening terrain and the availability

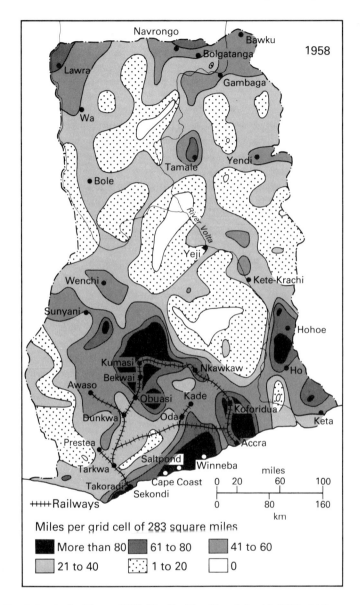

Fig. 9.9 Road density in Ghana, 1958 (Taaffe, Morrill and Gould, 1963, 512).

of complementary forms of transport. Kolars and Malin (1970), for example, used a corresponding figure of 25 miles in a study of accessibility to Turkish railways on the grounds that this represents the approximate limit of a day's caravan journey. Cartographic representations of network density have been supplemented by calculations which express route length relative to area. Ginsburg (1961) has done this for the road and rail networks of approximately 130 countries. He derived a mean density of 10.3 km per 100 km² for roads and a corresponding figure of 0.95 for railways. Two-thirds of the countries analysed were found to lie below each of these mean values. The distribution of countries relative to the mean suggests that those with above-average network densities are also more highly developed in economic terms. Thus European countries tended to have high densities whereas such African states as Ethiopia and Liberia were found at the other end of the spectrum. This correlation between network density and economic development at an international scale is paralleled by a similar association at the level of individual countries. Figure 9.9 shows the distribution of road densities in Ghana in 1958 (Taaffe, Morrill and Gould, 1963). Not surprisingly, the highest values are aligned along the coast, between the capital city of Accra and the major port of Takoradi, and are also focused on Kumasi, which is the principal centre of Ghana's cocoa industry. Correlations between network density and indices of development provide only circumstantial evidence of a causal link between the provision of transport facilities and economic growth. Further insight into the nature of this relationship may be gained by viewing networks as dynamic rather than as static elements of the landscape.

9.2 Evolution of Networks

That transport networks are subject to change is readily apparent in the form of abandoned routes such as disused canals and overgrown railway cuttings and also in the form of additional links such as new motorways and by-passes. What is less obvious is the fact that they display characteristic sequences of development. These sequences, which have been identified in various case-studies, have been formalized into a number of evolutionary models. Although such models run the risk of partitioning what is an essentially continuous process into a series of artificial stages, this weakness is more than offset by the insights which they provide into the nature of network change. The following section outlines two models relevant to situations in which demands for movement within an area are generated by (i) internal forces and (ii) external forces, and then discusses the relationship between (iii) network change and economic development.

9.2.1 Internal Movement and Network Change

Models of network change may either adopt a composite view in which the interrelationship between several kinds of transport route are examined or they may have the more restricted objective of analysing the sequential development of a network serving a single mode. Composite models acknowledge the fact that the orientation of a later network may be strongly influenced by an existing structure. For example, the first canals in England were extensions of the navigable river systems which penetrated inland from the estuaries of the Thames, the Humber and the Severn. Similarly, many of the early railways served merely as short feeder routes linking coal mines to the canal system. Subsequently, the canals were displaced by the railways, although one of the continuing problems facing governments is how to coordinate effectively the differing modes in a fully integrated national transport system. The complexities of this task emphasize the point that

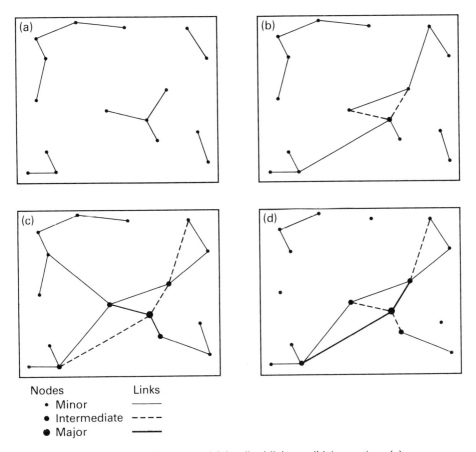

Nodes   Links
  • Minor   ———
  • Intermediate ----
  ● Major   ━━━

Fig. 9.10 A model of network change: (a) localized linkage; (b) integration; (c)
(c) intensification; (d) selection.

it is often easier to understand the forces which shape network development by
treating individual modes in isolation from one another. Figure 9.10 identifies four
stages in the evolution of such a single-mode network. This model incorporates
certain assumptions. Firstly, the area served by the network is regarded as a self-
contained unit in the sense that there is no interaction with places beyond its boundaries. This situation is difficult to find in reality. Although the UK is an island,
the structure of its road and rail networks reflects the significance of the major
ports in its overseas trade. A second assumption is implicit in the fact that the
network evolves around a fixed distribution of nodes. This suggests that routes
develop exclusively in response to demands for movement created by existing
nodes. However, the process may be reversed as spatial relationships are changed
by the extension of a network. This problem is discussed more fully in section
9.2.3. A final qualification relates to the distinction between the overall topological
properties of the network shown in Figure 9.10 and the characteristics of its individual links. These are represented as straight-line connections on an isotropic

surface, but differences in their quality and capacity are identified by adopting an arbitrary threefold classification which applies both to the routes themselves and the nodes which they connect.

The first stage of network development is initiated by the construction of short links between adjacent and complementary nodes (Fig. 9.10a). The structure is composed of isolated segments and overall connectivity is therefore low. During this phase of *localized linkage* there is no differentiation in the relative importance of the various nodes and individual links are of uniformly poor quality. The second phase of *integration* is self-explanatory (Fig. 9.10b). Both the connectivity and the density of the network are increased as previously independent sub-systems are joined up. Some differentiation begins to occur as certain nodes are able to take advantage of favourable locations within the embryo network. The *intensification* stage sees the conversion of branching structures into circuit networks thereby enabling direct movement between places that had formerly been connected only by round-about routes via other nodes. On the other hand, the improved connectivity which such developments imply is more than offset by the construction of feeder routes which ensure that even the most remote places are incorporated within a single comprehensive network (Fig. 9.10c). However, the life of these smaller branches tends to be short as the traffic proves inadequate to justify the investment. Consequently, the network is pruned in the final stage of *selection* as a high proportion of total movement is concentrated upon relatively few major routes and there is a return to a structure in which circuits rather than branches are the predominant characteristic (Fig. 9.10d). Certain peripheral nodes are eliminated from the network altogether, but this does not necessarily mean their total isolation as they may be served by another mode of transport.

Although this model may seem abstract and over-simplified, it closely matches the evolution of the railway network in Britain and the maps in Figure 9.11 may be regarded as analogous to each of the stages represented in Figure 9.10. In 1835 (Fig. 9.12a), the railways in Britain were restricted to short isolated links which reflected the actions of innovators who were quick to see the opportunities presented by the new mode of transport. Many of these early lines were built to move coal. The pioneering Stockton and Darlington Railway, for example, had its origins in a scheme to link the Durham coalfield with the jetties of the River Tees by means of a horse-drawn plateway. Several other short links, such as the Leicester and Swannington Railway, were specifically built to meet the demand for moving coal from the mines to nearby markets. The Liverpool and Manchester Railway was the most significant of these early enterprises because it represented the first attempt explicitly to cater for passenger traffic and was therefore the forerunner of many later developments which transformed the virtually blank railway map of 1835 into a rudimentary network with more than 2,000 miles of track by 1844 (see Dyos and Aldcroft, 1971). The network in 1845 (Fig. 9.11b), just before the 'railway mania' of the late 1840s which added a further 5,000 miles of line within the next seven years, corresponded to the integration phase of the model. Despite the existence of isolated segments in Cornwall, South Wales and Scotland, connectivity had improved and circuits were beginning to be established. Birmingham, for example, was located at the apex of two triangular networks linking Bristol and London in the south and Liverpool, Manchester and Leeds in the north. By 1914 (Fig. 9.11c), the British railway network had reached its maximum extent

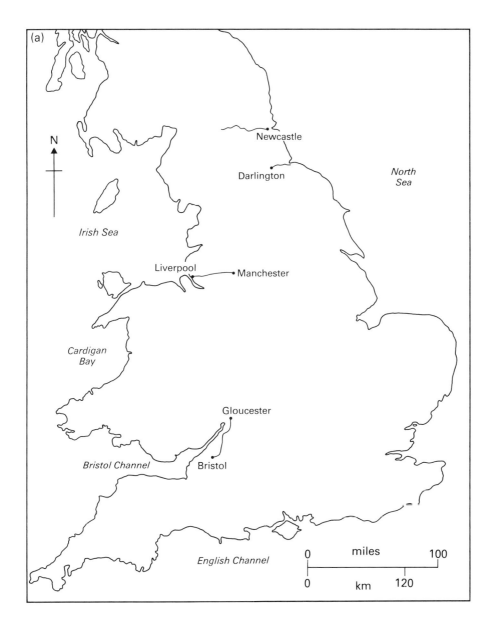

Fig. 9.11 The railway network in England and Wales in: (a) 1835; (b) 1845; (c) 1914; (d) 1978. (*Note:* Several minor lines and plateways are omitted from the maps for 1835 and 1845.)

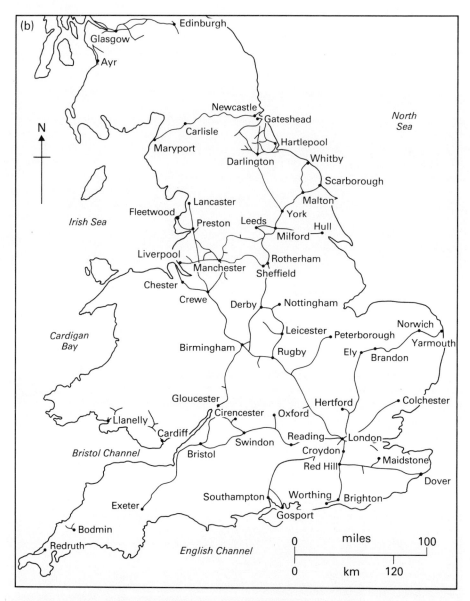

of over 23,000 miles. Connectivity between the major towns and cities had improved not only by virtue of the progressive transformation of branching structures into circuits, but also as a result of corporate amalgamations. Nevertheless, piecemeal development by separate companies had led to the duplication of routes between the major cities. Although the great density of lines in 1914 gives the impression of a highly integrated network, detailed examination indicates a substantial increase in the number of short branch lines as compared with 1845. Most of these lines were constructed around the turn of the century when the

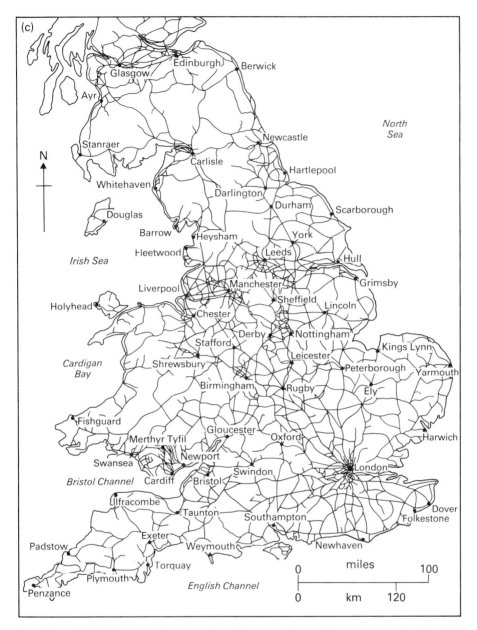

(c)

Edinburgh
Glasgow
Berwick
Ayr
North Sea
Stanraer
Newcastle
N
Carlisle
Hartlepool
Whitehaven
Darlington
Durham
Scarborough
Douglas
Barrow
Heysham
York
Fleetwood
Leeds
Hull
Irish Sea
Liverpool
Manchester
Grimsby
Holyhead
Sheffield
Chester
Lincoln
Derby
Nottingham
Stafford
Kings Lynn
Cardigan Bay
Shrewsbury
Leicester
Peterborough
Yarmouth
Birmingham
Rugby
Ely
Fishguard
Gloucester
Oxford
Harwich
Merthyr Tyfil
Newport
Swansea
Swindon
London
Bristol Channel
Cardiff
Bristol
Dover
Ilfracombe
Folkestone
Taunton
Southampton
Exeter
Newhaven
Padstow
Weymouth
Torquay
miles   100
Plymouth
English Channel
Penzance
0   km   120

benefits of the 'railway age' were enjoyed by even the smallest community. By 1975, however, many of these communities were once again dependent upon other forms of transport as the total length of the network had contracted to less than half of its 1914 peak (Fig. 9.11d). This contraction has been achieved not only by closing branch lines in rural areas, but also by eliminating certain main lines, such as the coastal link between North and South Wales, where the population is unable to sustain traffic at an economic level. Many duplicated lines have also been closed and British Rail has concentrated its investment upon improving the quality and

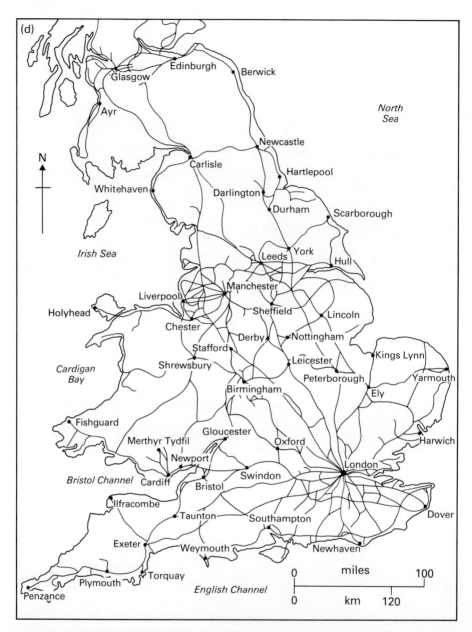

(d)

capacity of the principal inter-city routes which account for the bulk of the traffic carried on the network. Comparison of the situations in 1845 and 1975 reveals many similarities between the integration and selection stages of network development. The prestigious inter-city lines of the 1970s were nearly all in existence by the mid-nineteenth century and the importance of these routes to the contemporary finances of British Rail may be regarded as yet another illustration of positive feedback through time as the early establishment of rail links reinforced the advantages of the major urban centres.

9.2.2 External Movement and Network Change

An alternative model of network change is indicated in Figure 9.12. It differs in two respects from the one we have applied to the British railway system. Firstly, it is a composite model in the sense that the basic structure of road, railway and airline networks is assumed to be the same at successive points in time as the different modes of transport adopt common alignments. Secondly, a coastline is introduced into the model in order to demonstrate the way in which the evolution of a transport network may be oriented towards certain ports in response to demands for movement which are generated by external forces. This type of situation is best demonstrated by the experience of former colonies and the model outlined in Figure 9.12 is largely based upon empirical evidence assembled from West Africa (Taaffe, Morrill and Gould, 1963). However, transport development in

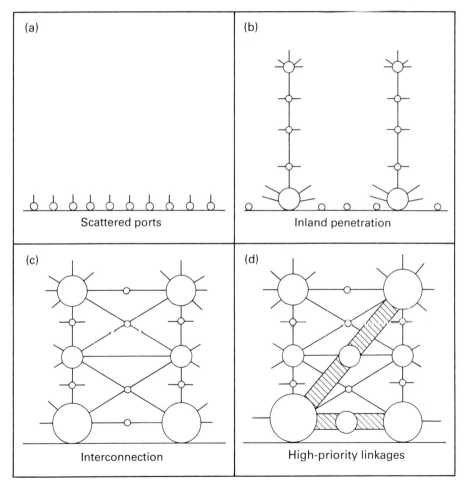

Fig. 9.12 A 'colonial' model of network change: (a) scattered ports; (b) inland penetration; (c) interconnection; (d) high priority linkages (Taaffe, Morrill and Gould, 1963, 504).

remote, underdeveloped areas within large countries may be similarly initiated by external forces. Thus it may be possible to identify certain critical nodes which are analogous to the coastal ports in so far as they represent the interface between the periphery and the rest of the country. The development of scheduled air services in northwestern Australia, for example, may be partially explained in terms of the 'colonial' model of network development (Holsman and Crawford, 1975). Yet another example is provided by the Trans-Siberian Railway in the USSR which has served as a baseline for the subsequent development of the Soviet Arctic.

The first *scattered ports* stage of the model is characterized by the existence of many small ports and trading stations along the coast (Fig. 9.12a). Any contact between these ports is achieved by coastal shipping, which is easier and cheaper than overland transport. The second stage sees the establishment of a few lines of *inland penetration* which link certain ports with interior market centres which themselves begin to serve as the foci of minor radial route systems (Fig. 9.12b). The stimulus to inland penetration in colonial territories was usually based on a combination of political and economic motives. The ability to move fairly quickly between the coast and inland centres was regarded as a prerequisite to the exercise of colonial power beyond a narrow coastal strip. In Ghana, for example, the first serious moves inland by the British were directed towards Kumasi, which was the capital of the rebellious Ashanti (Taaffe, Morrill and Gould, 1963). Similarly, rapid network development was viewed as essential to the achievement of the political objective of creating the Federated Malay States towards the end of the last century (Leinbach, 1975). Both of these countries also demonstrate the economic reasons for penetration associated with the tapping of agricultural and mineral resources. In the case of Ghana, cocoa and gold were the main attractions whereas profits from rubber and tin served as the commercial magnet in Malaya.

A contemporary example of the same kind of process is provided by the exploitation of Alaskan oil (Sugden, 1972). Figure 9.13 is a diagrammatic representation of the essential features of the transport and settlement pattern in Alaska. With the exception of Fairbanks, all the major settlements are located on the coast and therefore may be conceived as 'scattered ports'. In many senses, these settlements are outports of Seattle in Washington State. For example, there are more air services to Seattle from Anchorage, the largest centre in Alaska, and from Juneau, the state capital, than there are flights between these two settlements. Oil developments, initially focused on Cook Inlet on the south coast and more recently on the North Slope fringing the Arctic Ocean, have accentuated this pattern of external control. These developments have also emphasized the significance of the lines of communication which penetrate the Alaskan interior along a north–south axis between Fairbanks and Anchorage. The quality of the road link and the frequency of air services have improved as a result of increased traffic generated by activities on the North Slope. The construction of a winter road between Fairbanks and Prudhoe Bay and the eventual commissioning of the trans-Alaska oil pipeline in mid-1977 have extended this axis northward, but the purposes and patterns of movement in Alaska remain similar to those associated with the inland-penetration stage in former colonies.

Whatever the reasons for inland penetration, the initial routes favour one or two points at the expense of their competitors and provide the basic structure around which the network subsequently develops. During the third *interconnection*

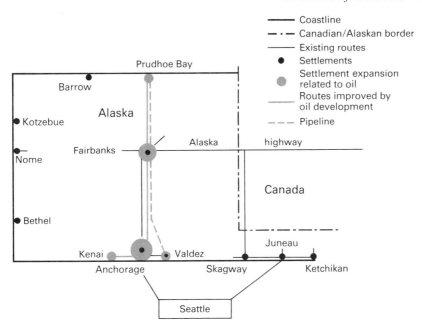

Fig. 9.13 Basic elements of transport networks in Alaska (Sugden, 1972, 228).

stage, feeder routes focused on centres situated at various points along the lines of inland penetration begin to join up so that lateral movement becomes possible (Fig. 9.12c). As the processes of interconnection and port concentration continue, the final stage in the sequence is reached with the emergence of certain *high-priority linkages* between a few dominant nodes (Fig. 9.12d). All of the principal forms of transport are most highly developed along these corridors, which become progressively more dominant as the principal arteries of movement. The final stages of the model are less easy to substantiate with empirical evidence than the early ones. This is partly because many developing countries have not yet achieved the degree of internal coherence in their economic structure which is implied by stage four. Nevertheless, there is no doubt that many countries currently find themselves somewhere between stages two and three. Some of the implications of such externally oriented transport networks in perpetuating the problems of unbalanced growth were discussed in chapter 5. However, transport networks need not necessarily be regarded as imposing a strait-jacket of the past on the pattern of development, but may also be viewed in a positive sense as a means of guiding future development.

9.2.3 Network Change and Economic Development

Models of network change regard the creation of individual links as responses to demands for movement. Thus *localized linkage* (Fig. 9.10a) reflected the existence of specific complementarities between adjacent places such as a coal mine and a nearby town and *inland penetration* (Fig. 9.12b) was related to the achievement of either political or economic objectives. However, networks may also be seen as causes as well as effects. The addition, modification and elimination of routes may bring about substantial changes in the accessibility of places relative to one another. The opening of a new bridge, the realignment of a trunk road and the closure of a railway line will all have a wide range of positive and negative consequences. For example, while the shopper and the motorist may welcome the construction of a by-pass around a congested market town, their feelings are not likely to be shared by shop- and garage-owners who stand to lose business. On the other hand, traders located in a quiet suburban backwater may suddenly find themselves occuping a highly profitable location along the new route. The consequences of new road schemes in urban areas may extend beyond the mere redistribution of traffic flows to the generation of increased overall levels of movement. Studies by Garrison *et al.* (1959) have emphasized the complexity of these impacts and have underlined the point that it may be equally plausible to regard transport investment as a result of a need for movement or as a generator of movement. The problem is very similar to the cycle of circular and cumulative causation described in chapter 5 as being responsible for the phenomenon of unbalanced economic growth. Indeed transport facilities and movement patterns represent an integral part of the cycle and the chicken-and-egg argument regarding the role of networks as lead or lag factors in the development process is therefore of more than academic interest.

Despite their explicit view of routes as effects rather than causes, the logic of models of network change implies that individual links also serve as generators of movement and a feedback mechanism is apparent in the relationship between the various stages. In the case of the 'colonial' model, the ports from and to which the first inland-penetration lines are directed may be selected fortuitously, but this initial choice is critical since it ensures their continued growth at the expense of others. This initial advantage also conditions the future structure of the network since the dominant routes at all stages in its development tend to be focused on the ports which were first established as export centres in the colonial period. This kind of positive-feedback effect is often reflected in the similar orientations of networks serving different modes of transport. For example, the pattern of eighteenth-century canals in England and Wales was closely paralleled by the early railways, and the contemporary motorway system follows essentially the same lines. The reasons for these similarities are self-evident. The major canals were constructed between industrial areas which generated high levels of traffic. The advantages of these areas were reinforced by the improved accessibility which the canals gave them and therefore it was logical that they should also attract the railways and, eventually, the motorways. This sequence of circular and cumulative causation which produces a reciprocal link between route development and movement patterns ensures that an initial network configuration tends to become resistant to change. However, this in itself suggests that some of the forces which create the problem of unbalanced growth may be harnessed to try to solve it. In particular, the construction of transport facilities in advance of demand has been seen as a means of modifying spatial relationships within a country and thereby generating new patterns of movement and growth. South America clearly demonstrates the nature of this problem and also offers some spectacular examples of the use of transport investment as a policy instrument.

Although most South American states gained independence from colonial rule earlier than their counterparts in Africa, existing transport networks in these countries display clear evidence of export orientation. For example, the railways of Argentina and Uruguay were principally designed to facilitate the shipment of meat and wool to Britain, whilst in Chile, Bolivia and Peru they have always been geared towards carrying copper, lead and tin to ports on the Pacific coast (see Gilbert, 1974). These export lines are often matched and reinforced by the orientation of major roads and many Latin American states still have an overall network structure which has advanced little beyond the inland-penetration stage. This situation has political as well as economic implications. The lack of transcontinental links has meant that commercial relationships between countries have been limited and 'Latin America appears as a complex of national space more closely tied to exogenous decision-making centres than to itself' (Melchior, 1972, 88). Support for this interpretation is provided by the fact that the number of telephone calls made from Latin American countries to the US is three times greater than the number of international calls within the continent (Melchior, 1972). Parallels to this situation may be observed within individual countries. Chile in particular has been faced with the problem of trying to integrate within its national territory enclaves dominated and, to a large extent, controlled by US-owned mining corporations (see Porteous, 1973). One of the factors enabling these 'company states' to retain their identity has been the relative lack of interconnecting transport links between the inland lines of penetration through which the mining companies have channelled their exports.

The Pan-American Highway, which more or less follows the axis of the western cordilleras from Ciudad Juarez near the US–Mexico border to Puerto Montt in southern Chile, is the only transcontinental road in South America. The development of east–west links is inhibited by the peripheral distribution of population around the coastal fringes of the continent and also, in many cases, by the mutual suspicion of neighbouring states regarding each other's military ambitions! Nevertheless, there have been several attempts to use new roads to promote economic integration within individual countries. Road transport is especially important in Brazil where successive governments have viewed new highways as a means of encouraging the dispersal of economic development away from the core region centred on São Paulo and Rio de Janeiro. Attention was initially focused upon extending the road network within São Paulo state. An analysis of the relationship between changes in the accessibility of individual nodes and the spatial pattern of population and industrial growth within this area between 1940 and 1960 has provided some support for the argument that transport improvements are the leading factor in the development process (Gauthier, 1968). Despite some evidence of spread effects (see section 5.2.1) within the southeast, the quality and extent of the network in this part of the country were unusual in a national context and elsewhere the Brazilian system of paved roads was still very rudimentary as late as 1964 (Fig. 9.14a). The first road scheme conceived on a national as opposed to a regional scale was the Belem–Brasilia Highway which, when completed in 1960, was the only main road between the vast Amazon region in the north of the country and the economic core in the southeast. This road has served as a focus for land settlement and Katzman (1975) estimates that, by improving accessibility relative to its northern and southern termini, it has attracted as many as

Fig. 9.14 Federal road network in Brazil in: (a) 1964; (b) 1974.

320,000 settlers along its length. This kind of impact has provided the economic justification for a spate of construction which has transformed the structure of the Brazilian road network over a period of only ten years (Fig. 9.14b).

The most ambitious projects have been associated with the policy of developing Amazonia, which occupies more than half the area of Brazil, but which contained only 8 per cent of the country's population and contributed a mere 4 per cent to the gross national product in 1975 (Kleinpenning, 1977). This policy is partly geared towards the attainment of economic and social objectives in that Amazonia not only contains substantial reserves of mineral and timber resources, but also provides possibilities for agricultural settlement. Thus the policy represents a conscious attempt to encourage emigration away from the overpopulated northeast and to offset the economic dominance of the southeast. Political and strategic factors are also important because it is argued that more effective integration of

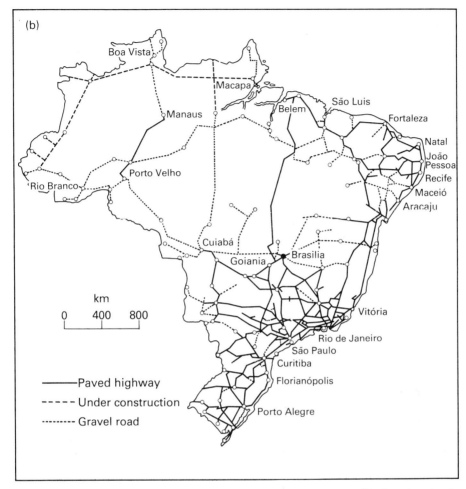

(b)

——— Paved highway

----- Under construction

········ Gravel road

Amazonia into the national territory is necessary to secure Brazil's frontiers in the north and west. Despite criticisms that road-building in Amazonia has displaced indigenous tribal groups, caused ecological damage to the tropical forest environment and benefited only big business corporations and land speculators rather than the underprivileged farmers and landless labourers whom these schemes were officially intended to help, the Brazilian government has pushed ahead with its plans (see Kleinpenning, 1977). The trans-Amazon Highway is a gravel road linking the Belem–Brasilia Highway in the east with the Peruvian border in the west – a distance of nearly 3,500 miles. Construction of a corresponding road on the northern bank of the river began in 1973 and it is eventually hoped to create a vast ring-road around the Amazon Basin which will be divided into two halves by a transverse route connecting Porto Velho in the south with Boa Vista in the north. Although agricultural settlement and cattle-raising have been promoted along the line of the Trans-Amazon Highway and various new industrial plants have been sited in Belem and Manaos, the Amazon road-building programme can only be regarded as a very long-term investment in which economic criteria are secondary to considerations of national power and prestige. Indeed, this programme cannot, because of the evidence that transport investment may stimulate economic development, be rejected out of hand, nor, because of the difficulties of deciding what represents a reasonable time scale over which to judge it, is it ever likely to become an obvious failure. This problem of evaluation is common to any programme of transport investment, although it is a problem which has obvious attractions to the politician since he can never be proved wrong, a situation which Gauthier (1970) cynically suggests may have something to do with the popularity of such programmes as instruments of development policy.

We began this chapter by regarding networks as static features of the landscape and ended it by returning to the familiar theme of circular and cumulative causation. Thus, in the case of developing countries, the lines of inland penetration, originally opened up to meet specific demands for movement, have, by determining the nature of spatial relationships within these countries, subsequently maintained and reinforced geographically unbalanced patterns of economic growth. On the other hand, the reorientation and/or extension of transport networks are seen to offer a possible means of escape from this dilemma. No matter whether networks develop in response to 'natural' economic forces or as a result of a deliberate policy commitment, it is clear that, when viewed through time, they serve the short-run purpose of permitting movement between points in space, but they have the long-run effect of modifying the spatial context within which decision making takes place.

Further Reading

GAUTHIER, H. L. 1968: Transportation and the growth of the São Paulo economy. *Journal of Regional Science* 8, 77–94.

A rigorous attempt to disentangle the cause/effect relationship between transport provision and economic development.

HAGGETT, P. and CHORLEY, R. J. 1969: *Network analysis in geography.* London.

The definitive work which deals with networks in both physical and human geography.

KANSKY, K. J. 1963: Structure of transportation networks. *University of Chicago, Department of Geography, Research Papers,* **84.**

The publication which is most closely associated with the application of graph theoretic concepts to the analysis of transport networks.

KOLARS, J. and MALIN, H. J. 1970: Population and accessibility: an analysis of Turkish railroads. *Geographical Review* **60,** 229–46.

An interesting case-study of the relationship between the characteristics of a network and the distribution of the population which it is intended to serve.

TAAFFE, E. J., MORRILL, R. L. and GOULD, P. R. 1963: Transport expansion in underdeveloped countries. *Geographical Review* **53,** 503–29.

The original version of one of the most 'tested' models in geography!

10 **Points**

It is logical to proceed from the study of linear features to a consideration of point patterns in the landscape. The movements which are directed along specific routes only have meaning in the context of origins and destinations which often exist at junctions on networks. These junctions are frequently associated with distinctive clusters of human activities which may be characterized in geometric terms as points. Settlements are normally represented in this way on maps, and the urban area is composed of features such as hospitals, schools and factories which are themselves essentially punctiform in character.

On a fundamental level, it is possible to identify certain common elements in any distribution in which phenomena are conceived as points in the landscape. In particular, the location of points with respect to one another is often determined by the relative strengths of opposing sets of forces – one set encouraging concentration or clustering, the other set encouraging uniformity or dispersal. Although these forces are implicit in a wide variety of point patterns ranging from the location of shops to the siting of industrial plants, their combined effect is most clearly seen in the distribution of settlements. This chapter proceeds, then, from the general to the particular by considering (i) the properties of point patterns and (ii) settlements as point patterns.

10.1 Properties of Point Patterns

There are certain conceptual problems in analysing spatial arrangements of points. It is possible to distinguish between the characteristics of a distribution which stem from the location of the points with respect to a specific area and those which stem from their location with respect to each other. In the former case, attention is focused on the number of points per area (i.e. density); in the latter, the emphasis is placed upon the distance between points (i.e. spacing). The importance of the density characteristics of point distributions was indirectly considered in chapter 4 in the context of a discussion of some of the problems associated with population pressure on resources (see sections 4.1.1 and 4.2.2). Consequently, we will now examine the significance of *spacing* as one of the basic attributes of any spatial distribution of points. A prerequisite to the analysis of such distributions is their accurate description. Thus we will review some of the problems of describing point patterns and then distinguish between (i) clustered patterns and (ii) dispersed patterns, as limiting cases at opposite ends of a distribution spectrum.

10.1.1 Describing Point Patterns

Figure 10.1 shows a series of point patterns. At one extreme the distance between the points is maximized in a dispersed or uniform distribution, whilst at the other this distance is minimized by placing them on top of one another at a single location. In between these two extremes is the case of a random distribution. The lack of any noticeable order or regularity in such a distribution reflects the fact that, expressed in probability terms, each point has an equal chance of occurring at any position within the area and is not influenced by the location of other points. Thus whilst situations of maximum dispersion or maximum clustering represent unique distributions, there is, for any given area, an infinite number of different distributions which nevertheless conform to this definition of randomness. The difference between clustered, dispersed and random distributions is easy to appreciate in the model situations represented in Figure 10.1, but in practice it is often difficult to distinguish effectively between different spatial arrangements on the basis of qualitative estimates of degrees of dispersion or clustering. This problem has stimulated the development of various techniques specifically designed to facilitate the objective comparison of point patterns. Nearest-neighbour analysis makes it possible to describe any point pattern in terms of a single statistic (Rn) on a scale ranging from 0 to 2.0.* The bottom of this scale corresponds to the situation of extreme clustering and the upper limit one of maximum dispersion, with the mid-point of 1.0 representing a random distribution. Although nearest-neighbour analysis may be criticized on the grounds that, with the exception of the limiting cases, a particular value on the scale does not describe a unique distribution, and also because of the difficulty of establishing the kind of deviation from 1.0 that is required to infer that a distribution is significantly different from random, the technique remains useful because it provides a numerical basis for the objective description and comparison of point patterns.

An interesting example of the application of nearest-neighbour analysis is provided by a study of settlement patterns in the US (King, 1962). Twenty sample areas representing widely differing parts of the country were selected and nearest-neighbour statistics were calculated to describe the characteristics of their respective settlement patterns. The results of this exercise are indicated in Figure 10.2 by plotting the position of each of the sample areas (identified by reference to the states in which they are located) on the Rn-scale. It is noticeable that the most marked tendency towards clustering is associated with the western states of Washington (Rn=0.71) and Utah (Rn=0.70) whereas it is in the midwestern states of Minnesota (Rn=1.38), Missouri (Rn=1.38) and Iowa (Rn=1.35) that the highest scores, indicating a tendency towards dispersed settlement patterns, are found. Physical factors seem to be largely responsible for the low scores in Washington and Utah where the arrangement of pairs of towns along river valleys in otherwise largely uninhabited areas has produced linear clustering. On the other hand, the higher scores in the Midwest are not entirely unexpected given the low relief and the historical legacy of a uniform method of land subdivision.

Although the extreme cases are interesting, they fall far short of the theoretical limits of the nearest-neighbour statistic and the most obvious feature of King's

---

* The upper limit is actually 2.149 for reasons which are explained by Taylor (1977, 133–73). This book provides a good discussion of the derivation and limitations of the nearest-neighbour statistic.

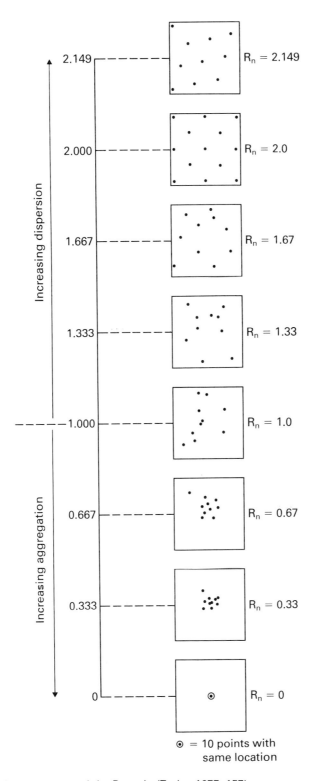

Fig. 10.1 Point patterns and the R_n scale (Taylor, 1977, 157).

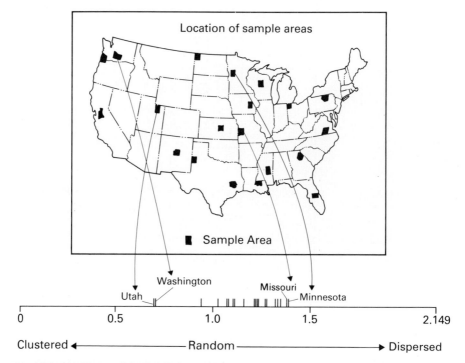

Fig. 10.2 Distribution of settlements in sample areas of the US (after King, 1962).

results is the fact that the vast majority of the sample areas are grouped around the mid-point of the scale. Similar results have been obtained in a corresponding study of settlement patterns in the USSR (Barr, Lindsay and Reinelt, 1971). Indeed practical applications of nearest-neighbour analysis have emphasized time and time again that the range of Rn values displayed by empirically observed point patterns is much more compressed than the theoretical limits would imply. From this it may be inferred that inexplicable chance factors reflected in irrational behaviour on the part of individual decision makers are the dominant influence upon spatial patterns in the landscape. An alternative view, however, might be that forces making for dispersion are balanced in most areas by others making for concentration so that the net result is an apparently random distribution. The validity of this latter interpretation may become more convincing after an examination of such forces in the light of the proposition that dispersion represents the ideal spatial arrangement for certain types of human activity whereas clustering is best for others.

10.1.2 Clustered Patterns

We have already noted a tendency towards clustering in the distribution of human activities. This was related in chapter 4 to the uneven distribution of environmental constraints and resources, and in chapters 5 and 6 to the operation of feedback mechanisms associated with various economic and social processes. All of these explanations rest upon the existence of place-to-place variations in the content of space. However, even if such variations are eliminated by means of the simplifying assumption of an isotropic surface, it is still possible to identify forces which promote clustering. These forces are embraced within the concept of *accessibility*.

Accessibility is an abstract notion which is difficult to define, but it is generally understood to describe the effort involved in getting to a place from other places (see Hansen, 1959; Forbes, 1964; Ingram, 1971). It is therefore a variable quality of location which may be measured in the same kind of units that we have already applied in our discussion of the effects of changes in transport technology upon urban form (see section 6.2.2). A further index of accessibility was introduced in the last chapter where different network structures were shown to benefit certain nodes more than others. The attribute of accessibility is closely related to the role of the principle of least effort as an influence upon human behaviour, and it is not difficult to show that the clustering of certain activities at particular locations represents the most efficient spatial arrangement in the sense that the need for movement is minimized. This may be demonstrated by reference to the role of accessibility in determining (i) land-use patterns within cities and (ii) the internal structure of shopping centres.

Land Use within Cities
The relationship between accessibility and land use has been an important theme in attempts to explain the internal structure of urban areas (see Alonso, 1964). Most cities possess a core area in which many shops and offices are concentrated. This area owes its distinctiveness to the clustering of similar individual establishments which may themselves be regarded as points. One approach to the explanation of these patterns is to regard the city centre, because of its position as the focus of the urban transport system, as the point of maximum accessibility within the built-up area. Thus it is possible to derive a model of urban land use in which different activities are arranged concentrically around the central point depending upon their relative needs for high accessibility with respect to the surrounding population. Land values are regarded as a surrogate measure of accessibility and the various land uses are differentiated on the basis of their ability to pay for the right to use land. Figure 10.3 indicates the way in which this competition between users is theoretically resolved through the operation of the land market. The rent/distance relationship for retail functions is steep because the economic viability of department stores and specialized shops depends upon accessibility to a large population of potential customers. Thus they are willing to pay high rents for a central location, but are not interested in peripheral sites. Similar arguments apply to commercial activities, whilst accessibility is shown in Figure 10.3 to be progressively less important for industrial and residential development. The intersection of each rent/distance line indicates the point at which one function is outbid by another and therefore defines the boundary of each land-use ring around the centre.

This land-economists' interpretation of urban land-use patterns makes several unrealistic assumptions (see Carter, 1972). We have already seen (section 6.2.2) how changes in transport technology have affected time/distance relationships within cities. It was shown that these changes are often oriented along the axis of transport routes. As Yeates (1965) has demonstrated with reference to Chicago, land values respond to these directional variations in accessibility and therefore

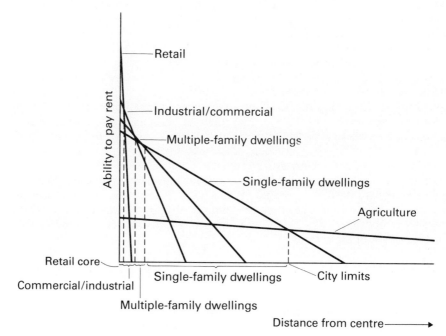

Fig. 10.3 Land values and urban land use.

distort the simple concept of a conical rent-surface rising uniformly to a central peak. Furthermore, the city centre is not always the most accessible point and the effects of increasing car ownership are apparent in the establishment of out-of-town hypermarkets which incorporate the kind of high-order functions associated with the retail core in the land-economists' model. Another weakness is the assumption that the internal structure of the city is a product of unfettered competition between the various land uses. This is at variance with the trend towards greater official intervention in the operation of the land market through the introduction of planning regulations. For example, amenity areas such as Central Park in New York could not survive in a free land market. Nevertheless, the model is not so far removed from the reality of the modern 'western' city, at least as far as its central-area functions are concerned, and Berry (1974) argues, on the basis of a study of land-use trends in Melbourne, that planning controls are generally ineffective in the face of the power of market mechanisms.

Internal Structure of Shopping Centres
The logic of land economics has also been employed on a smaller scale to account for the internal layout of shopping centres. Garner (1966) suggested that differences in the market thresholds (section 5.1.2) of various types of shop should create a concentric arrangement of establishments within shopping centres corresponding to the zonal land-use pattern postulated for the city as a whole. The essence of the argument is presented in Figure 10.4 for a small group of shops located at a crossroads. Three orders of retail establishment are identified with

(a) Shopping centre at crossroads

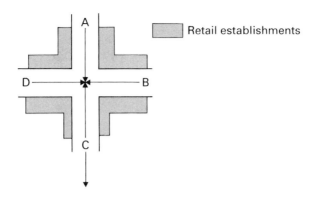

Cross-sections

(b) Accessibility to customers

(c) Sales volume (and bid rents) of three types of business

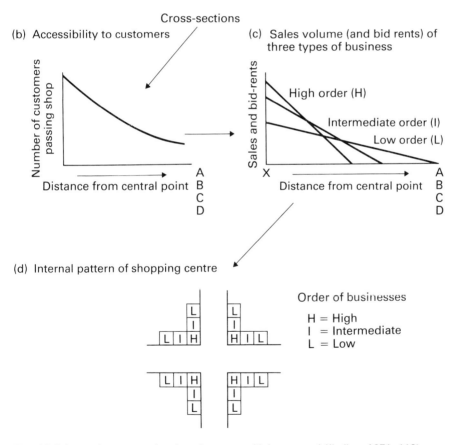

(d) Internal pattern of shopping centre

Order of businesses

H = High
I = Intermediate
L = Low

Fig. 10.4 Internal structure of a shopping centre (Johnston and Kissling, 1971, 118).

successively lower market thresholds. The corner locations at the junction are passed by the greatest number of potential customers and are therefore occupied by high-order businesses whilst intermediate and low-order establishments are arranged in sequence away from these points of maximum accessibility. Garner tested his model against several clusters of shops in Chicago ranging from small neighbourhood groupings to much larger regional centres. This was done by correlating the land value of a site with the threshold level of the establishment occupying it. Although correspondence with the predicted pattern was not always statistically significant, Garner was able to conclude that 'the empirical evidence ... tends to support the hypothesized internal structure of retail nucleations' (Garner, 1966, 165). Although this conclusion does not seem very convincing it would be surprising if a firmer one could be reached as the location of different types of shop is not exclusively determined by the relationship between threshold requirements and accessibility.

10.1.3 Dispersed Patterns

Just as the clustering of many human activities is promoted by considerations of accessibility relative to focal points, so the dispersal of other activities is encouraged by considerations of spacing relative to areas. Thus where individuals or institutions are effectively competing for the right to use space, they will tend to repel one another and thereby create a uniform or dispersed distribution pattern. The settlement of a frontier area is a good example in the sense that pioneer farmers will wish to stake a claim to their own piece of land, which must obviously be separate from existing holdings. The net result of this process, especially where there is some statutory control which ensures uniformity in the size of landholding, tends to be the kind of regular distribution of farmsteads established under the provisions of the Homestead Act during the colonization of the American Midwest. In many situations it is not so much competition for space itself which is important, rather competition for access to the content of space and, in the case of a wide range of economic activities, for access to the population which represents their markets. Thus although clustering is the rule where activities serve the *same* population, dispersal enables competing establishments to secure their own market area and thereby serve *different* populations. This influence upon point patterns may be illustrated by reference to (i) the market area of shops and (ii) the market area of factories.

Market Area of Shops
It is possible to identify certain types of shop that are complementary and which therefore tend to be drawn together in space whereas others are non-complementary and hence tend to be spatially dispersed. Although these shop types may be identified intuitively, attempts have been made to test these ideas more rigorously either by analysing the location of retail facilities relative to one another (see Parker, 1962; Rogers, 1965; Getis and Getis, 1968), or by studying patterns of shopping behaviour (see section 10.2.2). Parker examined the distribution of shops throughout Liverpool, with the exception of the city's central area. He developed indices of attraction and repulsion between different shop types by comparing the

actual incidence of adjacent locations* with the pattern that might have been expected if the shops had been randomly distributed. At one level of generalization, Parker's findings are in accord with Garner's model of the internal structure of shopping centres in so far as he identified retail clusters associated with different orders of function. Thus shops which tend to be patronized on a regular basis such as grocers, butchers and greengrocers are grouped together and 'occasional' shops selling higher-order items such as clothing, furniture and electrical appliances are likewise clustered. However, there are certain significant differences in spatial relationships between shops *within* these two broad groups.

In the case of 'occasional' shops, similar establishments are often drawn together because of the importance of comparison shopping or because they tend to serve a common clientele. Purchasers of items such as clothing and shoes often make their choices only after comparing prices and styles in several shops and it is easier to do this when competing shops are clustered together. Similarly, certain goods which are closely associated in the mind of the shopper are also frequently associated geographically. For example, one of the few strong spatial affinities which Getis and Getis (1968) discovered in their study of retail distributions in the central business districts of several US cities was between shops selling women's clothes and those selling accessories such as handbags and gloves.

Whereas 'occasional' shops of a particular type tend to compete directly for the custom of a common population by clustering in specific locations, lower-order 'daily' shops avoid competition by adopting a dispersed distribution with respect to similar establishments. Parker found that both greengrocers and grocers, for example, were widely dispersed throughout the shopping centres he studied and this was reflected in high indices of repulsion within these groups. Low-order shops which either overlap in function or offer products that are close substitutes may also be expected to repel one another. Butchers and fishmongers and greengrocers and florists represent such combinations and Parker was again able to demonstrate a tendency towards dispersal in these cases.

Market Area of Factories
Dispersed-location strategies designed to avoid competition are not adopted by low-order shops only and a similar approach may be employed in industry. We have already discussed certain principles of industrial location by reference to Weber's locational triangle (see section 6.1). Quite apart from its assumption of direct proportionality between distance travelled and transport costs, this model suffers from a number of other weaknesses. First, it treats the market as a single point whereas the products of most factories are widely distributed to a multiplicity of purchasers. Second, it refers only to the location of the individual plant and fails to recognize that the location of one factory may be influenced by that of another. This influence may either be positive, where linkages promote agglomeration (see section 5.1.1), or it may be negative, where competing plants are placed as far apart as possible in order to secure access to independent market areas.

* For the purposes of this study, adjacent location was defined as a next-door neighbour or a shop separated by not more than one postal number. This requirement of adjacency is very strict and it might be argued that, at this scale of study, shops separated by three or four intervening establishments along a street are sufficiently close to be regarded as 'neighbours'. Such problems associated with the definition of proximity are difficult to resolve in anything other than an arbitrary manner and they have an important bearing on the results, as Getis and Getis (1968) have shown.

The latter strategy enables each plant to supply a particular section of the market at a lower price than its rivals.

The theoretical basis of such spatial monopolies may be explained diagrammatically. In Figure 10.5, three factories selling identical products are located along the horizontal axis which is also assumed to represent the distribution of consumers. The price charged at any position on this line is composed of the costs of production at the factory plus the costs of delivery which are assumed to be directly proportional to distance. The intersection of the delivered price lines from each factory defines the boundary of their respective markets and it can be seen that plant B commands a smaller segment of the linear market by virtue of its

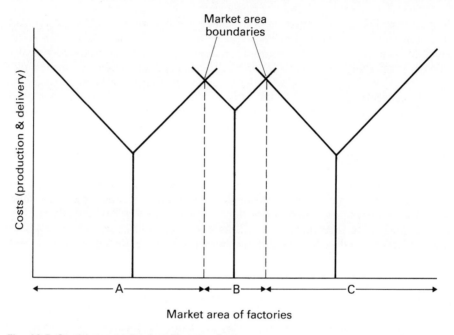

Fig. 10.5 Spatial monopolies in a linear market.

higher production costs. The one-dimensional representation of Figure 10.5 may be visualized in two-dimensional terms with each plant located at the centre of its own market area. In theory, more and more factories are introduced into the landscape serving smaller and smaller market areas until the minimum sales threshold is reached in each case. In practice, this equilibrium situation is never attained. For any industry, the structure of both production and transport costs as well as the distribution of customers are constantly changing so that the optimal spatial arrangement of factories and market areas is in a permanent state of flux. In particular, the combination of a trend towards larger units of production and a relative fall in transport costs is tending, in many industries, to enlarge market areas rather than reduce them (Smith, 1971).

Post-war developments in the brewing industry in the UK clearly reveal the inter-

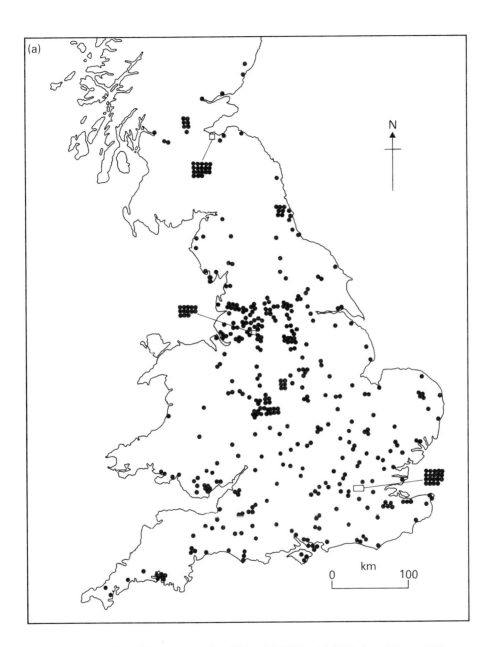

Fig. 10.6 Distribution of breweries in the UK in: (a) 1951; (b) 1971 (after Watts, 1977, 233).

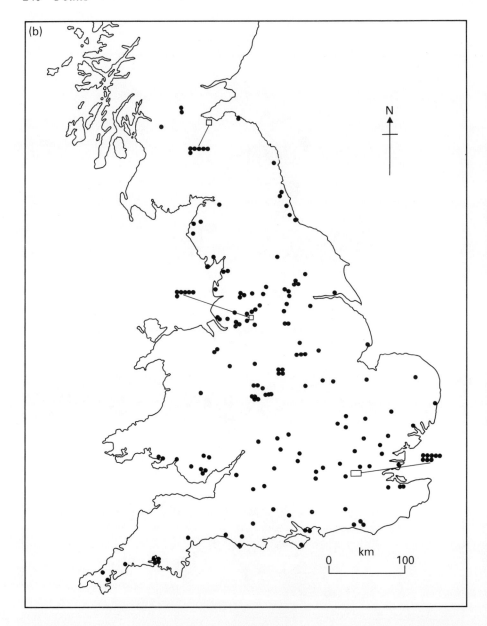

relationships between plant location and market areas (Watts, 1977). The distribution of breweries in 1951 closely reflected the distribution of population with major
concentrations in the big cities and a fairly even scatter throughout the rest of
the country (Fig. 10.6a). Output was mainly of traditional 'cask' beers which
deteriorated rapidly, thereby accentuating the need for a brewery to be close to
its market. Consequently, the typical brewery had a market area with a radius

of approximately 25 km which merged into the territory of adjacent plants at its perimeter. By 1971 the number of breweries had fallen to 170 as compared with 435 twenty years earlier. This change was mainly due to an increase in the optimum level of brewery output which made it possible to concentrate production at fewer locations. The switch to 'keg' beers was also important since not only are these of higher value than 'cask' beers and therefore better able to bear the cost of transport (see section 8.1.2), but they also retain their quality for a longer period and therefore do not have to reach the customer as quickly. Figure 10.6b suggests that the pattern of closures was largely at the expense of the non-metropolitan breweries. These were smaller anyway and also had higher distribution costs because they served a more dispersed population. Watts confirmed the visual impression of metropolitan concentration by statistical analysis and demonstrated that the survival rates of breweries in or near large population centres were significantly higher than for those in intermediate locations between the major cities. On the other hand, the most remote plants also had a better chance of survival because they were protected by distance from the competition of metropolitan breweries and thus closures in places such as Cornwall, west Wales and Cumbria were less drastic. The survival of these peripheral breweries underlines the validity of the concept of spatial monopoly despite the concentration of production in the cities. Indeed this in itself does not indicate that the relationship between plant location and market area which determines the spacing of breweries has become irrelevant, but is simply a reflection of the fact that this relationship is maintained over greater distances than in the past.

10.2 Settlements as Point Patterns

The changing distribution of breweries in the UK has largely been due to a general increase in the average size of the typical plant. This link between the output and location of breweries is paralleled in many other point patterns where spatial arrangements reflect a complex relationship between the size and spacing of the individual elements which contribute to the overall pattern. Nowhere is this more apparent than in the distribution of settlements. Casual observation suggests that villages are more numerous and closely spaced than towns, which themselves bear a similar relationship to cities. Although this situation is so familiar that it may easily be taken for granted, the study of settlements has traditionally occupied a central position within human geography. Indeed, an extensive literature is concerned with the spatial distribution of settlements. One of the most pervasive influences upon this literature has been the work of Walther Christaller, who developed his ideas in the early 1930s with reference to the settlement patterns of southern Germany. Christaller regarded towns and villages as 'central places' which provide goods and services to a surrounding hinterland and he derived a model of settlement location based on this premise. This is taken as a starting-point in the following section which compares (i) settlement patterns in the theory and (ii) settlement patterns in reality.

10.2.1 Settlement Patterns in Theory

Although central-place theory is generally associated with the original publication of Christaller (trans. Baskin, 1966) it is important to acknowledge the later contributions of others such as Lösch (1954) and Berry and Garrison (1958). However, these refinements and modifications have been extensively reviewed elsewhere (see Berry, 1967; Beavon, 1977) and an understanding of Christaller's basic model is sufficient to grasp the implications of central-place theory for the analysis of settlement patterns. Such an understanding may be gained by reviewing the assumptions of the model and by determining the logical consequences of these assumptions by deriving a theoretical central-place system.

The Assumptions of the Model
Christaller's central-place system is based on the relationship between a set of suppliers of goods and services and a larger set of consumers. The actions of each of these groups of decision makers can be understood through an appreciation of two fundamental concepts relating to the sale and purchase of any good or service – firstly, its population or sales *threshold*, and secondly, its *range*. The threshold concept was discussed in chapter 5 (section 5.1.2) and it refers to the minimum level of sales or equivalent population necessary to make the provision of a good or service an economic proposition. Whilst the threshold of a good is important to the supplier because it defines the margin between making a profit and making a loss, the behaviour of consumers in Christaller's system is determined by the range of a good. This is the maximum distance that a consumer is prepared to travel to purchase a particular good. It is based upon the proposition that most people will go further to buy an expensive item such as a piece of furniture than they will to obtain a less valuable commodity such as a loaf of bread. Thus for any good or service it is theoretically possible to identify two limits around a central place – the inner line defines the area which encloses the necessary threshold whilst the outer one indicates the range beyond which the consumer is unwilling to travel.

The notions of range and threshold as they apply to individual central-place functions provide the conceptual basis of Christaller's model, but the spatial implication of the interrelationships between many such functions can only be appreciated when certain assumptions are made regarding the behaviour of consumers and the nature of the environment in which they are placed. The principle of least effort governs the actions of purchasers, who therefore always travel to the nearest centre at which a particular good is available. Any incentive to go to a more distant centre is eliminated by assuming that there are no differences in price or quality between centres. Complications associated with variations in the content of space are similarly eliminated by postulating the existence of an isotropic plain upon which a population composed of consumers with identical purchasing power is evenly distributed. In the absence of any physical obstacles or transport systems, there are no directional constraints on movements which take the form of straight-line journeys to the nearest central place at which a specific commodity may be purchased. The availability of goods and services in different levels of central place is predetermined by specifying distinctive 'bundles' of functions with common threshold requirements.

A Theoretical Central-Place System
Given the starting conditions established by these assumptions, a series of events may be identified in the evolution of a theoretical central-place system. The structure of such a system incorporates a 'horizontal' component relating to the

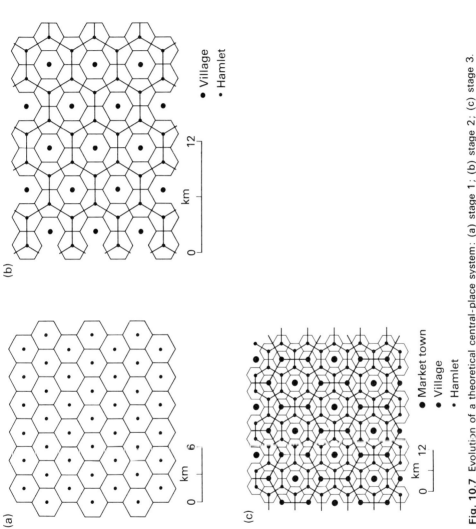

Fig. 10.7 Evolution of a theoretical central-place system: (a) stage 1; (b) stage 2; (c) stage 3.

spacing of central places and a 'vertical' component relating to their size. These two components are interrelated, but it is convenient to consider them separately.

The spatial arrangement of settlements begins with an even distribution of small central places which may be termed hamlets. Each hamlet provides a common set of services and lies at the centre of its own market area (Fig. 10.7a). This area takes the form of a hexagon because of the problems of overlap and unserved territory associated with circles. The size of this area, and hence the spacing of the hamlets, is determined by the threshold population required to support the services which they provide. The boundaries of the hexagons enclose sufficient consumers to ensure that the suppliers of central-place goods make just enough money to remain in business. It therefore follows that the hamlets are 'packed'

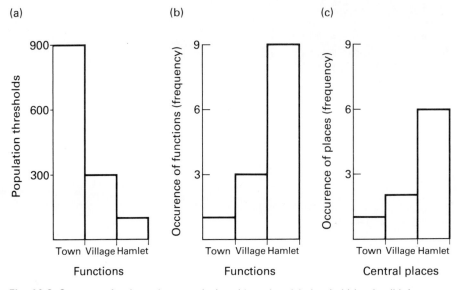

Fig. 10.8 Structure of a three-tier central-place hierarchy: (a) threshold levels; (b) frequency of functions; (c) frequency of central places.

as tightly as possible in the landscape so that the overall distance which the consumers have to travel is minimized. The hamlets supply only basic frequently demanded goods and a number of larger settlements (villages), which incorporate all these functions together with some additional services, may be expected to develop. The market areas of the villages absorb and enclose those of the hamlets in such a way that the regular arrangement of central places is maintained. Since the goods and services of the villages are needed less often, they not only have higher thresholds, but also have a greater range since consumers are willing to travel further. Consequently, the villages are more widely spaced than the hamlets. The final stage in Figure 10.7c is represented by a series of towns, although this process could obviously be extended to further levels of central place as Christaller demonstrated by identifying seven orders of settlement in his study area of southern Germany.

In addition to producing a distinctive spatial arrangement of central places, another logical consequence of the assumption of common thresholds for specific 'bundles' of goods is the emergence of a hierarchical progression in which there is a clear relationship between the size of a settlement and the number of times it appears in the landscape. This 'vertical' component of the central-place model may be demonstrated by considering the simple example of a three-level hierarchy corresponding to the hamlet–village–town sequence in Figure 10.7. For the purposes of explanation, we will assume that the services are provided to an island with a total population of 900. This is equivalent to the threshold of the town functions whilst the village and hamlet services have thresholds of 300 and 100 respectively (Fig. 10.8a). The occurrence of each order of settlement is predetermined by specifying the total population of the island and the thresholds of each set of functions. Thus one set of town functions are provided, three sets of village functions and nine sets of hamlet functions (Fig. 10.8b). Since a high-order place supplies all lower threshold functions, it follows that, in addition to a single town, the island will be served by two villages and six hamlets (Fig. 10.8c), thereby producing a stepped hierarchy of different sized settlements.

10.2.2 Settlement Patterns in Reality

The apparent simplicity of the central-place model has stimulated many attempts to establish its validity by empirical testing. Indeed, the location of central places is one of the most intensively studied aspects of human geography (see Berry and Pred, 1961) and any review of this work must necessarily be highly selective. Nevertheless, some of this literature is utilized in the following section, which considers the implications of testing the central-place model and tries to resolve some of the resulting contradictions between theory and reality by relaxing the assumptions of the central-place model.

Testing the Model
Although several variations of the basic central-place system represented in Figure 10.7 have been developed both by Christaller and by others, these modifications retain common spatial and structural regularities relating firstly to their 'horizontal' and secondly to their 'vertical' components. Thus they all reveal a consistent relationship between the size and spacing of central places and also indicate some form of stepped hierarchy. The 'horizontal' component always implies that larger places are more widely separated than smaller ones and that centres of the same size are located equidistant from one another at regular intervals throughout the landscape. The 'vertical' component always implies that some kind of arithmetic or geometric relationship, such as the 1–3–9 sequence outlined in section 10.2.1, is maintained between the number of centres at each level in the hierarchy. We will now examine how far these attributes of the central-place model are matched in reality by reference to (i) the spatial distribution of settlements and (ii) the size distribution of settlements.

Spatial Distribution – Numerous attempts have been made to identify in reality the uniform spatial arrangement of central places deduced theoretically by Christaller. The American Midwest has attracted particular attention because it approximates

Christaller's assumptions of a flat plain with a uniform population distribution.*
Berry (1967) provides examples from South Dakota, Iowa and Illinois whilst
Brush (1953) tested the model in Wisconsin. Brush calculated the mean straight-
line distances separating settlements in a three-tier hierarchy and found that hamlets were 5.5 miles from one another, villages were 9.9 miles apart and towns
occurred at intervals of 21.2 miles. In a later study, Brush and Bracey (1955) argued
that these distances were closely matched in a similar three-level rural settlement
hierarchy in southern England. Although these comparable results in widely differing areas are superficially impressive, they are less convincing when it is appreciated that Brush and Bracey employed no objective method for distinguishing
between the different levels in the hierarchy. The rigid classification of settlements
into hamlets, villages or towns obscures gradations in population size and
functional complexity which exist in reality. Thus the mean distances are based
upon the prior definition of 'unique' types of central place and the validity of the
distance calculations rests upon the validity of the classification scheme.

Thomas (1961) indicated a way out of this circular argument through the use
of correlation and regression analysis.† Rather than seek to establish precise distances between different levels of central place, Thomas set himself the more limited
objective of demonstrating the existence of a statistical relationship between the
size and spacing of settlements. With reference to a sample of settlements in the
state of Iowa, he measured the distance between each settlement and its nearest
neighbour of similar population size.‡ By analysing many such measurements, he
was able to show that 35 per cent of the total variation in the distances between
the sample settlements and their nearest neighbour was 'explained' by the relationship with population size. Although significant in statistical terms, this is nevertheless a fairly low level of explanation. Olsson and Persson (1964) obtained a very
similar result in a corresponding piece of work relating to central places in Sweden
and these studies emphasize that the spacing of settlements is not exclusively determined by their size as the Christaller model implies, but is also affected by other
variables.

One of the advantages of the technique of regression analysis employed by
Thomas is its ability to help identify these other variables. This may be illustrated
by reference to O'Farrell's (1970) study of the spacing of urban centres (i.e. with
populations exceeding 1,500 in 1966) in the Irish Republic. He began by attempting
to predict variations in the distance between these centres in terms of variations
in their size as suggested by the Christaller model. Approximately half the distance
variation could be 'explained' on this basis. However, when the actual distance
between a particular settlement and its nearest neighbour of equal or greater population size§ is compared with the value predicted by the regression equation, a
distinctive pattern emerges (Fig. 10.9a). Generally speaking, centres in the western
part of the country are more widely spaced than predicted whilst those in the east

* Yeates and Garner (1971) provide a good summary of North American work.
† See glossary.
‡ What is meant by 'similar' raises much the same kind of classification problems faced by Brush and
Bracey in distinguishing between towns, villages and hamlets. However, Thomas employs a more
rigorous approach, which clearly justifies the working definition adopted in his study.
§ Distance measurement to a larger centre, when this is nearer than a centre of similar size, is justified
by O'Farrell as being consistent with one of Christaller's principal postulates – that each higher-order
central place performs all the functions of lower-order central places.

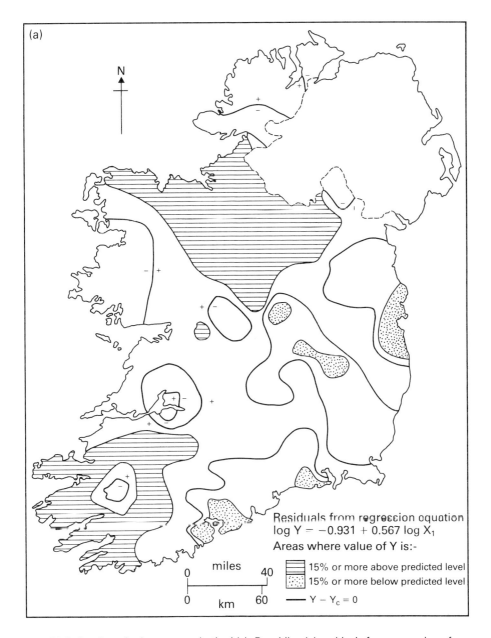

(a)

Residuals from regression equation
log Y = −0.931 + 0.567 log X₁
Areas where value of Y is:-

15% or more above predicted level
15% or more below predicted level
Y − Y_c = 0

miles
0   40

0   60
km

Fig. 10.9 Spacing of urban centres in the Irish Republic: (a) residuals from regression of spacing on settlement size; (b) residuals from regression of spacing on settlement size and income levels (O'Farrell, 1970, 283 and 285).

and south tend to be closer together. The counties of Sligo and Leitrim in the northwest and parts of Kerry, Cork and Limerick in the southwest show especially high positive residuals from regression.* These anomalies begin to make sense when it is remembered that the west of Ireland has been suffering from out-migration and economic stagnation ever since the 1840s whilst conversely Dublin and,

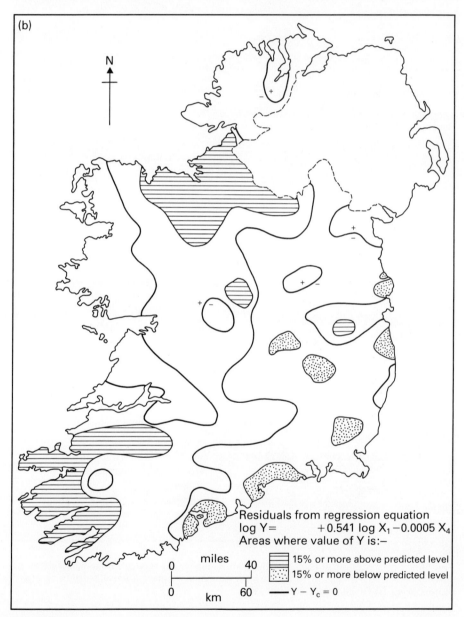

(b)

N

Residuals from regression equation
$$\log Y = \quad\quad + 0.541 \log X_1 - 0.0005 X_4$$
Areas where value of Y is:–

	15% or more above predicted level
	15% or more below predicted level
$Y - Y_c = 0$	

miles
0 — 40

0 — 60
km

* See glossary.

to a lesser extent, Cork have been the principal centres of population growth and industrial investment. This contrast prompted O'Farrell to introduce another factor into his regression equation – spatial variations in income. He hypothesized that centres may be expected to be more closely spaced in areas where consumers have greater purchasing power because a larger number of central-place functions may be sustained. Support for this argument was provided by the resulting multiple-regression equation which increased the overall level of 'explanation' to 60 per cent and, when translated into map form, reduced the area extent of the residuals (Fig. 10.9b).

The results of O'Farrell's study compare very favourably with a similar exercise carried out by King (1961) for a sample of 200 settlements throughout the US. Despite incorporating six factors in his equation, King was only able to achieve a 25 per cent level of 'explanation'. The discrepancy between the results of these studies is not surprising, however, when the vast difference in the size of the two countries is considered. Indeed, these discrepancies point to the principal reason why spatial arrangements of settlements in the real world do not match those postulated in Christaller's model. O'Farrell's results are better simply because Eire, with its more uniform physical environment, its predominantly agricultural economic base and its relatively even distribution of population, corresponds much more closely than does the US (taken as a whole) to the assumptions of the central-place model.

Size Distribution – Empirical studies have emphasized that, in practice, the spatial distribution of settlements does not conform to the regular hexagonal lattice of Christaller's model. O'Farrell and others have used regression analysis effectively to demonstrate that large centres are more widely spaced than small ones, but attempts to make more positive statements about mean distances between settlements of similar size run into the difficulty of establishing a satisfactory basis for the definition of such size-classes. As already noted with reference to the work of Brush and Bracey, there has often been a tendency to assume the existence of a hierarchy without really assembling evidence to justify such an assumption. Efforts to resolve this problem have adopted widely differing scales of study as some workers have scanned the evidence for urban-size 'jumps' between major cities whilst others have looked for similar discontinuities at the opposite end of the settlement spectrum.

The apparent conflict between the so-called *rank-size rule* and the central-place model has stimulated a number of international comparisons of city-size distributions in different countries. As originally formulated by Zipf (1941), the rank-size rule states that if all settlements in a country are arranged in descending order by population, the size of the *r*th settlement bears the following relationship to that of the largest one:

$$Pr = \frac{Pi}{R}$$

where *Pr* is the population of the *r*th settlement,
    Pi is the population of the largest settlement,
    R is the size-rank of the *r*th settlement.

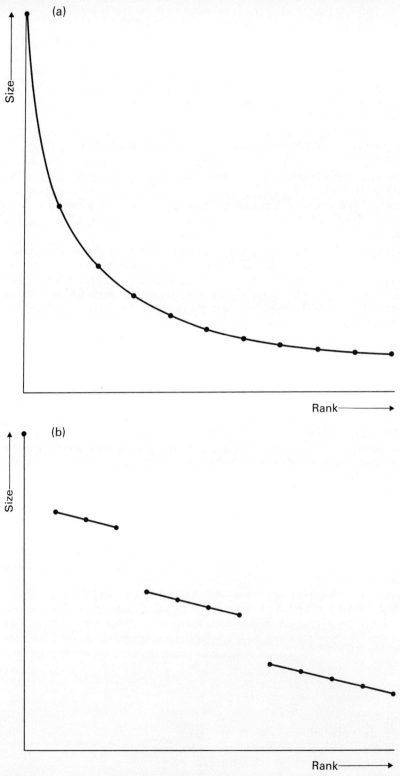

Fig. 10.10 Settlement size distribution implied by: (a) rank-size rule; (b) central-place model.

In verbal terms, this simply means that the second-largest settlement will be half the size of the first, the third will be one-third the size, the fourth will be one-quarter the size, and so on. When plotted on a graph, this relationship produces a smooth descending curve which becomes progressively shallower at its lower end (Fig. 10.10a). By contrast, Christaller's ideas imply the existence of a stepped hierarchy of distinctive functional groupings. Since functional complexity is positively correlated with the population of a centre, these groupings tend to correspond with particular size-classes and the central-place model may be expected to produce the kind of rank-size distribution indicated in Figure 10.10b.

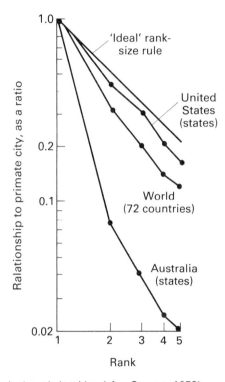

Fig. 10.11 Observed rank-size relationships (after Stewart, 1958).

The rank-size rule differs from the central-place model in the sense that Zipf regarded it as a generalization based on observation rather than as a logical structure deduced from a set of clearly stated assumptions. Despite its empirical foundation, tests of the rank-size rule have revealed great variation about the norm specified by the formula. Stewart (1958) examined the ratio between the populations of the five largest cities in each of 72 different countries. Some indication of the differences between them is provided by Figure 10.11. Both axes on the graph have been transformed into logarithmic form so that the rank-size curve of Figure 10.10a appears as a straight line. Whereas the US shows a reasonably close correspondence to this line, the ratio between the five largest Australian cities shows considerable divergence, with the centres below Sydney much smaller than expected. Although Stewart's study suggests that city-size distributions rarely accord with the predictions of the rank-size rules it nevertheless seems that these distributions take the form of a more or less smooth curve (albeit a curve which differs widely in slope from country to country)* rather than a stepped hierarchy.

This conclusion does not necessarily invalidate the logic of Christaller's argument and many attempts have been made to show that the rank-size rule and the central-place model are not incompatible (see Richardson, 1973). A common thread running through these studies is the proposition that the introduction of random or chance factors has the effect of blurring Christaller's hierarchy into a continuous relationship. These factors may often be interpreted simply as deviations from the restrictive assumptions of the model. For example, it is obvious that not all settlements function exclusively or even primarily as central places.

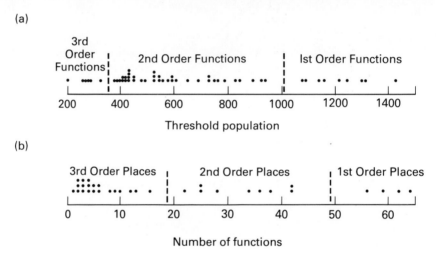

Fig. 10.12 Functional bases of central-place hierarchy in Snohomish County, Washington: (a) classification of functions by threshold population; (b) classification of places by number of functions (after Berry and Garrison, 1958).

Many towns and cities owe their origin and their growth to the rise of manufacturing industry (see section 5.1) and there is no reason why they should slot into a set of size-classes determined by the thresholds of different levels of central-place function. In these circumstances, it would be surprising to find a stepped settlement hierarchy at the national scale and it is only at regional and local scales that the necessary conditions are likely to occur.

We have already seen how the 'vertical' component of Christaller's model is a consequence of the prior specification of 'bundles' of goods with common threshold populations (see section 10.2.1). With reference to 33 settlements in Snohomish County, Berry and Garrison (1958) tried to establish whether such 'bundles' do indeed exist. The technique which they employed to derive the threshold population for each of 52 central functions was described in chapter 5 (section 5.1.2).

---

*An analogy may be drawn between variations in the slope of the rank-size curve and the way in which the distance/decay exponent varies between commodities (see section 8.1.2).

Table 10.1 reproduces data from Berry & Garrison. The full matrix of central places (columns) against central functions (rows) is shown below.

	Threshold Population	FIRST ORDER				SECOND ORDER									THIRD ORDER																		
		Marysville	Snohomish	Arlington	Monroe	Edmonds	Stanwood	East Stanwood	Lynnwood	Sultan	Mukilteo	Granite Falls	Darrington	Alderwood Manor	Lake Stevens	Beverly Park	Lowell	Silvana	Gold Bar	Startup	Warm Beach	Index	Machias	Cathcart	Maltby	Oso	Cedarhome	Bryant	Robe	Getchell	Florence	Trafton	Silverton	Verlot
Population		2460	3494	1915	1684	2996	720	390	500	850	900	974	600	600	2586	725	1600	300	325	300	314	220	200	175	700	200	100	150	25	50	300	25	15	20
Number of Activities		64	62	59	56	42	42	38	36	34	28	25	25	22	16	13	12	10	9	8	6	6	5	5	4	4	4	3	3	3	2	2	2	1

THIRD ORDER / CENTRAL FUNCTIONS

Function	Threshold Population
Filling Stations	196
Food Stores	254
Churches	265
Restaurants	276
Taverns	282
Elementary Schools	322

SECOND ORDER

Function	Threshold Population
Physicians	380
Real Estate Agencies	384
Appliance Stores	385
Barber Shops	386
Auto Dealers	398
Insurance Agencies	409
Bulk Oil Distributors	419
Dentists	426
Motels	430
Hardware Stores	431
Auto Repair Shops	435
Fuel Dealers (coal, etc.)	453
Drug Stores	458
Beauticians	480
Auto Parts Dealers	488
Meeting Halls	525
Animal Feed Stores	526
Lawyers	528
Furniture Stores, etc.	546
Variety Stores: 5 & 10	549
Freight Lines & Storage	567
Veterinaries	579
Apparel Stores	590
Lumber Yards & Woodworking	598
Banks	610
Farm Implement Dealers	650
Electric Repair Shops	693
Florists	729
High Schools	732
Dry Cleaners	754
Local Taxi Services	762
Billiard Hall & Bowling Alleys	789
Jewelry Stores	827
Hotels	846
Shoe Repair Shops	896
Sporting Goods Stores	928
Frozen Food Lockers	938

FIRST ORDER

Function	Threshold Population
Sheet Metal Works	1076
Department Stores	1083
Optometrists	1140
Hospital and Clinics	1159
Undertakers	1214
Photographers	1243
Public Accountants	1300
Laundries and Laundromats	1307
Health Practitioners	1424

Table 10.1 Central place/central function relationships in Snohomish County, Washington

Source: Adapted from Berry, B. J. L. and Garrison, W. L., The functional bases of the central place hierarchy, *Economic Geography* **34** (1958), 150.

Not surprisingly, no two functions were found to have identical thresholds and they extended from a figure of 196 to support a filling station to 1,424 to sustain a medical practice. However, when the functions were plotted as points along a line scaled between these two extremes (Fig. 10.12a), Berry and Garrison were able to identify three groups – using the criterion that every member of a group should be closer to some other member of that group than to any other point. The same technique was used to classify the settlements in terms of the number of different kinds of functions which they provided. In this case, the points ranged from a minimum of 1 (for a central place only able to offer a single service) to a maximum of 64. This scatter of points was also grouped into three classes (Fig. 10.12b) so that a cross-tabulation of functions against places could be produced in which the number of establishments providing each function in the different centres was recorded. For example, Table 10.1 indicates that Marysville possesses 9 filling stations, 3 drug stores and 1 accountant, whilst the corresponding figures for Lynnwood are 9, 1 and 0 and for Startup 2, 0 and 0. The final step involved trying to establish whether the three groups of functions were significantly associated with the three groups of central places. The incidence of values in Table 10.1 suggests such an association since members of the highest-threshold group tend to be found only in the first rank of central places, whilst those in the middle group occur both in the top and middle-rank places. Finally, the right-hand columns, relating to central places with the most limited range of functions, are largely blank in all but the top corner of the table, thereby indicating that their functions are restricted to those in the lower-threshold group. Berry and Garrison confirmed the visual impression given by Table 10.1 of a relationship between threshold levels and orders of central places by an analysis of variance* between the entries in the cells. Thus, by careful assembly and analysis of data in a small field area, they were able to provide empirical evidence in support of Christaller's assertion that the hierarchical structure of central places is a consequence of the existence of 'bundles' of functions with, if not identical, at least broadly similar thresholds.

Relaxing the Assumptions of the Model

Although real-world settlement patterns do not match exactly those of central-place theory, most of these discrepancies reflect the restrictive assumptions of the model rather than faulty logic in its construction. The model is essentially normative and therefore attempts to deduce an idealized spatial arrangement of settlements under certain specified assumptions rather than to predict reality. These assumptions may be grouped into three broad categories relating to (i) the homogeneity of the environment, (ii) the behaviour of consumers and (iii) change through time.

Homogeneity of the Environment – In Christaller's model, settlements are located on an isotropic plain which is not only devoid of place-to-place variations in the nature of the physical environment, but which is also characterized by a dispersed and uniformly distributed rural population. This requirement of homogeneity in both the physical and human environment is obviously unrealistic and common sense suggests that relaxing the assumption will inevitably produce modifications to Christaller's central-place systems. Figure 10.13 indicates the way in which dif-

* See glossary.

ferent types of localized resource may be expected to distort the regular distribution of seven settlements on an isotropic plain (a). In the second case (b), attempts to gain access to a zonal resource such as a coalfield result in a shift in the position of the settlements and a corresponding change in the areas which they serve. In the third case (c), the settlements are shown to respond to a linear resource such as a river, whilst in (d), a point resource such as a well or a defensive site is assumed. Although these examples are hypothetical, there is abundant evidence of the influence of uneven resource distributions upon settlement patterns. The coalfields, for example, have exerted a powerful influence upon the urban geography of the UK,

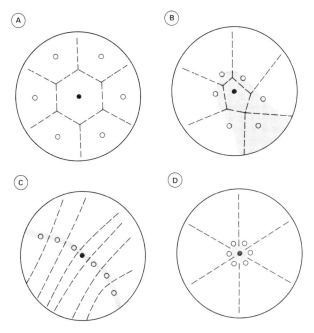

Fig. 10.13 Influence of resource distributions upon settlement patterns: (a) uniform resources; (b) zonal resource; (c) linear resource; (d) point resource (Haggett, Cliff and Frey, 1977, 105).

an influence which underlines the fact that, contrary to the assumptions of Christaller's model, not all settlements owe their origin or their continued existence to their role as central places.

There is often a strong correlation between variations in the physical content of space and uneven population distributions. Thus localized resources tend to attract population and stimulate further growth whilst population densities in rural areas partially reflect the nature of the agricultural system which is in turn related to the qualities of the physical environment. Such variations in population distribution do not invalidate the basis of the central-place model since the size and shape of market areas may be adjusted to ensure that they enclose sufficient consumers to attain the threshold sales necessary to support different levels of function. This implies that pairs of central places of equivalent status in the hierarchy will no longer be equidistant, but will be equally accessible to identical numbers of consumers. Where densities are higher, a given threshold population will be enclosed within a smaller area and settlements will be more closely spaced. This is apparent in Figure 10.14a which plots the distribution of high-order central places in England and Wales identified by Smith (1968). The map includes all the cities and major towns plus the main shopping centres in Greater London. The distribution is highly clustered with concentrations in the London, Lancashire and west Yorkshire areas which themselves account for a substantial proportion of the total population of England and Wales. In Figure 10.14b, the areal units have been transformed so that their size is proportional to the population they contain (Taylor, 1977).

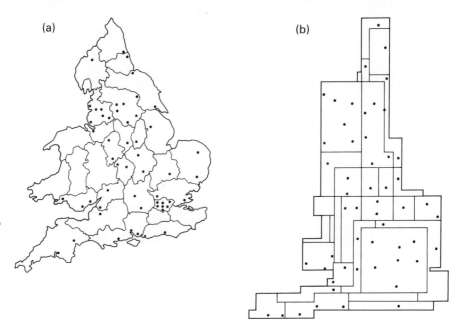

Fig. 10.14 High-order central places in UK in: (a) absolute space; (b) population space (Taylor, 1977, 154).

The shape and contiguity of the original units is maintained as far as possible and the location of the central places with respect to one another remains the same. There is an element of subjectivity in deriving these common relative locations, but the more uniform spatial arrangement apparent in Figure 10.14b emphasizes that clustered settlement patterns often reflect uneven population distributions which violate the assumptions, but not the principles of central-place theory.

Behaviour of Consumers – While the distribution of consumers is important in determining the spatial implications of the threshold concept, their behaviour affects the calculation of the range of specific goods and services. The central-place model rests upon the assumption that consumers will always travel to the nearest centre at which a particular good or service is available. Empirical studies suggest that consumers do not always behave in such a 'rational' manner. Similar results have been obtained in widely differing situations. For example, a survey of the shopping habits of the rural population of Iowa established that only one-third of the sampled households purchased groceries at the nearest centre (Rushton, Golledge and Clark, 1967). Slightly higher proportions were found by Clark (1968) in a study of intra-urban shopping patterns in Christchurch, New Zealand, although less than 50 per cent of the households patronized the shops nearest their home. Such behaviour is not necessarily inconsistent with the principle of least effort. Most shopping trips are made with the intention of purchasing more than one item. Consequently, a shopper may buy low-order goods during an expedition to purchase high-order ones. In this situation, a neighbourhood shop may be by-passed in favour of a multiple-purpose stop in the town centre. The effort or cost of movement is therefore divided between several commodities with the result that 'the effective range of goods purchased may be greater than the range of the same goods for single-purpose trips' (Yuill, 1967, 107).

A further modification to Christaller's assumption that consumers will always use the nearest centre is associated with the notion of indifference zones. This is based on the proposition that, at certain scales, shoppers will consciously travel further than necessary because a particular centre is thought to possess advantages which more than offset the extra effort involved in getting to it. Alternatively, they may be truly indifferent to the effect of distance and simply not appreciate that one shop is further away than another. The way in which choice of shop may be based on factors other than distance has been demonstrated by Day (1973) with reference to shopping patterns in a new town. In common with the other British new towns, the location of shopping facilities in Crawley was deliberately planned so that each neighbourhood would be served by its own complex of 'convenience' shops whilst higher-order goods would be obtained in the town centre. Despite the conscious application of central-place concepts in designing the town, Day found that many shoppers in Crawley rarely used the neighbourhood centres. The relative ease with which the town centre could be reached either by public transport or by private car meant that the additional time spent travelling was not regarded as a significant deterrent by most shoppers. Furthermore, any extra effort involved was thought to be justified in view of the better quality, wider selection and lower prices of goods in the town centre. Similar arguments were highlighted by Rushton, Golledge and Clark (1967) to account for the failure of many households surveyed in their Iowa study to patronize the nearest centre for low order goods. Clearly, the extent of indifference zones may be expected to increase with improved personal mobility. Car-ownership makes it possible for the housewife to choose between a wider range of alternative centres on the basis of criteria other than distance. These criteria are not always economic in nature and the relative attractiveness of centres may reflect preferences based upon other considerations.

Several studies have emphasized the significance of social or cultural factors in determining these preferences. We have already seen the way in which Protestants and Roman Catholics in West Belfast may walk further to patronize their own shops (see section 6.3.3). Similar behaviour had been observed by Ray (1967) in a rural part of eastern Ontario which is divided into French- and English-speaking areas. Thus some farmers located near the boundaries of these areas chose between alternative central places on the basis of their cultural associations rather than their distance. In another Canadian example, Murdie (1965) compared the shopping habits of Mennonites in southwestern Ontario with those of the rest of the population in the same area. The Mennonites are similar to the Amish people of Pennsylvania in their strict adherence to a traditional way of life. Old-order Mennonites continue to wear the same clothes as their ancestors and therefore have no interest in the new fashions which generally enter a rural area via the largest central place before 'trickling down' the urban hierarchy. Furthermore, the kind of comparison shopping which most people indulge in when buying clothes is not necessary for the Mennonites since their mode of dress permits little variation in styles. For this reason, Murdie found that Mennonites bought their

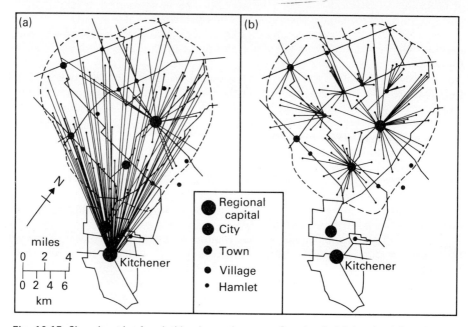

Fig. 10.15 Shopping trips for clothing in southwestern Ontario of: (a) 'modern' Canadians; (b) Mennonites (Murdie, 1965, 221).

clothes locally at the nearest centre, whereas modern Canadians display a much more dispersed pattern of shopping trips focusing upon Kitchener, which is the largest centre in the study area (Fig. 10.15a and b). Another factor contributing to these differences was the greater mobility of modern Canadians as compared with Mennonites, for whom distance remained a greater constraint because of their reliance upon traditional forms of transport.

This conclusion has important implications for the applicability of the central-place model since it suggests that closer adherence to the nearest-centre principle may be found in the less mobile societies of the developing world. Some support for this argument is provided by Wood (1974) in a study of home-to-market distances in the Meru district of Kenya where a combination of potential and gravity models (see section 5.1.2 and 8.2.2) incorporating size and distance variables was found to predict accurately over 90 per cent of the individual decisions relating to the choice of one market rather than another. The fact that all of these markets existed only on certain days of the week does not invalidate the inference that market users conformed very closely to the kind of 'rational' behaviour assumed by the central-place model. Indeed, periodic markets, which are a common feature of life in the developing world and which existed as travelling fairs in medieval Europe, may be regarded as mobile central places. By moving his stall, a vendor can reach, within the period of the market-cycle, a much larger population of potential consumers. If he were to remain at a single point, he might not achieve his sales threshold because of the limited range of his goods. Thus periodic markets represent a logical response to the constraints imposed by poor mobility, and their timing and location are determined by the same principles which govern the structure of a fixed central-place system.

Change Through Time – The functioning of periodic central-place systems depends upon the integration of spatial arrangements with temporal cycles, but time also serves as the dimension through which change takes place. Although Christaller did not make any explicit assumptions about this dimension, his model implicitly regards settlement patterns as static structures. This is obviously a limitation and, given the complexity of factors affecting their evolution, it would be surprising to find *any* system of cities, towns and villages at a given moment in time, in the state of equilibrium implied by the central-place model. We have already noted an example of a lag between change in relevant environmental circumstances and change in the physical fabric of central-place systems. Thus anomalies in the spacing of settlements in the Irish Republic were explained in terms of a contrast between areas of population decline and areas of population growth. Similarly, Berry, Barnum and Tennant (1962) regarded the apparent under-representation of hamlets in the settlement hierarchy of southwestern Iowa as symptomatic of their eventual disappearance in the North American rural landscape as widening car ownership extends the distance over which trips may be made.

Although the dynamic nature of settlement patterns often makes it difficult to match theory with reality, it does not undermine the basic principles of the central-place model. Indeed several studies which have regarded the spread of settlement as a form of spatial diffusion (see chapter 7) have indicated how the regular population distribution assumed by Christaller may be generated by the colonization of an uninhabited area. This evolutionary approach has been developed with reference to such diverse environments as Lappland in northern Sweden (Bylund, 1960), the American Midwest (Hudson, 1969) and the forest lowlands of Sierra Leone (Siddle, 1970). The latter area is reasonably uniform in its physical characteristics and is thought to have been largely uninhabited prior to the seventeenth century. Siddle developed a model of colonization in terms of the concept of a maximum economic radius around any settlement. This radius is determined by the outer range of the daily journey to work in surrounding fields (see section 6.2.1). He argued that the most likely response to increasing population pressure in the vicinity of a village located in an empty area is the foundation of a new settlement. Given the strength of kinship links, it is logical to assume that the new village would be located as close to the old one as the economic radii of both settlements would allow. The hypothesis of continuing social contact with the parent community suggests that any subsequent decisions to create further settlements are

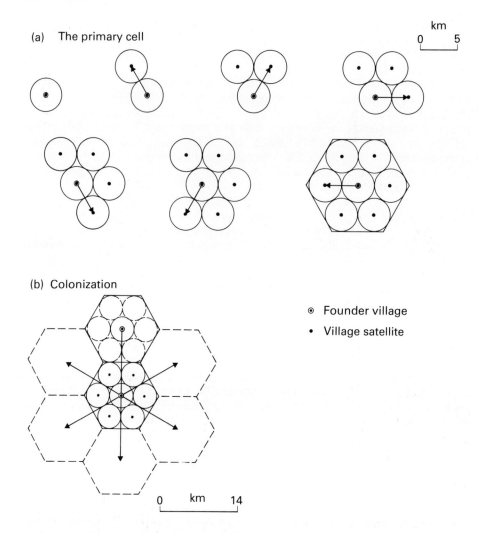

Fig. 10.16 A model of settlement colonization: (a) the primary cell; (b) colonization (Siddle, 1970, 81).

likely to be taken in the founder village which therefore eventually occupies a focal position in relation to a surrounding constellation of later settlements (Fig. 10.16a). As population growth and colonization continue, a whole series of such central-place 'cells' would encroach upon a wider and wider area, thereby producing the uniform population distribution which Christaller adopted as his starting-point (Fig. 10.16b). Siddle demonstrated that rural settlement patterns in Sierra Leone are consistent with this evolutionary interpretation. Nearest-neighbour analysis revealed 'a definite bias towards regularity of spacing' (Siddle, 1970, 87) and cer-tainly produced much higher Rn values than those associated with similar analyses of settlement patterns in more developed countries (see section 10.1.1). Indeed the most significant distortions of this largely uniform pattern have occurred as a result of the superimposition of such comparatively recent activities as diamond mining upon the pre-colonial system.

The inference that the central-place model works 'better' in pre-industrial societies underlines the fact that it represents only a partial explanation of settlement location. It is hardly surprising, therefore, that no single area replicates exactly the spatial and hierarchical arrangements deduced by Christaller. Nevertheless, the principles incorporated in the model have not only provided a theoretical basis for the study of settlement patterns, but have also found practical applications in, for example, planning the location of shops and other services in new towns (Burns, 1959) and, on a larger scale, in designing the layout of settlement schemes in virgin territory such as newly reclaimed polders in the Netherlands (Van Hulten, 1969). Even more significantly, Johnson (1970) has argued that the existence of an integrated central-place system along the lines postulated by Christaller is essential to the growth prospects of the developing countries, because, as we saw in chapter 7, such a system provides the link between urban and rural environments and hence the means by which the forces of change may be transmitted from core to periphery.

Further Reading

CHRISTALLER, W. 1966: *Central places in southern Germany*. Translated by C. W. Baskin. Englewood Cliffs, N.J.

A translation of Christaller's original work.

INGRAM, D. R. 1971: The concept of accessibility: a search for an operational form. *Regional Studies* 5, 101–7.

A discussion of the nature and measurement of accessibility.

JOHNSON, E. A. J. 1970: *The organization of space in developing countries*. Cambridge, Mass.

An impressive attempt to demonstrate the relevance of central-place concepts for the formulation of economic planning strategies in developing countries.

TAYLOR, P. J. 1977: *Quantitative methods in geography*. Boston.

Chapter 4 of this book provides a good discussion of the technical and conceptual problems involved in the analysis of point patterns.

11 Areas

Although many elements in the landscape may be conceived as lines and points, these one-dimensional forms are set within a broader frame of two-dimensional spaces or areas which are defined by boundaries of one sort or another. These boundaries may exist as physical barriers such as hedges or fences or they may be apparent only as lines enclosing a 'parcel' of territory on a map. It may be argued that a consideration of boundaries would be more appropriate under the general topic of 'lines' in chapter 9. However, the real significance of boundaries lies in their role in the partitioning of space into areas. The practical implications of such divisions become clear when, for example, it is remembered that location with respect to an international boundary can determine whether an individual lives in a communist state, a parliamentary democracy or under a military dictatorship. Similarly, living on one side of a street rather than the other may make all the difference between falling in the catchment area of a well-equipped, modern school and that of a dilapidated establishment of dubious academic reputation. Thus despite the fact that their boundaries cannot always be 'seen', areas are no less 'real' in their influence upon the way in which we organize our lives at the surface of the earth.

Any space enclosed by lines is an area. However, the kind of criteria which are employed in drawing the boundary lines provide the basis for a distinction between (i) field areas and (ii) territorial areas. Field areas are centred upon a focal point and are defined in terms of the relationship between this focus and the content of the surrounding space. The sphere of influence of a market town or the zone from which a hospital draws its patients are examples of field areas. By contrast, territorial areas are defined in legal and/or political terms and involve the notion of property or ownership. Furthermore, whereas field areas reflect and respond to changes in levels of spatial interaction between a centre and its hinterland, territorial areas often inhibit movement. Thus householders do not generally welcome the use of their gardens as public thoroughfares and similar kinds of proprietorial instincts ensure that movement across international frontiers is subject to differing degrees of restriction. The distinction between the two types of area is by no means watertight and it is not difficult to think of areas which incorporate the ideas of both territory and field in their delimitation. For example, local government areas provide a spatial framework for the provision of various services to a population and, to that extent, may be regarded as field areas. At the same time, these areas acquire a territorial significance which is underlined by the characteristically indignant reactions of their inhabitants to any proposed boundary changes, particularly if such changes involve surrendering a portion of land to an adjacent authority. Despite such situations in which areas cannot easily be categorized as field or territorial in nature, the distinction is employed in the following chapter which considers the properties and significance of areas as elements of spatial organization.

11.1 Field Areas

The definition of field areas ultimately rests upon the attenuating effect of the dimension of distance upon spatial interaction (see chapter 6), but their general properties can only be understood by reference to many concepts which we have already considered. Thus Figure 11.1 indicates the way in which movements are characteristically channelled into networks (lines) focusing upon nodes (points) which tend to develop at differential rates to form hierarchies. The remaining interstitial zones are integrated into the overall system and bound to the nodes by various types

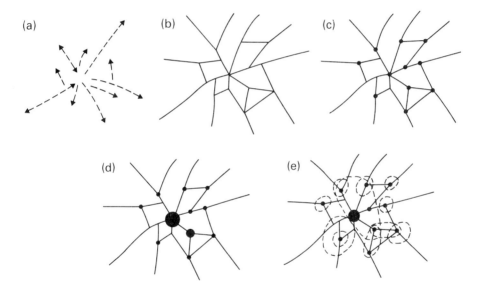

Fig. 11 1 The elements of spatial systems: (a) movements; (b) networks; (c) nodes; (d) hierarchies; (e) field areas (after Haggett, 1965, 18).

of interaction. For example, the dotted lines around the nodes in Figure 11.1e may define the outer limits of their respective commuting hinterlands so that each one lies at the centre of its own journey-to-work field area which may overlap with that of an adjacent node. At a higher level of resolution, it becomes apparent that these settlement nodes are themselves composed of many smaller nodes such as shops and schools which contribute to the aggregate pattern of movement and serve as the focus of their own field areas. At this scale, the official definition of catchment areas has important consequences for the general accessibility of public facilities and some of these issues are considered in the following section which analyses (i) the boundaries of field areas and (ii) the role of field areas in the organization of space.

11.1.1 Boundaries of Field Areas

Since an area can only be said to exist if an enclosing boundary can be identified, either visually or conceptually, some insight into the general properties of field areas may be gained by focusing our attention upon the problems involved in defining their boundaries. These problems emphasize the elusive nature of field-area boundaries that are specific to a particular form of interaction which may itself be subject to changes in intensity and direction through time. These difficulties may be better understood by discussing the interrelated issues of (i) boundary definition and (ii) boundary change.

Boundary Definition
The distance/decay curve characteristically slopes downward very rapidly at first and then levels off to a slow, almost imperceptible decline as the distance from the origin increases (see chapter 6). Thus an absolute limit or boundary may be very misleading. For example, a local newspaper may have a very restricted circulation area apart from a few copies that are posted overseas to homesick emigrants! Nevertheless, such exceptional cases do not invalidate the field-area concept and two alternative approaches may be adopted in the search for meaningful boundaries. The first is essentially based upon the gravity model (see section 8.2.2) whereas the second relies upon direct measurement of actual movements. These approaches identify respectively (i) break-even boundaries and (ii) mean field boundaries.

Break-Even Boundaries – Intuitively, it seems reasonable to postulate that the extent of a field area will be directly proportional to the significance of the node upon which it is focused. Thus if two cities of equal population size are assumed to be linked by a straight-line transport route, the boundary between their respective field areas will lie midway between them. Where the two cities are of unequal size the break-even line will be displaced towards the smaller city by a distance which reflects the size-ratio between them (Fig. 11.2). This common-sense logic is consistent with the ideas contained in the gravity model (see section 8.2.2) from which the following formula for the calculation of break-even distances between two nodes is derived (Reilly, 1931):

$$d_j k = \frac{d_{ij}}{1 + \dfrac{P_i}{P_j}}$$

where $d_j k$ represents the distance from j to the break even point k,
    d_{ij} is the distance between node i and node j,
    P_i is the population of node i,
    P_j is the population of node j.

Although the application of gravity concepts represents a theoretical approach to the definition of field areas, the comparison of actual movement patterns with predicted break-even boundaries helps to identify the variables other than mass

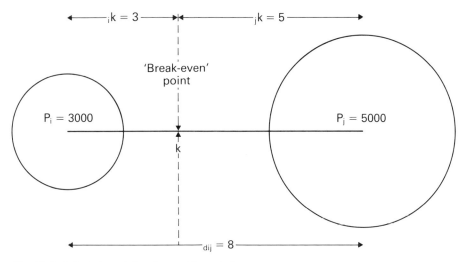

Fig. 11.2 Calculation of 'break-even' boundaries.

and distance which affect the level of spatial interaction between a node and its hinterland. In addition to its value in comparative studies, the normative* approach may also be used in planning future patterns of spatial organization. Huff (1973) employed a sophisticated version of the break-even formula to define theoretical field areas focused upon 73 first-order urban places in the US. He argues that the adoption of this division as an administrative framework would reflect the essentially metropolitan-oriented patterns of contemporary life in the US.

Mean-Field Boundaries – One way of overcoming the problems involved in establishing absolute spatial limits to the interaction between a centre and its hinterland is to draw lines enclosing a specified proportion of these movements. For example, the commuting 'mean' field of a centre defines the area accounting for 50 per cent of all journey-to-work movements to that centre. This type of approach has been widely used, especially in attempts to define urban spheres of influence. In this context, it is obviously directly related to the notion of range (see section 10.2) in that it indicates how far individuals are prepared to travel to patronize central-place services. The use of questionnaires, in which a sample of households at varying distances from a centre are asked where they purchase specific items, makes it possible to produce maps such as Figure 11.3a – in which areas enclosing successively higher proportions of the total number of shoppers travelling from outside Exeter to use retail facilities in the city centre are plotted. The production of such maps obviously involves a considerable amount of survey work, and Figure 11.3b indicates a less precise but more common representation, in which no value is attached to the various boundary lines which are nevertheless understood to enclose 'most' movements to the specified central-place functions. The lack of correspondence between these lines not only reflects differences in the ranges of the respective functions, but also emphasizes that, strictly speaking, any field area is specific to a particular form of interaction.

* See glossary.

Although most studies of the field areas of settlements focus upon the movements of people such as shoppers and commuters to a centre, such field areas may also be defined in terms of the movement of commodities. In the developing world, for example, even the largest city often depends upon a surrounding agricultural area for its supply of perishable foods. The transferability of such commodities is frequently limited by a poorly integrated national transport system and a lack of refrigerated vehicles. Figure 11.4 indicates those administrative districts around Calcutta which contribute at least 1 per cent to the city's daily supply of various

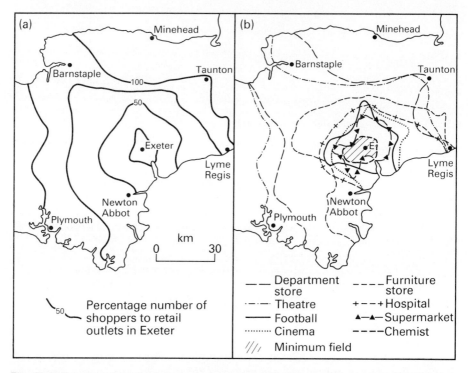

Fig. 11.3 Field-area boundaries around Exeter, 1970, defined in terms of: (a) percentage fields based on retail customers; (b) miscellaneous central-place functions (Toyne, 1974, 8).

commodities (Dutt, 1972). It is clear that the size and shape of the 'daily influence areas' differ between each commodity. Transferability is important in determining the size of these areas with milk (Fig. 11.4c), which is highly perishable in the Indian climate, being drawn from a much more restricted zone than either fruit (Fig. 11.4d) or vegetables (Fig. 11.4e). Differences in the shape of field areas reflect the influence upon interaction of variations in the content of space. Thus directional variations in the availability of transport facilities and the existence of barriers of various types all ensure that field areas identified by empirical observation are characteristically much more irregular in shape than those defined by applying the criteria of the break-even formula. A further factor apparent in Figure 11.4 is the existence of local specializations in the production of the various commodi-

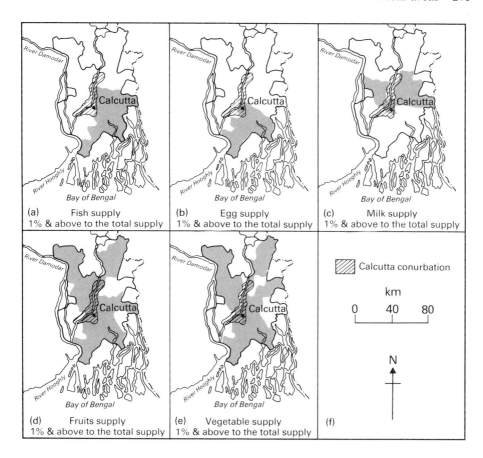

Fig. 11.4 Field area of Calcutta defined in terms of administrative districts contributing at least 1 per cent of metropolitan: (a) fish supply; (b) egg supply; (c) milk supply; (d) fruit supply; (e) vegetable supply (after Dutt, 1970, 35).

ties, with a large proportion of Calcutta's fish traditionally being drawn from the Salt Lake district to the east of the metropolis (Fig. 11.4a).

Boundary Change

In view of the close relationship between transferability and field-area size at any point in time, it is not surprising to find that changes in transferability produce corresponding changes in the size of field areas through time. The overwhelming trend is towards a progressive extension of these areas about their respective nodes. This trend is perhaps best illustrated by the increasing range of daily commuting into employment centres. In addition to its affect upon urban form (see section 6.2.2), increasing personal mobility is extending the economic influence of cities well beyond the margins of the continuously built-up area so that in the US, for example, very few areas east of the Mississippi and west of the Rockies do not lie within the commuting field of a large urban centre (Fig. 11.5). The significance

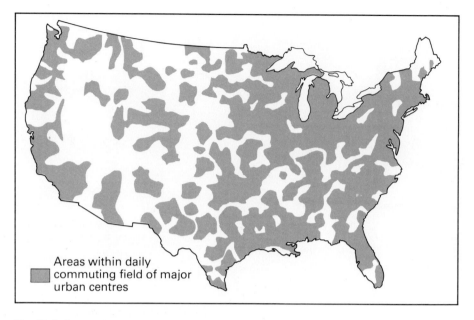

Fig. 11.5 Commuting field areas in the US (after Berry, 1970, 27).

of these areas becomes even more apparent when it is appreciated that they contained 95 per cent of the nation's population in 1960 (Berry, 1970). The increasing scale of metropolitan influence has necessarily involved ever more complex patterns of movement which are reflected in the overlapping commuting fields of adjacent centres. Indeed, it has often been argued that the northeastern US functions as a single metropolitan system extending from Boston in the north to Washington in the south (see Gottmann, 1961). This situation is not unique to the US and similar phenomena, which are ultimately composed of a complex hierarchy of interlocking urban field areas, may be observed elsewhere in less extensive forms such as the Merseyside, southeast Lancashire and west Yorkshire conurbations in northern England (see Lawton, 1967) and the urban agglomerations of the Witwatersrand in South Africa (see Fair, 1975).

11.1.2 Field Areas and the Organization of Space

Since field areas are defined in terms of movement, the relationship between the principle of least effort and movement minimization outlined in chapter 8 is an important factor affecting the role of field areas in the efficient organization of space. This relationship is implicit in two types of problem. Firstly, deciding where to locate a particular facility such as a school or hospital in relation to a fixed distribution of population. Secondly, deciding where to draw boundaries given a fixed distribution of facilities. In both cases, the reciprocal relationship between a central point, which represents the focus of movement, and its surrounding area is basic to the solution of the problem. Nevertheless, differing insights into the nature of this relationship are provided by considering separately some of the issues involved in (i) locating public facilities and (ii) defining administrative boundaries.

Locating Public Facilities

Decisions concerning the location of such facilities as schools, hospitals and play-grounds are often made by public officials. Although such so-called *location–allocation problems* relate explicitly to the positioning of point-like facilities in the landscape, they can only be solved by reference to the concept of a surrounding catchment or field area. First impressions suggest that the problem should not be too difficult to solve and it bears some resemblance to Weber's locational triangle (see section 6.1). However, appearances can be deceptive. For example, Schneider (1971) faced the evaluation of over 19 million theoretical possibilities in selecting optimal locations for 5 ambulance depots from a set of 77 sites. Several variables contribute to the mammoth proportions of the location–allocation problem. Very often it is not only a question of choosing a location, but also a matter of deciding how many facilities, possibly of differing size, should be provided in order to minimize the total cost of supplying a service to a surrounding population. Furthermore, the locations need not necessarily be fixed and the existence of such facilities as mobile libraries, which may be regarded as analogous to periodic markets (see section 10.1.2), adds a new dimension to the problem. The ability of modern computers to perform the kind of comparative calculations involved in location–allocation problems has made it feasible to seek more or less optimal solutions and much research has been devoted towards the derivation of suitable algorithms* (Massam, 1975).

The importance of such research is underlined by evidence from a wide variety of cultural situations that the accessibility of public facilities relative to the population that they are intended to serve influences the usage which they get. Gould (1971) has noted the operation of the distance/decay effect upon school attendance in tropical Africa. Similarly, Jolly and King (1966) have observed a decline in the level of medical care with increasing distance away from the Mitwani hospital in Uganda and the same phenomenon was described by Fuller (1974) with regard to attendance at a birth-control clinic in Santiago, Chile. These examples of the influence of accessibility upon the behaviour of 'consumers' of public services emphasizes the importance of the location decision in ensuring that the limited funds available for such investments in developing countries are used to greatest effect. Although standards of public-service provision are generally much higher in the developed world, the same problem remains. It is especially relevant in remote, rural areas where a sparse and often declining population is in direct opposition to a trend, based on considerations of economies of scale, towards larger individual units of provision. This conflict makes it difficult to attain the thresholds required to maintain a viable service.

The very uneven distribution of Sweden's population, together with that country's comprehensive welfare system, has presented many opportunities for geographers to become involved in the formulation of location strategies for public facilities (see Pred, 1973). Figure 11.6 illustrates the implications of this population distribution for the provision of a theoretical service with a range of 30 km (Öberg, 1976). The cost effectiveness of successive units declines sharply as lower and lower

* See glossary.

(a)

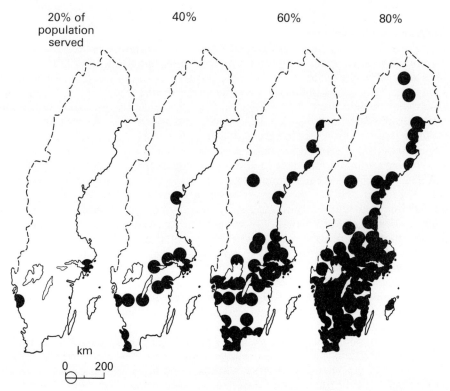

20% of
population
served
    40%   60%   80%

km

0   200

Fig. 11.6 Provision of a service with a 30-km distance radius to the Swedish population, 1960: (a) areas with access to supply; (b) relationship between supply points and population served; (c) distances to nearest supply points (Öberg, 1976, 105, 106 and 107).

population increments are served by the addition of each new facility (Fig. 11.6b). This relationship is expressed in a different way in Figure 11.6c, which indicates, for different numbers of units, the proportion of the total population lying within a specified distance radius. These graphs appear to establish a clear set of investment priorities with Stockholm and Göteborg qualifying first and second respectively before turning to the lesser population centres. Such a sequence would be the most cost-effective, but would not necessarily be the most equitable. Determining investment priorities on the basis of the urban hierarchy tends to accentuate differentials in the quality of public services between urban and rural environments and a case may be made on the grounds of regional equality for adopting a more dispersed location strategy.

The difficulties involved in locating public facilities are not confined to reconciling the often conflicting goals of equality and efficiency. Other factors frequently result in distributions which bear little relationship to either of these goals. Political influence and favouritism may determine the location of desirable facilities. Brunn (1974) quotes several examples from the US where elected officials have repaid

(b)

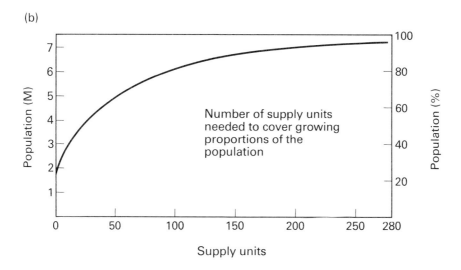

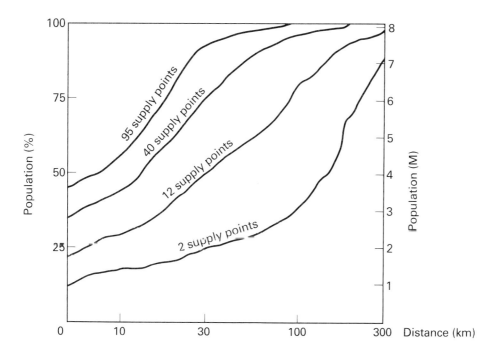

political debts by directing facilities such as community centres and swimming pools to particular areas. This practice is by no means unique to the US and Gould (1971) emphasizes that decisions regarding the location of education facilities in developing countries are often made primarily on political rather than economic grounds. The arguments may be reversed in the case of undesirable facilities. Thus sewage works, mental hospitals and prisons are frequently associated with low-income areas which lack the influence and the resources necessary to resist such developments (see Mumphrey and Wolpert, 1973).

We have so far adopted an essentially static approach to the problem of siting public facilities and it is clear that no matter what criterion is adopted to define the 'best' solution – this solution will change through time. For example, Lawrence (1972) observed that the location of hospitals in the Sydney metropolitan area had failed to keep pace with the outward movement of population with the result that the inhabitants of the peripheral suburbs were 'under-provided' with hospital beds as compared with inner-city residents. In addition to such changes in the content of space, improvements in levels of personal mobility and a tendency towards in-creasing scales of operation in the provision of public services also ensure that the 'best' location strategy is specific to a set of circumstances which may be of limited duration. The implications of these kinds of change are not restricted to location–allocation problems, but are also apparent in the whole question of defining local-government boundaries.

Defining Administrative Boundaries

The significance of the spatial organization of local government has been empha-sized in many countries as urban areas have expanded beyond existing administra-tive boundaries both in terms of their physical growth and the extent of their daily commuting systems (see section 11.1.1). This trend has often resulted in the division of administrative responsibility for a single urban or metropolitan system between several authorities. Such divisions create many difficulties. A particular problem in the UK was associated with the implementation of housing policies in the 1950s and 1960s as the attempts of city authorities to move families from inner-city slum-clearance zones into new estates on the urban fringe were frustrated by the unwill-ingness of the 'rural' counties to provide the necessary land. In the US, the migra-tion of industry and the middle classes beyond the city limits is leaving behind a residual population of the poor and under-privileged in decaying urban com-munities which are losing their principal sources of tax income. The adverse con-sequences of inappropriate local-government units are not confined to the cities. Remote rural areas can often neither meet critical threshold levels nor raise, from a limited and frequently declining population base, the funds required to finance high-cost public services.

Ad hoc municipal annexations and the consolidation of adjacent rural areas represent the usual responses to these kinds of problem, although comprehensive national revisions of administrative boundaries are occasionally undertaken. Such a revision occurred in the UK in 1974. This provided the opportunity to apply the field-area concept by the administrative integration of urban centres and their surrounding hinterlands in single city-region authorities. We will now consider the extent to which this opportunity was taken by examining the changes that were introduced in northwest England. This part of the UK is an interesting case-study for a number of reasons. Firstly, it incorporates a wide range of situations from the sparsely populated areas of the Lake District in the north to the metropolitan centres of Liverpool and Manchester in the south. Secondly, the complex pattern of daily movement associated with these centres underlines the difficulties involved in defining discrete field areas (Fig. 11.7a). Thirdly, the pre-1974 local-government map typifies the kind of fragmentation of administrative responsibilities which created the need for reform in the first place (Fig. 11.7b).

A Royal Commission was set up in 1966 to make recommendations for the reform of local government in England (Royal Commission, 1969). Its suggestions for the Northwest are indicated in Figure 11.7c. The difference between these proposals and the old pattern of administrative boundaries may be explained in terms of the application by the Commission of several principles. Recognition of the need to create larger metropolitan authorities reflecting the increased range of daily movement patterns is apparent in the expansion of the administrative areas focused on Liverpool and Manchester. A further important factor influencing the Commission was its belief in the existence of certain optimum population sizes, ranging from a minimum of 250,000 to a maximum of 1,000,000, for the provision of certain services such as education and social welfare. Rigid application of the minimum threshold necessarily involved the disappearance of many small authorities whilst the upper limit required the subdivision of the large, city-oriented authorities into second-tier districts which were to be autonomous for certain functions, but which were to fall under metropolitan control for others. The acceptance of thresholds obviously implies an inverse relationship, which may be observed in northwest England, between population density and the size of administrative areas. In practice, optimum population sizes are very difficult to establish because they vary between functions. Indeed these problems are so great that one of the members of the Commission produced a dissenting report (Royal Commission, 1969, Vol. 2) in which he argued that notional thresholds should not be allowed to constrain the application of the field-area concept as the primary determinant of a revised local-government structure. Consequently, the author of this report was prepared to accept much larger authorities with the result that the eight top-tier authorities recommended for northwest England by the majority report were reduced to only four in the minority report. In addition to the significance of movement patterns and population thresholds as guiding principles, the Commission also attempted to utilize the old boundaries as far as possible. This partly reflected a desire to minimize the problems of changing to the new system and partly a wish to retain the loyalties and traditions associated with the existing pattern. Nevertheless, some divergences from the alignment of former boundaries were recommended in order to create areas of more compact shape. For example, the Commission suggested that the Furness district, which had previously been physically separated from the county of which it was an administrative part, should be incorporated within a single coherent unit. Such an arrangement tends to reduce the cost of providing services by improving accessibility to an administrative centre and also diminishes the scope for policy differences between adjacent authorities by reducing boundary length relative to area.

Despite the lengthy deliberations of the Commission, the reform of local government which ultimately took place in 1974 differed considerably from its recommendations (cf. Fig. 11.7c and d). A two-tier system has been adopted throughout

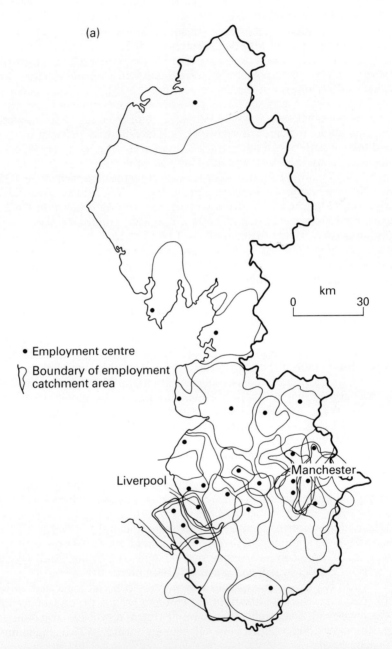

(a)

km
0   30

• Employment centre

Boundary of employment
catchment area

Liverpool

Manchester

Fig. 11.7 Reform of local government boundaries in northwest England, 1974: (a) commuting field areas, 1966; (b) pre-1974 local government boundaries; (c) boundaries proposed by Royal Commission (majority report); (d) boundaries introduced in 1974 (map of commuting field areas from Royal Commission, 1969, Vol. III).

(b)

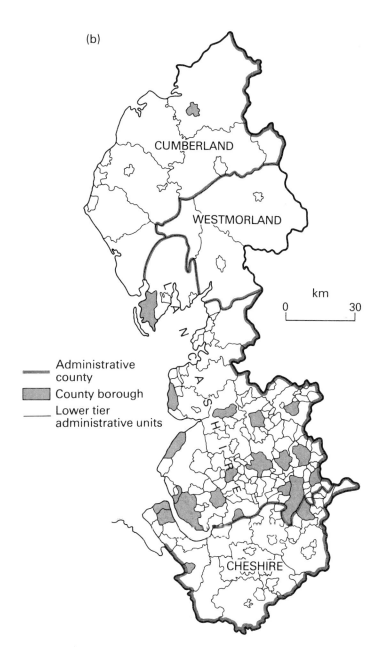

CUMBERLAND

WESTMORLAND

LANCASHIRE

CHESHIRE

km
0   30

Administrative
county
County borough
Lower tier
administrative units

(c)

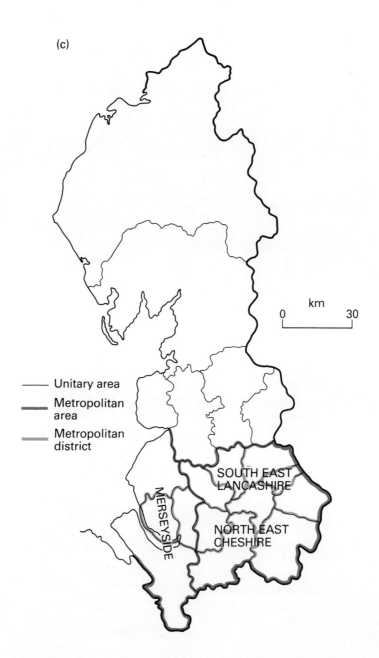

km

0   30

—— Unitary area

—— Metropolitan area

—— Metropolitan district

SOUTH EAST LANCASHIRE

MERSEYSIDE

NORTH EAST CHESHIRE

(d)

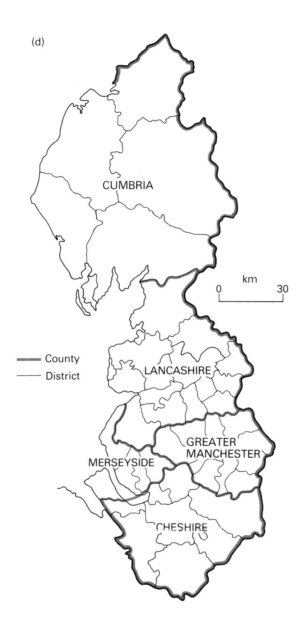

CUMBRIA

km

0   30

County

District

LANCASHIRE

GREATER
MANCHESTER

MERSEYSIDE

CHESHIRE

the country, rather than exclusively in metropolitan areas, in the belief that certain services may be better provided within the framework of smaller spatial units. Nevertheless, it has been estimated that the changes made have not only achieved a 44 per cent decline in the overall length of administrative boundaries in England, but have also produced much greater uniformity in their population size (Chisholm, 1975). On the other hand, the expansion of the metropolitan authorities has fallen far short of the recommendations of the Commission. Indeed, the new boundaries for Liverpool and Manchester do not even enclose the existing built-up areas let alone incorporate the daily flows to these employment centres. Nevertheless, the field-area principle has not been abandoned altogether and many intermediate urban centres such as Preston, Lancaster and Chorley have become the foci of expanded administrative areas which more closely reflect daily movement patterns (cf. Fig. 11.7a and d).

In attempting to account for the failure to implement the field-area concept at the metropolitan scale, it is necessary to recognize that administrative units are governed by elected representatives. This political dimension probably encouraged the Conservative government which actually introduced the present system to ensure that the former shire counties, many of which traditionally returned Conservative councils, retained their identity. Thus in the Northwest, Lancashire and Cheshire, which virtually disappeared under the Commission's proposals, have survived more or less intact. This political aspect of local-government reform emphasizes the territorial functions of administrative areas in that it is related more to a fixed distribution of voters rather than the fluid distribution of commuters which provided the starting-point for the Commission's deliberations (Fig. 11.7a).

11.2 Territorial Areas

Whereas field areas are theoretically defined in terms of movements, territorial areas are defined in relation to static (at least in the short term) distributions. Despite this fundamental difference, the framework adopted in the preceding section may also be employed to structure our discussion of the nature of territorial areas and we will therefore consider (i) the boundaries of territorial areas and (ii) the role of territorial areas in the organization of space.

11.2.1 Boundaries of Territorial Areas

The properties of territorial areas may be understood, to a large extent, by concentrating attention upon their boundary characteristics. The boundaries of field areas are largely created by movement, but those of territorial areas often direct or constrain rather than respond to movement. The implications of these differences are discussed in the following section which reviews (i) the problems of boundary definition and (ii) the nature of boundary effects.

Boundary Definition
The boundaries of territorial areas are generally defined with reference to the distributions which make up the content of space. Although these distributions change through time, they generally provide a more stable basis for boundary definition

than the essentially fluid movement patterns which are employed to demarcate field areas. Consequently, changes in the boundaries of territorial areas tend to be infrequent. Indeed, these boundaries often acquire an inertia which ensures that they are even more resistant to change than the distributions to which they were originally matched or related. The influence of these distributions upon the definition of territorial areas may be considered by reference to (i) the physical content of space and (ii) the human content of space.

Physical Content of Space – One of the most obvious influences of the physical environment on the definition of territorial areas is provided by the existence of 'natural' boundaries created by such linear features as mountain ranges and rivers. The permanence of the Rhine and the Pyrenees, for example, has been an obvious advantage in a continent such as Western Europe, which has experienced a very turbulent political history. In some cases, the permanence of the feature proves illusory, as in the celebrated example of the Rio Grande which has shifted its course on a number of occasions thus necessitating adjustments in the US–Mexico boundary (see Hill, 1965). International agreement along even the most obvious physical barrier may not always be easy to reach, especially where there is the kind of mistrust and hostility between the two parties evident in Sino-Indian relations over their common frontier in the Himalayas (see Kirk, 1960). Although the barriers to movement created by such features represent the clearest illustration of 'natural' frontiers, it is important to remember that space itself is also a barrier to movement which may reinforce the effectiveness of physical obstacles. In an historical context, uncertainties concerning the position of distant and remote frontiers have not seemed particularly important. However, as the 'shelter' function of distance declines in a 'shrinking world' there is a tendency for states to wish to define more precisely the margins of their areas of authority. This desire is often stimulated when a blurred frontier zone is thought to contain valuable resources, and Bolivia and Brazil, for example, finally resolved the last section of their common frontier as recently as 1958 when the possibility of oil deposits in the Andean Piedmont made it necessary to draw a line through the isolated forests and swamps of the Mato Grosso (see Fifer, 1966).

The coastline is a linear feature which has a special significance in defining the boundaries of countries. As the volume of international trade has increased, so the possession of a coastline has become more important to the political and economic security of any country. States such as Paraguay in South America and Chad in Africa must rely upon the goodwill of others in permitting the passage, either overland or via major river systems, of their goods to coastal ports. This situation has precipitated many conflicts as landlocked states have attempted to gain access to the sea by altering the *shape* of their territory. For example, Poland's only link to the sea during the inter-war years was provided by a 'corridor' to the port of Danzig on the Baltic (see Hartshorne, 1937). However, whilst this arrangement was of benefit to Poland, it had the effect of isolating East Prussia from the rest of Germany – a situation which was unacceptable to Hitler and which he attempted to change in 1939. Many contemporary 'trouble-spots' provide illustrations of similar access corridors. In the Middle East, the southward extension of Israel to the Gulf of Aqaba provides an outlet to the Indian Ocean and the Far East which eliminates Israel's need to use the Suez Canal.

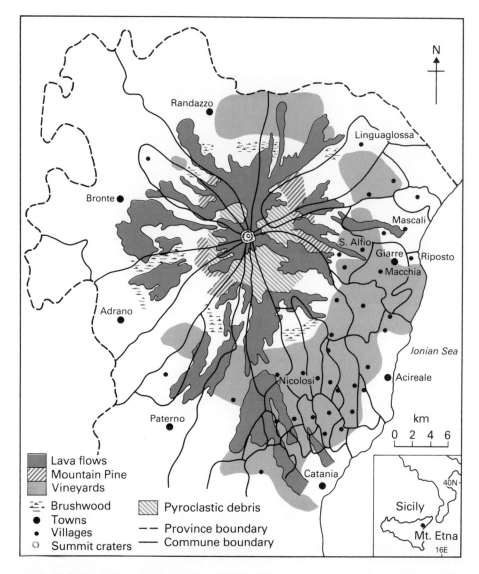

Fig. 11.8 Relationship of commune boundaries to physical patterns on Mount Etna, Sicily (after Clapperton, 1972, 161).

It is not only linear components of the physical environment such as mountain ranges, rivers and coastlines which are employed in defining the boundaries of territorial areas. Spatial variations in such attributes as soil and vegetation conditions, which typically form areal rather than linear distributions, may also be important. The influence of such distributions upon human activity is often readily apparent in the spatial organization of agricultural communities. For example, parish, commune or township boundaries may reflect local variations in environmental conditions. The historical origins of such boundaries are frequently obscure, but their orientation often suggests that they have been drawn to ensure that each community is allocated a similar share of different types of environment. Figure 11.8 shows commune boundaries on Mount Etna in Sicily. Many of these boundaries run parallel to the slope of the volcano and it seems reasonable to infer that this pattern reflects a deliberate attempt to allocate the altitudinal land-use zones equitably between the various communes (Clapperton, 1972). A similar situation, in a very different cultural context, is represented in Figure 11.9, which

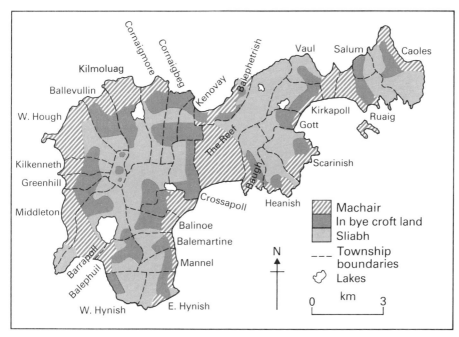

Fig. 11.9 Township boundaries on Tiree, Inner Hebrides (Coull, 1962, 19).

shows the location of township boundaries on the island of Tiree in the Inner Hebrides. Generally speaking, each township contains three different types of environment within its boundaries: a strip of coastal machair and beach which has traditionally provided seaweed for both animal and human consumption as well as serving as grazing land, the in-bye croft land which is used for arable purposes, and finally, the areas of *sliabh* (raised beach and rock outcrop) which are suitable only for rough grazing (Coull, 1962). The arrangement of boundaries not only influences the allocation of land types between townships, but also ensures that each community has access to the sea for fishing.

Human Content of Space – Whereas the achievement of diversity in environmental circumstances may be an important objective when defining territorial boundaries with reference to the physical content of space, homogeneity is usually the dominant criterion when the human composition of an area is more important than its physical characteristics. Notwithstanding the undeniable importance of 'natural' frontiers, one of the most powerful influences upon the evolution of the political map of the world has been the concept of the nation state, which rests upon the basic ideological force of nationalism – the drive of a particular group for a territory of its own.* The Treaty of Versailles following the First World War was perhaps the most spectacular demonstration of the concept as new states such as Czechoslovakia, Austria, Hungary and Yugoslavia were carved out of the German and Austro-Hungarian empires. Theoretically, these states were conceived as culturally homogeneous entities, although in practice they represented varying amalgams of many different groups. Even in countries with relatively stable frontiers there are often internal pressures promoting their fragmentation into smaller political units which more closely reflect human distributions. The activities of the Scottish and Welsh nationalists in the UK and the divisions between Flemings and Walloons in Belgium are typical examples of such pressures in two countries which are relatively small when viewed on a global scale.

Given these problems in Western Europe, in which the concept of the nation state originated, it is not surprising to find serious difficulties in the political organization of space in the developing world, where the concept is not only alien, but where it has also been superimposed upon other types of organizational structure (see Soja, 1971). The situation is frequently aggravated by the permanence of national frontiers inherited from the colonial period. In Africa, many of these frontiers date back to the nineteenth-century 'scramble' for the continent when boundaries were drawn in ignorance of physical and human distributions. Some of the implications of these divisions for the independent states may be illustrated by reference to Nigeria. Not only do the boundaries of Nigeria cut across the distributions of many groups whose members recognize some common social bond or link, but they also enclose many such groups in a country with an area almost four times that of the UK (Fig. 11.10a). There is a long tradition of antipathy between many of these groups which encouraged the colonial administration to adopt a federal system of government based upon three Provinces which broadly reflected the distribution of the principal ethnic groups of the Hausa-Fulani, the Ibo and the Yoruba. This structure continued after independence, although the Provinces were renamed Regions and the non-Yoruba part of the former Western Province was hived off to form the midwest Region (Fig. 11.10b). In 1967, the military government, which had gained power in the previous year, replaced these four Regions with 12 States (Fig. 11.10c). Despite this attempt to provide the various tribal groups with greater autonomy, the east-central State broke away in the same year to form the core of the Republic of Biafra which survived until 1970. As part of its efforts at reconciliation following the civil war, the government set up a Commission to consider the possibilities of creating further states to take greater account of local interests. The results of this exercise are apparent in Figure 11.10d and the progressive fragmentation of the Nigerian federal structure from three units at independence to 19 by 1976 reflects successive attempts to match the spatial framework of the country's political system to the complexities of its tribal distributions.

---

*There are clear parallels between nationalism and the territorial instincts implicit in certain aspects of human behaviour in social space (see section 6.3).

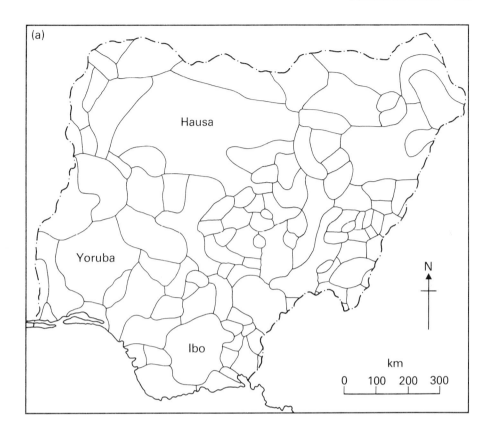

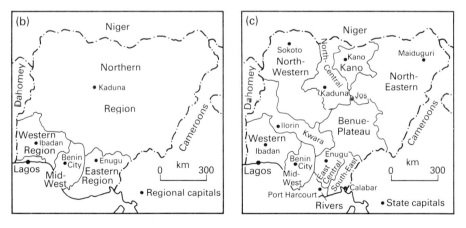

Fig. 11.10 Administrative boundaries and community distributions in Nigeria: (a) principal community groups; (b) federal boundaries, 1960–1967; (c) federal boundaries, 1967–1976; (d) federal boundaries, 1976–   (map of principal community groups after Murdock, P. G., *Africa: its peoples and their culture history*, McGraw-Hill, New York, 1959).

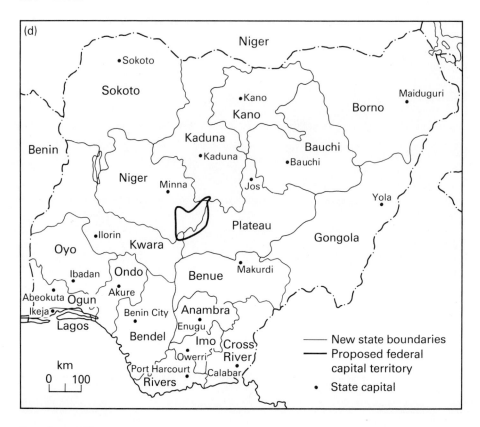

Boundary Effects
The emphasis has so far been placed upon the relationship between boundary
definition and the properties of territorial areas. However, these boundaries have
certain properties of their own which derive from their effect upon (i) spatial processes and (ii) spatial patterns.

Boundaries and Spatial Process – We have already seen how the boundaries of
territorial areas influence both diffusion and interaction. International frontiers,
for example, may limit the spread of ideas or culture traits (see section 7.1.2) and
may also restrict the flow of goods or people as a result of the imposition of tariffs,
quotas and immigration controls (see section 6.1.2). The inhibiting effect of boundaries upon movement is often most clearly seen in situations where nodal centres
are separated from their hinterlands or field areas by political boundaries. For
example, the partitioning of Germany following the Second World War had an
adverse effect upon the subsequent development of several cities such as Hamburg
and Lübeck located adjacent to the new boundary. On a smaller scale, a study
of the shopping habits of residents of New Brunswick living adjacent to the border
with Maine suggested that they had better knowledge of possibilities on the
Canadian side, but perceived the opportunities as being greater in the US
(Reynolds and McNulty, 1968). This feeling that the 'grass may be greener on

the other side' is sometimes justified and boundaries may actually stimulate move-ment. US citizens, for example, can save money by crossing into Mexico to buy certain goods whereas many Mexicans move in the opposite direction in search of better paid jobs.

Boundaries and Spatial Patterns – The influence of boundaries upon movement is often reflected in the structure of transport networks which are frequently trun-cated in the vicinity of international frontiers. For example, only four officially recognized crossing points exist along the entire 435-mile length of the border between Nigeria and Benin. In a study of this boundary, Mills (1973) confirmed the existence of a distinctive frontier zone in which settlements tend to be smaller and rates of population growth slower than in the areas which are completely enclosed by the respective national transport networks. These characteristics are relatively recent boundary effects since the Nigeria–Benin frontier is a colonial creation rather than a traditional ethnic divide. Although a denser population and a more sophisticated transport network together ensure that similar frontier zones are less evident in Western Europe, the EEC Commission nevertheless attaches considerable importance to the need for more effective coordination of the trans-port systems of member states. The absence or non-integration of transport net-works in frontier zones contributes to their typically stagnant economies which also reflect their peripherality relative to national markets and the political un-certainties with which they are frequently associated. The tension surrounding the border between East and West Germany, for example, has certainly deterred indus-trial investment.

Despite the generally negative influence of boundaries upon economic develop-ment, they may occasionally have the opposite effect. The unique juxtaposition of a highly developed country and a 'third world' nation has produced some spec-tacular effects along the US border with Mexico, where many American companies have established plants within a 20-km zone on the southern side of the frontier (see Dillman, 1970). Cheap labour and various tax incentives offered by the Mexi-can authorities enable these firms to take advantage of lower production costs whilst the host country gains new employment opportunities in a peripheral area. This type of development reflects the role of boundaries in defining the spatial margins of different political and economic environments and policy differences may, for example, be reflected in agricultural land-use patterns. In physical terms, the plains of Manitoba and Saskatchewan are much the same as those of Montana, North Dakota and Minnesota, but Reitsma (1972) used census and fieldwork data relating to the early and mid-1960s to identify significant differences between the US and Canada in the relative importance of the various crop and livestock combi-nations. Although wheat is the dominant crop on both sides of the border, barley is clearly the second-rank crop in the US whereas oats occupies this position in Canada (Fig. 11.11a to c). The reversal in the role of the two subsidiary crops is mainly a consequence of a deliberate policy on the part of the US government to control or reduce wheat output. Faced with these restrictions, most American farmers switched many wheat fields to barley. This had the effect of depressing the price of barley in *both* countries, which in turn brought about a reduction in its acreage in Canada. The greater importance of oats to the north of the border is to some extent due to the role of this crop as an animal feed since livestock

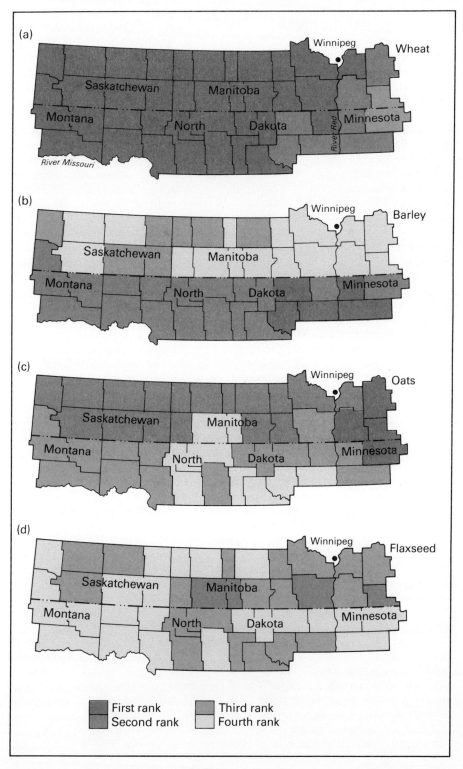

Fig. 11.11 Agricultural land use along US–Canada frontier, 1959–1961. Rank distribution of: (a) wheat; (b) barley; (c) oats; (d) flaxseed (Reitsma, 1971, 218).

densities are higher in Canada, a situation that itself partly reflects government policy, which has been geared towards encouraging agricultural diversification amongst Prairie farmers. The importance of flaxseed along sections of the Canadian border area (Fig. 11.11d) reflects the role of the frontier as a cultural divide, since the Mennonites for whom this is a traditional crop have not settled in this part of the US.

11.2.2 Territorial Areas and the Organization of Space

Practical applications of the territorial-area concept are typically concerned with the allocation of the contents of space between different individuals or groups. Since it has already been noted that the concept implies ownership or possession, issues of equity are often involved when space is partitioned into territorial areas. The significance of such divisions in resolving questions of 'who gets what' may be illustrated with reference to the physical and human content of space respectively, by examining problems of (i) resource allocation and (ii) political representation.

Resource Allocation
We have already described several situations in which the drawing of boundary lines between territorial areas has a bearing on the allocation of resources. The fragmentation into separate parcels of individual holdings in rural communities is often motivated either by a desire to achieve a fair division of land types or as an insurance against environmental hazards (see section 4.1.2). We have also described the operation of similar principles in the definition of community boundaries in Sicily and Scotland (see section 11.2.1). At an international scale, attempts to extend territorial sovereignty with the objective of annexing resources have resulted in many conflicts between countries. The War of the Pacific (1879–1883) between Peru, Bolivia and Chile was essentially a dispute over the ownership of nitrate deposits in the Atacama Desert. More recently, the existence of valuable phosphates in the former colony of Spanish Sahara was an important factor in its subsequent, not entirely amicable, division between Mauritania and Morocco in 1976. Although these disputes focused on the possession of land-based resources, the question of access to the resources of the oceans is probably the most important contemporary illustration of this type of problem. These resources fall into two main categories – firstly, mobile and renewable biotic resources, and secondly, fixed and non-renewable mineral deposits. In the former case the issue centres upon attempts to regulate the rate of exploitation in order to maintain fish and whale stocks; in the latter case it is a matter of deciding who should be responsible for extraction and how the economic benefits should be distributed. Although there is clear evidence of over-exploitation in many of the world's fishing grounds, it is the quest for mineral deposits, mainly oil and gas under the continental shelves and manganese nodules on the deep ocean beds, which has precipitated recent efforts to reach international agreement on the division of seas. We may consider some of the implications of this debate at the scale of (i) the world's oceans and (ii) the North Sea.

The World's Oceans – There has been a progressive erosion since 1945 of the 'freedom of the seas'. The principle has not always been applied, but it has certainly been widely accepted since the nineteenth century (see Prescott, 1975). The so-called Truman Declaration in 1945 whereby the US effectively claimed sovereignty over the resources of its surrounding continental shelf set in motion a chain of events which seems likely to culminate by the end of the 1970s in the universal adoption of 200-mile zones within which coastal states will have exclusive economic rights to any resources contained in the sea itself and on or below the seabed. The Truman Declaration was primarily motivated by anticipated discoveries of oil and gas on the continental shelf and the trend towards the marine extension of national jurisdiction has been based upon the attainment of economic rather than political objectives.

Coull (1975) draws an interesting analogy between the origins and development of the common-field system and recent events regarding access to the resources of the oceans. In both cases 'the organization of resource use becomes more defined in a situation of pressure' (Coull, 1975, 103) and the restriction of access by the demarcation of territorial areas is an essential component of this organization. Thus just as the growth of population leads to a filling-in of the settlement map and a need to reorganize systems of cultivation, so advances in the technology of fishing and mineral exploitation are enabling the 'global village' to reach out to the limits of its territory. It is not unreasonable to regard the oceans as the last earthbound frontier open to human exploration and exploitation and it seems to be following the precedent set by other frontiers in which a 'free-for-all' is replaced by more rigid forms of control.

Despite the growing acceptance of extended areas of national economic jurisdiction as the basis of such control, many problems remain. For example, this type of arrangement tends to benefit island states and others with long coastlines whilst at the same time denying land-locked states access to resources in areas which had previously been regarded as commons. In addition to conflicts of interest based upon accidents of territorial shape and location, there is a fundamental division between the countries of the developed and the developing world (see Leipziger and Mudge, 1976). The technology to exploit offshore mineral deposits is largely confined to North American and European multinational corporations. This places such organizations in a strong bargaining position in their dealings with the governments of developing nations which fear that most of the benefits of offshore mineral exploitation will accrue to the multinationals and to the countries in which they are based. This concern has been reflected in discussions at successive Law of the Sea conferences regarding the feasibility of establishing some kind of international tax-collecting agency with responsibility for the redistribution of wealth created by seabed mining operations.

The North Sea – The territorial division of the North Sea has, by comparison with the difficulties faced in reaching agreement at the global scale, been relatively easy to achieve. Two levels of territorial subdivision associated with the search for oil and gas may be identified. At the international scale, the North Sea is divided between five countries for the purposes of offshore exploration (Fig. 11.12a). However, these national sectors are further subdivided into the licence units to which the mining legislation of each country relates (Fig. 11.12b). Whilst the international

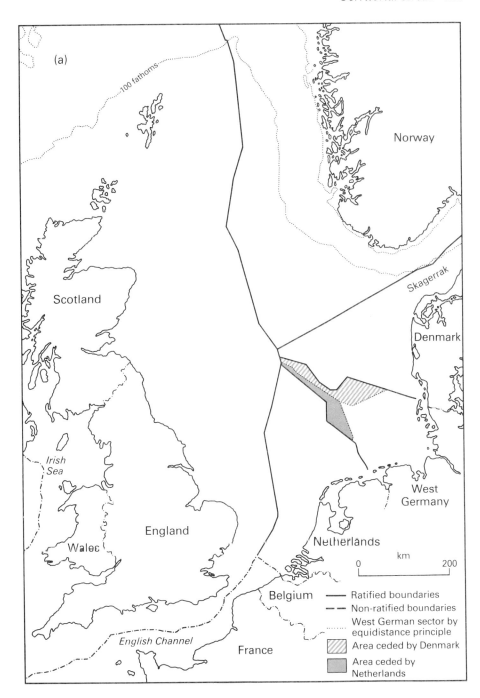

Fig. 11.12 Territorial division of North Sea: (a) between countries; (b) for offshore mining legislation.

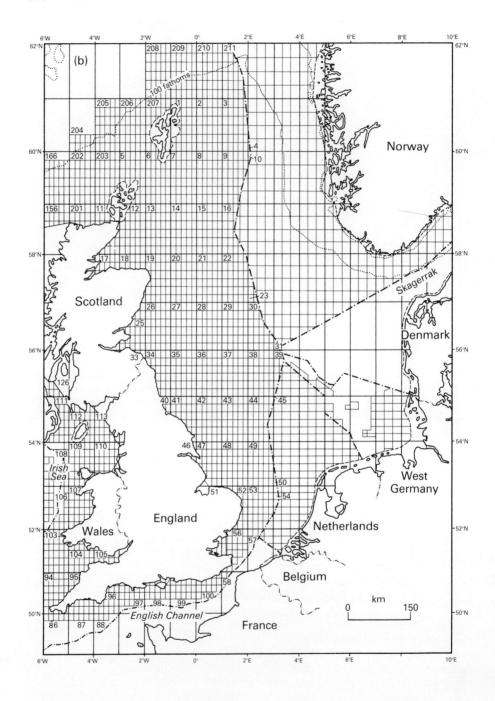

division was an essential prerequisite to the commencement of exploration, the licence units have provided the respective governments with an important measure of control over the subsequent pattern of offshore activity (see Chapman, 1976).

Most of the national sectors in the North Sea were defined by the application of a formula whereby a median line is drawn equidistant from a set of base lines paralleling the respective coastlines. The only exception was that of West Germany. Ostensibly, the West German government was unhappy with this procedure because a base line drawn across the concave Heligoland Bight would yield a smaller offshore area than an allocation based on a ratio proportional to coastline length. However, West Germany was as much interested in the shape of its territory as its size. At the time these negotiations were proceeding in the mid-1960s, geological prospects in the central North Sea were regarded as especially promising. As a result of the agreement ultimately reached, West Germany gained some territory in this area by means of a finger-like extension which may be regarded as analogous to a coastal access corridor on land (Fig. 11.12a). The fact that no major discoveries have since been made in this territory ceded by Denmark and the Netherlands underlines the point that, in contrast to the definition of community territories in rural societies (see section 11.2.1), the division of offshore areas normally takes place *before* the precise distribution of the resources is known. As events have turned out, the two countries which gained the largest proportions of the North Sea by virtue of their long coastlines, the UK and Norway, also possess the bulk of the proven oil and gas reserves. However, this is not necessarily a function of the allocation mechanism, which is best described as a 'resource lottery'.

The individual licence units within the various national sectors may themselves be viewed as territorial areas in the sense that the right to search for oil and gas is granted by the appropriate government to the holder of the licence. These units therefore incorporate the idea of possession or ownership – albeit a temporary one which extends for the duration of the licence. Most of the North Sea states have adopted a chessboard system of licensing based upon individual 'blocks', although Denmark has divided its entire sector between only two exploration consortia. The size of the 'blocks' adopted by the remaining countries are all different with the UK having the smallest and Norway the largest (Fig. 11.12b). Generally speaking, the views of industry and government diverge on what represents the optimum size – the former prefer 'blocks' to be larger, the latter prefer them to be smaller. This difference is related to the scope for tighter government control over oil-company activities that is implicit in smaller licence units. The fine spatial framework provided by the 'block' system makes it possible for governments to use the licence allocation procedure to influence the location and speed of exploration by the selective release of territory and to control the pattern of commercial involvement by discriminating between applicants.

Political Representation

Just as the partitioning of space may affect the allocation of resources, so the creation of areal units for the purposes of political representation may influence the allocation of power. Most electoral systems involve a procedure whereby votes are cast on some kind of constituency basis. The successful candidate(s) theoretically represent at some higher level, which may be a regional or national legislature, the interests of the population residing in these territorial units. Intuitively, it seems reasonable to assume that the composition of these assemblies should closely reflect the voting preferences of the electorate. This is not always the case. With reference to general elections in the UK, Taylor (1973) notes that a 44 per cent share of the vote resulted in a landslide defeat for the Conversatives in 1906, 40 per cent of the House of Commons' seats for the Liberals in 1910 and a parliamentary majority for Labour in 1964. The most important factor contributing to such apparent contradictions is the areal pattern of constituencies, which provides the spatial framework for the organization of elections. Two principal sources of distortion may be identified. The first concerns the ratio within the constituency of voters to representatives; the second concerns certain political characteristics of its population. Both of these issues may be resolved by redrawing boundaries to alter (i) the size of constituencies and (ii) the shape of constituencies.

Size of Constituencies – A basic principle in any parliamentary democracy should be equality in the effectiveness of votes. Such equality implies the maintenance of a more or less constant ratio in different constituencies between the number of voters and the number of representatives which they elect. The classic 'rotten borough' of Old Sarum in which a deserted town site returned two members of parliament until 1832 may be of interest only to political historians, but this type of situation is by no means confined to the 'bad old days'. A Supreme Court ruling in the US in 1962 opened up a Pandora's Box of similar, if less extreme, electoral abuses. This suit was brought against the state of Tennessee by a group of voters who alleged that the electoral constituencies in that state ensured that the value of votes in certain urban counties was 'debased' relative to those in some rural areas because of widely differing voter/representative ratios. In fact the number of inhabitants per legislator in certain urban constituencies was as much as 19 times greater than in less populous rural areas, but this subsequently appeared a relatively mild distortion when it was revealed that a corresponding ratio of 978 to 1 existed in Vermont (Silva, 1965)! In some cases, these situations were deliberately maintained by a particular group for its own political advantage. Representatives of rural areas, for example, were frequently unwilling to legislate themselves out of a job by promoting the necessary boundary changes (see Bushman and Stanley, 1971). However, imbalances in the voter/representative ratio ultimately reflect a failure to readjust constituency boundaries to changes in population distribution. Evidence for this is provided by the frequent over-representation of rural and agricultural interests in the representative assemblies of many democratic states.

The problem is sometimes aggravated by policy measures which accelerate the process of population redistribution. Prior to the 1974 general election in the UK, constituency size ranged from almost 100,000 voters in the case of Billericay to less than 30,000 in Ladywood. Each of these two constituencies typifies differing aspects of intra-metropolitan population change. Thus whilst Ladywood contains extensive slum-clearance zones within the inner areas of Birmingham, Billericay is one of many rapidly growing commuter centres around London. Quite apart from creating a need for boundary change to ensure equality of representation, such trends have interesting implications for future general-election results in the UK. Inner-city areas such as Ladywood have long been Labour strongholds. Rehousing policies which transfer much of their population to estates on the urban fringe therefore have the effect of introducing new Labour voters into areas of traditional Conservative support in the outer suburbs. Similarly, boundary changes in inner-city constituencies necessitated by such shifts of population may tend to reduce their political homogeneity. Both of these inferences suggest a reduction in the number of 'solid' seats and a corresponding increase in the number of 'marginals' (see Rowley, 1970).

Despite the complexities of the process, it is now generally agreed in most democratic states that there is a need for a mechanism to adjust constituency boundaries on a regular basis to take account of population change. Following the 1962 Supreme Court verdict, the criterion of equality of population size has been vigorously applied in the US where reapportionment in the wake of this decision has drastically reduced the variation in population size between the largest and smallest electoral districts within every state of the union. For example, variations of 53.4 per cent and 87.1 per cent in Florida and Rhode Island were reduced, under changes introduced in 1970, to 0 1 and 0.16 per cent respectively, and a figure of 106.3 per cent in California fell to 1.65 per cent (Brunn, 1974). Such variations are very small when compared with the tolerance limit of plus or minus 25 per cent of the mean constituency size within which the UK Boundary Commission was asked to operate under the terms of the Act which created it in 1944. In practice, the Commission has not even adhered to these guidelines because it has tended to regard the existence of constituencies with often ill-defined community associations as a more important principle than equality of population size (see Rowley, 1975).

The US and UK have plural or 'first past the post' electoral systems in which a party may theoretically obtain 49 per cent of the popular vote and yet gain no representatives if it fails to get a majority in any one constituency. Systems based upon proportional representation are designed to overcome this weakness by enabling the direct translation of a given proportion of the popular vote into a corresponding percentage of the seats in a representative assembly. However, constituency size can have a decisive influence upon the extent to which such a proportional relationship is actually achieved. The existence of a single national electoral district as employed in Israel and the Netherlands guarantees direct proportionality, but the adoption of smaller constituencies tends to undermine this relationship. The Republic of Ireland has a proportional-representation system based upon many such sub-national constituencies which have been progressively reduced in size towards the constitutional limit of 3 representatives per constituency (Paddison, 1976). In 1923, there were 30 separate constituencies returning an average of 5.1 members; 50 years later there were 42 constituencies each of which was represented by an average of 3.5 members. This trend is related to the fact that only 51 per cent of the vote is needed in a 3-member constituency to secure 2 out of the 3 seats (i.e. 66 per cent); whilst conversely a popular vote as low as 42 per cent in a 4-member constituency will also yield 2 seats (i.e. 50 per cent). This kind of arithmetic ensures that 3-member constituencies are advantageous in areas where a party is strong whereas 4- and 5-member constituencies are preferable where it expects to do less well. Since the periodic review of constituency boundaries in Eire is carried out by the government of the day rather than by an independent commission, there is a strong temptation to manipulate these relationships to party advantage. Figure 11.13 indicates the ratio between the votes and seats gained by

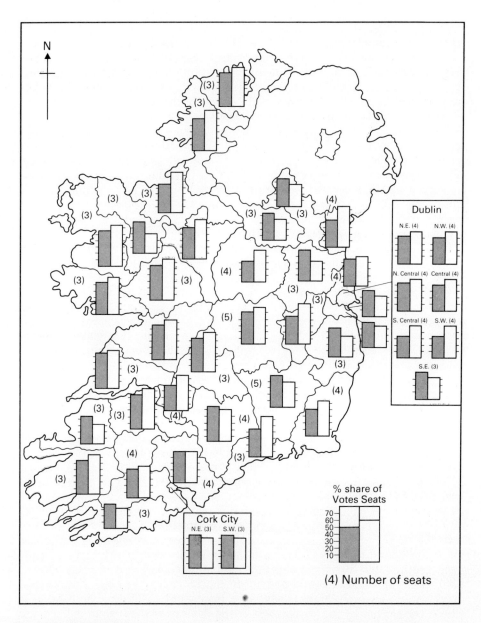

Fig. 11.13 Fianna Fail party's share of votes and seats in Irish general election, 1969 (Paddison, 1976, 234).

the ruling Fianna Fail party at the 1969 general election. It is noticeable that Fianna Fail gained a higher proportion of seats than votes in most constituencies by the concentration of 3-seat constituencies in the west where it is traditionally strong and 4-seat constituencies in the Dublin area where the opposition Fianna Gael party generally has more support.

Shape of Constituencies – Notwithstanding this evidence of electoral manipulation in Eire by means of changes in constituency size, such manipulation is more frequently associated with modifications to constituency shape. The so-called

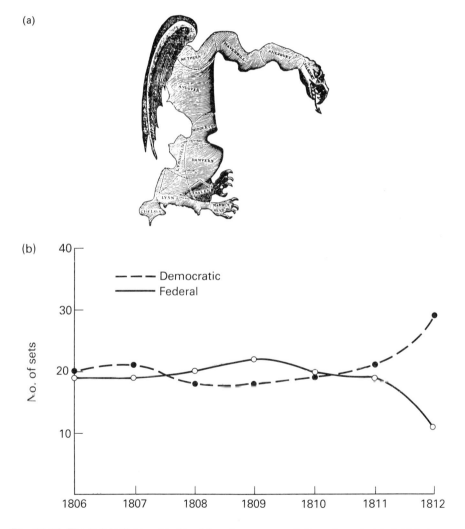

Fig. 11.14 The 'original' gerrymander: (a) cartoon representation of senatorial districts in Massachusetts, 1812 (*Boston Gazette*, 26 March, 1812); (b) party representation in Massachusetts Senate, 1806–1812 (Taylor, 1973, 128).

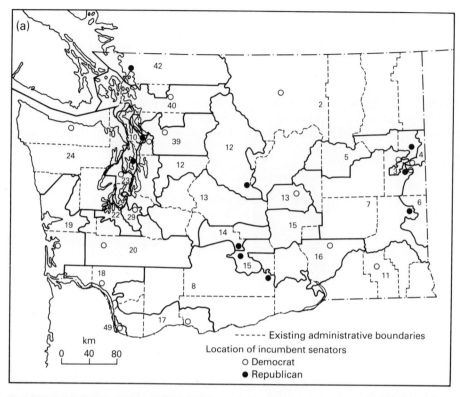

Fig. 11.15 Alternative redistricting proposals for the state of Washington, 1972 (excluding Greater Seattle area): (a) Democratic proposal; (b) Republican proposal; (c) Court proposal (The numbers identify the electoral districts.) (Morrill, 1973, 470, 472 and 473).

gerrymander rests upon the fact that voting behaviour normally reveals distinctive spatial patterns with concentrations of support for a particular party in specific areas. This provides the opportunity to alter the shape of constituencies on the basis of a known or presumed spatial distribution of party support. Two basic strategies may be identified: one which splits the opposition vote in such a way as to minimize the number of constituencies in which it may be expected to achieve a majority; and a second which concentrates the opposition vote in specific districts where it is wasted on 'overkill'. Application of either of these strategies tends to produce irregularly shaped rather than compact districts. This is apparent in Figure 11.14a, which is a cartoon representation of the original gerrymander in Massachusetts. The success of this device was revealed by the 1812 election results in which, after a series of close contests, the Democrats gained a landslide victory despite securing a minority of the total votes cast (Fig. 11.14b)! This notorious case underlines the potential significance of such spatial manipulations for the allocation of political power.

Paradoxically, regular and well-intentioned attempts to ensure population equality between electoral districts increase the opportunities for gerrymandering. Figure 11.15 is typical of a succession of proposals for the redrawing of electoral

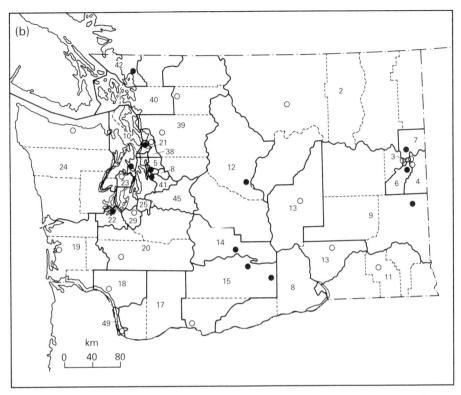

districts through the US following the Supreme Court verdict of 1962. It demonstrates the way in which the two political parties produced very different suggestions for the division of Washington state into electoral districts of equal population size. Both the Republican and Democratic proposals had the dual objectives of meeting this principle and maximizing the effectiveness of their own votes in terms of representation in the state legislative chambers (Morrill, 1973). As a result of these differences, a 'neutral' solution was devised on the ruling of the Federal Court (Fig. 11.15c). In addition to equality of population, this solution took account of such criteria as the need to ensure that the districts were reasonably compact in shape, that they reflected existing county boundaries and that they took account of the 'natural' frontiers created by such features as Puget Sound. The reconciliation of such diverse criteria is not always possible. The 'neutral' solution indicated in Figure 11.15c was derived intuitively, but various computer programs have been developed which seek to solve this kind of redistricting problem (Taylor, 1973). Nevertheless, it is important to recognize the limitations of computers in this respect and any attempt to devise an impartial arrangement of constituency boundaries must take account of the spatial distribution of voting patterns if unintentional, but no less significant, gerrymanders are to be avoided.

Areas may be regarded as bounded spaces. Such partitions of space may possess the characteristics of either field or territorial areas, but more frequently they combine the properties of both. No matter whether areas are defined in terms of the

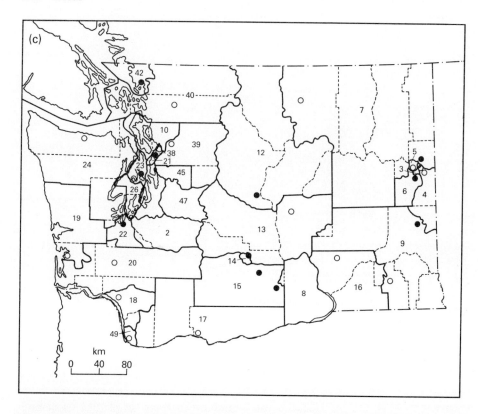

effect of the dimension of distance upon movement or with reference to the physical and human distributions which make up the content of space, it is clear that they are not simply geometric abstractions and that they have important practical consequences upon the daily lives of individuals and upon the organization of society as a whole.

Further Reading

BERRY, B. J. L. and HORTON, F. E. 1970: Urbanization and environment: changes in the nature of the urban system. In Berry, B. J. L. and Horton, F. E. (Eds.), *Geographic perspectives on urban systems*, Englewood Cliffs, N.J., 20–63.

A good historical account of the evolution of metropolitan field areas in the US.

GOTTMANN, J. 1973: *The significance of territory*. Charlottesville.

A stimulating collection of essays concerned with the nature of territorial areas at the international scale.

MASSAM, B. 1975: *Location and space in social administration*. London.

A thorough treatment of the practical significance of location–allocation problems.

TAYLOR, P. J. and JOHNSTON, R. J. 1979: *Geography of elections*. Harmondsworth.

A section of this book considers the potential sources of electoral distortion inherent in the use of areal units as bases for political representation.

Conclusion

We have considered a wide range of topics in the pages of this book and it may be helpful to try and identify certain general themes implicit in the selection, organization and presentation of the material contained within it. The role of man as a decision maker lies at the heart of our interpretation of the spatial arrangement of human activities at the surface of the earth. In view of the fact that individuals may be very unpredictable in their behaviour, such a focus may appear to provide a very insecure foundation upon which to base any generalizations about these spatial arrangements. However, although we may find it difficult to explain and predict the actions of individuals, we can often make probability statements about the way in which the majority of people will react in a given situation.

The most fundamental principle of spatial organization is related to the dimension of distance and its influence upon movement as expressed in the form of various distance/decay relationships. This observed effect of distance upon spatial interaction and spatial diffusion itself rests upon an even more basic notion – the principle of least effort. The conjunction of the essentially behavioural principle of least effort with the physical properties of distance as a barrier to movement underpins our approach to the explanation of the spatial distribution of human activities. This approach also involves a recognition of the need to interpret spatial arrangements in the context of the functional systems which they represent. Thus settlement patterns, for example, can only be fully understood in relation to the existence of a functional hierarchy based upon the provision of goods and services to surrounding hinterlands of varying size.

The dynamic nature of spatial patterns is a further important theme. These patterns are not instant creations and, in our attempts at explanation, we are almost inevitably drawn into evolutionary statements of causality. Closely related to this is the reciprocal nature of the relationship between process and pattern. The influence of past and present spatial arrangements upon the future options and actions of decision makers has been emphasized at several stages in this book, not least in the context of the problem of geographical variations in levels of economic development. Consideration of this latter issue underlines the point that the study of human geography need not be regarded as an end in itself, but may also be seen as contributing to our understanding of many very real economic and social problems. Notions of efficiency, for example, are implicit in the siting of industrial plants and public facilities. Such problems are basically concerned with locating and organizing human activities in such a way as to maximize financial and/or other less tangible social or psychological returns. Notions of equality also have a spatial component. Gross inequalities in living conditions and opportunities between people situated in different places may be observed at every scale of analysis. The reduction or, in a utopian world, the elimination of such contrasts is obviously not an exclusively geographical problem, but it does represent a worthwhile objective towards which our attempts at the explanation of spatial systems may be directed, since it is only through such understanding that we can hope to control the forces responsible for these inequalities.

Further reading

SMITH, D. M. 1979: *Where the grass is greener*. Harmondsworth.

A good introduction to the spatial dimensions of inequality at various geographical scales.

Glossary of Technical Terms

Algorithm – A term used in computing science to refer to a collective sequence of interrelated steps for the solution of a particular problem such as the derivation of a minimum-distance path through a network.

Analysis of variance – The variance of a data set is a measure of the extent to which individual values vary about its overall mean value. Analysis of variance is a procedure which makes it possible to compare the variances of two data sets with a view to establishing if any statistically significant difference exists between their respective means. Thus analysis of variance isolates two components of variability – that which may be expected *within* a data set and that which may be found *between* two data sets with differing mean values.

Correlation – Correlation refers to the relationship between two variables. A positive correlation indicates that an increase in the value of one variable is accompanied by an increase in that of another variable. A negative correlation exists when a rise in one is matched by a decline in the other. A correlation coefficient is a single value which describes the degree or strength of any relationship.

Factor analysis – Factor analysis is a technique which may be used to identify complex relationships between many variables. Large data sets are reduced to a limited number of factors which account for a large amount of the total variability in the original data set. The existence of these factors suggests that some of the variables behave in a similar fashion and are therefore probably related. Factor scores may be calculated which plot the position of individual observations with respect to linear scales relating to each factor.

Linear programming – This is one of a number of techniques which have been developed to provide a quantitative basis for decision making. The word 'programming' is a synonym for planning and the adjective 'linear' is employed because, in its simplest form, the technique is used to solve problems in which there is a straight-line relationship between one variable and some other variable(s) – that is, as the value of one variable increases by one unit, so the value of another variable which is related to it rises (or falls in the case of a negative relationship) by a consistent amount. Such relationships are, for example, implicit in the problem facing an industrial firm when deciding how to distribute its products at minimum total transport costs from a fixed arrangement of plants of known capacity to a given pattern of markets of known size (i.e. the 'transportation problem').

Normal distribution – This implies a symmetrical arrangement of individual observations about the mean of a data set, with the majority of cases concentrated about this mid-point.

Normative – The normative approach to explanation attempts to establish what *should* occur in a particular situation defined by a set of carefully specified assumptions. It therefore provides a yardstick or norm against which reality may be measured.

Principal-components analysis – This technique is similar to factor analysis in its approach and its application.

Regression – Just as correlation measures the *strength* of a relationship between two variables, so regression describes its *form*. Thus a regression equation may be calculated which indicates the average amount by which one variable changes (up or down) per unit of change in the other variable.

Residuals from regression–The regression equation permits the prediction of one variable from a known value of the other variable – the former is said to be *dependent* on the latter. A residual from regression represents the difference between the predicted value of the dependent variable and its actual or observed value. A negative residual exists when the equation overpredicts, a positive residual is the result of underprediction.

Standard deviation–This is another index of variability within a data set and is the square root of the variance term. Standard-deviation units may be calculated which locate the position of individual values with respect to the mean of the data set to which they belong.

Utility–This term was originally conceived by economists to aid their understanding of the way in which individuals make choices between, for example, buying a washing machine and a hi-fi system. It is an index of the satisfaction which the consumer receives from each purchase. Such an abstract concept is obviously difficult to measure and it is normally converted into a more tangible criterion, such as income, which may be empirically identified.

Bibliography

ABLER, R., ADAMS, J. S. and GOULD, P. 1971: *Spatial organization: the geographer's view of the world.* Englewood Cliffs, N.J.

ADAMS, J. G. U. 1971: London's third airport. *Geographical Journal* **137**, 468–93.

— 1972: Life in a global village. *Environment and Planning* **4**, 381–94.

ADAMS, J. S. 1969: Directional bias in intra-urban migration. *Economic Geography* **45**, 302–23.

— 1970: Residential structure of mid-western cities. *Association of American Geographers, Annals* **60**, 37–62.

ALEXANDER, J. W., BROWN, S. E. and DAHLBERG, R. E. 1958: Freight rates: selected aspects of uniform and nodal regions. *Economic Geography* **34**, 1–18.

ALLAN, J. A. 1976: The Kufrah agricultural schemes. *Geographical Journal* **142**, 48–56.

ALONSO, W. 1964: *Location and land use.* Cambridge, Mass.

APPLETON, J. H. 1963: The efficacy of the Great Australian Divide as a barrier to railway communication. *Institute of British Geographers, Transactions* **33**, 101–22.

ASCHMANN, H. 1970: The natural history of a mine. *Economic Geography* **46**, 172–89.

BAKER, A. R. H. 1973: Adjustments to distance between farmstead and field: some findings from the southwestern Paris Basin in the early 19th century. *Canadian Geographer* **17**, 259–73.

BALDWIN, A. 1975: Mass removals and separate development. *Journal of Southern Africa Studies* **1**, 1215–27.

BARBOUR, K. M. 1977: Rural road lengths and farm-market distances in north-east Ulster. *Geografiska Annaler* **59** (B), 14–27.

BARR, B. M. and FAIRBAIRN, K. J. 1974: Some observations on the environment of the firm: locational behaviour of Kraft pulp mills in the interior of British Columbia. *Professional Geographer* **26**, 19–26.

BARR, B. M., LINDSAY, I. J. and REINELT, E. R. 1971: Patterns of urban spacing in the USSR: analysis of order neighbour statistics in 2 dimensional space. *Journal of Regional Science* **11**, 211–24.

BARRACLOUGH, S. and DOMIKE, A. L. 1966: Agrarian structure in seven Latin American countries. *Land Economics* **42**, 391–425.

BARTLETT, H. H. 1956: Fire, primitive agriculture and grazing in the Tropics. In Thomas, W. L. (Ed.), 692–720.

BAUER, F. H. 1963: Significant factors in the white settlement of Northern Australia. *Australian Geographical Studies* **1**, 39–48.

BAYLISS, B. T. and EDWARDS, S. L. 1970: *Industrial demand for transport.* London.

BEAVON, K. S. O. 1977: *Central place theory: a reinterpretation.* London.

BERGMANN, E. F. 1973: The multi-national corporation. *Professional Geographer* **25**, 255–60.

BERRY, B. J. L. 1961: City-size distributions and economic development. *Economic Development and Cultural Change* **4**, 573–87.

— 1967: *Geography of market centers and retail distribution.* Englewood Cliffs, N.J.

— 1969: Relationships between regional economic development and the urban system: the case of Chile. *Tijdschrift voor Economische en Sociale Geografie* **60**, 283–307.

— 1970: The geography of the United States in the year 2000. *Institute of British Geographers, Transactions* **51**, 21–54.

— 1972: Hierarchical diffusion: the basis of developmental filtering and spread in a system of growth centres. In Hansen, N. M. (Ed.), *Growth centers in regional economic development*, New York, 108–38.

BERRY, B. J. L. and GARRISON, W. L. 1958: The functional bases of the central place hierarchy. *Economic Geography* **34**, 145, 154.

BERRY, B. J. L. and PRED, A. 1961: *Central place studies: a bibliography of theory and applications*. Bibliography Series 1, Regional Science Research Institute, Philadelphia.

BERRY, B. J. L., BARNUM, H. G. and TENNANT, R. J. 1962: Retail location and consumer behavior. *Regional Science Association, Papers and Proceedings* **9**, 65–106.

BERRY, B. J. L. *et al* 1966: Essays on commodity flows and the spatial structure of the Indian economy. *University of Chicago, Department of Geography, Research Papers* **111**.

BLACK, W. R. 1972: Interregional commodity flows: some experiments with the gravity model. *Journal of Regional Science* **12**, 107–18.

BLACKBOURN, A. 1972: The location of foreign-owned manufacturing plants in the Republic of Ireland. *Tijdschrift voor Economische en Sociale Geografie* **63**, 438–43.

— 1974: The spatial behaviour of American firms in Western Europe. In Hamilton, F. E. I. (Ed.), *Spatial perspectives on industrial organization and decision-making*, London.

BLAIKIE, P. M. 1971: Spatial organization of agriculture in some north Indian villages. *Institute of British Geographers, Transactions* **52**, 1–40.

BLAINEY, G. 1968: *The tyranny of distance*. Melbourne.

BOAL, F. W. 1968: Technology and urban form. *Journal of Geography* **67**, 229–36.

— 1969: Territoriality on the Shankill–Falls divide, Belfast. *Irish Geography* **6**, 30–50.

BOARD, C. 1976: Spatial structure of labour migration. In Smith, D. M. (Ed.), *Separation in South Africa*, Occasional Paper No. 6, Department of Geography, Queen Mary College, London, 63–76.

BOWEN, E. G. 1966: The Welsh colony in Patagonia 1865–1885: a study in historical geography. *Geographical Journal* **132**, 16–27.

BRAEKHÜS, K. 1976: Oslo: past, present, future. *Norsk Geografisk Tidsskrift* **30**, 127–38.

BRAY, J. 1969: The craft structure of a traditional Yoruba town. *Institute of British Geographers, Transactions* **46**, 179–93.

BROEK, J. O. M. 1932: *The Santa Clara Valley, California*. Utrecht.

BROOK, A. 1976: Spatial systems in American history. *Area* **8**, 47–52.

BROOKFIELD, H. C. 1975: *Interdependent development*. London.

BROWETT, J. G. 1976: The application of a spatial model to South Africa's development regions. *South African Geographical Journal* **58**, 118–29.

BROWN, L. A. and COX, K. R. 1971: Empirical regularities in the diffusion of innovations. *Association of American Geographers, Annals* **61**, 551–9.

BROWN, L. A. and MOORE, E. G. 1969: Diffusion research in geography: a perspective. *Progress in Geography* **1**, 119–58.

BROWN, P. and BROOKFIELD, H. C. 1967: Chimbu settlement and residence: a study of patterns, trends and idiosyncrasy, *Pacific Viewpoint* **8**, 119–51.

BRUNN, S. D. 1974: *Geography and politics in America*. New York.

BRUSH, J. E. 1953: The hierarchy of central places in southwestern Wisconsin. *Geographical Review* **43**, 380–402.

BRUSH, J. E. and BRACEY, H. E. 1955: Rural service centers in south-western Wisconsin and southern England. *Geographical Review* **45**, 559–69.

BUNGE, W. 1962: *Theoretical geography, Lund Studies in Geography* (Ser. C) **1.**

BURNS, W. 1959: *British shopping centres*. London.

BURTON, I. 1963: *Accessibility in northern Ontario: an application of graph theory to a regional highway network*. Ontario.

BURTON, I. and KATES, R. W. 1964: The perception of natural hazards in resource management. *Natural Resource Journal* **3**, 412–41.

BUSHMAN, D. O. and STANLEY, W. R. 1971: State senate reapportionment in the Southeast. *Association of American Geographers, Annals* **61**, 654–70.

BYLUND, E. 1960: Theoretical considerations regarding the distribution of settlement in inner north Sweden. *Geografiska Annaler* **42**, 225–31.

CAMERON, G. C. and CLARK, B. D. 1966: *Industrial movement and the regional problem.* Glasgow.

CAMERON, J. M. R. 1974: Distortions in pre-settlement land evaluation: the case of Swan River, Western Australia. *Professional Geographer* **26**, 393–8.

CARROTHERS, G. A. P. 1969: An historical review of the gravity and potential concepts of human interaction. In Ambrose, P. (Ed.), *Analytical human geography*, London, 226–42.

CARTER, H. 1972: *The study of urban geography*. London.

CHAPMAN, K. 1973: Agglomeration and linkage in the United Kingdom petro-chemical industry. *Institute of British Geographers, Transactions* **60**, 33–68.

— 1974: The structure and development of the oil-based industrial complex at Grangemouth. *Scottish Geographical Magazine* **90**, 98–109.

— 1976: *North Sea oil and gas: a geographical perspective*. Newton Abbot.

CHISHOLM, M. 1962: *Rural settlement and land use*. London.

— 1975: The reformation of local government in England. In Peel, R., Chisholm, M. and Haggett, P. (Eds.), *Processes in physical and human geography*, London.

CHISHOLM, M. and O'SULLIVAN, P. 1973: *Freight flows and spatial aspects of the British economy*. Cambridge.

CHRISTALLER, W. 1966: *Central places in southern Germany*. Translated by C. W. Baskin. Englewood Cliffs, N.J.

CHRISTOPHER, A. J. 1973: Environmental perception in Southern Africa. *South African Geographical Journal* **55**, 14–22.

CLAPPERTON, C. M. 1972: Patterns of physical and human activity on Mount Etna. *Scottish Geographical Magazine* **88**, 160–7.

CLARK, C., WILSON, F. and BRADLEY, J. 1969: Industrial location and economic potential in Western Europe. *Regional Studies* **3**, 197–212.

CLARK, W. A. V. 1968: Consumer travel patterns and the concept of range. *Association of American Geographers, Annals* **58**, 386–96.

COATES, B. E. and RAWSTRON, E. M. 1971: *Regional variations in Britain*. London.

COLE, H. S. D., FREEMAN, C., JAHODA, M. and PAVITT, K. L. R. (Eds.). 1973: *Thinking about the future*. London.

COMMISSION ON THE THIRD LONDON AIRPORT 1971: *Report*. London.

CONNELL, J. 1974; The evolution of Tanzanian rural development. *Journal of Tropical Geography* **38**, 7–18.

COULL, J. R. 1962: The island of Tiree. *Scottish Geographical Magazine* **78**, 17–32.

— 1975: The big fish pond: a perspective on the contemporary situation in the world's fisheries. *Area* **7**, 103–7.

COUPER, A. D. 1968: Indigenous trading in Fiji and Tonga: a study of changing patterns. *New Zealand Geographer* **24**, 50–60.

— 1972: *The geography of sea transport*. London.

COX, K. R. 1965: The application of linear programming to geographic problems. *Tijdschrift voor Economische en Sociale Geografie* **56**, 228–35.

CURRY, L. 1963: Regional variation in the seasonal programming of livestock farms in New Zealand. *Economic Geography* **39**, 95–117.

CYERT, R. M. and MARCH, J. G. 1963: *A behavioural theory of the firm*. Englewood Cliffs, N.J.

DACEY, M. F. 1962: Analysis of central place and point patterns by a nearest neighbour method. *Lund Studies in Geography* (Ser. B)**24**, 55–75.

DAHLKE, J. 1975: Evolution of the wheat belt in Western Australia: thoughts on the nature of pioneering along the dry margin. *Australian Geographer* **13**, 3–14.

DARBY, H. C. 1956: The clearing of the woodland in Europe. In Thomas, W. L. (Ed.), 183–216.

— (Ed.) *The Domesday Geography of England*, Cambridge (6 vols.).

DAVIES, G. W. 1976: The effect of a subway on the spatial distribution of population. *Journal of Transport Economics and Policy* **10**, 126–36.

DAWSON, A. H. 1977: Costs of production and location of British industry. *Geography* **62**, 93–6.

DAY, R. A. 1974: Consumer shopping behaviour in a planned urban environment. *Tijdschrift voor Economische en Sociale Geografie* **64**, 75–83.

DEMAINE, H. and DIXON, C. 1972: Land tenure patterns and agricultural development in North-east Thailand: a case study of the Lam Pao irrigation area. *Journal of the Siam Society* **60**, 45–60.

DENNIS, A. S. and KREIGE, D. F. 1966: Results of ten years of cloud seeding in Santa Clara County, California. *Journal of Applied Meteorology* **5**, 684–91.

DENT, W. 1966: Optimal wool flows for minimization of transport costs. *Australian Journal of Agricultural Economics* **19**, 142–57.

DEPARTMENT OF TOWN AND COUNTRY PLANNING, UNIVERSITY OF MANCHESTER. 1966: *Regional shopping centres in North West England, Part Two: A retail shopping model*. Manchester.

DE SMIDT, M. 1966: Foreign industrial establishments located in the Netherlands. *Tijdschrift voor Economische en Sociale Geografie* **57**, 1–19.

DICKASON, D. G. and WHEELER, J. O. 1967: An application of linear programming: the case of Indian wheat transportation. *National Geographical Journal of India* **13**, 125–40.

DICKEN, P. 1971: Some aspects of the decision making behaviour of business organizations. *Economic Geography* **47**, 426–38.

DIENES, L. 1972: Investment priorities in the Soviet regions. *Association of American Geographers, Annals* **62**, 437–54.

DIETVORST, A. G. J. and WEVER, E. 1977: Changes in the pattern of information exchange in the Netherlands 1967–1974. *Tijdschrift voor Economische en Sociale Geografie* **68**, 72–82.

DILLMAN, C. D. 1970: Commuter workers and free zone industry along the Mexico–US border. *Association of American Geographers, Proceedings* **2**, 48–51.

DURY, G. H. 1977: Likely hurricane damage by the year 2000. *Professional Geographer* **29**, 254–8.

DUTT, A. K. 1972: Daily influence area of Calcutta. *Journal of Tropical Geography* **35**, 32–40.

DYOS, H. J. and ALDCROFT, D. H. 1971: *British transport*. Leicester.

ENGBERG, H. C. and HANCE, W. A. 1969: Growth and dispersion of branch banking in Tropical Africa 1950–1964. *Economic Geography* **45**, 195–208.

EVANS, W. D. and HOFFENBERG, M. 1952: The inter-industry relations study for 1947. *Review of Economic Statistics* **34**, 97–142.

EVERSLEY, D. E. C. 1965: Social and psychological factors in the determination of industrial location. In Wilson, T. (Ed.), *Papers on regional development*, Oxford, 102–14.

FAIR, T. J. D. 1975: Commuting fields and the metropolitan structure of the Witwatersrand. *South African Geographer* **5**, 7–15.

— 1976: Polarisation, dispersion and decentralisation in the South African space economy. *South African Geographical Journal* **58**, 40–56.

FAIR, T. J. D. and SCHMIDT, C. F. 1974: Contained urbanization: a case study. *South African Geographical Journal* **56**, 155–66.

FIFER, J. V. 1966: Bolivia's boundary with Brazil: a century of evolution. *Geographical Journal* **132**, 360–71.

FORBES, J. 1964: Mapping accessibility. *Scottish Geographical Magazine* **80**, 12–21.

FOUND, W. C. 1971: *A theoretical approach to rural land-use patterns.* London.

FREMLIN, J. H. 1964: How many people can the world support? *New Scientist* **24**, 285–7.

FRIEDMANN, J. 1966: *Regional development policy: a case study of Venezuela.* Cambridge, Mass.

— 1972: A general theory of polarized development. In Hansen, M. (Ed.), *Growth centers in regional economic development,* New York, 82–102.

FULLER, G. 1974: On the spatial diffusion of fertility decline: the distance-to-clinic variable in a Chilean community. *Economic Geography* **50**, 324–32.

GARNER, B. J. 1966: The internal structure of retail nucleations. *Northwestern University Studies in Geography* **12.**

GARRISON, W. L. 1960: Connectivity of the interstate highway system. *Regional Science Association, Papers and Proceedings* **6**, 121–37.

GARRISON, W. L., BERRY, B. J. L., MARBLE, D. F., NYSTUEN, J. D. and MORRILL, R. L. 1959: *Studies of highway development and geographic change.* Seattle.

GARST, R. D. 1974: Innovation diffusion among the Gusii of Kenya. *Economic Geography* **50**, 300–12.

GAUTHIER, H. L. 1968: Transportation and the growth of the Sao Paulo economy. *Journal of Regional Science* **8**, 77–94.

— 1970: Geography, transportation and regional development. *Economic Geography* **46**, 612–19.

GERASIMOV, I. P. 1976: Problems of natural environment transformation in Soviet constructive geography. *Progress in Geography* **9**, 73–100.

GETIS, A. and GETIS, J. M. 1968: Retail store spatial affinities. *Urban Studies* **5**, 317–32.

GILBERT, A. 1974: *Latin American development.* London.

— 1975: A note on the incidence of development in the vicinity of a growth centre. *Regional Studies* **9**, 325–33.

GINSBURG, N. 1957: Natural resources and economic development. *Association of American Geographers, Annals* **47**, 196–212.

— 1961: *Atlas of economic development.* Chicago.

GLACKEN, C. J. 1967: *Traces on the Rhodian shore.* Berkeley and Los Angeles.

GODDARD, J. B. 1971: Office communication and office location: a review of current research. *Regional Studies* **5**, 263–80.

GODDARD, J. B. and PYE, R. 1977. Telecommunications and office location. *Regional Studies* **11**, 19–30.

GOTTMANN, J. 1961: *Megalopolis.* Cambridge, Mass.

GOULD, P. R. 1963: Man against the environment: a game theoretic framework. *Association of American Geographers, Annals* **53**, 290–7.

— 1970: Tanzania 1920–1963: the spatial impress of the modernization process. *World Politics* **22**, 149–70.

GOULD, P, and WHITE, R. 1974: *Mental maps.* London.

GOULD, W. T. S. 1971: Geography and educational opportunity in Tropical Africa. *Tijdschrift voor Economische en Sociale Geografie* **42**, 82–9.

GRUNIG, J. E. 1970/71: Communication and the economic decision making process of Colombian peasants. *Economic Development and Cultural Change* **19**, 580–97.

HÄGERSTRAND, T. 1952: The propagation of innovation waves. *Lund Studies in Geography* (Ser. B) **4.**

— 1957: Migration and area. In *Migration in Sweden, Lund Studies in Geography* (Ser. B) **113.**

— 1967: *Innovation diffusion as a spatial process.* Translated by A. R. Pred. Chicago.

— 1970: What about people in regional science. *Regional Science Association, Papers and Proceedings* **24**, 7–21.

— 1973: The domain of human geography. In Chorley, R. J. (Ed.), *Directions in geography,* London, 67–87.

HAGGETT, P. 1975: Simple epidemics in human populations: some geographical aspects of the Hamer-Soper diffusion models. In Peel, R., Chisholm, M. and Haggett, P. (Eds.), *Processes in physical and human geography*, Bristol.

HAGGETT, P. and CHORLEY, R. 1969: *Network analysis in geography*. London.

HALL, J. M. 1970: Industry grows where the grass is greener. *Area* **3**, 40–6.

HALL, P. *et al.* 1973: *The containment of urban England* (2 vols.). London.

HAMILTON, F. E. I. 1971: Decision making and industrial location in Eastern Europe. *Institute of British Geographers, Transactions* **52**, 77–94.

— 1976: Multinational enterprise and the EEC. *Tidjschrift voor Economische en Sociale Geografie* **67**, 258–78.

HAMILTON, P. 1977: *Overpopulation in the central Andes of Peru*. Unpublished Ph.D. thesis, University of Aberdeen.

HANSEN, W. G. 1959: How accessibility shapes land use. *Journal of the American Institute of Planners* **25**, 73–5.

HARDWICK, P. A. 1972: Salisbury's urban transportation problems in the light of current overseas trends. *Geographical Association of Rhodesia, Proceedings* **6**, 20–31.

HARRIS, D. R. 1974: Tropical vegetation: an outline and some misconceptions. *Geography* **59**, 240–50.

HARTSHORNE, R. 1937: The Polish corridor. *Journal of Geography* **36**, 161–76.

HARVEY, D. 1969: *Explanation in geography*. London.

— 1973: *Social justice and the city*. London.

HARVEY, M. E. and GREENBERG, P. D. 1972: Development dichotomies, growth poles and diffusion processes in Sierra Leone. *African Urban Notes* **6**, 117–36.

HAY, A. M. 1971: Connection and orientation in three West African road networks. *Regional Studies* **5**, 315–19.

— 1976: A simple location theory for mining activity. *Geography* **61**, 65–76.

HAYTER, R. 1975: Farmers' crop decisions and the frost hazard in east-central Alberta. *Tijdschrift voor Economische en Sociale Geografie* **66**, 93–102.

HEAL, D. W. 1974: *The steel industry in post-war Britain*. Newton Abbott.

HENSHALL, J. D. and MOMSEN, Jr, R. P. 1974: *A geography of Brazilian development*. London.

HILL, A. G. 1973: Segregation in Kuwait. In *Social patterns in cities*, Institute of British Geographers Special Publication No. 5, 123–42.

HILL, J. 1965: El Chamizal: a century-old boundary dispute. *Geographical Review* **55**, 510–22.

HIRST, M. A. 1973: A functional analysis of towns in Tanzania. *Tijdschrift voor Economische en Sociale Geografie* **64**, 39–51.

HOLLAND, S. 1976: *Capital versus the regions*. London.

HOLSMAN, A. J. 1975: Interstate interaction patterns in Australia. *Australian Geographical Studies* **13**, 41–61.

HOLSMAN, A. J. and CRAWFORD, S. A. 1975: Air-transport growth in under-developed regions. *Australian Geographer* **13**, 79–90.

HORTON, F. E. and REYNOLDS, D. R. 1971: Effects of urban spatial structure on individual behaviour. *Economic Geography* **47**, 36–48.

HUDSON, J. C. 1969: A location theory for rural settlement. *Association of American Geographers, Annals* **59**, 365–82.

HUFF, D. L. 1973: The delineation of a national system of regions on the basis of urban spheres of influence. *Regional Studies* **7**, 323–9.

HUFF, D. L. and LUTZ, J. M. 1974: The contagion of political unrest in independent Black Africa. *Economic Geography* **50**, 352–67.

HUGHES, J. W. and JAMES, F. J. 1975: Changing spatial distribution of jobs and residences. *Growth and Change* **6**, 20–5.

HUNTER, J. M. and YOUNG, J. C. 1971: Diffusion of influenza in England and Wales. *Association of American Geographers, Annals* **61**, 637–53.

HUNTINGTON, E. 1915: *Civilization and climate*. New Haven.

INGRAM, D. R. 1971: The concept of accessibility: a search for an operational form. *Regional Studies* **5**, 101–7.

ISARD, W. and SMITH, T. E. 1967: Location games: with applications to classic location problems. *Papers, Regional Science Association* **19**, 45–80.

JACKSON, J. C. 1969: Mining in 18th century Bangka – the pre-European exploitation of a tin island. *Pacific Viewpoint* **10**, 28–54.

JAMES, B. G. S. 1964: The incompatibility of industrial and trading cultures. *Journal of Industrial Economics* **13**, 90–4.

JANELLE, D. G. 1968: Central place development in a time–space framework. *Professional Geographer* **20**, 5–10.

JEFFERSON, M. 1928: The civilizing rails. *Economic Geography* **4**, 217–31.

JEFFREY, D. 1975: Spatial imbalance in the Australian regional economic system: structural unemployment 1955–1970. *Australian Geographer* **13**, 146–54.

JOHANSEN, H. E. 1971: Diffusion of strip-cropping in southwest Wisconsin. *Association of American Geographers, Annals* **61**, 671–83.

JOHNSON, E. A. J. 1970: *The organization of space in developing countries*. Cambridge, Mass.

JOHNSTON, R. J. 1976: *The world trade system*. London.

JOLLY, R. and KING, M. 1966: The organization of health services. In King, M. (Ed.), *Medical care in developing countries*, Nairobi.

JONES, G. 1964: *The Norse Atlantic saga*. London.

JONES, P. N. 1970: Some aspects of the changing distribution of coloured immigrants in Birmingham, 1961–1966. *Institute of British Geographers, Transactions* **50**, 199–219.

KANSKY, K. J. 1963: Structure of transportation networks. *University of Chicago, Department of Geography, Research Paper*, 84.

KATES, R. W. 1963: Perceptual regions and regional perception in flood plain management. *Regional Science Association, Papers and Proceedings* **11**, 217–27.

— 1971: Natural hazard in human ecological perspective: hypothesis and models. *Economic Geography* **47**, 438–51.

KATZMAN, M. T. 1975: Regional development policy in Brazil: the role of growth poles and development highways in Goias. *Economic Development and Cultural Change* **24**, 75–108.

KAUFMANN, A. 1968: *The science of decision making*. London.

KEEBLE, D. E. 1967: Models of economic development. In Chorley, R. J. and Haggett, P. (Eds.), *Models in geography*, London.

— 1969: Local industrial linkage and manufacturing growth in outer London. *Town Planning Review* **40**, 163–88.

— 1972: The South East and East Anglia. In G. Manners *et al.* (Eds.), *Regional development in Britain*, London.

KING, L. J. 1961: A multivariate analysis of the spacing of urban settlements in the United States. *Association of American Geographers, Annals* **51**, 222–33.

— 1962: A quantitative expression of the pattern of urban settlements in selected areas of the United States. *Tijdschrift voor Economische en Sociale Geografie* **53**, 1–7.

KIRK, W. 1960: The Sino-Indian frontier dispute: a geographical review. *Scottish Geographical Magazine* **76**, 3–13.

— 1963: Problems of geography. *Geography* **48**, 357–71.

KISSLING, C. C. 1969: Linkage importance in a regional highway network. *Canadian Geographer* **13**, 113–29.

KLEINPENNING, J. M. G. 1977: An evaluation of the Brazilian policy for the integration of the Amazon region (1964–1974). *Tijdschrift voor Economische en Sociale Geografie* **68**, 297–311.

KNOX, P. L. 1975: *Social well-being: a spatial perspective*. London.

KOLARS, J. and MALIN, H. J. 1970: Population and accessibility: an analysis of Turkish railroads. *Geographical Review* **60**, 229–46.

KRUMME, G. 1969: Towards a geography of enterprise. *Economic Geography* **45**, 30–40.

KWOFIE, K. M. 1976: A spatio-temporal analysis of cholera diffusion in western Africa. *Economic Geography* **52**, 127–35.

LAKSHMANAN, P. P. 1972: Regional patterns in commodity flows in India. *Environment and Planning* **4**, 59–72.

LANGDALE, J. V. 1976: Australian urban and regional development planning: a regional centre strategy. *Australian Geography* **13**, 264–71.

LAWRENCE, R. J. 1972: Social welfare and urban growth. In Parker, R. S. and Troy, P. N. (Eds.), *The politics of urban growth*, Canberra, 110–12.

LAWTON, R. 1967: The journey to work in Britain: some trends and problems. *Regional Studies* **2**, 27–40.

LEINBACH, T. R. 1972: The spread of modernization in Malaya: 1895–1969. *Tijdschrift voor Economische en Sociale Geografie* **63**, 262–77.

— 1975: Transportation and the development of Malaya. *Association of American Geographers, Annals* **65**, 270–82.

— 1976: The impact of accessibility upon modernizing behaviour. *Tijdschrift voor Economische en Sociale Geografie* **67**, 279–88.

LEIPZIGER, D. M. and MUDGE, J. L. 1976: *Seabed mineral resources and the economic interests of the developing countries*. Cambridge, Mass.

LEVER, W. F. 1974: Regional multipliers and demand leakages at establishment level. *Scottish Journal of Political Economy* **21**, 111–22.

LINNEMANN, H. 1966: *An econometric study of international trade flows*. Amsterdam.

LOGAN, M. I. 1968: Work residence relationships in the city. *Australian Geographical Studies* **6**, 151–66.

LOGAN, M. I. *et al.* 1975: *Urban and regional Australia: analysis and policy issues*. Melbourne.

LÖSCH, A. 1954: *The economics of location*. Translated by W. Woglom, New Haven, Conn.

MABOGUNJE, A. L. 1973: Manufacturing and the geography of development in Tropical Africa. *Economic Geography* **49**, 1–20.

MCNEE, R. B. 1970: Regional planning, bureaucracy and geography. *Economic Geography* **46**, 190–8.

MANNERS, G. 1967: Transport costs, freight rates and the changing economic geography of iron ore. *Geography* **52**, 260–79.

— 1971: *The changing world market for iron ore 1950–1980*. Baltimore.

MARBLE, D. F. and NYSTUEN, J. D. 1963: An approach to the direct measurement of community mean information fields. *Regional Science Association, Papers and Proceedings* **11**, 99–109.

MARCHAND, B. 1973: Deformation of a transportation surface. *Association of American Geographers, Annals* **63**, 507–21.

MASSAM, B. 1975: *Location and space in social administration*. London.

MAYFIELD, R. C. and YAPA, L. S. 1974: Information fields in rural Mysore. *Economic Geography* **50**, 313–23.

MEADOWS, D. H., MEADOWS, D. L., RANDERS, J. and BEHRENS, W. W. 1972: *The limits to growth*. London.

MEINIG, D. W. 1962: A comparative historical geography of two railnets: Columbia Basin and South Australia. *Association of American Geographers, Annals* **52**, 394–413.

MEIER, R. L. 1962: *A communications theory of urban growth*. Cambridge, Mass.

MELAMID, A. 1959: The geographical pattern of Iranian oil development. *Economic Geography* **35**, 199–218.

MELCHIOR, E. R. 1972: The integration of space in Latin America. *Latin American Urban Research* **2**, 85–100.

MILLS, L. R. 1973: The development of a frontier zone and border landscape along the Dahomey–Nigeria boundary. *Journal of Tropical Geography* **36**, 42–9.

MORAWSKI, W. 1967: Balances of interregional commodity flows in Poland: a value approach. *Regional Science Association, Papers and Proceedings* **20**, 29–41.

MORGAN, W. B. and MUNTON, R. J. C. 1971: *Agricultural geography*. London.

MORRILL, R. L. 1963: The development of spatial distributions of towns in Sweden: an historical predictive approach. *Association of American Geographers, Annals* **53**, 1–14.

MORRILL, R. L. 1965: The negro ghetto: alternatives and consequences. *Geographical Review* **55**, 339–61.

— 1968: Waves of spatial diffusion. *Journal of Regional Science* **8**, 1–18.

— 1970a: The shape of diffusion in space and time. *Economic Geography* **46**, 259–68.

— 1970b: *The spatial organization of society*. Belmont, Calif.

— 1973: Ideal and reality in reapportionment. *Association of American Geographers, Annals* **63**, 463–77.

MORRILL, R. L. and PITTS, F. R. 1967: Marriage, migration and the mean information field. *Association of American Geographers, Annals* **57**, 401–22.

MUMPHREY, A. J. and WOLPERT, J. 1973: Equity considerations and concessions in the siting of public facilities. *Economic Geography* **49**, 102–21.

MURACO, W. A. 1972: Intraurban accessibility. *Economic Geography* **48**, 388–405.

MURDIE, R. A. 1965: Cultural differences in consumer travel. *Economic Geography* **41**, 211–33.

MYRDAL, G. 1957: *Economic theory and underdeveloped regions*. London.

NEUTZE, G. M. 1974: The case for new cities in Australia. *Urban Studies* **11**, 259–75.

NYSTUEN, J. D. 1963: Identification of some fundamental concepts. In Berry, B. J. L. and Marble, D. F. (Eds.), *Spatial analysis*, Englewood Cliffs, N.J., 35–41.

NYSTUEN, J. D. and DACEY, M. F. 1961: A graph theory interpretation of nodal regions. *Regional Science Association, Papers and Proceedings* **7**, 29–42.

ÖBERG, S. 1976: Methods of describing physical access to supply points. *Lund Studies in Geography* (Ser. B) **43**.

ODINGO, R. S. 1971: Settlement and rural development in Kenya. In Ominde, S. H. (Ed.)., *Studies in East African geography and development*, London, 162–76.

O'FARRELL, P. N. 1970: A multivariate model of the spacing of urban centres in the Irish Republic. In Stephens, N. and Glasscock, R. E. (Eds.), *Irish geographical studies*, Belfast.

OJO, G. J. A. 1968: Hausa quarters of Yoruba towns with special reference to Ile-Ife. *Journal of Tropical Geography* **27**, 40–9.

— 1973: Journey to agricultural work in Yorubaland. *Association of American Geographers, Annals* **63**, 85–96.

OLIVER, J. 1975: The significance of natural hazards in a developing area: a case-study from north Queensland. *Geography* **60**, 99–110.

OLSSON, G. and PERSSON, A. 1963: The spacing of central places in Sweden. *Regional Science Association, Papers and Proceedings* **12**, 87–93.

PADDISON, R. 1976: Spatial bias and redistricting in proportional representation election systems: a case-study of the Republic of Ireland. *Tijdschrift voor Economische en Sociale Geografie* **67**, 230–41.

PARKER, H. R. 1962: Suburban shopping facilities in Liverpool. *Town Planning Review* **33**, 197–223.

PARR, J. B. 1973: Growth poles, regional development and central place theory. *Regional Science Association, Papers and Proceedings* **31**, 173–212.

PATERSON, J. H. 1972: *Land, work and resources*. London.

PEDERSEN, P. O. 1970: Innovation diffusion within and between national urban systems. *Geographical Analysis* **2**, 203–54.

PERPILLOU, A. V. 1966: *Human geography*. London.

PORTEOUS, J. D. 1973: The company-state: a Chilean case-study. *Canadian Geographer* 113–26.

PRED, A. R. 1969: *The spatial dynamics of US urban-industrial growth 1800–1914*. Cambridge, Mass.

— 1971: Urban systems development and the long-distance flow of information through pre-electronic US newspapers. *Economic Geography* **47**, 498–524.

— 1973: Urbanization, domestic planning problems and Swedish geographic research. *Progress in Geography* **5**, 1–76.

— 1974: *Major job-providing organisations and systems of cities*. Association of American Geographers, Commission on College Geography, Resource Paper 27.

— 1976: The inter-urban transmission of growth in advanced economies: empirical findings versus regional planning assumptions. *Regional Studies* **10**, 151–71.

PRESCOTT, J. R. V. 1975: *Political geography of the oceans*. Newton Abbot.

PRESTWICH, R. 1975: America's dependence on the world's metal resources: shifts in import emphases, 1960–1970. *Institute of British Geographers, Transactions* **64**, 97–118.

PRINCE, H. C. 1964: The origin of pits and depressions in Norfolk. *Geography* **49**, 15–32.

PYLE, G. F. 1969: The diffusion of cholera in the United States. *Geographical Analysis* **1**, 59–75.

RAY, D. M. 1967: Cultural differences in consumer travel behaviour in eastern Ontario. *Canadian Geographer* **11**, 143–56.

REES, J. 1974: Decision making, the growth of the firm and the business environment. In Hamilton, F. E. I. (Ed.), *Spatial perspectives on industrial organization and decision making*, London, 189–212.

REILLY, W. J. 1931: *The law of retail gravitation*. New York.

REITSMA, H. J. 1972: Areal differentiation along the US/Canada border. *Tijdschrift voor Economische en Sociale Geografie* **63**, 2–10.

RETEYUM, A. 1976: Transformation scene in Central Asia. *Geographical Magazine* **48** (11), translated by D. J. S. Shaw), 682–6.

REYNOLDS, D. R. and MCNULTY, M. L. 1968: On the analysis of political boundaries as barriers: a perceptual approach. *East Lakes Geographer* **4**, 21–38.

RICHARDSON, H. W. 1973: Theory of the distribution of city sizes: review and prospects. *Regional Studies* **7**, 239–51.

RIDLEY, T. M. and TRESIDDER, J. O. 1970: The London transportation study and beyond. *Regional Studies* **4**, 63–71.

ROBINSON, D. J. 1971: Venezuela and Colombia. In Blakemore, H. and Smith, C. T. (Eds.), *Latin America: geographical perspectives*, London, 179–246.

ROBINSON, G. and SALIH, K. B. 1971: The spread of development around Kuala Lumpur: a methodology for an exploratory test of some assumptions of the growth-pole model. *Regional Studies* **5**, 303–14.

ROBSON, B. T. 1973: *Urban growth: an approach*. London.

RODWIN, L. 1970: *Nations and cities*. Boston.

ROGERSON, C. M. 1975: Industrial movement in an industrializing economy. *South African Geographical Journal* **57**, 88–103.

ROGERS, A. 1965: A stochastic analysis of the spatial clustering of retail establishments. *Journal of the American Statistical Association* **60**, 1094–1103.

ROSE, H. M. 1972: The spatial development of black residential subsystems. *Economic Geography* **48**, 43–65.

ROWLEY, G. 1970: Elections and population changes. *Area* **2**, 13–18.

— 1975: The redistribution of parliamentary seats in the UK: themes and opinions. *Area* **7**, 16–21.

ROYAL COMMISSION 1969: *Local government in England 1966–1969* (3 vols.), London.

RUSHTON, G., GOLLEDGE, R. G. and CLARK, W. A. V. 1967: Formulation and test of a normative model for the spatial allocation of grocery expenditures by a dispersed population. *Association of American Geographers, Annals* **57**, 389–400.

SAARINEN, T. F. 1966: Perception of drought hazard on the Great Plains. *University of Chicago, Department of Geography, Research Paper*, 106.

SADLER, P. 1974: The economic effects of large industrial undertakings on rural areas. *Omega* **2**, 497–507.

SARGENT, JNR, C. S. 1972: Towards a dynamic model of urban morphology. *Economic Geography* **48**, 357–74.

SAUER, C. O. 1952: *Agricultural origins and dispersals*. New York.

SCHAEFFER, K. H. and SCLAR, E. 1975: *Access for all*. London.

SCHNEIDER, J. B. 1971: Solving urban location problems: human intuition versus the computer. *Journal of American Institute of Planners* **37**, 95–8.

SEGAL, A. 1967/68: The politics of land in East Africa. *Economic Development and Cultural Change* **16**, 275–96.

SEWELL, W. R. D. (Ed.). 1966: Human dimensions of weather modification. University of Chicago, Department of Geography, Research Papers 105.

SIDDLE, D. J. 1970: Location theory and the subsistence economy: the spacing of rural settlements in Sierra Leone. *Journal of Tropical Geography* **31**, 79–90.

SILVA, R. C. 1965: Reapportionment and redistricting. *Scientific American* **213**, 20–7.

SIMMONS, I. G. 1974: *The ecology of natural resources*. London.

SJOBERG, G. 1960: *The pre-industrial city*. Glencoe, Illinois.

SMITH, D. M. 1966: A theoretical framework for geographical studies of industrial location. *Economic Geography* **42**, 95–113.

— 1971: *Industrial location*. New York.

— 1973: *The geography of social well-being in the United States*. New York.

— 1977: *Human geography: a welfare approach*. London.

SMITH, R. D. P. 1968: The changing urban hierarchy. *Regional Studies* **2**, 1–9.

SMITH, R. H. T. 1970: Concepts and methods in commodity flow analysis. *Economic Geography* **46**, 404–16.

SOJA, E. W. 1968: *The geography of modernization in Kenya: a spatial analysis of social, economic and political change*. Syracuse Geographical Series No. 2, Syracuse, New York.

— 1971: *The political organization of space*. Association of American Geographers, Commission on College Geography, Resource Paper No. 8.

SPOEHR, A. 1956: Cultural differences in the interpretation of natural resources. In Thomas, W. L. (Ed.), 93–102.

STEWART, C. T. 1958: The size and spacing of cities. *Geographical Review* **48**, 222–45.

STEWART, J. Q. 1947: Empirical mathematical rules concerning the distribution of equilibrium of population. *Geographical Review* **37**, 461–85.

STILLWELL, F. J. and HARDWICK, J. M. 1973: *Regional development in Australia*. Sydney.

STOHR, W. 1975: *Regional development experiences and prospects in Latin America*. Paris/The Hague.

STUTZ, F. P. 1973: Distance and network effects on urban social travel fields. *Economic Geography* **49**, 134–44.

SUGDEN, D. E. 1972: Piping hot wealth in a sub-zero land. *Geographical Magazine* **44**, 226–9.

SWAN, S. B. ST C. 1967: Paddy crops failure and variable yields in Ceylon. *Pacific Viewpoint* **8**, 159–74.

SYMONS, L. 1972: *Soviet agriculture*. London.

TAAFFE, E. J. and GAUTHIER, H. L. 1973: *Geography of transportation*. Englewood Cliffs, N.J.

TAAFFE, E. J., MORRILL, R. L. and GOULD, P. 1963: Transport expansion in under-developed countries. *Geographical Review* **53**, 503–29.

TARRANT, J. R. 1975: Maize: a new United Kingdom agricultural crop. *Area* **7**, 175–9.

TAYLOR, M. J. 1973: Local linkage, external economies and the ironfoundry industry of the West Midlands and East Lancashire conurbations. *Regional Studies* **7**, 387–400.

TAYLOR, M. J. and WOOD, P. 1973: Industrial linkage and local agglomeration in the West Midlands metal industries. *Institute of British Geographers, Transactions* **59**, 127–54.

TAYLOR, P. J. 1973: Some implications of the spatial organization of elections. *Institute of British Geographers, Transactions* **60**, 121–36.
— 1977: *Quantitative methods in geography.* Boston.
THOMAS, E. N. 1961: Towards an expanded central-place model. *Geographical Review* **51**, 400–11.
THOMAS, W. L. (Ed.). 1956: *Man's role in changing the face of the Earth.* Chicago.
THORNGREN, B. 1970: How do contact systems affect regional development? *Environment and Planning* **2**, 409–27.
THROWER, N. J. W. 1966: *Original survey and land sub-division.* Chicago.
TIMBERS, J. A. 1967: Route factors in road networks. *Traffic Engineering and Control* **9**, 392–4, 401.
TORNQVIST, G. 1968: Flows of information and the location of economic activity. *Lund Studies in Geography* (Ser. B) **30**.
— 1970: Contact systems and regional development. *Lund Studies in Geography* (Ser. B) **35**.
— 1973: Contact requirements and travel facilities – contact models of Sweden and regional development alternatives in the future. In Pred, A. R. and Tornqvist, G., *Systems of cities and information flows. Lund Studies in Geography* (Ser. B) **38**.
TOWNROE, P. M. 1969: Locational choice and the individual firm. *Regional Studies* **3**, 15–24.
ULLMAN, E. L. 1956: The role of transportation and the bases for interaction. In Thomas, W. L. (Ed.), *Man's role in changing the face of the Earth*, Chicago, 862–80.
— 1958: Regional development and the geography of concentration. *Regional Science Association, Paper and Proceedings* **4**, 179–206.
— 1974: Space and/or time: opportunity for substitution and prediction. *Institute of British Geographers, Transactions* **63**, 125–139.
UNITED NATIONS (ECONOMIC COMMISSION FOR EUROPE) 1967: *Criteria for location of industrial plants.* New York.
VAN HULTEN, M. H. M. 1969: Plan and reality in the Ijsselmeer-polders. *Tijdschrift voor Economische en Sociale Geografie,* **60**, 67–76.
WALLACE, I. 1974: The relationship between freight transport organization and industrial linkage in Britain. *Institute of British Geographers, Transactions* **62**, 25–44.
WARNTZ, W. 1961: Transatlantic flight paths and pressure patterns. *Geographical Review* **51**, 187–212.
WARREN, K. 1973: *Mineral resources.* Newton Abbot.
WATSON, J. W. 1955: Geography: a discipline in distance. *Scottish Geographical Magazine* **51**, 1–13.
— 1969: The role of illusion in North American geography: a note on the geography of North American settlement. *Canadian Geographer* **13**, 19–27.
WATTS, H. D. 1974: Spatial rationalisation in multiplant enterprises. *Geoforum* **17**, 69–76.
— 1977: Market areas and spatial rationalization: the British brewing industry after 1945. *Tijdschrift voor Economische en Sociale Geografie* **68**, 23–34.
WEBBER, M. 1963: Order in diversity: community without propinquity. In Wingo, L. (Ed.), *Cities and space*, Baltimore, 22–54.
— 1964: Culture, territoriality, and the elastic mile. *Regional Science Association, Papers and Proceedings* **13**, 59–69.
WEBER, A. 1929: *Alfred Weber's theory of the location of industries.* Translated by C. J. Friedrich. Chicago.
WEINAND, H. C. 1973: Some spatial aspects of economic development in Nigeria. *Journal of Developing Areas* **7**, 247–63.
WERNER, C. 1968a: Research seminar in theoretical transportation geography. *Northwestern University, Studies in Geography* **16**, 128–70.
— 1968b: The role of topology and geometry in optimal network design. *Regional Science Association, Papers and Proceedings* **21**, 173–89.

WESTAWAY, J. 1974: Contact potential and the occupational structure of the British urban system 1961–1966: an empirical study. *Regional Studies* **8**, 57–73.

WHITBY, R. H. 1971: Technical progress in aviation. *Regional Studies* **5**, 117–20.

WHITE, L. 1967: The historical roots of our ecological crisis. *Science* **155**, 1203–7.

WHITELAW, J. S. and ROBINSON, S. 1972: A test for directional bias in intra-urban migration. *New Zealand Geographer* **28**, 181–93.

WHITTLE, A. W. R. 1978: Resources and population in the British neolithic. *Antiquity* **52**, 34–43.

WILBANKS, T. J. 1972: Accessibility and technological change in northern India. *Association of American Geographers, Annals* **62**, 427–36.

WILLIAMS, A. V. and ZELINSKY, W. 1970: On some patterns in international tourist flows. *Economic Geography* **46**, 549–67.

WILSON, A. G. 1971: A family of spatial interaction models, and associated developments. *Environment and Planning* **3**, 1–32.

WILSON, M. G. A. 1968: Changing patterns of pit location in the New South Wales coalfield. *Association of American Geographers, Annals* **58**, 78 90.

WOLPERT, J. 1964: The decision process in a spatial context. *Association of American Geographers, Annals* **54**, 537–58.

WOOD, L. J. 1974: Spatial interaction and partitions of rural market areas. *Tijdschrift voor Economische en Sociale Geografie* **65**, 23–34.

WOOD, P. 1969: Industrial linkage and location. *Area* **2**, 32–9.

YEATES, M. H. and GARNER, B. J. 1971: *The North American city*. New York.

YUILL, R. S. 1967: Spatial behavior of retail customers: some empirical measurements. *Geografiska Annaler* **49** (B), 105–15.

ZELINSKY, W. 1966: *A prologue to population geography*. New York.

— 1974: Selfward bound? Personal preference patterns and the changing map of American society. *Economic Geography* **50**, 144–79.

ZIMMERMAN, E. W. 1964: *Introduction to world resources* (ed. by H. C. Hunter). New York.

ZIPF, G. K. 1941: *National unity and disunity*. Bloomington, Ind.

— 1949: *Human behaviour and the principle of least effort*. Reading, Mass.

ZOBLER, L. 1962: An economic historical view of natural resource use and conservation. *Economic Geography* **38**, 189–94.

Index

Index